# Quakers on the
# American Frontier

# Quakers on the American Frontier

*A History of the Westward Migrations,*
*Settlements, and Developments of Friends*
*on the American Continent*

Errol T. Elliott

The Friends United Press
Richmond, Indiana

Copyright 1969

by

**The Friends United Press**

Grateful recognition is extended to the following for permission to
quote from materials copyrighted by them as noted in the footnotes:

The State Historical Society of Iowa, Iowa City, Iowa
The University of Oklahoma Press, Norman, Oklahoma
The Joseph Rowntree Charitable Trust, York, England, present
holders of the rights to the works of Rufus M. Jones published by Macmillan of London

Efforts have been made to determine the current copyright validity
of all quoted selections. Any oversights have been unintentional.

PRINTED IN THE UNITED STATES OF AMERICA
BY THE BRETHREN PRESS, ELGIN, ILLINOIS

Dedicated

to

Elisha M. and Alice Elleman Elliott
and their daughter Lela

# CONTENTS

# ILLUSTRATIONS

# FOREWORD

One of the outstanding characteristics of the Quaker movement has been the testimony of experience. The powerful influence of the Journals of George Fox, John Woolman, and great numbers of other Friends can be attributed in large measure to their written witness.

In similar fashion, periodically, some outstanding Quaker personality would sense the importance of setting down an account of the spiritual journey of the Society of Friends, gathering together the experiences of a people and recording something of the values, attitudes, and events which shaped their history.

When the concern was expressed in the Executive Council sessions of the Five Years Meeting (now Friends United Meeting) about a decade ago, it was quite natural and appropriate that the Council should decide to authorize a history of the westward movement of Friends, bringing up to date their spiritual pilgrimage. A committee was appointed to carry forward this concern and to clarify the purposes of such a project. They recommended that the proposed work should record the migrations west of the Allegheny mountains, the impact of pioneer life in molding the character of Friends and their Meetings, and something of the changes and adjustments which occurred within the life of the Society.

The progress of the committee was slow and discouraging for a time, partly because of the enormity of the task and partly because of the responsibility involved in the production of a book which would interpret with honesty and fairness the complex and intricate story of Friends on the American frontier.

In 1965 the project was given a tremendous new thrust when Errol T. Elliott, one who had given a lifetime to service among midwestern Friends, accepted the challenge and was appointed to the assignment. Providence had drawn together the right man and the great task. Financial assurances were arranged in order that the work might not be delayed or interrupted.

Errol Elliott brought to this effort impressive qualifications and capabilities. His academic, pastoral, and administrative experience prepared him well for the monumental task of research and the selection and weaving of the historical data into a meaningful and exciting story. But more importantly, as a child of the frontier, who with his family had experienced crossing the prairies westward by covered wagon, he writes with the empathy and sensitivity of one who sees not only facts but meanings.

As one who understands something of the motivations and hardships which helped to shape the frontier spirit, Errol Elliott brings to his work a remarkable blend of reporting with interpretation. He records the facts of the migrations, the amalgamations, and the schisms with a combination of objectivity and insight. The reader of this volume will appreciate Butterfield's reminder that "we go to the past not to discover facts only but significances." History is made not only by man's relation to the natural world but also by the values and attitudes of all his relationships. The author of this book has told the story of the westward movement of Friends as it was, a spiritual as well as a physical adventure, with fact and value inseparable.

A volume of this size must necessarily avoid meticulous detail. Rather, as with the broad strokes of an artist, he outlines the main features of a great scene on the Quaker landscape. With characteristic mastery of words he provides us with an overview which enables us to see the main stream, the chief emphases and questions, the relentless problems and tensions, and the major concerns and contributions of the Quaker movement up to the present time.

It is with appreciation to Errol Elliott that we commend this book to those who would learn from the past. We publish it in the hope that it will be widely read and used in classrooms and church groups as a significant chapter in the experience of a people who are part of the continuing drama of history.

*— Lorton G. Heusel*

# PREFACE

While members of the Religious Society of Friends publish a great deal, through periodicals, mimeographed reports, pamphlets, and occasional books, they do not produce as many historical studies as we need. Furthermore, much of the historical writing tends to be either genealogical or antiquarian and does not make a substantial contribution to our knowledge or to scholarship.

The serious historical work which is done tends to focus upon the first generation of Quakerism or the colonial experience, while little effort is made to study and interpret the nineteenth and twentieth centuries. In the Rowntree series, Charles W. Braithwaite wrote two thick books on the period before 1715, and then Rufus M. Jones prepared two smaller volumes entitled *The Later Period of Quakerism,* covering the next two centuries! He also produced *Quakers in the American Colonies,* with assistance from Isaac Sharpless and Amelia Mott Gummere, which did not go beyond the eighteenth century.

Other Quaker authors tend to stay in the same period. Hugh Barbour has recently published a volume on *Quakers in Puritan England,* D. Elton Trueblood has written a new biography of Robert Barclay, and Dean Freiday has edited a new edition of the *Apology.* My own volume on the founding of Pennsylvania, entitled *William Penn's "Holy Experiment,"* emphasizes another leader of the first generation, while Frederick B. Tolles has published several volumes on eighteenth-century Friends, most notably *Meeting House and Counting House.* Non-Quaker scholars have written about George

Fox and William Penn, and one has prepared a new edition of the journal of John Woolman.

It is difficult to draw up a list of books on Quaker history in the nineteenth and twentieth centuries. The superb volume on Joseph John Gurney, by David Swift, does not do justice to Gurney the Quaker, tending to emphasize other aspects of his career. There have been several studies of Rufus Jones, of which some have been published, but most remain on microfilm. Occasionally a volume appears about John Greenleaf Whittier or Lucretia Mott, but these stress their reform actions rather than their Quakerism. One would not say that the volumes about Herbert Hoover, A. Mitchell Palmer, or Richard Nixon emphasize their Quakerism.

There has not been a general history of Friends in the United States since the volume by Allen C. Thomas, which first appeared in 1894 and was last revised in 1930. Elbert Russell in *The History of Quakerism* (1942) did some work on the later period, and Walter R. Williams' *The Rich Heritage of Quakerism* (1962) also made some effort in this direction. Howard Brinton's *Friends for 300 Years* (1952) did not emphasize American Quaker history, nor did D. Elton Trueblood's *The People Called Quakers* (1966). The slender volume prepared for the Fourth World Conference of Friends, *American Quakers Today,* made a beginning in this direction.

Perhaps all of this is a very indirect way of welcoming the present volume by Errol T. Elliott on the westward movement of Quakers. Although he begins with southern Friends in the colonial period, and makes some references to the beginnings of Quakerism in England and to members of the sect in the other colonies before the American Revolution, most of this volume is devoted to the period after 1800.

While the book is about American Quakers in the nineteenth and twentieth centuries, it does not pretend to be about all American Friends of this period of time. With his emphasis upon Quakers west of the Appalachians, the author makes only passing references to Friends on the east coast and even more infrequent comments about those in England. The thesis of this volume, the western movement of Friends, means that he has focussed his study upon midwestern and western Quakers.

There were few regional or geographical differences within American Quakerism in 1800, but they developed as the century progressed.

It might be true to say that Friends were virtually the same, whether they lived in North Carolina, New Jersey, Rhode Island, or in old England at the time of the Napoleonic wars. This could not be said by midcentury, and differences became more pronounced in the years that followed. Some of the distinctive qualities could be traced to theological positions which corresponded with the various branches of Friends created by the schisms of the nineteenth century. There were also subtle environmental differences and Errol Elliott has illuminated these in his book.

The various theological groups were represented in western America, and, although he has emphasized the so-called Gurneyites, he examines all branches of the Society and analyzes the way each group related to the others. Thus one gains a fairly comprehensive understanding of American Quakers, even though the volume is by definition limited to the western scene.

Errol Elliott was reared on the plains of Kansas, received his education and spent most of his working years in the West, but does not have a parochial view of Quakerism. During his time as General Secretary of the Five Years Meeting and editor of the *American Friend,* he served Quakers in all parts of the United States, on both sides of the Appalachians. Furthermore, as chairman of the Friends World Committee for Consultation he served a much wider constituency. He not only knows all kinds of Friends; he loves them and has an appreciation for them that transcends the differences which exist. During the months he was at Haverford for research and writing, he was a most acceptable member of the Haverford Meeting and his ministry was deeply appreciated. I am sure that he found the Meeting satisfying even though it was quite different from the one he attended as a boy in Kansas, or the Meetings he served as pastor. The Quakerism of Errol Elliott is deep and broad, and he has written this volume out of that kind of background and experience.

In this book Errol Elliott has developed the thesis that Quakerism in the West is different from what it had been or what it became in other places, because of the western influence. He has accepted the environmental emphasis of Frederick Jackson Turner, and has attempted to show that the frontier influence has shaped and modified the Quakerism which Friends took with them across the mountains. He believes that the struggle with the elements made a profound impact on Quakerism; he feels that the self-reliance of the men and women on the frontier added a new dimension to the tension between the individual and the corporate group. And he concludes that the adventurous spirit, the search for something new and better, also molded and changed western Quakerism. He makes a good case for these conclusions, and it is stimulating to study this period of Quaker history as seen through this thesis.

The reader will be struck by the way in which history sometimes seems to repeat itself. The description of the controversy regarding the Underground Railroad is strongly reminiscent of the current discussion over sending medical supplies to the Vietnamese of the National Liberation Front and Hanoi. Friends in the *ante bellum* years divided sharply over the issue of breaking the law for a good reason, over obedience to a "higher law," and there were splits in western Yearly Meetings over the question. As one reads of the efforts to administer the Indian policy of President Ulysses S. Grant in the 1870's one is reminded of the conflicts in Pennsylvania in the 1750's.

Seemingly there are times when Friends, with all the goodwill in the world, are unable to succeed in their efforts, because of political conditions and external powers beyond their control. The differences which evolved between younger and older Friends indicate that the "generation gap" was not invented in the 1960's. The current concern for a corporate witness, when viewed in the historical perspective of this volume, is seen to be a revival of a position Friends took in an earlier day before the emphasis on individualism and tolerance became a popular stance. We need to view the present in terms of the past, and this book will perform a valuable function in this regard.

Many Friends will enjoy reading a description of how their ancestors conquered the wild and unfriendly environment of the old Ohio Territory, the land beyond the Mississippi obtained through the Louisiana Purchase, or the regions on the west coast which were wrested from neighbors of the United States by force. The readers will be able to visualize the westward migration of several generations of some families, such as the Coffins from Nantucket, the Nicholsons from New England, or the Mendenhalls from Pennsylvania, all of whom went west by way of North Carolina. There is a noble, pioneering spirit in this story, and Errol Elliott has made the most of it. It will also be apparent that the evangelical zeal of these Friends drew many new converts to the fold. There are some stalwart names which keep appearing in each generation, but far more new names are added than old ones perpetuated. It is apparent that there was a healthy mixture of birthright and convinced Quakers in the westward movement.

In a volume of this size the author could not deal in a detailed manner with every aspect of Quaker history; in fact, it was seldom possible for him to discuss any subject in a definitive way. Perhaps he is at his best in writing about the organization of the Five Years Meeting, and the work of this body and its successor, Friends United Meeting. His own involvement in this important element in American Quakerism has given him an advantage in analyzing and discussing this subject. He has devoted a great deal of effort to gaining a comprehensive view of Friends and education in the area west of the Appalachians, and this chapter, supplemented by appendices, will be most useful. His sections on various other concerns of Friends will also be valuable, for he has combined thorough research with the exercise of his own mature judgment and reflection in discussing these topics.

While Errol Elliott has benefited from monographs, from local histories, and from personal conversations with various persons, he has largely relied on his own research and interpretation. This pioneering effort to encompass the history of the westward movement of Friends and their development once they had settled in the West will place all future students in his debt. While not trained as a professional historian, he has made a serious and largely successful effort to adopt the techniques and the attitudes of the professional. His long and active career in western Quakerism has given him a unique vantage point for this study. His careful footnoting of his material, plus the invaluable information gathered in his appendices, will also serve as stepping-stones for those who follow. This will be a useful volume for many years to come.

*— Edwin B. Bronner*

# ACKNOWLEDGEMENTS

## *Those Who Helped*

History such as this could not be written without help from a large number of persons friendly to its purpose and generous in spirit. From coast to coast I have had responses to my appeal for help. These have come in the forms of letters loaned from family collections, pamphlets, theses written for academic credits, books, and suggestions. Indispensable was the help given by the librarians of our Friends colleges: Guilford, Earlham, Wilmington, Malone, William Penn, Friends University, George Fox, Whittier, Haverford, and Swarthmore. I am especially indebted to Haverford College with its large Quaker Collection, and to the T. Wistar Brown Fund, which made possible an extended research into the background of literature.

The Friends United Meeting has given major support to this venture, and the Friends World Committee (American Section) has helped to make possible the necessary visitations to the areas included.

It was a rare privilege to have access to the letters of the late Rufus M. Jones made possible by the generosity of his daughter, Mary Hoxie Jones. The counsel of Henry J. Cadbury was invaluable. D. Elton Trueblood, well-known author, was a helpful counsellor.

At my request a committee was appointed by the Friends United Meeting to counsel and to read critically most of the manuscript. I am thereby indebted to the five who have been closely associated with me in the entire production. They are: Edwin B. Bronner, who was raised in a Friends pastoral home in California and, now Professor of History and Curator of the Quaker Collection at Haverford College, is associated with Philadelphia Yearly Meeting; Charles F. Thomas, experienced in pastoral service in Iowa, North Carolina, and Indiana Yearly Meetings, now Assistant Professor of Applied Theology in the Earlham School of Religion; Wilmer Cooper, raised in Ohio Yearly Meeting (Conservative), now a member of a pastoral Meeting in Indiana and Dean of the Earlham School of Religion; Opal Thornburg, archivist for the Lilly Library of Earlham College, who, out of her background of experience in historical writing and knowledge, has read my writing chapter by chapter and sentence by sentence, making suggestions for clarity and structure; and Dorothy Gilbert Thorne, who has aided me in the research on North Carolina Yearly Meeting. Edwin Bronner as a trained historian has been of special help.

Lorton G. Heusel, General Secretary of the Friends United Meeting, has been a trusted counsellor, representing that body of Friends under whose concern the writing of this volume was initiated and supported. All other members of the Friends United Meeting staff have been indispensable when information on Quaker affairs and on their respective departments of work was required. David O. Stanfield, Associate Secretary for Administration, with special concern for publications, carried much of the responsibility in the work of publishing arrangements and the preparation of illustrative materials.

Many other Friends have helped by reading certain chapters pertaining to their respective fields of interest. For this help I am indebted to Everett L. Cattell, President of Malone College; Arthur Roberts, Professor of Philosophy and Religion, and Myron Goldsmith, Professor of History, both of George Fox College; Fred Littlefield, Superintendent of Kansas Yearly Meeting; Sheldon G. Jackson, Kansas Quaker historian; Merle A. Roe, Superintendent of Rocky Mountain Yearly Meeting; Jack Willcuts, Superintendent of Oregon Yearly Meeting; Frederick B. Tolles, Director of Friends Historical Library, Swarthmore College; and Harold B. Winn, President of the Evangelical Friends Alliance.

Algie I. Newlin, professor in Guilford College, North Carolina Quaker historian, not only made a major contribution in his map of trails and accompanying explanations but has also made important suggestions for the chapters on North Carolina and Ohio Yearly Meetings. Maurice Creasey, Director of Studies at Woodbrooke College,

England, while a lecturer in residence at the Earlham School of Religion, has given valuable suggestions on the aspects which might be of special interest to British and European Friends.

Rare indeed was my privilege to have conversation with those whose memory and whose correspondence made their contributions very personal. Levi T. Pennington, with his long years of wide experience, was a remarkable resource of information. I sat with him for several hours during two weeks at Newberg, Oregon, and skimmed choice experiences from his very live memory covering the Five Years Meeting (Friends United Meeting), Pacific College (now George Fox College), Oregon Yearly Meeting, and Pacific Yearly Meeting. Herbert C. Jones of San Jose, California, has contributed much both by letters and in conversation, from his memory and from his Quaker family background.

The Friends World Committee, the American Friends Service Committee, and the Friends Committee on National Legislation have been responsive to my requests for information.

Though the contributions of many Friends have been generously given I bear responsibility for all that has been included or omitted in the content of these pages. In the last analysis I had to make the decision on what was to be included and how it was to be told.

Carol James Anderson has brought more than her characteristic efficiency to copying and correcting my none-too-legible script. Her devotion to this work has been contagious when it was most needed.

From the wall of the Haverford College library the portrait of Rayner W. Kelsey looked down, as with concern for my work. I remembered that he, Harlow Lindley, and Walter C. Woodward were kindred Quaker historians of their day and close friends of each other. Walter C. Woodward was my predecessor in the Five Years Meeting office. It was both sobering and inspiring to work as if these three observed and cared about what I was doing.

Above all, my wife, Ruby Kelly Elliott, brought that depth of supporting spirit just when patience and endurance were essential. Our four children, with their questions and ideas, helped in a measure to bridge the generation gap on what is important and unimportant in the backward-forward look of present-day life.

—*E. T. E.*

# QUAKERS AND THEIR HISTORY

## An Introductory Statement

When requested by the Five Years Meeting (now the Friends United Meeting) to write this account I was asked to confine it, in the main, to the areas west of the Allegheny Mountains. Friends of the northeastern area have been included in many historical accounts, whereas those of the Midwest and the Pacific coast have had no inclusive review of their life and development. The agreement on the geographic limitations for this volume is by no means separatist in intention, but rather the opposite. The aim is to bring a neglected aspect of Quaker history into the total perspective.

It should be noted that this book is *not* a series of histories of the Yearly Meetings involved, for the focus of this writing is on Friends of the American frontier *as a distinct development,* though within the whole Society of Friends. Therefore those aspects of each Yearly Meeting which offer distinctive contributions to the larger story are included.

Where to begin the story was a primary question. To start with Friends in the southern states, especially those of North Carolina, seemed to be the obvious answer. The great majority of Friends migrating to the West came from this area. The experiences of Friends in the South who faced the issues of slavery and war explain their main reason for going west. Quakerism was in the crucible, and the experiences of that period and in that area represent a great turn in the history of American Friends. Present-day North Carolina

Quakerism is, in faith and practice, more western than eastern even while being southern. North Carolina Yearly Meeting is like a peninsula of the Quaker West. It would have been impossible to give an intelligent explanation of Friends west of the Alleghenies without including those of the southern states. This history must therefore include the vast area from Albemarle Sound to Puget Sound.

It is readily understood why the development of Friends life in the Mississippi valley and on the Pacific coast has not been brought into a total American Quaker story. America is new, as world history goes, and the occupying of a great continent was not easily accomplished. Now the broad valleys are teeming with people, in large cities and on vast ranges and farms. Within this expanding frontier American Friends have pioneered in helping to shape the American future even while they were being refashioned by the new conditions around them.

### THE QUAKER DIVERSITIES

That there should have been changes from the original patterns of Quaker faith and practice would be expected, for change is the course of all life. How significant are the resulting diversities is another question now facing the entire Society of Friends. Can all of the present forms be rightly included under the name *Quaker?*

This question may find illustration in the true story of a small Quaker boy. He felt too much at home with his rosarian neighbor and collected the small labels from his rosebushes, proudly displaying them to his parents. Obviously the labels could not be placed back, each on the bush from which it came. To that small boy Gertrude Stein's definition, "A rose is a rose is a rose," was adequate, but not to a rosarian. The diversities of Friends would hardly suggest the simple statement that "a Quaker is a Quaker is a Quaker."

Yet Friends are not without some common marks of historical identity. What one body of Friends may have lost another may have retained, though in a new form or expression. It hardly needs emphasizing that no Friends Meeting today is a close replica of the original, but that there is a common depth in which Friends are rooted becomes increasingly clear. The first need is that Friends of varied persuasions shall understand each other and be understood by their non-Quaker neighbors.

It can be readily seen that a writer of one volume, covering the space and time involved, would have to make some difficult, if not agonizing, choices as to what could be rightly included or excluded from the account. Every Yearly Meeting of Friends presented in these pages merits at least one volume. This must be left to other Quaker historians.

Painting only in broad strokes, I found it necessary to elect from available material those aspects which did most to shape the character, qualities, and forms of western American Friends.

### THE HISTORICAL VIEW

Historical writing can never be purely objective, for it is not a kind of photography; yet the historian must try to distinguish between fact and nonfact, between fact and wishful thinking. He must also distinguish between fact and truth, for they are not to be identified as one and the same. As Collingwood in his *The Idea of History* says, "the events of history are never mere phenomena, never mere spectacles for contemplation, but things which the historian looks not *at,* but *through,* to discern the thought within them . . . all history is the history of thought." This approach is required of both writer and reader. George Buttrick in his *Christ and History* says of the historian, "His net of words cannot catch the sorrow of a feudal serf or Saint Joan's rapture in her martyrdom." It is equally true that a writer or a reader of Quaker history cannot enter fully into the distress of those who suffered for conscience' sake, or sense the joy of anticipation of those who looked westward from some Appalachian height into the "Canaan" toward which they moved. He can, in spirit, move with them as the wagons make their precarious way over trails hardly worthy of being called roads.

There was no posing before the camera of history by that body of Friends of North Carolina as they went through the exacting tests on the issues of slavery and war, nor by those who crossed mountains and penetrated the forests to make their homes in the West. To tell the facts about them would not of itself tell the truth about who they were or why they responded to the circumstances around them. He who writes or reads must, so to speak, help push their covered wagons over the hills, chock their wagon wheels, sit by their campfires, then help them clear their land and build their houses.

He must also remain in North Carolina with that heroic remnant that did not migrate. It is the opinion of this writer that not the Appalachians or the frontiers of the new lands, but the farms of the Carolinas were the more peculiar testing grounds for the Quaker way of life. One who writes or reads about those Friends should raise the question whether he would have the same spiritual stamina to hold firm when every pressure of slavery and war was asking him to yield. Only in this can the truth rise out of the facts.

One who reads history must also see that it is not simply an account of events of the past. The reader is *in it,* for history is an unfolding creation. He too is making history and should feel his involvement in the total drama. If God, as the eternal reality, is Alpha and Omega they who would know Him in experience should be concerned for the full range of His creative work, past and future. We are one with those who preceded and those who will follow us. If we are not aware of this we shall be like people who do not know where they are going because they do not know where they have been!

### IN THE AMERICAN EXPANSION

Friends were not alone in the streams of caravans that flowed westward. Indeed, they were but a fraction of the larger movement. This was the "Westward Ho!" of the nation. Everyone going west was in a race getting there *first* to get the *best,* in a great rivalry. The frontier has affected the American vocabulary. The first, the largest, the tallest, the most comfortable are not solely American superlatives, but there are probably more of them in our thought and speech than we recognize.

The late-to-bed-and-early-to-rise schedule of those who cleared the timber for Ohio, Indiana, and Iowa farms, broke the sod and built houses of it on the prairies of Kansas and Nebraska, and turned deserts into well-watered gardens on the Pacific Coast, did not lend itself to an extended contemplation that was possible in the more settled communities and urban centers. Here a new kind of life was evolving with a fresh contribution to be made. In that period every range of territory was "out there," ahead, and the backward look meant less than getting into the conquest of the farm-to-be and the home-in-the-making.

Friends were in an unmade land and it called not only for long hours of work, but also for ingenuity. In the main, little was given them; they had to make it, from the tools they used to the houses they built and the farms they tilled. It would be strange indeed if they had not developed some spiritual innovations to meet their new conditions. Either they would change or perish. Some Meetings did not change and ceased to exist while others moved to new patterns and survived.

The moving frontier had to settle finally, develop institutions, turn and face the world neighborhood on a shrinking planet, and awaken to the idea that world one-ness is a fact; that men cannot run from it into forests or onto broad, self-sufficient plains. Settling into a new awareness is also a part of the western story. Friends were there, sharing in it, contributing to it, and being shaped by it. They have brought into the world Society of Friends an authentic life of their own, feeling that they have both conserved and contributed something of basic value to the Quaker future.

In the story here related, parts of the history of America and of the Society of Friends in the West are brought into focus and given illustration in the life experiences of those who faced new tests of freedom and came through to write a new chapter in the history of Friends as they lived their part in the American epic.

There is a parallel between the history of the early Hebrews and that of Friends in western America. Each, moving from an area of slavery, came to and through a wilderness of both physical and spiritual kinds. Each acted as if God were alive in history. They could not believe Him failing. Every event was in some way a religious event in its deeper meaning, and Friends, like the Hebrews, stood on the rim of a new land and sought to conquer it, though not with weapons but with tools of peacemaking. "Canaan" was out there, unknown but calling.

Perhaps our story should start as did many of their stories: "And it came to pass in those days that. . . . "

# Chapter 1

## A HINGE IN QUAKER HISTORY
### *Friends in the Southern States*

To that quiet Quaker Meeting, deep in the bush country of South Carolina, his voice must have come like a peal from Sinai. The Meeting had gathered in silence, but was charged with expectancy, for the coming of Zachariah Dicks was not simply that of another visiting Friend. Like Zachariah of old he was a "seer" of the old school. To some of the waiting Friends his presence may have seemed as authentic as if he had stepped out of the pages of the Old Testament and taken his seat on the facing bench.

Out of the silent waiting he rose and intoned his message, "O Bush River! Bush River! How hath thy beauty faded away and gloomy darkness eclipsed thy day." That was not all that he said, but it was enough, for it was the heart of his message. Bush River was doomed![1]

---

[1] Stephen B. Weeks, *Southern Quakers and Slavery,* Johns Hopkins Press, 1896; p. 307 (footnote). This volume is an excellent history covering the period of southern Quaker settlements and the westward migrations.

The result was electric. Many of his listeners were by no means unprepared for his warning. They knew well the times in which they were living, and the message of Zachariah was like a catalyst in a supersaturated atmosphere. Perhaps never since George Fox had the voice of a Quaker minister been so effective in the outward response of a Friends Meeting. It loosened the ties that held Friends to their hard-won farms, turned their faces northwestward, and started wagons moving toward the great Northwest Territory. Soon all traces of Friends Meetings in that area were gone.

There was some precedence for what occurred at Bush River. In 1799 Joseph Dew visited Ohio Territory and in prophetic language reported to Trent River Friends, "I see the seed of God sown in abundance, extending far northwestward." Trent River Meeting responded, opening the way for migration, but not with a complete exodus as did Bush River, where the entire Monthly Meeting consisting of about seven local Meetings had, by 1808, moved as a body to the new territory.[2]

Though Quaker history made a sharp turn at this time this was not panic. A century-and-a-half had led to this decision and made the great migrations of Quakers from southern states all but inevitable. Nor did the response to Zachariah represent undue regard for the special insights of a seer. These Friends were too long schooled in group discipline to respond to a voice detached from the circumstances of the times or from the decision of a Quaker Meeting. They discerned truth in his words, for they too could see the ominous trend of events.

## How It Came to Be

As with a storm, a movement does not start with a burst of thunder, but "gathers" as the elements combine to create it. History sets well her stage before that dramatic moment in which the spirit of man responds to some inner compulsion. A storm was gathering out of the preceding years and the Quakers had been alerted to its coming.[3]

To understand this turn in Quaker history we must go farther

---

[2] Rufus M. Jones, *The Later Periods of Quakerism,* Vol. I, Macmillan and Co., Ltd., London, 1921; Chapter XI, "The Great Migration," p. 377.
[3] For a list of writings on early Quaker history see Appendices.

back to trace the course which led to the events at Bush River, and to the general migrations of Friends from the southern states.

Where, indeed, did it begin? In a profound sense it started with the Quaker movement which rose with artesian power in mid-seventeenth-century England. Like an eruption within the established order it challenged many religious traditions and battled the social evils of the day. Its center was inward, with an emphasis on the immediate and personal experience of God, and its outward expression issued in a call to "sound the day of the Lord." It was not, at first, concerned to establish its own identity. It carried no name beyond that of "friends of truth" and that given by its enemies, *Quakers*, a name more accurate than either friends or enemies knew, for this was a quaking movement. Enemies of a movement are often more accurate than its friends, in the sense that they observe what it does rather than what it claims to be.

The record of the expanding Quaker movement cannot be reviewed here. It has been told many times by many writers. Our purpose here is to catch the main points of that movement as it affects the story in the following pages. It came into being during an age of exploration, a century-and-a-half after America was discovered and the great era of expansion had begun.

The Quaker movement struck the American shore shortly after its beginning in England and Quaker communities were soon created on the shores of New England and spread into what is now New York, New Jersey, and Pennsylvania. Those areas were the base from which more migrations came as the frontier was pushed farther back to the west and to the south. American Quakerism cannot be fully understood apart from a knowledge of Friends in the Northeast, in states extending westward to the Alleghenies and southward to the Potomac River. It is a development fully told by many writers and, though not within the chief purpose of this history, its importance will be evident many times in the following pages.

### Experiences in Virginia

Though the main purpose of the following story is to present the migrations to areas west of the Alleghenies we must review briefly the movements and difficulties of Friends as they moved southward and settled in Virginia, the Carolinas, Georgia, and Tennessee. These are the areas from which the main migrations of Quakers later came into the expansive area of the West.

The first Friend to lift the Quaker standard in the South, before Quaker southern settlements developed, was Elizabeth Harris from England. In 1656 she visited the frontier settlements in Virginia, preaching chiefly to non-Friends with evident success. She followed her visit by correspondence and by sending books to the newly won converts. Josiah Coale and Thomas Thurston, who shortly followed her, were imprisoned as a wave of persecution began. A law of 1643, enacted during the Civil War in England, to "suspend and silence" any minister in Virginia not ordained by the Church of England did not promise an easy life for Friends and other religious bodies.

Thus the Quakers again came into conflict with the church much as they had in England. The non-Quaker colonizing of Virginia had as its purpose the transplantation in America of the high-class English way of life with its established church. Here the Quakers, having no appointed clergy, met their old enemy, the tithe, assessed for the support of what they called a "hireling" ministry. They were assessed heavy fines for nonattendance, for not having their children baptized, for failure to pay tithes, and for unauthorized preaching.

In 1659-1660 laws made specifically against Friends as "an unreasonable and turbulent sort of people, commonly called Quakers," started a persecution hardly less severe than that in Massachusetts. Mary Tompkins and Alice Ambrose, visiting about 1662, were whipped "with thirty-two stripes, with a whip of nine cords, and every cord with three knots; they were handled so severely that the very first lash drew blood and made it run down from their breasts."

Other visiting Friends were those coming over from England on Robert Fowler's *Woodhouse*. One of these was William Robinson, who later wrote to George Fox from a Boston jail regarding his Virginia experience, "There are many people convinced and some there are brought into the sense and feeling of Truth in several places." The next year William Robinson was hanged on Boston Common.

Friends grew in numbers and firmness in the face of persecution. These included both immigrating Friends from the North and those newly convinced. Josiah Coale reported in 1660 that he "left Friends in Virginia very well and fresh in the truth," and in 1676 William Edmundson found Friends "finely settled."

The laws of Virginia were, in part, aimed at protecting the colony from the spying French, with whom they were at war. Dissenters were suspected of disloyalty. The suspicion of Friends as a disloyal element is shown in a report of the Henrico County Court to the Governor. It stated that there was a meetinghouse

> to which several persons deemed Quakers do Resort upon Sunday & Thursday in Every week under pretence of Religious worship, but have no constant preacher. Except Mrs. Jane Pleasants (widow) whose qualification & Lycence we know not we are also informed that of late there have been monthly meetings, kept (by these persons deemed Quakers) at ye house of William Porter Jun in the County, and that several Wandering Strangers Come here as Preachers, and upon pretense of Religion, Resort to the two meeting places.[4]

The adherents of the established church in Virginia were so superior in numbers and in power that Friends were mainly involved in securing concessions and exemptions from tithes and from military fines. Virginia Yearly Meeting's advice of 1707 represents their stand in urging Friends to be faithful in the testimony against tithes "either for themselves or servants and that the Monthly Meeting do deal with such offending persons in the power of Truth." These fines were taken generally in tobacco, which Friends were raising as did their neighbors. As much as five hundred pounds of tobacco were taken as a fine from one Friend for "priests dews" (sic!).

Friends, following the example of their English forebears, besieged the Assembly and Governor for redress of these injustices. They were not alone in this, the Presbyterians perhaps having more influence than did Friends because of superior numbers. In many cases a parallel story of the efforts of other religious bodies could be told. Thomas Jefferson estimated that, at the time of the Revolution, two-thirds of Virginians were dissenters.

Friends were tireless in their work for freedom and justice. Certainly time and truth were with them. The course of unjust laws in Virginia could not last forever. In 1776, the year of the Declaration of Independence, a Bill of Rights was adopted by the legislature ending the battle on "church rates" and separating church and state.

---

[4] Weeks, *op. cit.*, p. 147-148. Also Chapters II and III on the migrations from north to south, and life in the southern area.

The fiery champion of liberty, Patrick Henry, was the author of this bill. In its support he said that

> religion, or the duty which we owe to our Creater, and the manner of discharging it, can be directed only by reason and conviction, not by force or violence, and therefore all men are equally entitled to the free exercise of religion, according to the dictates of conscience; . . . it is the mutual duty of all to practice Christian forebearance, love and charity towards each other.

In spite of persecutions Friends grew both in numbers and in firmness of fellowship. Not all settlements or Meetings can be reviewed here, but those having the greater significance in the Quaker movements should be noted.

In 1730 Friends from New Jersey and Pennsylvania settled on the Monocacy River. The settlement expanded with the securing in 1732 from the Governor and the Council of Virginia of 100,000 acres. Hopewell Monthly Meeting of Friends, established in 1735, and Fairfax Meeting, set off in 1744, along with other Meetings constituted Fairfax Quarterly Meeting under Philadelphia Yearly Meeting. In 1789 the Quarterly Meeting was transferred to Baltimore Yearly Meeting.

### LIFE IN THE CAROLINAS

As Friends had filtered through the timber and the brush to Virginia, over roads that were little more than trails, they then continued their migrations farther south. They came to the Carolinas like an overflow from Virginia, settling along the coast until the frontiers were pushed westward and inland settlements of a century later were possible.[5]

The first Quaker family settling in North Carolina may well have been that of Henry Phillips on Albemarle Sound. In 1672 George Fox and William Edmundson visited them. Overjoyed at this visit, the Phillips family remarked that they had not seen other Quakers for seven years. This suggests that they may have arrived in 1665. North Carolina Yearly Meeting assumes 1672 as a firm date for the first Quaker settlement, and observes three centuries of Quakerism in the state.

---

[5] Besides the references previously given, J. Floyd Moore, *Friends in the Carolinas,* prepared for observance of the "Tercentenary of North Carolina Quakerism," gives a summary of their history.

William Edmundson called a meeting for settlers of the area, consisting almost wholly of non-Friends. This gathering did not offer, as he saw it, a very promising prospect. These were people living in isolation from established communities, and social life of an elevating kind was largely lacking. Educational facilities did not readily follow those who came mainly in quest of land and had little motivation besides the making of a living. Of these first neighbors of Friends it was said that "they sat looking earnestly at the preacher, their elbows on their knees, their faces in their hands, their pipes in their mouths, and their hats on their heads." Edmundson, writing of them, confirmed this view and added, "Yet several of them were tendered and received the testimony."

Friends of today have not overlooked the first settlement, nor the first Quaker visitors on Albemarle Sound. A granite marker, with a bronze tablet, has been placed eight miles from the present city of Hertford honoring the first Quaker visitors who held a religious meeting in the home of Henry Phillips. The bronze tablet inscription is as follows:

Edmundson-Fox Memorial

Near this spot William Edmundson, an English Friend, held in May, 1672, the first religious service on record in Carolina.

Six months later George Fox, founder of the religious Society of Friends, also visited this section and held Meetings among the colonists. Here were the beginnings of the religious life of a great State.

Unlike the Friends in Virginia, those in North Carolina had an open prospect from the beginning, for their numbers were superior to those of their opponents and in the Quaker Governor, John Archdale, they had a friend in power. Their opponents were no less zealous than those in Virginia, but they were not so strong. This is evident in an appeal from Carolina to officials in England, written in 1703 by a representative of the established church.

To the Lord Bishop of London: . . . My Lord, I humbly beg leave to inform you, that we have an Assembly to sit the 3d November next, and there is above one half of the burgesses that are chosen are Quakers and have declared their designs of making void the act of establishing the Church; if your lordship, out of your good and pious care for us, doth not put a stop to their growth, we shall the most part, especially the children born here, become heathens. I humbly entreat your lordship to send some worthy, good man amongst us to regain the flock, and so perfect us in our duty to God, and establish us by his doctrine, life, and conversation in the fundamentals of our Christian profession, that we in our time, and those as come hereafter, may bless God that he has raised up so noble a pillar as your lordship to regain those who are going astray, and put a stop to the pernicious, growing principles of the Quakers. . . .

> Your most humble and obedient servant,
> Henderson Walker.[6]

The struggle between the established church on the one hand and Quakers and other Christian bodies on the other was not nearly so severe as in Virginia. This was due, in the main, to superior numbers of Quakers, Presbyterians, and others as contrasted with those of the Church of England.

The appointment of a Quaker Governor gave great political prestige to Friends. John Archdale was a thoroughgoing, convinced Quaker when in 1694 he was appointed Governor of Carolina.[7]

There is even more evidence of Quaker political power in an appeal five years later by a representative of the Church of England.

To the Secretary of the Society for the Propagation of the Gospel:

The Quakers, though not the seventh part of the inhabitants, yet by the assistance and contrivance of Archdale, a Quaker and one of the lords proprietors, have in a manner the sole management of the country in their hands, and of late years have at their pleasure procured a revolution of government as often as he that sat at the helm seemed to favor our Church, or endeavored to make any provision for a ministry; and if the grievances of the country be not speedily redressed by the proprietors, the Quakers, in conjunction with the Presbyterians (who always, in hope of preferment, side with those who are in capacity to promote their interest), will bear down the Church. . . . being turned out of the council and places of trust, for no other reason but because they are members of the Church of England, and that shoemakers

---

[6] Zora Klain, "Quaker Contribution to Education in North Carolina," a doctoral thesis for the University of Pennsylvania, 1924, p. 34, 35.
[7] *Ibid.*, p. 33, 34.

and other mechanics should be appointed in their room, merely because they are Quaker preachers and notorious blasphemers of the Church; . . .

> Your most obedient servant,
> James Adams[8]

As the migrations proceeded southward from Virginia, Friends had become experienced in the ways of conflict with church and state. Many Friends did not stop in Virginia except for counsel and supplies, particularly in the later migrations. Many of these later migrants were from Nantucket Island off the coast of Massachusetts where, at one time, it was estimated that two-thirds of the Nantucket population were Quakers.[9] The main movement from that area to the Carolinas came in the decade immediately preceding the War of Independence. Migrations from Pennsylvania came down the Great Valley.

Their reason for coming to Carolina was by no means that which impelled their descendants to leave the Carolinas a hundred years later. Elijah Coffin said that their reason was "soil"! There was nothing wrong, necessarily, with their economic motives, nor even with the lure of adventure that may have drawn many of them. What they brought with them, in a spiritual sense, we can hardly appraise. They brought themselves, their faith in freedom, and their ways of thought and worship. By 1750 Quakers were said to be the most numerous and the only organized body of dissenters in any of these southern provinces.

It was nearly a century from the organization of the Yearly Meeting in 1698[10] until 1791, when the first Yearly Meeting sessions were held at New Garden, around which several new Meetings had been established. The frontier had moved inland from the coast. The name *New Garden* has followed Friends settlements across the continent, as have other names. The original New Garden was in County Carlow, Ireland, but the name came at this period directly from the Meeting in Chester County, Pennsylvania. In the year 1751, when

---

[8] *Ibid.*, p. 35.

[9] Weeks, *op. cit.*, p. 107, 108. The list of Friends in this migration southward includes the names of Coffin, Macy, Starbuck, Gardner, Worth, Wickersham, Reece, Gifford, Bunker, Swaim, and Dixon.

[10] Elbert Russell, *The History of Quakerism*, The Macmillan Company, 1943, p. 113, 114; Chapter 10 gives a context of history within which North Carolina Yearly Meeting was established in 1698.

Cane Creek was set off as a Monthly Meeting, New Garden was established as a Meeting for Worship; in 1754 it became a Monthly Meeting.

While Meetings were being set up across North Carolina during the middle and later periods of the eighteenth century, many Quaker immigrants bypassed these settlements, going into South Carolina and Georgia. One of these settlements that came to prominence was Bush River, referred to at the beginning of this chapter. As early as 1762 some Friends had settled in the area. It was established as a Monthly Meeting in 1770. Bush River was surrounded by other Meetings that grew up rapidly in the area.

The dates of growth and decline caused by migrations to and from the Meetings in Virginia roughly paralleled those of North Carolina. For Virginia Friends the decline meant death of the Yearly Meeting as such. With the concurrence of North Carolina and Baltimore Yearly Meetings, and after fourteen years of joint review, Virginia Yearly Meeting was laid down in 1844, becoming a Half-Yearly Meeting reporting to the new parent, Baltimore Yearly Meeting.

Friends came to the Carolinas, built homes and meetinghouses, and improved their farms. What were their ideas, their daily life, their characteristics in the eighteenth century?

The most evident was their solidarity. In any period this has seemed a mystery to non-Friends. How could they command loyalty to the Meeting and firmness in their testimonies in such large measure when the influences around them challenged their way of life? There was no bishop, no ruling personality, no authority at the top. Yet there was order and organization that rested on the entire Meeting, the Quarterly Meeting, and the Yearly Meeting.

This kind of corporate life had generally been true from the beginning of the Quaker movement in England. Certainly there would be, and there were, deviations from the group control. Generally these defections came singly or in small groups and were met, as a last step, by disownments. Preceding steps were taken before disownment, in which such members were "labored" with by elders or persons appointed by the Meeting.

Solidarity might be held in older established Quaker communities, but would it hold on the frontier when Friends families and Meetings were widely scattered? Would the spirit of independence rise and threaten dissolution of their corporate life?

The answer is to be understood by the circumstances they faced. Spiritual unity and group solidarity are always better maintained when under test, and in the Carolinas they were faced with issues that continually challenged every aspect of their traditions as Friends. The heart of their group experiences will be more clearly seen when we come to their witness against slavery and war. Rarely has a Quaker group come through with a firmer witness than did these Friends during the latter half of the eighteenth century, and on through the Civil War.

They were concerned, as Henry Cadbury has well stated, with the reputation of the Society.

> They felt its solidarity in a way we do not. They did not take the easy view that each Friend should do that which is right in his own eyes. Trust in individual guidance and faithfulness did not go so far as to do away with all corporate testimony. Without excessive authoritarianism they developed a real society of Friends, whose radiating influence brought benefit to many of the best movements in the community.[11]

Before coming to the great issues of slavery and war that put their testimonies in the crucible, let us see some of the characteristics that have marked Quakers in the minds of their neighbors as a peculiar people. These were not new to Carolina Friends for they had characterized Quakers from the beginning. Whether peculiar or not, the characteristics grew out of a deeper principle which, at its best, made little distinction between the sacred and the secular. Life was *one,* whether in the meetinghouse or in the market. However, some of the early Quaker peculiarities are worthy of review.

Like their forebears these Friends believed in a democracy which should be witnessed to even in the cemetery. The Monthly Meetings were asked to continue "their labors in love with those that have 'artificial' gravestones in our graveyards to have the same removed." Regardless of wealth or position a Friend was a Friend. As they addressed all men in the levelling speech of the singular *thee* and *thou,* so should the graveyard give witness to that faith that a man is a man and should not be given special honors either by addressing

---

[11] Henry J. Cadbury, *The Church in the Wilderness,* "The Historical Lecture," North Carolina Yearly Meeting Session, 1948, p. 13.

him in the plural *you* because of his status or by singling him out for honors above others, even in death.

They were still faithful to the Quaker witness when giving testimony in court or in legal matters, by avoiding the oath.[12] "Swear not at all" leaped out of the New Testament as a command to them. They would not thereby practice a double standard of truth, one for the courtroom, where penalties could be assigned for falsehood, and another standard for daily life. Truth and integrity were their hallmarks. *Yea* and *nay* were enough for them.

The oath of allegiance had a special implication for it raised the question, "To what or to whom does one owe supreme allegiance?" This was especially critical, in their view, during the War of the Revolution. To refuse an oath or an affirmation of allegiance during that time seemed to colonial authorities to place Friends on the British side, and left them open to a charge of disloyalty. From the Quaker view it was a principle of owing allegiance to neither side, lest it imply a violation of their testimony against all war and their chief allegiance to God. More than "to swear or not to swear" was involved. Often in Quaker history the question of oath or affirmation has involved a principle beyond the oath, as such.

Their basic view as expressed in 1783, when the war was past, quite clearly indicated their main emphasis.

> Friends taking under consideration a former minute of this meeting, which was a prohibition of taking any test to either of the powers while contending, do apprehend that the said order is not now in force, but that Friends are now at liberty either to take or refuse the said test according to the clear freedom of their own minds.[13]

Far from refusing allegiance to state and nation, they went so far as to suggest a form that would be satisfactory to them. The question of affirmation of loyalty was subordinate to the object of loyalty. Their highest loyalty was to God.

---

[12] Fernando G. Cartland, *Southern Heroes*, Cambridge, Riverside Press, 1895, p. 123, 124. Governor William Graham opposed requiring Friends to renounce allegiance to the United States and taking the oath of allegiance to the Confederacy. The alternative was banishment of those who refused. Governor Graham declared, "It would amount to a decree of wholesale expatriation of the Quakers, and on the expulsion of such a people from our midst the whole civilized world would cry 'shame.'"
[13] Weeks, *op. cit.*, p. 193.

This quality of integrity permeated their commercial life. In 1803 Friends decided that the bankrupt law could not excuse them from paying their debts. They worked with members whose financial affairs threatened Quaker integrity, and sometimes helped them pay their debts. The Meeting cared about the member and about the reputation of the Society.

They were watchful over their young people and held to a strict line on marrying "after the manner of Friends." This was due in part to their aversion to the "hireling ministers" by whom a mixed marriage (a Friend with a non-Friend) was performed. It was also due in part to their faith in the Quaker way of life that could thereby become diluted with the "ways of the world." The disownments that took place for "marrying out of Meeting" did, in many cases, irreparable damage to the Society of Friends. We can understand their attitude in a time when the Society felt itself to be almost under siege by the world.

Their concept of civic responsibility shifted during the eighteenth century from that of the Archdale period, when political life was more nearly in keeping with their principles. When the political situation changed and state and local authorities required compromise, their attitude was all but reversed. In 1809 a proposal came to North Carolina Yearly Meeting "that any Friend, who holds office as a member of the Federal or State Legislature, as justice of the peace, clerk of the court, coroner, sheriff or constable, should be disowned."[14] Government was far from going their way and it seemed to them impossible for a Friend to carry responsibility in office and at the same time be true to Quaker principles. A far cry from the Archdale period!

They were also committed, as were Friends at their beginning, to plainness in "dress and address." We have indicated above their use of *thee* and *thou* as a principle which gave every person equal status, whether nobleman or peasant. They would not address prominent persons with the plural *you* and the peasant with the singular *thee* and *thou.*

This plainness in speech and in dress often ran into trivial requirements. If in any traits Quakers were sometimes "queer" it was

---

[14] *Ibid.,* p. 129.

in these. In some instances their requirements were, to our views, quite humorous. A certain Friend appeared in Meeting wearing a pea-green coat and pink pants; nonetheless he was dressed "plain" because the *cut* was right![15] When some Friends became wealthy, they kept the cut right but bought expensive materials. Such are the foibles of a people when outward rules replace inward spirit.

In earlier years the First Day Meetings were supplemented by gatherings in homes and meetinghouses for reading of tracts and study of the Bible. These later became First Day Schools for religious training of children. With the end of the Civil War and the reconstruction period, First Day Schools came to be regularized as permanent programs for the Meetings.

Meetings for Gospel ministry were also set up as general meetings. These were, at first, very similar to the First Day or Sunday meetings for worship, with an emphasis on preaching. As the Wesleyan evangelical wave swept America these came to be a "series of meetings," and yet later "revival meetings" calling for conversions. As yet the pastoral system had not begun, but the evangelistic trend opened the way for it. We shall see more of this development later, in the western areas.

Preaching, even in the days of the strictly open meeting for worship, had been encouraged by the needs and the expectations of Friends. Visiting ministers through the years had come in considerable numbers from England, Ireland, New England, Pennsylvania, and other areas of the North. They had come under concern, having been released by their local Meetings and Yearly Meetings for Gospel service among Friends.

Friends visiting "in the love of the Gospel" have always been an important part in holding the Society of Friends together in fellowship and in keeping alive the Quaker testimonies.[16] These visitors, it may be assumed, helped in a large way to save Friends from extinction in new territories and to keep them spiritually deepened and identified as Friends Meetings.

Some of these important visitors were Thomas Chalkley, John

---

[15] Dorothy Lloyd Gilbert (Thorne), *First Friends at New Garden in North Carolina,* a monograph, p. 11.

[16] Weeks, *op. cit.,* p. 90ff., gives an example of Quaker individuals in earlier visitations.

and Samuel Fothergill, John Churchman, John Woolman, William Reckitt, Catherine Peyton, Mary Peisley, and, much later, Mary Moon Meredith.

The value of the travelling Quaker ministry can hardly be overstated. One of the great losses in migrations westward was the lessening of visitations as great distance over rough roads made travel more difficult. One of the main barriers in American Quakerism has always been the isolation and therefore the insulation from the Quaker currents of life. During all these years of stress and strain North Carolina held, and it continues to hold, a commendable spirit of unity. When divisions were rending other Friends bodies, this Yearly Meeting experienced no great schism.

There was one slight exception. When the Five Years Meeting, in 1902, adopted a discipline a small group of Friends in North Carolina withdrew. Friends from Rich Square in Eastern Quarterly Meeting were not satisfied with the trend toward the pastoral and programmed activities of Friends and decided to form their own Yearly Meeting. Thus was born in 1903 the North Carolina Yearly Meeting (Conservative) which since 1904 has met annually at the Cedar Grove meetinghouse in Woodland, North Carolina.

A third diversity in the North Carolina area is represented, not by a separation, but by the extension of Ohio Yearly Meeting. There are ten Meetings in the state affiliated with the Piedmont Quarterly Meeting of Ohio Yearly Meeting.

Today high tribute can be paid to North Carolina Yearly Meeting for its spirit of unity and solidarity. While some other Yearly Meetings in America have had a continuing tension along lines of faith and practice, North Carolina Friends have exemplified the victory that comes when, though having as great diversities as any other Yearly Meeting, Friends could transcend those differences and finally resolve such defections as might arise.

### GEORGIA AND TENNESSEE SETTLEMENTS

Another Quaker settlement was in Georgia. In 1758, some Friends families moved to a point about seven miles north of Augusta and, believing that an Indian war was threatening, stayed only a short time. In 1770, a settlement was formed on a grant made to Friends by the General Assembly of Georgia. Here the town of Wrightsborough was started, the name honoring Sir James Wright, Governor of the colony.[17]

The Wrightsborough Meeting reported to Bush River Quarterly Meeting in South Carolina. In 1799 there were ten Meetings in South Carolina and three in Georgia. These Friends early took the trail north, scarcely leaving any traces of what were once thriving Meetings. In 1803 the last evidence of the Georgia Friends indicates that they had left for the Ohio area. Bush River Meetings followed near the same time.

There had been a migration from North Carolina Yearly Meeting to eastern Tennessee as early as 1784.[18] Lost Creek was the first important settlement there, and later New Hope. In 1802 those two were constituted as a Quarterly Meeting. This movement to Tennessee was firmly resisted by the home Meetings partly because of their fear that it was the result of worldly interests, but also because Friends were uncertain whether the land had been rightly acquired from the Indians. They had seen government and other agencies driving sharp bargains with the Indians, and Friends had defended Indian interests.

Restraints were urged by the older Meetings and Friends were exhorted to seek counsel and secure consent before moving. Friends were generally fearful of a restless, roving spirit not "in divine ordering" but rooted in the desire for worldly possessions. This was reflected in a minute of Western Quarterly Meeting of North Carolina Yearly Meeting in 1792.

> Taking into consideration the case of Friends removing to the back settlements & the difficulties and danger some have been reduced to and trouble they have brought on Friends thereby, for preventing of which this meeting do give it as our sense & judgment that no Friend do remove and settle out of the limits of a Monthly Meeting without first applying to and having consent of the Monthly and Quarterly Meeting to which they belong. . . ."[19]

The journals of Friends visiting these frontier settlements reflect certain fears that the home Meetings in the Carolinas had recorded.

---

[17] *Ibid.*, p. 117-124. A review of Friends settlements in and the emigration from Georgia.
[18] *Ibid.*, p. 251ff. Tennessee Settlements of Friends. Also *Journal* of William Williams, 1828; a good review by this visiting Friend.
[19] *Ibid.*, p. 252.

Joshua Evans, when he was visiting Friends of Tennessee in 1797, wrote:

> . . . my concern was increased, on beholding brethren and fellow professors too incautious in respect to such hasty removals . . . . I was likewise concerned to caution Friends against a disposition that leads to unsettlement, and to ramble farther out into remote places . . . suffering their minds to be captivated with the love of a rambling lazy life, or going to new settlements to seek a maintenance by hunting. . . . .[20]

Nothing could restrain Friends from moving with the receding frontier. The settlements in Virginia, the Carolinas, Georgia, and Tennessee had been made with a view of establishing permanent homes and Meetings. There were probably several reasons for the decision to move again, but there was one purpose that outweighed all other considerations. To that purpose we shall now direct our attention.

### THE BIRTH OF A TESTIMONY: FRIENDS AND SLAVERY

Though Friends were ahead of their times on the question of slavery, why did it require a century for them to awaken to its evils and renounce it? Their spiritual insight led them to renounce war from the beginning of the Quaker movement. Why not slavery? They had urged living wages for servants. What of the servants who received *no* wages and had no rights beyond the will of their masters?

This is one of the mysteries within Quaker history. Perhaps the main explanation is that they, like many present-day Christians, had social "blind spots." Custom at any period of history often has the appearance of necessity, and what is "necessary" is not readily seen as immoral. There is ever a tendency of people to be very selective in their identification of sins.

It should also be noted that in England Friends were not exposed to the forms of slavery existing elsewhere in the world. They were quite overwhelmed with the problems raised by their opponents which resulted in tensions, conflicts, and persecution. They were fully occupied with the immediate problems that were pressed upon them. Not until they came to America were they exposed to the growing,

---

[20] *Ibid.,* p. 254.

massive evil of slavery. The question still remains: Why did they not instinctively cry out against it as they had in the case of war? To find the answer to that question we would do well to raise it for our own day, when the final phase of the emancipation is upon us!

There were some background reasons for their attitude. Slavery is as old as human history. It predated the Christian era by many centuries and became so much a way of life that people could not readily isolate it as an evil. The New Testament does not condemn slavery as an institution. Masters are counselled to be kind to their slaves and slaves are exhorted to be obedient to their masters. The principle of brotherhood proclaimed in Philemon and throughout the New Testament would finally destroy slavery, though there was no attack on the total system. It is evident that Greek slaves were in the fellowship of the early church. There was precedent for the attitude of Friends.

### The Southern Experience

The long road by which Friends of the southern states came to a complete renunciation of slavery wound slowly upward, over a century. It was not a well-defined road; they had to build it even as they travelled on it. In the end it became a highway of the spirit. A full review of the course by which the Society of Friends came to the higher moral level of practice cannot be given here, but some steps will be indicated as they developed in the South.

George Fox on his visit to America in 1671-1672 probably saw slavery at its worst on the island of Barbados, where the sugar industry relied heavily on slave labor. Friends had colonized on the island and, like their neighbors, owned slaves. Though Fox did not condemn the institution of slavery itself he urged steps that could lead eventually to emancipation. He suggested to Friends not only kindness to their slaves but also treating them as indentured servants to be set free after a certain period of service.

The visit of Fox to Barbados started an agitation that was unwelcomed by non-Friends slaveholders.[21] When accused by Barbados authorities of inciting slaves to rebellion, Fox stoutly denied such a motive as "wicked slander." Friends knew that rebellion would mean

---

[21] Thomas E. Drake, *Quakers and Slavery in America*, Yale University Press, 1950; p. 2, footnote, offers sources on Fox in Barbados.

bloodshed which offered no answer to the plight of the slaves. Instances of rebellion appeared occasionally through this early period illustrating the futility of violence as an answer.

Though Friends on Barbados owned slaves they rose above the commonly held ideas and tried to educate and Christianize their own slaves. To do so they openly violated the law. Education of slaves was prohibited. Education is always dangerous to the vested interests within every tyranny and, as viewed by the authorities on Barbados, threatened the peace and well-being of the existing order. Friends came to be thought of as a dangerous people and captains of ships were forbidden to bring in any more Quakers. This may explain why the colony of Friends on Barbados finally disappeared. They may have emigrated to the mainland of America, returned to England, or ceased to be Friends.

The message of Fox was beamed toward all Friends in America when in 1676 he wrote:

> And so now consider, do not slight them, to wit, the Ethiopians, the blacks now, neither any man or woman upon the face of the earth; in that Christ died for all, both Turks, Barbarians, Tartarians, and Ethiopians; he died for the tawnies [Indians] and for the blacks as well as for you that are called whites. . . .

His letter became more specific and practical as he suggested:

> It will doubtless be very acceptable to the Lord, if so be that masters of families here would deal so with their servants, the Negroes and blacks, whom they bought with their money, to let them go free after a considerable term of years, if they have served them faithfully; and when they go, and are made free, let them not go away empty-handed. This, I say, will be very acceptable to the Lord.[22]

Once the light began to break it came into greater glow in the minds of some individuals of the Society of Friends. One such Friend was William Edmundson, who had been closely associated with George Fox in his visit to Barbados and to the Friends in the Carolinas and Virginia.

In 1676 Edmundson wrote in a letter to Friends in America:

---

[22] *Ibid.*, p. 6, both quotations.

And it would be acceptable with God, and answer the witness in all, if you did consider their [the Negroes'] condition of perpetual slavery, and make their conditions your own, and so fulfill the law of Christ. For perpetual slavery is an aggravation, and an oppression upon the mind, and hath a ground; and Truth is that which works the remedy, and breaks the yoke and removes the ground. So it would do well to consider that they [the slaves] may feel, see, and partake of your liberty in the gospel of Christ, . . . [that] they may see and know the difference between you and other people, and your self-denial may be known to all.[23]

Then Edmundson struck with a question that would require an answer in which Friends would be forced to concede. "And many of you count it unlawful to make slaves of the Indians, and if so, then why the Negroes?"[24] The Quaker conscience was being penetrated by an invincible logic, for the Friends abhorred the enslaving of Indians.

Edmundson was a century ahead of his time. He was a "voice crying in the wilderness," but his voice was not wasted. It would later be echoed again and again from Friend to Friend. What was now the voice of one man finally became a chorus of Quaker voices.

Chief among the Friends who later visited Virginia and the Carolinas and felt burdened by their slaveholding was John Woolman. He had a very sensitive spirit and felt deeply the difference "in general betwixt a people used to labor moderately for their living, training up their children in frugality and business, and those who live on the labour of slaves." He felt so keenly the danger of his own involvement with the evil that when, as a guest in the home of a slaveholding Friend, he resolved to pay his host, though the man might be a person of wealth. He wanted not only to raise his voice against slaveholding; he also felt that "conduct is more convincing than language" and he did not want to be restrained in his plain speaking with a host by being beholden to him as a guest.[25]

Woolman's interest was broader and deeper than the issue of slavery alone. He was an apostle of the simple life and a saint in

[23] *Ibid.*, p. 9, 10.
[24] *Ibid.*, p. 10.
[25] *Journal*, of John Woolman, a classic in Quaker literature. Amelia Mott Gummere; The Macmillan Company, 1922. The relation of Woolman to the early antislavery movement among Friends was very penetrating. P. 190-199.

the consistency of his practice. He, like other visiting Friends, was concerned for the degenerating influence of slavery on the slaveholder as well as on the slave. The low spiritual state reported of many Friends Meetings was attributed largely to the blight of slaveholding. Woolman was convinced that "the love of ease and gain are the motives in general of keeping slaves, and men are wont to take hold of weak arguments" as they rationalize their practices.

His concern is well summarized in a paragraph from an epistle to Friends of New Garden and Cane Creek in 1757.

> Where slaves are purchased to do our labour numerous difficulties attend it. To rational creatures bondage is uneasy, and frequently occasions sourness and discontent in them which affects the family and such who claim the mastery over them. Thus people and their children are many times encompassed with vexations, which arise from their applying to wrong methods to get a living.

Though antislavery conviction was not born with Quakerism, it was inherent in the Quaker faith. The nature of their faith regarding God and man would not let Friends rest in the face of this social evil. There was, in theory, no break between their religious and their secular life. Life was in some deep sense of one piece. Therefore problems could not be left to be solved somewhere in the great beyond while Friends remained safely resting in religious experience.

Even when they were tempted to relapse into acceptance of the world as it was, and failed to respond to great issues, they had (if nothing more) the words, the message, and the testimonies so well fastened in their personal and corporate memories that they would be forced to consider their meaning and to give answers. The decision regarding slavery would finally be faced as clearly as was the challenge of Elijah. It must be God or Baal!

Friends in the North came more quickly to a clear antislavery stand. This was partly due to their commercial and industrial life. The types of farming in the South were conducive to slavery. The coming of large cotton plantations opened the way, and when Eli Whitney's cotton gin came into use there was a call for cheap labor as cotton became the major export. This led to an increase in the slave traffic as ships plied the waters from Africa to America bringing thousands of unwilling workers in shackles to be sold to the highest bidder.

When slavery was observed in this stark form, like cattle being placed on the auction block, the Quaker conscience rebelled. This was the *first step* in their antislavery development: *Friends must not traffic in slaves for gain!* To hold them and be kind to them, to educate and perhaps sometime free them seemed a long way from buying, selling, and trading in order to make money on the flesh and blood of human beings. One step after another was taken, each approaching nearer and nearer the ultimate object of letting the oppressed go free.

Further steps were generally expressed in "Queries" sent down to the Monthly Meetings. Before 1759, New York Yearly Meeting had written the Query asking whether Friends were clear of importing or purchasing Negroes as slaves. By 1787 there was not a slave in the limits of New York Yearly Meeting. We shall not here trace the developments that came earlier in the northern areas, but should remember that through visiting ministers, of whom there were many, and through communications and epistles, impact on the thinking of southern Friends was very great, indeed crucial.

The development of a clear testimony on slavery came as if inch by inch, certainly year by year. *The next step* was the issue of Friends' buying or selling Negroes *for any reason,* but this raised questions regarding exceptions. If a Friend buying a slave could keep mother and child from being separated or keep a man with his family, would such a transaction be justified? Their answer placed the welfare of the slave first.

In trading with non-Friends they felt involved in the motivations of those with whom they dealt and hence a further restriction was made in which "it was now agreed that no Friend should buy a slave of any other person than 'a Friend in unity,' except it be to prevent the parting of man and wife, of parent and child, or for other good reasons approved by the monthly meeting; and that none should *sell* a slave to any person who makes a practice of buying and selling for the sake of gain." This idea of buying only from a "Friend in unity" was obviously designed, in part, to keep all transactions under Quaker scrutiny. Friends were living near a thin ethical line where close choices were necessary. This new restriction brought

Friends toward a clearer view and a complete testimony, yet in its birth stages.

It is important to note that while they were evolving their ultimate position they took time at every step to encourage the state legislature in doing the same. In their efforts they did not stop with the North Carolina Assembly. They knocked at the doors of the British throne only four years before the Declaration of Independence. They were quick to seize an opportunity afforded by a more advanced attitude in Virginia. We quote their action here at some length in the words of their Standing Committee to the Assembly of North Carolina in 1772.

> Being fully convinced in our minds and judgments beyond a doubt or scruple, of the great evil and abomination of the importation of Negroes from Africa . . . we are impressed with abhorrence and detestation against such a practice in a christian community. . . . Morality and true piety are much wounded where slave-keeping abounds, to the great grief of true christian minds.
>
> And therefore, we cannot but invite our fellow subjects and especially the Representatives of North Carolina (as much lies at their door for the good of the people and prosperity of the Provinces) to join with their prudent brethren — the Burgesses of the Colony of Virginia in presenting an address to the throne of Great Britain, in order to be as eyes to the blind, and mouths to the dumb (and whether it succeed or not we shall have the secret satisfaction in our own minds of having used our best endeavors to have so great a torrent of evil effectually stopped at the place where it unhappily had permission to begin).

They called on the Meeting for Sufferings of London Yearly Meeting for aid in this move.

> Dear Friends: We think proper to acquaint you, that we have been informed by our friends of Virginia that the members of the House of Burgesses in their colony had agreed to present an address to the throne of Great Britain, desiring that an effectual stop may be put to the iniquitous practice of importing negroes from Africa to the colonies. . . . We have, therefore, taken care to make known to several members of the House of Burgesses in our province the steps taken in Virginia on that account. . . . We shall be glad to hear that Friends with you, if they find

freedom, exert what influence they can to forward so good a work.[26]

This was like a foregleam of the Friends Committee on National Legislation which would be organized one hundred seventy-one years later. North Carolina Friends were in themselves a "committee" on legislation. Friends have rarely been silent when appeals to government were deemed to be in order. How and when they should appeal may be argued, but that Friends have assumed an obligation on every level of responsibility can hardly be denied. If some Friends today feel that other Friends are too persistent, too active in that field, let them read the story of North Carolina Friends for a century before the Civil War, both on slavery and on peace. Those Friends would not take *no* for an answer. Year after year they all but besieged government for redress of wrongs and for justice through law.

As Friends began to accept the position of complete divorcement from slavery they freed their slaves only to discover that they were seized and sold again. The Yearly Meeting raised money, employed lawyers, went to court and won. But the victory did not last long, for the Assembly passed a law making it illegal to free slaves except for good services, and this to be judged by the court. It was now legal for officials to seize freed slaves and sell them again.

In a letter of near-desperation Friends wrote the Meeting for Sufferings in London for advice, adding it as a paragraph in the letter referred to above:

> As there is an act of Assembly in this province which prohibits any person from setting a negro free except for meritorious services to be judged of by the County Court — under penalty of said negro being seized and sold to the highest bidder, for the benefit of the parish — such Friends as desire to liberate their slaves from principles of justice and christianity are under a great difficulty on that account. So we would be glad of your friendly advice and assistance if any steps appear to you that might be taken with prudence and safety.[27]

Whatever advice they may have received, they had to work out

---

[26] *Slavery Within Its Limits*, a narrative, reviewing the course of thought and work by North Carolina Yearly Meeting; published by Swaim and Sherwood, Greensboro, N. C., 1848, p. 7-9. An excellent review.

[27] *Ibid.*, p. 9.

their problems for themselves. It was indeed for them a moral dilemma. They deplored the system, but they loved Negroes more. What were the options? In the first place they might have declared their principles, freed their slaves, and left them at the mercy of the system. In one sense they would have been clear of guilt, but they would by no means have been clear in conscience, for they knew children would be torn from their mothers' arms and families would be separated never to meet again. They knew also the cruel life the slaves would have under hard taskmasters. Here again, in a more sharply etched situation, they must choose, and they chose the welfare of their Negroes. What did the papers, the bills of sale, or deeds at the courthouse matter when the destiny of human lives was at stake!

They answered their dilemma by appointing trustees or agents from their membership who could receive transfers of ownership from individual members. This may seem, at first glance, like deepening the guilt by putting the Meetings into the slave business, while relieving individuals of responsibility. Though this appears to be an example of "situational ethics" it can hardly be called "moral relativism." They took the only moral course open to them and penetrated or transcended the system and its legalisms with a testimony of love and justice for Negroes as fellow human beings.

They could not be rightly accused of assuming this corporate responsibility with a profit motive. Their self-restrictions forbade making financial gain out of Negroes. They could now bring group decisions to bear on the difficult choices to be made. Friends had from their beginning relied on group worship and thought and in their business meetings had solved problems through finding the "sense of the meeting." There was wisdom in group thought and leading, beyond that of the individual member.

This action of corporate responsibility had followed years of effort. They had urged emancipation of slaves by their members. Indeed, they were now prepared, after nearly a hundred years, to disown members who refused to comply. Should they now reverse themselves under the plea of necessity? The system was there and must be faced. They could not ignore it, and they could not condone compliance by their members.

They had spent many hours in their Meetings, had passed on their problems to the Quarterly Meetings which in turn had gone to the Yearly Meeting for counsel. This had meant agonizing hours and days that were added into years, giving advice to their members, revising their queries, restricting the trade in slaves, and then prohibiting buying or selling or ownership of Negroes. They had encouraged Meetings to invite "the blacks" (as they often called Negroes) into meetings for worship and to set up special meetings for them.

They had set up schools for educating their slaves and slave children, but the state met this also with prohibitions — educated Negroes would be restless Negroes. Slavery required ignorance! Again Friends had protested to their State Assembly year after year, with no relieving legislation. The state could not be convinced that implanting Christian virtues through religious instruction was desirable. Christianity was also dangerous, as it always is when human heads and hearts are imbued with it.

Surely Friends today could hardly suggest a better way, one that was more in keeping with Christian moral principles. This was not a hand-to-mouth ethical and moral philosophy. Inwardly Friends had long ago freed their Negroes, though outwardly the papers at the courthouse recorded them as slaves.

The counsel of Paul to Philemon, and of Fox to Friends everywhere, had come to its full meaning — to treat the Negroes as brothers. The meaning of basic Quaker testimonies came through the test. Up to the time of the North Carolina witness the testimony had been tested, but not on the large scale that occurred here.

Though it took more than a century, Friends had "arrived" in their witness. They were solidly committed to their stand, with few if any dissenting. Friends were willing to wait for the sense of the Meeting, even for a century. Though they waited long, yet they were ahead of their contemporaries. Many representatives of other churches agreed with them, but could not claim the backing which Quakers had from their own official body.

Some slaves wanted to bind themselves for life to a Quaker master as a security against being sold, but the Yearly Meeting, knowing it involved permanent slaveholding, discouraged this. Furthermore, in case of the death of the owner the property would become estate and there was no certain prediction of what the heirs might do. This was a hazard they would not allow.

Another response was to get their slaves to the North and to freedom. This was possible, though not always easy. By 1819 Vestal Coffin and Levi Coffin initiated the "Underground Railroad" (as it was later called), a system for helping runaway slaves to cross the Ohio River and make their way to Canada.[28] We shall review this activity in a later chapter.

In short, the Quakers were a "holy nuisance" to the existing order! They saw and practiced the peace principle as it related to those who opposed them. They had written after several years of struggle, "Another lesson taught here is that of charity — charity for those who continue to hold slaves. Hasty and harsh condemnation of those who differ from us can seldom fail to prove injurious."

Here indeed was the moral crisis — to hate the system, to believe in peaceful means of solving problems, to use every imaginative means when only relatively good answers were available, and yet to respond in such ways as they could *peaceably*. No available answer was the *right* answer, not in the *ultimate* sense.

By 1848 the Meeting for Sufferings of North Carolina Yearly Meeting, in a pamphlet reviewing the course of antislavery development in the Society of Friends, wrote this clear declaration:

> That slavery is inconsistent with the requisitions of Christianity we think will be manifest to every person who will examine the subject with candor. We confess that while we believe critical investigations into the meaning of Greek and Hebrew words [of the Bible] may afford an answer to those who build their right of slavery on such a sandy foundation, we do not rely on them to prove that slavery is wrong. What says the conscience?
>
> In the secret of thy own bosom does it not raise its still voice and chide thee for using thy fellow men for thy benefit and aggrandisement? Does it not whisper even when thou hast sought for arguments to justify slaveholding — they will not do! We call on professing Christians to beware how they press a few texts of scripture into justification of slavery, and proceed thereon to erect a structure the foundations of which are laid in the groans and tears and blood of their colored brethren.[29]

---

[28] Levi Coffin, *Reminiscences*, Robert Clark & Co., Cincinnati, Ohio, 1880; p. 21. This deals almost solely with the Underground Railroad as conducted both in the South and in the North. Chapter I, "The Beginnings."

[29] *Slavery Within Its Limits, op. cit.*, Preface, p. 3, 4.

This clear coinage of faith had come out of the furnace of affliction. It cost something to write those words and to live them out in
daily life.

Now it can be understood why the visit of Zachariah Dicks at
Bush River, as related at the beginning of this chapter, carried such
force. Friends were tired and largely hopeless. They had stood
firm, but uprisings and violence had occurred in several areas. Who
could blame them if they sought a land of freedom! Bush River was
but a vanguard of the movement. Across the entire Yearly Meeting
wagons now began to roll. And though many Meetings discouraged
the movement it could not be stopped until a Yearly Meeting of
several thousands was reduced to the heroic one-tenth or less of
Friends who had faced the storm that was destined to break into
the Civil War.[30]

The story of that experience is told in a later chapter. We shall
now take up the account of North Carolina Friends following the
Civil War.

### RECONSTRUCTION IN THE POSTWAR PERIOD

When the war ended, destruction of property, loss of lives, and
the breakdown in the usual order of political and economic life left
the South in shambles. Sherman's march from Atlanta to the sea had
left a wake of desolation in its path. At a time when he was needed
most, Lincoln was not there to lend his benevolent spirit to the
prostrate "enemy." Secession had been defeated and the slaves were
no longer slaves — they were henceforth freedmen. Carpetbaggers of
the North moved in and chaos reigned.[31]

That is a dismal and pitiful story told often by historians. Our
concern here is with the condition of Friends. Property, equipment,
clothing, food, everything needed to start life again, had been largely
lost or greatly depleted. Whereas Friends who migrated westward
before the war had gone to escape the slave environment, many
Friends now began to move in a desperate attempt to escape poverty

---

[30] Cartland, *op. cit.*, p. 67, suggests 25,000 Friends in the southern states before
the migrations began, which threatened North Carolina Yearly Meeting with extinction.
From 1,000 to 2,000 has been estimated as the number of Friends remaining in the
South.

[31] *Ibid.*, Chapter XXIV reviews the reconstruction period under the Baltimore
Association following the Civil War.

and find some place of hope. Friends in Ohio and Indiana invited them. The door of welcome was open, but the means of feeding and clothing themselves during the trip was sadly lacking.

Whether equipped for the journey or not, many Friends started west. Some of them got as far as Baltimore, where they were discovered by Friends in a deplorable condition, unable to go farther, hardly able to return. The response of Baltimore Friends was heartening and generous. Francis T. King, a retired Baltimore Friends businessman who had earlier acquainted himself with their needs even while the war was on, urged them to return to their homes where relief could be sent to them. He was held in high esteem by his contemporaries and allowed privileges by the military forces of the North so that he could minister to the needs of Friends behind the lines of war.

Abraham Lincoln had written a "passport" for him which is reproduced here from Lincoln's pen.[32]

Not only had Francis T. King penetrated war lines and ministered to southern Friends; he had also been entrusted with $20,000 from southern sympathizers of his border state to relieve the needs of southern prisoners in northern prisons, despite his being a strong Union man. Earlier he had come under the influence of Joseph John

---

[32] *The Friend*, Philadelphia, Vol. 97, No. 12, p. 140.

Gurney,[33] a visitor in his father's home, and he had accompanied him on his journeys in that area.

In 1865, after the war ended, he again visited North Carolina Friends, advising them to open such schools as they could while a plan of substantial help was being made. Their meetinghouses had deteriorated until some were little more than sheds and barns. Many of the school buildings no longer existed or had been abandoned.

After the Baltimore Association was formed in 1865, its first order was to furnish relief, food, clothing, and the barest essentials. Those who had travelled as far as Baltimore were urged to return to North Carolina, where they could be helped. Even while this relief was coming, a plan for rehabilitation of schools was under way. The New Garden Friends Boarding School had not closed its doors, thanks to Nereus Mendenhall and others. Though it had operated under all but impossible difficulties it was there and furnished a base for the new efforts. Not only were school buildings in disrepair, but few Friends were prepared to be teachers. For the preparation of teachers some time would be required. During this first year of reconstruction the Baltimore Association helped to renovate existing buildings inside and out and secure equipment for teaching. At the same time Friends teachers in the North were enlisted for service, the New Garden Boarding School building was completely restored, and a normal school was added to prepare teachers from North Carolina Friends.

Joseph Moore, then a teacher of science in Earlham College, was secured to supervise the educational system of Friends. His genius for the work quickly put new life into the entire area. Part of the time he lectured on scientific themes of interest and awakened among Friends the appetite for knowledge. The sagging morale was renewed. With lantern slides he drew large attendance and kindled new interest in schools. Friends in local areas organized to repair and build schoolhouses with the financial aid of the Baltimore Association.

New Garden School, the heart of it all, was not only preparing teachers and bringing new currents of life to the new schools established over the Yearly Meeting; it was also a source of leadership in rebuilding the Meetings spiritually. Allen Jay of Indiana, following the work of Joseph Moore, encouraged the organization of Bible

---

[33] See Chapter 2.

Schools and the preparation of teachers for their classes (a forerunner of the Sunday Schools and the present-day Christian Education program).

By 1866, Friends New Garden School had no debts, had one hundred twenty-six students, and was training no fewer than one hundred potential teachers. By 1868 the miracle had occurred — there were forty schools with over 2,500 pupils of whom more than 1,400 were Friends children. Probably no poor children were overlooked. By 1870, forty-one schools were reported with nearly 2,800 pupils, and nearly one-half were Friends children.

There was at this time no public school system and Friends furnished, for all practical purposes, the entire public education in their areas. Governor Jonathan Worth said that this movement was the most important program of reconstruction he had seen.

By 1872 the Baltimore Association could cease most of its work, for North Carolina Friends were now able and willing to carry responsibility. The crisis was past but a great need remained as the Association turned over to the care of the Yearly Meeting thirty-eight schools with sixty-two teachers and 2,400 pupils. By 1887 the financial accounting showed over $138,000 raised and spent for the work of reconstruction.

Though the Association rightly carried the name of Baltimore, it represented very generous gifts from London Yearly Meeting, Philadelphia, New England, and other Yearly Meetings to the north, and from Friends in Ohio and Indiana. This was not the first time, nor would it be the last, when the bonds of loving fellowship felt by Friends everywhere would be expressed. Famine and drouth in Kansas would later call out a great response by Friends in all of these areas. If Friends today could realize how much had been shared among them in meeting the needs of one another it would give them a greater sense of historical gratitude.

The movement westward could hardly be understood but for the history of nearly two centuries within the Carolinas, out of which it came. North Carolina Quaker experience represents an important turn in the history of the Society of Friends in America.

We cannot rightly move from this area without recognizing these heroic Friends who stayed in the South. "These are they who came out of great tribulation" might well describe them. There were "tall" men and women who stood close together in order that they might stand! They included Nereus Mendenhall, responding to the inner voice and forsaking the lure of a more comfortable life in the great Northwest; Jeremiah Hubbard, refusing to yield in his determination to educate; Nathan Hunt, patriarch and steadying personality — these and others who preceded and followed them. Holding a unique place in the story were Francis T. King of Baltimore and those who worked closely with him.

North Carolina Friends would face a new level of life, rising from the ashes of the postwar period like a phoenix. From fewer than 2,000 members during the war they have become the largest Yearly Meeting within the Friends United Meeting on the American continent.

We must now return to the period of the migrations, near the opening of the nineteenth century. Here is the beginning of a movement destined to change a large part of Quaker history.

### NOTE

Family names of Friends migrating south from Nantucket Island include the following (for a more nearly complete account of Friends moving from northern areas to the South, see Weeks, *op. cit.,* p. 96-108): Barnard, Bunker, Dixon, Folger, Gardner, Gifford, Hussey, Macy, Reece, Starbuck, Swain, Wickersham, and Worth. The migrations were largely ended by the War for Independence.

# Chapter 2

## WAGONS WESTWARD!
### *To the Ohio Valley*

Somewhere over that distant range of mountains freedom's drums were beating. Soon the *clop-clop* of hoofs and the bumping of wagon wheels were caught in the rhythm of a new history-in-the-making. What began as a dream of the few became a contagion, and vehicles which at first moved singly or in small caravans formed road streams nearly a century long. The Quaker part in that movement reached its peak shortly before the Civil War.

These Friends were following no will-o'-the-wisp. Nor were they climbing the mountain "because the mountain was there," but because of what was beyond the mountain. They felt that they were in step with the future. A few intrepid Friends had been over there. It was a land of streams, forests, and good soil. It was waiting for those who had the faith and the fortitude to claim it.

The star of empire was moving west and thousands of Americans were responding in this "Westward-Ho" of the nation. This spirit doubtless caught the minds of Friends. Beyond the usual motivations,

Friends had a religious concern in this movement. The preceding chapter has presented the oppressive conditions of the slavery environment. Friends had faced it, labored against it, and had lost their case year after year. The prison walls of that environment were closing in on them. They were pushed by the conditions back of them and lured by the prospects ahead.

We cannot know who should have stayed or who should have left, but we can try to understand both groups. The smaller number remained in North Carolina, some of whom chose to stay as under divine leading. We shall see them in a later chapter when their peace testimony was tested during the Civil War. Perhaps many were simply caught in the web of circumstances. We have seen them through some of their trials, but now we turn to that larger number who moved out of the discouraging circumstances to what appeared to be a land of freedom and opportunity.

The Ordinance of 1787, by which the vast Northwest Territory was to be a land forever free from slavery, swung open the gate to the West. It provided that not fewer than three nor more than five states should be created out of the new territory. The five, not long afterward admitted to the Union, were Ohio, Indiana, Illinois, Michigan, and Wisconsin,[1] the first two attracting a high concentration of Quakers. The main tide of Friends to the new territory did not crest until the turn into the nineteenth century. The phrase *forever free* rang in Friends ears for it answered their deepest concern.

No Red Sea was split open before them, nor were the mountains rent asunder for their passing; but with whatever difficulties attending, they came. In spirit it was as if they bore the "Ark of the Testimony" bumping along in a covered wagon!

This was indeed a Quaker "Exodus." They came by foot, on horseback, by wagons, and in sundry vehicles that were drawn by oxen or horses. It was chiefly the day of the covered wagon — a period that would lengthen out into a century, as the numerous covered wagons continued moving farther, farther, farther on to their "promised land."[2]

---

[1] John A. Krout, *United States to 1865;* College Outline Series; Barnes & Noble, Inc., New York (reprint 1963); p. 54.

[2] Stephen B. Weeks, *Southern Quakers and Slavery;* The Johns Hopkins Press, 1896. Chapter X, "Southern Quakers and the Settlement of the Midwest," gives a full story of migrations and settlements.

At first they followed buffalo trails. Where the buffalo, deer, and Indian could go a horse could go. Then with the occasional wars, beginning with the French and Indian War (1756-1763), trails were widened into roads for military vehicles. These were often little more than cart roads until better ones made wagon travel feasible. In a few cases Friends floated on rafts or sailed on the rivers. By diverse ways of travel Friends came into their "Canaan."

Later migrations were aided by railroads which were slowly forming their network across the East, into the South, and far into the West. In 1804 Oliver Evans of Philadelphia built the first American steam locomotive, and in 1826 the first railroad was operated in the United States. From there on the development was rapid, the transcontinental line being completed in 1869.[3] Before the westward migrations of Friends were completed, many had come not only by wagon, raft, or boat, but also by rail.

Of necessity migrations of Friends ended temporarily with the coming of the Civil War; but after its close they started again. Addison Coffin of North Carolina, inveterate traveller that he was, made three trips to Indiana on foot. After the war he organized migrations by train. He reported that between 1866 and 1872 he directed ten trains of emigrants each year.[4] Railroads were interested in populating the new Northwest and gave every encouragement through special rates. Of the several thousands of emigrants led by Addison Coffin, only about five hundred were Friends.

PROBING AND PROVING THE NEW LAND

Though our interest just here must center, in the main, on those movements of Friends from the South to the land beyond the Ohio River, we must look farther back in the story and also farther north to catch the whole sweep of Quaker migrations.[5]

In 1773 Zebulon Heston and John Parrish ventured into Ohio Territory to visit the Indians, for whom Friends always had a great concern. Whether these Friends were in any sense scouting the new land we do not know, but they doubtless later reported their impressions. In 1777 Thomas Beals and William Robinson, with others,

---

[3] Stewart Holbrook, *The Story of American Railroads;* a comprehensive review of railroad development, contemporary with the migrations.

[4] Addison Coffin, *Life and Travels;* William G. Hubbard, publisher, 1897.

[5] Rufus M. Jones, *Later Periods of Quakerism I,* Ch. XI, "The Great Migration."

visited in southern Ohio and returned with a good report. Before 1800 Thomas Beals had come with his family to Lawrence County, later moving up the Scioto valley near the site of present-day Chillicothe, where he died in 1801. Joseph Dew, in 1799, had scouted the Ohio Territory and returned inspired with what he thought was a great opportunity.

Even earlier, Henry Beeson settled in 1768 in southwestern Pennsylvania near Redstone Creek, in the Monongahela valley, initiating the first settlement west of the Alleghenies though east of the Ohio River. Here he laid out a town known as Beeson's Town (later, Union Town).[6]

Near the same time Rees Cadwallader settled in this area at what was later known as South Brownsville. Friends following these two pioneers formed settlements there and also on the west side of the Monongahela River, at a point known as Westland. These two settlements of Friends were later established as Redstone and Westland Monthly Meetings, and in 1797 were set off as Redstone Quarterly Meeting by Baltimore Yearly Meeting.

With available water power these Friends started a grist mill, a saw mill, a paper mill, and later a woolen mill, a tannery, and an iron works. The latter, developed in connection with mining in the area, later became a contributing part to the industry at Pittsburgh.

They had come to this area despite warnings that their safety from Indian attacks could not be assured. Having a tradition of friendship with the Indians, they had less fear of them than did their neighbors. Their "broad brims" were probably their best protection.

Redstone Quarterly Meeting became a way station for migrating Friends coming from the East and the South on their way to Ohio. These Meetings of the Monongahela received the certificates of many Quaker families and later transferred them to new Meetings beyond the Ohio River.

As those new Meetings grew and desired recognition as Monthly Meetings, their requests came to Redstone Quarterly Meeting. When at last they asked for a Yearly Meeting to be established it was through Redstone that the appeal came to Baltimore Yearly Meeting. Redstone

---

[6] Levinus K. Painter, "The Rise and Decline of Quakerism in the Monongahela Valley"; the *Bulletin of Friends Historical Association* (spring 1956), Vol. 45, No. 1, p. 24-29.

Th
south
Virgi
ward
came
Moun
into c

La
where
land
it led
the ci

Se
of thi
ness l

Ea
was t
were
berlan
Virgir
Natio
Ohio

Th
that l
major

Ma
eastern
westw
land.
in Oh

Quarterly Meeting was transferred to Ohio Yearly Meeting as one of the five Quarterly Meetings constituting the new Yearly Meeting established in 1813.

These settlements, being in the line of traffic from south to north to west, were also caught in the movement and later disappeared. In 1862 the following minute was made: "The representatives to the Yearly Meeting are requested to lay before Friends the propriety of laying down Redstone Quarterly Meeting." There were no records after 1870. The settlements had faded into history after some sixty years.

This story was similar to that of many other Friends Meetings. They had been established on a frontier and were presumed to be permanent. But the frontier was moving. It was as if irresistible forces caught these Meetings as they were dissolved and swept on by the westward stream.

Another westward migration was in northern New York State, moving from the Atlantic seaboard to the Great Lakes area, south into Ohio, and on to Michigan Territory. Cornwall Monthly Meeting, set up in 1788, the first Meeting west of the Hudson, was settled by Friends moving from Massachusetts.[7]

The War of 1812 had cleared southern Michigan for settlement and in 1825 the Erie Canal was opened for traffic. Darius Comstock in 1825 became the pioneer Friend in the Raisin River area, settling northeast of the present city of Adrian. He was followed by Friends from New York, Philadelphia, and other eastern areas. Here, in 1859, Raisin Valley Seminary (a common school) was established, with Moses Sutton as the chief benefactor. One of the principals, later prominent in educational work farther west, was Benjamin F. Trueblood. The school was closed after the first decade of the twentieth century. This area is still a strong Friends center and constitutes one Quarterly Meeting in Ohio Yearly Meeting. This northern movement also branched into Canada and laid the basis for a Canadian Yearly Meeting. These earlier movements of Friends from older to newer territory were often made without concern and support by their Meetings.

No restraints exerted by Friends Meetings could ultimately stop

---

[7] Jones, *op. cit.,* p. 430-434.

the westward stream. Some Friends complied and remained. Others apologized, but did not return to their home Meetings. With or without acknowledgement of disobedience large numbers joined the historic movement.

### FRIENDS — SETTLED AND UNSETTLED

Paradise is always a receding place. It is just ahead, shining with some kind of alabaster walls. Those who seek it want to settle, not next door, but in the next county or the next state. It has been said that if these settlers could see the smoke from their neighbor's chimney they felt crowded! Within this new undiscovered continent many Americans were seeking that never-never land which is always just beyond. Friends were not immune to that contagion.

It requires imagination to sense the life they were compelled to live in a new land that had to be conquered foot by foot and day by day. Primitive conditions always bring out something primal in the human spirit. These Friends had to start with bare essentials such as they could bring in a wagon over long, rough miles. There was little or no diversion from toil in the beginnings of this life on the frontier. They lived by the axe, the spade, and the sickle. They had to make what they needed, whether it was shelter, food, clothing, social life, or entertainment. There were not many choices. Conditions required ingenuity and hard work. Whatever they possessed came as the fruit of their hands. Nothing came as from an assembly line — they did it all!

Their next need was for more Quaker neighbors. The immediate relationship with a neighbor was that of mutual helpfulness. They loaned and borrowed tools and traded labor with each other until a cabin was finished, a field plowed, or a harvest gathered and stored.

Beyond physical necessities these Friends, isolated on the frontier, hungered for fellowship with other Friends. How eagerly they must have welcomed a new wagonload of Quakers! We can understand why such warm invitations were extended to Friends east and south and we can feel the lure which those letters of invitation must have created. To have a Friends Meeting required only a place of meeting and the attendance of two or three Friends. Meetings that were settled later and became official Monthly Meetings with meetinghouses had started first of all in cabin homes.

The second development that followed closely was that of schools for their children. The first schools were generally conducted in cabin homes turned into schoolrooms for certain hours of the week. The teacher was anyone of their members best prepared for such service. Education came hand in hand with religious development.[8]

The first main settlement was in the Miami valley in southwestern Ohio. Thomas Beals, referred to above, who moved with his family into southern Ohio, was soon followed by others settling farther west.

In 1803 Miami Monthly Meeting was set off by Redstone Quarterly Meeting. In the meantime other meetings were being started in this area. Leesburg was set up in 1807 with Monthly Meeting status. By 1809 Miami Quarterly Meeting was established including these and other constituent Meetings of the area. More Meetings and Quarterly Meetings quickly followed.[9]

During the four years following the founding of Miami Monthly Meeting no fewer than eight hundred and twenty-six certificates of membership were received by these Meetings, over one hundred coming from Bush River and Cane Creek in South Carolina, and from Georgia.

Practically paralleling in time the settlements of Friends in southwestern Ohio were those in the eastern area of the new territory across the Ohio River from Wheeling. Though the first settlement of Friends was in the Miami valley, the first Monthly Meeting was established in eastern Ohio. In December 1801 a committee appointed by Redstone Quarterly Meeting visited Concord and Short Creek Preparative Meetings, which had developed from the early settlements, and agreed that their request for a Monthly Meeting be granted. In the same month Concord Monthly Meeting was held; it was the first Monthly Meeting in Ohio, consisting of its constituent Preparative Meetings.

Meetings multiplied rapidly, moving in their standing from meetings for worship as Indulged Meetings to Preparative Meetings within a Monthly Meeting group. In turn the Monthly Meetings were formed into Quarterly Meetings, as Meetings proliferated in a widening geographic circle.

---

[8] See Chapter 9, "Education and Schools."
[9] Harlow Lindley, "A Century of Indiana Yearly Meeting"; bulletin of *Friends Historical Society* (Philadelphia), spring 1963, Vol. 12, No. 1.

Very early it became necessary to assign responsibility for Meetings in each geographic area of Ohio. In 1803, even before Miami Quarterly Meeting was established, it was agreed that Miami Friends should have as their boundaries of concern the Ohio River on the south and the Hocking River on the east. Concord was to have the area from the Hocking River east to the mountains.

It is necessary to omit much interesting history in the Ohio Quaker story, such as the development of new Meetings and their organizational life and interrelationships. Some Meetings ended shortly after they began because of continued movements of Friends. The centers around which they clustered sometimes shifted from one Meeting or settlement to another.[10]

### FIRST YEARLY MEETING IN THE WEST — OHIO

There were requests to Redstone Quarterly Meeting for recognition of new Meetings and for setting off new Quarterly Meetings. The first Quarterly Meeting to be established was Short Creek, set off by Baltimore Yearly Meeting in 1806. This called for an adequate building in which the Quarterly Meeting could be held, and in 1807 a building was approved to be erected at Mt. Pleasant.

In this same year the expanding Meetings to the southwest, by this time including Miami, Leesburg, Center, West Branch, and others, requested Quarterly Meeting status. This too was granted by Baltimore Yearly Meeting. By 1808 Ohio Friends felt ready to request a division of Baltimore Yearly Meeting, thereby creating a new Yearly Meeting mainly west and north of the Ohio River.

The request was received by Redstone Quarterly Meeting and referred to Baltimore Yearly Meeting. Action was deferred year by year until 1812 when the request was granted. By this time there were four Quarterly Meetings in Ohio, one of which extended into Indiana Territory. These were Short Creek, Salem, Miami, and West Branch — the latter including Whitewater [Richmond], which later became a separate Quarterly Meeting. All this occurred within a period of about fifteen years.

The establishing minute of Baltimore included these words:

---

[10] *Friends Miami Monthly Meeting Centennial,* 1903.
C. Clayton Terrell, *Quaker Migrations to Southwest Ohio,* 1967.

. . . believing that in our deliberations we have been favored with a degree of solemnity, we are free to propose that the Quarterly Meetings west of the Allegheny Mountains within the verge of this Yearly Meeting be at full liberty to convene together at Short Creek on the 3rd First day in the 8th month, next (1813) in the capacity of a Yearly Meeting.

The opening minute of the new Yearly Meeting stated:

At Ohio Yearly Meeting for the state of Ohio, Indiana Territory and the adjacent part of Pennsylvania and Virginia, first opened and held at Short Creek the 14th of the 8th month 1813. Hatton Howard was appointed clerk and Isaac Wilson assistant clerk.

They adopted the Baltimore Yearly Meeting discipline as their own and a Meeting for Sufferings was appointed. The first Yearly Meeting west of the Alleghenies and the first to be established in more than a century opened a new era in the forming of new Yearly Meetings. None had been established in the eighteenth century.

As history goes, the coming into existence of the Meetings, the Quarterly Meetings, and the Yearly Meeting on the raw frontier within a period of fifteen years seems like a whirlwind development. Yet the minutes of these Meetings reveal a sense of caution with real concern for "right ordering" in the steps taken. Initial requests for recognition by new bodies of Friends were not always approved by a superior body. After "weighty deliberation," action on many requests was deferred or even refused. The refusal of a superior Meeting was accepted without any apparent tensions within the existing bodies. It was taken for granted that the action of a superior body was final.

This is a commentary on the Quaker way in business procedure at that period. The statements of discipline provided the methods by which Meetings were set off but could not provide the spirit which bound Friends together across time and space. Contrary to popular concepts, Quakerism, though it was personal, was by no means an individualistic form of religious faith and practice. Quaker history is replete with examples. The individual was guided in his concerns by the weighty deliberations of the Meeting. In turn the local Meeting was not wholly autonomous in spirit, but waited for the decisions of the superior body. New Yearly Meetings were not established without consultations with other Yearly Meetings. It took four years for Baltimore Yearly Meeting to consider and approve the establishing of Ohio Yearly Meeting.

This relationship was like a nerve system that spread from London Yearly Meeting through American Yearly Meetings and to other parts of the Quaker world. As Yearly Meetings were set off in the expanding American frontier they had the blessing of London and other Yearly Meetings. Exceptions to this did not occur until very recent years in Quaker history. Quakerism was like an organism and therefore sensitive. It was not simply structural or mechanical. Such a body might be slow-moving, almost overdeliberate, but it was in a spiritual sense *one body*.

## CONTROVERSIES AND SEPARATIONS

Strangely enough, the first damaging influence to the corporate life of Friends on the frontier came not from the West or from their immediate environment, but from the East — from Philadelphia and London and other Yearly Meetings in northeastern America. Had it not been for this "storm" rolling in from the Atlantic their future might have been very different as Friends moved on toward the Pacific. Too much emphasis can hardly be placed on this invasion of trouble from the East. The Orthodox-Hicksite separation of 1827 and 1828 and the Gurneyite-Wilburite separation of 1845 and 1854 caused a major change in Quaker history, opening the way for some extremes that followed. We cannot retrieve the losses in our history by any retroactive means, but we can recognize where responsibility lay, historically.

Today Friends take pride in the achievements of their ancestors but do not accept so readily a sense of historical guilt in their failures. If there is historic guilt for the events that ultimately brought a sense of separateness in America between East and West in Quaker faith and practice, it is no less on Friends of the East than on those of the West. Baron Von Hügel said that Quakers lack in historical gratitude. It could be added, with much more evidence, that they lack in historical humility! In accepting their history Friends need to think in the first person plural.

The history of this first great separation in the Society of Friends has been told many times by many Friends writers. We shall not review here in detail the developments that led to the schisms or the painful experiences that came first to Philadelphia and other Yearly Meetings in the East. It would not be a profitable use of time and space to recall here fully all aspects of that experience. They are presented in considerable detail by other writers.[11] The main aspects of it as it affected the new Ohio Yearly Meeting and thereby the new Meetings yet-to-be in the expanding West must be reviewed.

The disturbance centered on the question of authority in the realm of faith. In what measure was Quaker life and thought to take its direction from the Inward Light, and in what sense was the Bible to be accepted as the authority? It seems clear that Fox and his contemporaries accepted both. The fact that Fox urged an experience of that life "out of which the Scriptures came" did not mean that he made the Scriptures secondary. The nature and the meaning of dual guidance, by the Inner Light and by the scriptures, was not a simple question. The answers which at first were mainly a matter of emphasis became polarized — it must be one or the other!

The separation came first in Philadelphia Yearly Meeting in 1827, at which the supporters of Elias Hicks represented the inward emphasis on authority and the elders of Philadelphia Yearly Meeting held to the emphasis commonly called the orthodox position. There were important factors other than the question of inward and scriptural authority, but the directions taken were toward a "liberal" and an "orthodox" division. It is difficult to be both brief and fair to the positions of these two bodies of that time, but in the main that was the line of separation.

Elias Hicks[12] of New York and Thomas Shillitoe of England attended the sessions of Ohio Yearly Meeting in 1828, the year following the separation in Philadelphia. Shillitoe represented the orthodox view. Each was convinced that the other was betraying the faith of Friends. This set the stage for the opposing alignments. The conflict finally focused on the choice of clerks, representing the two views. There seemed to be no way to resolve the problem, in view of the adamant spirit that each side maintained. The sessions ended in complete separation, with about an even number on each side.

It would be only conjecture to depict what the future of Friends

---

[11] Jones I, *op. cit.*, Ch. XII.
[12] Bliss Forbush, *Elias Hicks, Quaker Liberal;* Columbia Press, New York, 1956.

in the West might have been had this separation not taken place. It did not take place in North Carolina. Perhaps they were too busy practicing their faith and facing the issues of antislavery and other problems to have time for it. Their avoidance of that division kept a balance in that Yearly Meeting which Ohio also needed.

The orthodox branch faced further testing. Another controversy and separation occurred later, during the sessions of 1854, within the orthodox branch of Ohio Friends. The issues in that division were somewhat different from those of 1828. The leaders were different and the issues were more in points of emphasis and due to frontier conditions than were the former. This separation was also imported — that is, it came from the East to the West. The chief protagonists were John Wilbur, New England Friend, and Joseph John Gurney of London Yearly Meeting.

Following the previous separation the course of orthodoxy had moved yet farther in reliance upon the Bible while at the same time casting doubt upon the historic position of inward spiritual authority. Bible study, which at one time was considered "creaturely activity," was now becoming popular. Those who opposed this new movement were not opposed to the Bible itself. Indeed, some Friends felt as if analytical study of it was a form of irreverence. It was somewhat like laying human hands upon the Ark of the Lord.

Again, we have in this controversy a mixture of elements. The evangelical movement had caught in many areas of America but was felt especially in the rural areas and on the frontiers of the West. With the separation of the Hicksites from the orthodox group in Ohio, the restraints of that influence were gone. The wave of religious enthusiasm among non-Friends had, in some cases, gone into extremes but was at the same time drawing in converts. Local churches were emerging with new members. Methodists, Baptists, and others were thriving in this multiplication of churches.

These new churches and their influence were nearer geographically to Friends of the new territory than were Friends of the Eastern Yearly Meetings. Furthermore, Friends of London Yearly Meeting were at this time closely aligned in spirit with the orthodox evangelical movements of the day. They had divorced themselves completely from the Hicksite "separatists" in America and were near in spirit to the orthodox Friends in the new West. To have the blessing of

Benjamin F. Trueblood

Joseph John Gurney

London seemed to validate the direction Ohio orthodoxy had taken. Stephen Grellet, Thomas Shillitoe, William Forster, and others from England had come preaching, and they were evangelical in spirit and message. The form of ministry which they had sensed in the life of early Friends was lifted up and accented.

In Ohio the strains from Friends' early history and from the evangelical movement around them united to form a relatively new expression of religious life and zeal. Though Joseph John Gurney would hardly have approved adoption of the revival methods that followed in the wake of his ministry, he had opened the way for it. The important part that he played in the future of midwestern Quakerism calls for a somewhat closer glimpse into his background in England.

Born in 1788, he was a member of a family of eleven children. On his mother's side he was a descendant of Robert Barclay.[13] His father was a wealthy banker and the home life was affluent. He had the better opportunities for education, and was scholarly in his attitudes while being at the same time deeply religious.[14]

Certain ministers of the Church of England had a great influence over him and helped to give a bent to his life in the direction of a Bible-centered orthodoxy. This, however, did not lead him wholly away from the concept of spiritual inwardness. These two influences were united in him as a scholar and preacher of great power.

There was much in the life of London Yearly Meeting at that time which gave encouragement to this development in his ministry. There was, however, a conservative group of Friends in London Yearly Meeting who had serious doubts about his views. These opposing views came very much into conflict in the sessions of 1836, and it seemed doubtful what the outcome would be. The influence of the Gurney view is readily seen in the London General Epistle for that year.

> It has ever been, and still is, the belief of the Society of

---

[13] Robert Barclay (1648-1690) was an apologist for the Quaker faith and practice. He has been given fresh interpretation through two very recent volumes: D. Elton Trueblood, *Robert Barclay* (Harper & Row, N. Y., 1968) and Dean Freiday, *Barclay's Apology* (in modern English; private printing, 1967). This classic systematic statement of the Quaker faith has been given utter clarity in this translation.

[14] See Jones I, *op. cit.*, Ch. XIII, for the backgrounds of Gurney and Wilbur and the history of the second separation.

> Friends, that the Holy Scripture of the Old and New Testaments
> were given by the inspiration of God: that therefore the declara-
> tions contained in them rest on the authority of God Himself and
> there can be no appeal from them to any other authority what-
> soever; and they are able to make us wise unto salvation through
> faith which is in Christ Jesus . . . that they are the only divinely
> authorized record of the doctrines which we are bound as Chris-
> tians to believe . . . that whatsoever any man says or does which
> is contrary to the Scriptures, though under profession of the
> immediate guidance of the spirit, must be recorded and accounted
> a mere delusion.

The evangelical spirit, despite the conservative influence, was
running stronger in London Yearly Meeting than among most American Friends. The tension in the Yearly Meeting came sharply to the
fore when Gurney asked for a minute liberating him to visit Friends
in America. The Yearly Meeting was not united, but finally granted
his request. His coming to America brought a turn in the history of
Western Friends. He was a man of good physical appearance, pleasant
personality, and scholarship, and was also an effective evangelical
preacher. He encouraged Bible study at a time when attention was
turning that direction under the evangelical influences in America.

Opposing Gurney was John Wilbur. Born in 1774, he was not
reared in the kind of climate out of which Gurney came. His education and outlook were more limited, but he was a man of great
integrity. He adhered to the older ways of life and thought, as he
viewed them, in Friends history. Inwardness rather than outwardness
was the accent of his ministry. Although as fully convinced of the
authenticity of the Scriptures as was Gurney, he deplored the development of Bible Societies as expressions of "the creature." In his view,
Gurney was leading Friends from the original depth of experience into
words and was following the course of the "hireling clergy." Wilbur
opposed foreign mission activity as the undue activity of men.

Theologically he was as "sound" as the most orthodox. He held
firmly to faith in the death of Christ as the propitiation for sin, but
felt that the teaching of Gurney was an attempt to place salvation in
the realm of belief alone. The Hicksites, he thought, had denied "the
work of Christ without us," and now the followers of Gurney were
slighting "the work of Christ within us."

The spirit that separated the followers of these two Friends was reflected first in 1845 in New England Yearly Meeting where, after an extended period of dissension, Wilbur was disowned but took with him about five hundred Friends out of the seven thousand in the Yearly Meeting. This, of itself, would not have affected seriously other Yearly Meetings but for the fact that both groups claimed to be New England Yearly Meeting and as such sent epistles to all Friends orthodox bodies. Which was the proper Yearly Meeting to recognize became an immediate problem.

The Yearly Meetings did not resolve this dilemma in the same way. London withheld recognition from the Wilbur group while recognizing the larger body in New England. This gave encouragement to the pro-Gurney Friends of Ohio. They now felt that they had the blessing of the parent Yearly Meeting.

Like other Friends bodies, Ohio Yearly Meeting was faced with these two epistles from the two groups in New England each calling itself New England Yearly Meeting. Again the problem hinged on the selection of a clerk for Ohio Yearly Meeting, whether he should be one who was favorable to the smaller or to the larger body in New England. They were unable to agree on a clerk, and the existing one was continued in office for several years. In 1845 Epistles were read from both Yearly Meetings. In the following year neither of them was read.

In 1854, with Eliza P. Gurney, widow of Joseph John Gurney, present and with Thomas B. Gould, second only to John Wilbur in the conservative cause, also attending, the issue came to a climax. Ohio Yearly Meeting experienced a second separation, and again presented to other Yearly Meetings the same dilemma: which one was to be recognized as the official Ohio Yearly Meeting? Philadelphia Yearly Meeting, in order to avoid a separation in its own ranks, decided to suspend epistolary correspondence with both bodies. A very small group in Philadelphia Yearly Meeting withdrew, calling themselves Primitive Friends. London Yearly Meeting, while recognizing the Gurney body, also experienced in their own ranks a very small conservative separation. The separated groups were known as the Fritchley Friends.

Later separations from Western, Iowa, and Kansas Yearly Meetings helped to augment the Conservative bodies and partially explain their influence among western American Friends. These are reported in other chapters.

The Orthodox-Hicksite controversy had more doctrinal ground for separation than did the Gurney-Wilbur division. The difference in the latter was mainly one of emphasis, with the differing accents of inwardness and outwardness in faith and practice. After the separation the two diverged sharply, particularly in outward practices.

With the two separations, the former balance that had characterized Ohio Yearly Meeting was completely gone. Now there were three bodies with three rather distinct accents, and each tended to become more extreme in its way of thought and practice. The future marked them off with considerable distinction from each other. They began at once to grow further apart, accenting the differences that had led to the separations. The Conservatives, as the Wilbur branch came to be known, were like the Gurney branch in basic theology, but like the Hicksite branch in manner of worship and outward expression. The measure of liberalism that characterized the inner group around Elias Hicks led toward more liberal views in that branch. The Gurney branch became more intensely evangelical in faith and practice, while the Wilbur group moved more deeply into inwardness and its historic uniqueness.

What if trouble from the East had not invaded Ohio? Whether a united Quaker body could have weathered the circumstances of the frontier and remained united would be only conjecture.

None of these three branches thought of themselves as "separatists." Such labels belonged only to the other two branches! At the beginning each was, in its own estimation, simply a Friends Yearly Meeting, holding to certain traditional Quaker practices which the other bodies had forsaken. Despite the embittered separations, for several years the same meetinghouse at Mt. Pleasant was used by the three branches for their Yearly Meeting sessions, held at different times of the year.

It is of interest to note that whereas the Hicksite and Wilburite branches settled into their future courses without further large separations, the Gurney branch continued to have them. These came mainly after the formation of the Five Years Meeting in 1902, and were due chiefly to questions of faith.

## TRENDS AFTER THE SEPARATIONS[15]

### Wilburite Friends

The Wilburite branch, now known as Conservative Friends, avoided what it thought were the extremes of Hicksism and Gurney-ism and settled into a form of life and expression distinctively its own. Its members were convinced that they were in the one continuing line of original Quakerism. Their ways of life did not change. Simplicity of dress and speech, the silent basis of meeting for worship, the separate business meetings for men and women, the avoidance of all corporate activities done "in the will and wisdom of man," and detachment from the ways of the world — these were the outward marks of their branch.

They spurned foreign missions, formal Bible study, and all programs that seemed to them to rise from the overactive will of man. This attitude continued until early in the twentieth century when, as one of their historians has said, "most of Conservative Quakerism has left its museum-like isolation and has rejoined the World Society of Friends." They now participate in all Friends activities and encourage "Christian education programs which they once spurned."

They declined in numbers, from six Yearly Meetings in 1935 to three at the present time, in Ohio, Iowa, and North Carolina. A few isolated Meetings are to be found in other states, and there is one in Costa Rica.

They retained their interest in the education of their children. Olney Friends School at Barnesville, Ohio, and Scattergood School at West Branch, Iowa, show evidence of their interest. The schools have been opened to Friends of the other branches and have graduated many young Friends who have taken their places within many Meetings of the Society of Friends.

Despite the quaintness of their outward life for the several years following the separation, they have conserved certain elements of Quakerism. Their depth of spirit and integrity of life have been their hallmarks. They have been warmly received by other Friends bodies and now have an influence that may well be out of proportion to their numbers. They have contributed perhaps more than their proportion of peace workers, both in time of war and in time of peace. They

---

[15] *American Quakers Today,* edited by Edwin B. Bronner, gives brief reviews by representative Friends of the three branches, as of 1967.

cooperate actively with the Friends World Committee, the American Friends Service Committee, and the Friends Committee on National Legislation, and share in All-Friends conferences.

William Taber, a present-day Conservative Friend, indicates the trend of this branch.

> . . . wide differences can be found among individuals and meetings in the Conservative groups. Among them one may find extremes of activism and quietism, rigidity and openness, provincialism and cosmopolitan alertness. Wide differences in theology may also be found, though the average conservative does tend to agree on the importance and necessity of Divine Guidance, and on the need for depth — regardless of the words used — in worship. A few conservatives may limit their social concerns to the Temperance Committee and the Book Committee, while most of them are increasingly active in other concerns, such as race relations.

### The Gurneyites in Ohio

The future of the Hicksite Friends in the Midwest is considered in another chapter. Our attention now turns to the Gurneyite Friends, who became the largest body west of the Alleghenies. It is not possible to write about the future of these three separated groups without seeming to assume that one of them was the main stream and the others separatists. Because the Gurney division became the largest body in the West numerically, their course will be followed without the repeated label of Gurneyite.

The Ohio Yearly Meeting (Gurneyite) with which we are now concerned was greatly weakened. Its numbers were depleted, but the spirit of evangelism which swept frontier America moved in as the old restraints were gone. Walter Robson, an English Friend, visited most of the American Yearly Meetings in 1877. He was impressed favorably with the evangelical spirit which he found in most Yearly Meetings of the orthodox branch, but was disquieted with what seemed to him the emotional excesses of Ohio Yearly Meeting. He wrote about a "sweet talk with dear Sarah Satterthwaite" of England, who was also in attendance:

> . . . we both feel that the Ohio Yearly Meeting is in a most peculiar position & the question is "where-unto will this grow?" A church of earnest labourers, all wanting to preach & pray &

sing let loose rejoicing in their freedom & impatient of any control. Well, I love to see life, but I would not for anything see London Yearly Meeting copy from Ohio. . . . Our meeting of Ministers & Elders [Ohio] this morning could do no business, there was such a rush of religious exercise — about 26 prayers & preaching interspersed till the clerk . . . just read the opening minute & at once adjourned. . . . The groaning-responding — 'Amen Brother' 'God help thee sister' were just kept up all the while. These meetings are very exercising to me — I almost dread them & I think you had need pray that I may overcome my too keen sense of the ludicrous [!][16]

That Robson was himself a thorough evangelical in faith is indicated by his many references throughout his visits to American Yearly Meetings. He finds one relieving experience in Ohio Yearly Meeting in which he also indicates his evangelical position. He attended

. . . the . . . meeting of Ministers and Elders. . . discussing the ground-work of our most holy faith. I think I never attended a more intensely interesting meeting. . . . The fact is, Hicksism has a little hold with a few of the Ministers & Elders of Ohio & hence the necessity of great plainness of speech & great clearness of doctrine & soundness of view — in speaking — writing or preaching of Christ & His atonement.

Though distressed with some aspects of Ohio Yearly Meeting sessions he was favorably impressed with some of the ministry. He reports that there was a visiting Negro Friend, William Allen, "a recorded minister with a certificate from one of the Westerly Yearly Meetings . . . a 'son of thunder', and also a lady Friend, Esther Frame (very young) [who] spoke for an hour and a half — the most finished wonderful sermon I ever heard."

He was also impressed with David B. Updegraff, "who is looked on as one of the finest [Friends] ministers in America." Updegraff seems to have been the most influential Friend of the Yearly Meeting, his voice generally bringing diverse discussion to focus and to a decision.

This year, 1877, twenty-three years after the Wilburite separation,

---

[16] Walter Robson, Papers; a review of his travels in America, in 1877. (Haverford College library.)

may well represent the crest of the emotional wave in the evangelical expression of Ohio Yearly Meeting. Just when and how it receded we cannot know, but certainly the later record presents a more constructive period in which new levels of spiritual stability were attained.

What occurred in Ohio Yearly Meeting did not end there but sent a line of division racing through other Meetings and set new courses of faith and practice through the West.[17]

### NOTE

Family names of Friends moving to Ohio include the following (for a more nearly complete list with points of origin and settlements, see Weeks, *op. cit.,* p. 272-280):

*To Eastern Ohio:* Bailey, Ballard, Bates, Binford, Bond, Butler, Cadwalader, Cox, Draper, Fisher, Gregg, Harris, Hicks, Hunnicutt, Jordan, Lewis, McPherson, Macy, Moorman, Morgan, Morlan, Outland, Parsons, Patterson, Peebles, Peele, Pidgeon, Reece, Richards, Schooley, Stanton, Stratton, Walthal, Whitaker, Wildman, and Wright.

*To Southwestern Ohio:* Anderson, Burgess, Butterworth, Carter, Cloud, Dillon, Doan, Edwards, Hadley, Harvey, Hobson, Holloway, James, Johnson, Kenworthy, Moore, Morman, Morrow, Newlin, Ozburn, Stanton, Stout, and Terrell.

---

[17] For a record of Hicksite Friends see Chapter 4.

# Chapter 3

## THE INDIANA COMPLEX OF MEETINGS

Watching a sunset must have suggested to Ohio Quakers not so much of beauty as of adventure. Beyond the horizon — what unknown lands with their resources may lie out there? This land is good, but perhaps out there it is better! No longer could it be said that Friends were motivated simply to move from slave lands to free soil. If so they might well have stopped — all of them — in Ohio. But as new areas became inhabited the price of land rose and the economic factor played a part. Farther on there would be room, and land at lower cost.

It was a great day for prospecting, and scouting parties often probed the frontier for newer, better locations. It must have been, in part, the scouting interest of David Hoover which led him to the banks of the Whitewater River in eastern Indiana. In 1802 his family had come from North Carolina and camped on the Stillwater River, about twelve miles north of Dayton, Ohio. In 1806, in a party of five, he made his way through the wilderness of trees and underbrush directly westward to the Whitewater River. It seemed to be a promising place, and their report to Friends farther east soon brought others to the site which would sometime later become Richmond, Indiana.[1]

Following David Hoover the earliest settlers were Jeremiah Cox and John Smith. Other Friends came to the new area in sufficient numbers that in the next year, 1807, an Indulged Meeting was granted with over eighty members, adults and children. Harlow Lindley indicates that "the meeting appears to have been 'indulged' by West Branch Monthly Meeting." The meeting was held in the cabin of Jeremiah Cox until the next year when a log meetinghouse was built. In 1809 Whitewater was set off as a Monthly Meeting from West Branch Monthly Meeting.

The succession of Friends Meetings in western America, if fully listed, would look like the *begats* of the Old Testament. Hardly would a Meeting become recognized officially as a Monthly Meeting until it was called upon to set off another Meeting, generally to the west. Such was the proliferation of new Meetings as hundreds of Friends came year after year from east and south into the new territory whose western bounds were yet to be defined.

An illustration of how one Monthly Meeting "begat" another is seen in the list given by Opal Thornburg, in the succession that issued in Whitewater Monthly Meeting.[2]

Chester M. M. [in Pennsylvania] was established in 1681 as a
     self-constituted meeting.
Newark from Chester (Pa.), in 1686
New Garden from Newark (Delaware), 1718. This Monthly
     Meeting was later Kennett M.M. (Pa.)
Nottingham from New Garden (Chester, Pa.), 1730
Hopewell from Nottingham (Cecil County, Md.), 1735
Westland from Hopewell (Winchester, Va.), 1785
Miami from Westland (Brownsville, Pa.), 1803
West Branch from Miami (Waynesville, Ohio), 1807
Whitewater M. M. set off from West Branch M. M. (West
     Milton, Ohio) in 1809.

If the succession were completed it would branch out in several

---

[1] Harlow Lindley, "A Century of Indiana Yearly Meeting," 1921; the *Bulletin of Friends Historical Society* (Philadelphia), spring 1923, Vol. 12, No. 1.

[2] Opal Thornburg, *Whitewater, Indiana's First Monthly Meeting, 1809-1959*, p. 17.

directions with a much larger number of Meetings, extending to the Pacific coast. Monthly Meetings became Quarterly Meetings which in turn were formed into Yearly Meetings. A "genealogy" of Friends Meetings would make an interesting chart.

### INDIANA YEARLY MEETING DEVELOPMENT[3]

Before Ohio Yearly Meeting was established (in 1813), two Quarterly Meetings which would be constituent parts of Indiana Yearly Meeting had been set off by Baltimore Yearly Meeting. They were Miami (1809) and West Branch (1812). Ohio Yearly Meeting then set off Fairfield (1815), Whitewater (1817), and Blue River (1819). Request for a division of Ohio into two Yearly Meetings was made in 1820 by the above five Quarterly Meetings. The request was granted and in 1821 Ohio Yearly Meeting, conferring with other Yearly Meetings, consented. Indiana Yearly Meeting held its first session that year.

Indiana Yearly Meeting, from this limited beginning, was destined to be a center of midwestern and far-western American Quakerism. New Meetings, uniting to form Quarterly Meetings, spread rapidly across the state and into Illinois, north into Michigan, farther west into Iowa and Kansas, and on to the north Pacific coast, until other Yearly Meetings were formed later in those areas. Since its first year a total of thirty-five Quarterly Meetings, in six states, have at one time or another belonged to Indiana Yearly Meeting, most of them going into the four Yearly Meetings that were set off by Indiana — Western (1858); Iowa (1863); Kansas (1872), set off jointly with Iowa; and Wilmington (1892).

Despite the loss of over 21,000 members to these Yearly Meetings, Indiana Yearly Meeting had a substantial number left. One hundred years later, in 1921, there were over 17,000 members.[4]

The opening minute of the new Yearly Meeting, assembled at Richmond, stated:

> Indiana Yearly Meeting for the states of Indiana, Illinois and the western part of Ohio, opened and held at Whitewater, the eighth day of Tenth month, 1821, agreeably to the request of the several Quarterly Meetings constituting the same, and united with by Ohio Yearly Meeting.

---

[3] Lindley, *op. cit.*, p. 4-5
[4] See "Parallels of History" in the appendices for a record of historical events.

S. B. Weeks says of this area of Indiana, "No section in the West represents, perhaps, more distinctly the effects of this southern migration than does Wayne County, Indiana, and White Water Monthly Meeting. . . . "[5]

It has been estimated that by 1821 there were no fewer than 20,000 Friends west of the Allegheny Mountains. That figure would make an average increase through immigrations and accessions of roughly 1,000 a year. Rufus Jones suggests, "We should perhaps be not far from the truth if we put one quarter of the whole number, i.e., five thousand, to the account of Philadelphia Yearly Meeting." The others came from southern Meetings. To one counting the wagons that later moved on the National Road through Richmond it might seem as if the whole nation were moving west. Over one hundred wagons a day were counted, at one time, moving through Richmond to areas beyond.[6]

When the first session of Indiana Yearly Meeting was held there were few roads and hence few vehicles on the Yearly Meeting grounds. Friends came, for the most part, by horseback and on foot. With no public inns or hotels large enough to accommodate them, the hundreds who came were crowded into homes of Friends overnight, sleeping on floors in all rooms available and in barns. Pallets made of quilts and blankets were sufficient. Many non-Friends of the community helped to absorb the numbers in their homes. When improved roads made travel by vehicles possible, many Friends came in covered wagons. These were quite as comfortable for overnight sleeping as were most homes. Tents erected on the grounds cared for many more. Even today some Yearly Meeting grounds in midwestern America blossom into tent villages for the duration of the sessions.

## Conditions on the Frontier

What were the conditions, material and spiritual, that characterized the life of Friends during these first few years in Indiana? Visiting Friends from London, Philadelphia and other Yearly Meet-

---

[5] Stephen B. Weeks, *Southern Quakers and Slavery;* The Johns Hopkins Press, 1896; p. 280. See also p. 272-280 for a listing of family names, with the Meetings from which they came and those in which they settled beyond the Ohio River.

[6] Rufus M. Jones, *Later Periods of Quakerism I;* Macmillan and Co., Ltd., London, 1921; Ch. XI for an extended account of the migrations.

ings were doubtless generous and restrained in their letters and journals as they described the frontier life of Friends. One can read much between the lines of William Forster of England regarding the lack of comfortable hospitality such as he would have been accustomed to at home.[7]

> We were guests to our Friend Benjamin Bailey [at Spring Creek on the Wabash] and his worthy wife, who had not been previously visited by Friends. I think they did their best to keep us warm; but the cabin being without a window, we were obliged to have the door open for light, and the logs not being well plastered, *it required some watchfulness to suppress the rising of a murmur* [!] [italics added].

As to the spiritual state of Friends on the Wabash, in western Indiana, Forster wrote:

> . . . their number is not large, and certainly, as to that which constitutes the life and power of religion, the Society must be considered to be in a low state. There is no Friend acknowledged as a Minister among them; and I had to fear that the discipline is far from being supported in the authority of Truth, and that the attendance of meetings for worship was regarded by many Friends with great indifference. . . .

On his visit to Richmond in 1821 he spoke of Whitewater Meeting as "one of the largest meetings in the state, containing, I suppose, not less than 120 or 130 families, forty of whom live in Richmond, which is a thriving village. . . . "

Stephen Grellet, a great evangelical Friends minister, attended Indiana Yearly Meeting in 1824. He was always sensitive on questions of orthodoxy and readily sensed any defections in doctrine. He wrote concerning Indiana Yearly Meeting of that year (four years before the Hicksite separation):

> That Yearly Meeting was very large; the immigration from slave states to these parts is great; it renders them however a very mixed company, and it will require time before they can rightly understand one another, and get over their various early prejudices. Their business was conducted harmoniously. There are some here

---

[7] *Ibid.*, p. 416ff., gives a report by visiting English Friends in Indiana.

also who have made strong efforts to sow the seed of infidelity, and have succeeded in many cases.[8]

One's imagination can readily sense the contrasts that would appear as Friends visiting from older and well-established Quaker communities in London and eastern America came in contact with Friends who, for at least one generation, had been mainly on the move and had carved out primitive homes on the frontier. In a manner of speaking, western Friends had not caught up with themselves in a spiritual sense. It required time for them to get beyond the sheer material circumstances and settle into the fellowship that makes a community out of a neighborhood, and a mature Quaker Meeting out of an assembly of Friends. This maturing was taking place as Friends of Indiana moved into their future.

The records of the early decades of Indiana Friends history, as shown in their minutes, reveal much the same problems as were indicated previously for Ohio Yearly Meeting. Disownments for infractions of discipline were common. Some were for more serious moral and ethical offenses and others for trivial defections.

Though the records of Meetings indicate a large number of disownments, and of labors with deviating members, it should be recognized that there was a strong spiritual core of leading Friends who kept the heart of the Meetings sound. Then, as now, defections make news whereas loyalty to principles seldom does. The soul of the Quaker movement was sound and the position firm. It was this center within the Quaker settlements that would issue in a stable future.

Let us now look further at the material conditions in which a high level of heroism is shown and which, as background, help us to see the influence on the spiritual life of the period. A paragraph by Harlow Lindley, Quaker Hoosier historian, gives a good picture of the primitive conditions.

> They made a very serviceable plow with a wooden mould-board, which was made of the best hardwood obtainable. They made a very serviceable harrow entirely of wood. The horse collars were made mostly of corn shucks plaited in large rope-like sections, and sewed together hard and fast with leather thongs.

---

[8] *Ibid.*, p. 424, 425, for the above quotations.

They also made collars of rawhide, cutting it in the proper shape, and sewing the edges together, stuffing it on the inside to make it hold its shape. The bridle was made of rawhide. Hames were made from the lower part of the tree, including a part of the root for the proper crook. A wagon that was termed a truck was made from cutting four large wheels from a large tree, usually a black gum. Oxen were the usual teams that were hitched to these crude but serviceable wagons. A heavy wooden yoke went on the oxen's necks. The pitchforks for all purposes on the farm were made of wood and wooden rakes were made of strong seasoned wood. A good spade was made of seasoned hickory.[9]

It requires little imagination to see how fully occupied were these Friends on the frontier. Outwardly their life was primitive, while inwardly some primary qualities of the human spirit were being rediscovered. In some sense it might seem that the Society of Friends as a spiritual movement must begin anew, that it must be reborn and started toward maturity under greatly different influences. We cannot know in what fine sense a spiritual heritage is carried from one generation to another, while at the same time new and authentic experiences shape a new people under new circumstances for service that they must pursue.

We must now break the story of the expansion of Indiana Yearly Meeting and come to the exciting interlude of service in the Underground Railroad and the postwar relief of freedmen.

## THE UNDERGROUND RAILROAD

There was a heritage of faith and love of freedom for all men that came with Friends to their frontier. Moving from slave states to the free territory of the then-Northwest did not close the door to antislavery work. In fact, it opened new opportunities not readily available to the South. Yet the beginning of helping fugitive slaves to freedom started on the southern side of the boundary. In 1819 Vestal Coffin had started at Guilford, North Carolina, what came later to be called the Underground Railroad.[10]

---

[9] Harlow Lindley, *Whitewater Centennial*, p. 49.
[10] Levi Coffin, *Reminiscences;* Robert Clark & Co., Cincinnati, Ohio. The account of the Underground Railroad in this chapter is based upon the autobiography of Levi Coffin.

In Indiana, Vestal Coffin's cousin, Levi Coffin, became the chief Quaker figure in this work. So cleverly managed was this work and so obscure the routes used through Ohio, Indiana, and Michigan to Canada that slave hunters, frustrated in their search for fugitives, referred to the system as an underground railroad and to Levi Coffin as its president.

Friends did not wholly agree on this method of antislavery work. To some it presented a moral dilemma. They were definitely and unalterably opposed to slavery and had taken every possible step to protect the interests of individual slaves, even to the point of turning slave ownership to the Society, but this had been done openly. They were hiding nothing. Integrity of speech and behavior had been a hallmark of the Society of Friends from the beginning. The coming of the underground method introduced secrecy and placed this particular work of Friends under cover. It invited making a virtue of falsehood, though clever answers to slave hunters might avoid the spoken lie. In the minds of some Friends, integrity was at stake.

North Carolina Yearly Meeting, in order to state clearly its position, in 1843 declared "utter disapproval of such interference in any way whatever" and disapproved of Friends who had given "shelter improperly" to slaves. Rich Square Monthly Meeting (North Carolina) had declared its position more clearly and emphatically.

> Whereas it is a well known testimony of the Society that they do not allow their members to hold slaves or in any way interfere with the system of slavery further than by petitions, reason, and remonstrance in a peaceable manner . . . some one or two of the members . . . have suffered themselves to be so far overcome through sympathy as to allow and give shelter improperly to one or more slaves . . . we have therefore thought it due to ourselves and to the people at large . . . to make known our long established practice and utter disapproval . . . while at the same time we do not in the least degree relinquish our testimony to the injustice of slavery.[11]

These admonitions did not stop individual Friends from following their own consciences. In Indiana there were fewer pressures of restraint than in North Carolina where community attitudes affected

---

[11] Weeks, *op. cit.*, p. 242n.

the Quaker response. Many of the Friends in Indiana, only a few years before, had been leaders in the antislavery forces in the South. They were now on the receiving end of the fugitive slave line of work. Though there were some proslavery non-Friends around them, Friends felt more freedom in their service to the escaping slaves.

Antislavery work in Indiana Yearly Meeting included more than helping fugitive slaves. Friends were equally concerned for the education of Negro children. By 1863 the Yearly Meeting reported that "few if any colored children in our limits were without literary instruction." Friends also attacked the "Black Laws" which in various ways restricted people of color. But the work which claimed the widest attention and was most dramatic was that of helping refugee slaves to freedom.[12]

Levi Coffin, the leader in this work, was born in Guilford County, North Carolina, in 1798 and spent his early years in that area. He had been deeply moved by the suffering of slaves. He had seen them chained together in coffles when being taken from one area to another. He had seen them on the auction block by which families were separated. He later stated that *Uncle Tom's Cabin*, by Harriet Beecher Stowe, had hardly overdrawn the pictures of suffering. Levi Coffin dated his conversion to antislavery in an experience at the age of seven.

> Free negroes in Pennsylvania were frequently kidnapped or decoyed into these States, [Carolinas], then hurried away to Georgia, Alabama, or Louisiana and sold. The gangs were handcuffed and chained together, and driven by a man on horseback, who flourished a long whip, such as is used in driving cattle, and goaded the reluctant and weary when their feet lagged on the long journey. One day I was by the roadside where my father was chopping wood when I saw such a gang approaching. . . . The coffle of slaves came first, chained in couples on each side of a long chain. . . . My father addressed the slaves pleasantly and then asked, "Well, boys, why do they chain you?" [They answered,] "They have taken us away from our wives and children, and they chain us lest we should make our escape and go back to them." My childish sympathy and interest were aroused, and when the dejected procession had passed on, I turned to my father

---

[12] *Minutes,* 1863.

and asked many questions . . . my father explained to me the
meaning of slavery. . . .[13]

When Levi Coffin married and moved to Indiana in 1826 he had
been thoroughly conditioned against slavery and was quite ready to
continue the work of the Underground Railroad. He settled at Newport (now Fountain City), Indiana, ten miles north of Richmond,
where he entered business as a merchant and manufacturer of linseed
oil. Here he lived near a settlement of free colored people who had
been settled there by committees of North Carolina Friends. This
colored settlement had aided fugitive slaves. They needed help in this
work and Levi Coffin gave it his careful management.

His home came to be a "station" on the Underground Railroad
where escapees, singly or in groups, found rest, food, shelter, and
needed clothing and were conveyed on to the next station on their
way to Canada and freedom.

Two years after settling at Newport he made a trip to North
Carolina, taking with him some horses for sale. While there he
attended an auction where slaves were being sold. If any further
conversion to the antislavery cause was needed, this was enough. The
slaves stood together where they were examined by prospective buyers
who looked over their bodies to see whether they were scarred by
marks of the whip or torture. Their teeth were examined, and their
bodies gone over much as horses would be. Standing on the platform,
the auctioneer described the quality of the slaves being sold. Here
are Levi Coffin's words:

> . . . a woman was placed upon the stand, with a child in her arms
> apparently a year old. . . . The auctioneer recommended her as a
> good cook, house servant and field hand. . . . She was industrious,
> honest and trustworthy, and above all, she was a Christian, a
> member of the church — as if the grace of God would add to her
> price! The bidding was lively and she sold for a high price. I
> supposed that the child was included in the sale, but soon saw
> that it was to be sold separately. The mother begged her new
> master to buy her child, but he did not want it and would not
> listen to her pleading. The child was torn from her arms and
> she was dragged away screaming, "My child, my child!"[14]

---

[13] Coffin, op. cit., p. 12, 13.
[14] Ibid., p. 126-128.

Levi Coffin returned home with these cries in his ears, "resolved to labor in this cause until the end of my days." It can be understood how the finer points of moral decisions were lost in the overwhelming concern for these victims of cruelty. The greater good was what mattered!

We cannot here retell the many stories of narrow escapes on the Underground Railroad. In them we see "truth stranger than fiction" as the desperation of slaves, singly and by families, was met with the kindness and the encouragement of Friends and others. It should be remembered that Friends were not alone, though they were leading in this service.

### The Abolition Separation

It might seem that the work of the Underground Railroad would have drawn Friends together so sympathetically and fully that a division of forces would be impossible. Though there appears to have been little opposition by Friends in Indiana to the methods of the Underground Railroad itself, it should not be assumed that Indiana Yearly Meeting was of one mind on all methods of antislavery work.[15]

There was no doubt about their unity on the issue of emancipation, but there was considerable lack of unity on how it was to be achieved. Perhaps by looking at our own times and the differing accents on how to complete the emancipation as of the mid-twentieth century under the caption of "civil rights," we can see the issue which then and now (and perhaps for any time) is much the same. Today there are Friends who feel that what is called "direct action" is incumbent upon them. This may be expressed in marches, vigils, and various kinds of demonstrations. There are others who take the slower approach and are commonly called "gradualists."

So it was with Friends of 1843. There were those who felt deeply the plight of the slaves. They had been closer to the persons suffering than had many other Friends. Direct action in freeing the slaves was their vocation and they were restive with the slower-moving body of Friends who seemed to them overcautious or even unconvinced of the urgency of the antislavery movement. The insurgents were fewer

---

[15] *Ibid.*, Ch. VII, for the view of Levi Coffin. *Minutes* of Indiana Yearly Meeting, 1843, for the opposing point of view.

in numbers and they found little trouble in thinking and moving together in their work.

The leaders of the underground work had not confined their activities and associations to Friends alone. They had encouraged and joined abolition societies made up of non-Friends and including persons and attitudes which the main body of Indiana Yearly Meeting held under suspicion. Within and connected with these societies were persons and activities which seemed to more conservative Friends to be extreme. *Abolition* came to be a "loaded" word, attached to the extremists. Many Friends feared their own Society was being led from its ancient testimony of peace and peaceful answers to the problem at a time when war was being discussed as the answer to slavery.

They were sensitive to all forms of political action, as threatening the Quaker way. The "zealots," if we may so designate them, within their ranks disturbed them. In some cases meetinghouses were being used for abolition speakers and this seemed to lend the properties of Friends to a dangerous course of action.

To the smaller body of abolitionist Friends this fear seemed absurd. In their view the work was not getting out of hand or threatening Quaker methods but, instead, was a witness of the Quaker sense of responsibility. The danger they feared was that Friends would do nothing or, worse yet, drift with prevailing ideas of the times and lose the fire of inward concern that had marked past periods of their history.

The zealots had Whittier, the poet, on their side and, so they assumed, the Friends of London Yearly Meeting. Joseph Sturge of England had been very progressive in this antislavery work, and Whittier had given evidence of his interest in the abolition movement. He had written Sturge that "this cause has been to me what the vision on the house-top was to Peter — it has destroyed all narrow sectarian prejudices and *made me willing to be a man among men.*"[16] He had crossed the line separating Quakers from others into a cause that was greater than the dividing barriers.

What would John Woolman of the preceding century have thought about the Underground Railroad with its undercover operations? What would he have counselled regarding the new issue that

<hr/>

[16] Jones II, *op. cit.*, p. 586, quoting from *Memoirs of Joseph Sturge*, p. 229.

now confronted Friends? Each side, the conservatives and the abolitionists, thought they were in the train of Woolman. His position was made a point of reference for both of them. He was integrity incarnate and, at the same time, far in front of the Friends of his day on the question of slavery. What he would have advised or chosen as a way of practical action within the alternatives of the 1840's no one can tell.

Indiana Yearly Meeting had precedent for its conservative position. Virginia Yearly Meeting in 1836 had said that abolition societies, in the excitement they had aroused, had obstructed the very cause they wished to promote and had "closed the door of usefulness" to the cause of the Negro.[17] Other Yearly Meetings had expressed conservative views. Following this line of thought, Whitewater Monthly Meeting had called attention to the "excitement which agitates [the] public mind on [the] subject of slavery," and had warned that "Friends should not join abolition and colonization[18] societies but should take the matter up from their own peculiar religious ground and not from any political consideration."

It is not difficult to see and to feel the tension that was developing. It was like crosswinds blowing. To which should Friends lift the sail? The need to hold the Yearly Meeting together on the one hand, and concern for a cause that ran deeper than organizational structures on the other hand, called for decision. It was not easy to discern the deeper reality — that each body with its differing accent was needed. What were reconcilable views moved farther apart and presented to many Friends a dilemma.

The issue was brought to a head when in 1841 the Yearly Meeting sent down to the Quarterly Meetings a communication advising against joining antislavery societies or opening their meetinghouses to antislavery lectures. The statement continued:

> As the subject of slavery is producing great excitement in our land, we again tenderly advise our dear friends not to join in associations with those who do not profess to wait for divine direction in such important concerns; lest if we overact the part called for at our hands, we injure the righteous cause, and

---

[17] Weeks, *op. cit.*, p. 216. See also Walter Edgerton, *A History of the Separation in Indiana Yearly Meeting of Friends;* printed in Cincinnati, Ohio, 1856.

[18] Some freedmen were being taken to Liberia, West Africa, for colonization.

suffer loss ourselves; comparable to what is said of Ephraim of
old, "he mixed himself among the people [and] strangers have
devoured his strength and he knoweth it not."[19]

The advice was presumably ignored and in the next sessions,
those of 1842, the Yearly Meeting passed an enforcing minute which
forbade the appointment of abolitionist Friends on committees or to
positions of responsibility. This disqualified some leading Friends
such as Charles Osborn and Levi Coffin. This group, now excluded
from important service in the Yearly Meeting organization, sought to
hold a meeting to consider their future. The meetinghouse was
refused them. They met early the next year and established their own
Indiana Yearly Meeting of Anti-Slavery Friends, with headquarters
at Newport.

They carried with them numbers variously estimated from several
hundred to two thousand. One of the Quarterly Meetings going out
with them was that of Salem, Iowa, then a part of Indiana Yearly
Meeting. Impatience had taken its toll, and, though numerically small,
another separation had occurred among Friends.

The new Yearly Meeting turned hopefully to London Yearly
Meeting, whose advanced position on antislavery issues was well
known. They were disappointed in the response of London, which
advised them to return to the main body and appointed a deputation
to carry the message and to meet with Friends in Indiana. London
Yearly Meeting, though sympathetic with Newport Friends, thereby
threw their influence against separation.[20]

This led to a sharp reaction from the Anti-Slavery Yearly Meeting, who later wrote to London Yearly Meeting charging that they
had shown "less regard for consistency and truth, than for the forms
of order" and less "concern for the promotion of the great cause of
justice and mercy, than for the preservation of the external bonds of
union." The communication went on to a more serious charge:

> . . . your Yearly Meeting has practically recognized (however you
> may discard it in theory) the doctrine of the infallibility of the
> Church or else that equally absurd and dangerous position, that

---

[19] *Minutes*, 1841, 1842.
[20] Coffin, *op. cit.*, p. 234ff.
Jones II, *op. cit.*, p. 589ff. See also Chapter V of *Quakers on the American
Frontier*, the chapter subdivision entitled "Abolition Separation in Iowa."

no matter how corrupt and oppressive the Church may become, those members who desire to have it otherwise, are bound to submit to the corrupt and anti-Christian measures of the dominant party, to preserve the external forms of order and the appearance of harmony.

Fuel was added to the fire when in 1842 Henry Clay was invited to attend a public meeting of Indiana Yearly Meeting. This kindled a sharp reaction as indicated in the words of the venerable Charles Osborn.

> On the first day in the time of the Yearly Meeting, Henry Clay, a noted slaveholder, and one who it was understood was seeking the Whig nomination to the Presidency, attended the public meeting, and as I have been told by many, such assurances of respect and a hearty welcome was perhaps never before given to any man on his first visit to a meeting of Friends. Also, I have been further informed, that before he left the City of Richmond, particular care was taken by some Friends, to let him know that Friends had no sympathy for, neither did they take any part with, the abolitionists.[21]

When the London committee came to Indiana they were given hospitality by the larger body of Friends. Levi Coffin managed to have them visit in his home, where he presented fourteen fugitive slaves to the committee. He placed a slave baby in the arms of a member of the London committee (quite a disarming act!) and said, "For pleading the cause of innocent babies like the one thou held in thy arms and sheltering the fugitives, such as you have seen, we have been proscribed."

The London committee probably did more to heal the breach than the writings of the times would indicate. Indiana Yearly Meeting relented in its restrictions, the emotions of both sides cooled, and the separatist group reunited with the main body in 1856, thirteen years after the separation. The memory of their schism doubtless served to bring a new balance into Indiana Yearly Meeting.

The work of Levi Coffin has been given extended attention here because it constituted an important part in the history of the midwestern movement, but there were other Friends similarly engaged.

---

[21] Charles Osborn, *Journal*, p. 418. See also Jones II, *op. cit.*, p. 588n.

Perhaps no other antislavery Quaker leader of the period is more prominent than Benjamin Lundy, who organized the first abolition society in 1815. In 1821 he issued the first printing of *The Genius of Universal Emancipation* at Mt. Pleasant, Ohio. He enlisted the interest of William Lloyd Garrison, later editor of *The Liberator*. Lundy was joined by Whittier in the publication of the *National Enquirer*. Benjamin Lundy died in Illinois in 1839 and was buried in the Friends Cemetery at McNabb. It was a Kansas journalist (non-Friend), Victor Murdock of Wichita, also a representative in Congress from that state, who aroused interest in marking his grave with a granite stone and who said of him, "Before Garrison, and Lovejoy, before Seward and Lincoln, Lundy took up the cudgel for liberty." Whittier wrote of Lundy, "It was his lot to struggle, for years almost alone, a solitary voice crying in the wilderness; yet, amidst all, faithful to his one great purpose, the emancipation of the slaves."[22]

Charles Osborn was another Friend in antislavery literary work like that of Lundy. He took his place with the antislavery group at Newport. Levi Coffin and his brave little group did not lose their cause in reuniting with the Yearly Meeting; they brought their foresight and fortitude into the larger body. They, in part, illustrate again the importance that concerned minorities have within all progress. They held, in their own way, the spirit of John Woolman, Benjamin Lundy, and a number of other Friends, valiant for an oppressed people called slaves on the long, hard road to freedom.

In this separation and reunion there is an example of two attitudes that always mark reform movements — that of the gradualists and that of those whom we might call today the activists, or those urging a course of direct and immediate action. Each can generally defend logically its own position and each helps to save the other from its own kind of extreme.

### SERVICE WITH FREEDMEN

The way was now open for the Yearly Meeting to unite in one of the most important services of Quaker history. The gap between the conservatives and the abolitionists had been largely closed. A new relationship with London Yearly Meeting had been established, the

---

[22] *Benjamin Lundy, Pioneer Quaker Abolitionist, 1789-1839;* monograph.

Levi Coffin

Timothy Nicholson

abundant evidence of which was soon to appear in their support of Levi Coffin and his work with freedmen.

The second phase of Quaker service suddenly opened during the war. Slaves often "flocked within the Union lines, as the armies advanced through Tennessee . . . and were protected . . . many of the slaveholders fled farther south taking able-bodied slaves with them, and leaving the women and children, aged and sick ones"[23] to their fate. Armies had swept over the land and few provisions were left. Hordes of slaves were left in a destitute condition. The Underground Railroad had come to an end, and a relief operation for these deserted slaves (now freedmen) was needed.

Large numbers of these Negro refugees came north through Cincinnati and Cairo and were met by Friends under the leadership of Levi Coffin and ministers of other Christian churches. Under these conditions, as well as in the earlier work with fugitive slaves, ecumenism (though the word had not yet been coined) became a reality as superficial differences were swept away and Baptists mingled with Quakers in a common service. Levi Coffin, with a touch of mingled humor and seriousness, referred to the work of J. B. Rogers, a Baptist minister who "had, I believe, not only been baptized with water but with the Holy Ghost" [!] It required non-Friends to bring the therapy of song to these assembled masses of desperate people, and as they were led in song Levi Coffin reported, "I thought of the day of Pentecost." The feeling was reciprocated in the words of Rogers, the Baptist: "These Friends . . . seemed to me divested of everything like . . . sectarian prejudice. I saw the difference between talking Christianity and acting it."

Christian church bodies were represented in the Western Freedmen's Aid Commission. Materials were collected and General Grant gave free transportation of supplies. At Helena, Arkansas, a school was started which later would develop into Southland Institute.

The idea of a Freedmen's Bureau was presented to President Lincoln, who called together representatives of Freedmen's Associations, by whom it was formed. Women Friends of Philadelphia united to help in relief work. Levi Coffin attended their meeting at

---

[23] Coffin, *op. cit.*, Ch. XIX, "Work Among the Freedmen," p. 619.

Arch Street and visited other interested groups in the East. He stood
on the famous Plymouth Rock "with Samuel J. May, Wendell Phillips and others of my old co-laborers in the anti-slavery cause. This
was a jubilee meeting of the old abolitionists." He returned with
$2,000 collected for work with freedmen.

Under the Western Freedmen's Aid Commission he visited England, securing his passport through a recommendation of Secretary
Salmon P. Chase of Lincoln's Cabinet and carrying a letter of recommendation from Henry Ward Beecher. He was warmly received by
British Friends — of whom he wrote as "this once despised and persecuted people, now a wealthy and influential body of Christians" —
such as "John Bright, Samuel Gurney, William Edward Forster,
Henry Pease, and others being members of Parliament."

Friends responded fully, calling together persons of influence in
government and representatives of "the principal London papers."
Levi Coffin writes of a meeting at Samuel Gurney's as "quite
aristocratic in character, being largely composed of lords, dukes,
bishops, and members of Parliament."

The London Freedmen's Aid Society was formed with Sir Thomas
Fowell Buxton as president. Through the American ambassador in
London and Secretary Chase, duty-free imports for clothing and other
supplies were secured. The railroads charged no freight to Liverpool,
and steamships gave free transportation. Irish Friends also gave Levi
Coffin hearty support, calling a meeting at which the Lord Mayor of
Dublin presided. A home meeting was held in Paris, attended by
"most prominent Protestants in Paris, and by a few Catholics."

A letter to him from the London Freedmen's Aid Society in
June 1865 expresses the feeling for the work of Levi Coffin and the
Friends and others associated with him in the work for freedmen.

> . . . you have in kindly words pointed to the condition and sad
> necessities of four millions of men, gradually shaking off their
> fetters and rising to the hopeful condition of freedom. . . . And
> now, thou apostle of Liberty, we bid thee farewell!
>
> [Signed]
> T. Fowell Buxton,
> Bart. Chairman
> Samuel Gurney, M. D.[24]

---

[24] *Ibid.*, p. 705 (excerpts from farewell letter).

Levi Coffin attended Indiana, Western, and Iowa Yearly Meetings the same year and received their wholehearted support. He also made later visits to Europe for aid.

Though the Underground Railroad had come to its close, the good work which it started had not. "When the colored people of Cincinnati[25] and vicinity celebrated the adoption of the Fifteenth Amendment of the Constitution, I thought it was a fitting time to resign my office as President of the Underground Railroad," wrote Levi Coffin.

A closing meeting was held at Cincinnati. Judge Taft, among others, was on the platform and speaking on that occasion. Levi Coffin, having held the position for over thirty years, wrote that the "government had now taken the work of providing for the slaves out of our hands . . . the road was of no further use. . . . I resigned my office and declared the operation . . . [at an end]."[26]

The Underground Railroad and the work for freedmen was a monumental accomplishment. In breaking the chains of the slaves Friends were breaking their own chains. The old clichés, such as "the hireling ministry," and the fear of linking their forces with other people, were giving way. The protective walls of a century which hemmed them in as a "peculiar people" were being shattered.

As we shall see in later chapters, this exposure was not without its hazards, but the old structures could not hold forever.

### WESTERN YEARLY MEETING ESTABLISHED

The West was unfolding mile by mile and year by year. The trails of immigrants were, in general, from east to west, but they zigzagged, crossed and recrossed, as rumors of opportunities "farther on" or "back there" were circulated at stopping places along the way.

When entire settlements or colonies moved, as in the case of Friends, they tended to resettle in family groups or colonies. Invitations from Friends farther west gave a sense of reassurance in an unknown land and set a goal for the long, long trail, and an end to the tiresome journey, as the pilgrims became settlers.

The courses taken in some of these movements of Friends are

---

[25] Levi Coffin later moved to Cincinnati, Ohio, where he continued to aid escaped slaves and dealt in "free labor" goods, to encourage "the abstaining from the gains of oppression."

[26] *Ibid.*, p. 712.

easily traced on a map of Indiana. The settlements at Whitewater (Richmond) and in southern Indiana, taking place at about the same time, represented parallel movements over separate trails. In 1806 John Hollowell of Wayne County, North Carolina, ventured alone into southern Indiana. He found a cave and a spring of water and for a while made his home in the cave. He returned to North Carolina and the next year came with his family. He is credited with being the first white settler in Orange County.[27]

In 1811 Jonathan Lindley with his family and a small caravan of Friends from Orange and adjoining counties in North Carolina came through on their way to Vigo County, to a site south of Terre Haute. Hearing of threatened Indian uprisings in that area, they were persuaded to settle in the Blue River area instead, with the Hollowells. Other Friends came and soon the settlement developed a Meeting which was set off in 1813 from Whitewater Monthly Meeting as Lick Creek Monthly Meeting.

With few roads and difficult travel, short distances were long distances, and new Meetings were opened for the convenience of Friends. In 1819 these were set off as Blue River Quarterly Meeting of Ohio Yearly Meeting, and the trend toward what would later become Western Yearly Meeting was set in motion.

Another lineage of Friends Meetings now begins. Hardly had Friends settled at Blue River when farther north and west new settlements were being made. Not all of these can be traced. Some of them did not continue for long, as Friends relocated or moved farther west. One settlement which became permanent, next in line after Blue River, was White Lick, in the vicinity of the present-day Mooresville, in Morgan County, a few miles southwest of Indianapolis.

Dates are not dull when they are seen as stepping stones by which Friends moved within a short time from one settlement to another, extending Indiana Yearly Meeting and thereby bringing Western (Indiana) Yearly Meeting toward birth. The usual growth of new Meetings occurred and in 1831 White Lick Quarterly Meeting was set off by Indiana Yearly Meeting, following the recognition of Monthly Meetings by Blue River Quarterly Meeting.

---

[27] *Semi-Centennial Anniversary, Western Yearly Meeting of Friends Church,* 1908. Starting with Blue River Meetings, this volume presents the expansion of Friends settlements and Meetings that constituted Western Yearly Meeting in 1858.

Farther north and west in Park County another settlement of Friends from North Carolina and Virginia had been forming from 1823 onward. White Lick Quarterly Meeting was the parent body as the Meetings of this area developed. In 1838 these Meetings were set off as Western (Bloomingdale) Quarterly Meeting.

Two more Quarterly Meetings — Union (Westfield), 1849, and Concord (Thorntown), 1852 — completed the first five Quarterly Meeting bodies which existed when the request for a new Yearly Meeting was made. Western Yearly Meeting was set off by Indiana Yearly Meeting and held its first session in 1858. In less than thirty-five years following the establishment of Western Yearly Meeting eleven other Quarterly Meetings were established making the sixteen that now constitute the Yearly Meeting.

## THE CONSERVATIVE SEPARATION

The gradual changes in faith and practice introduced by the evangelical awakening were moving in almost every area of Western Quakerism toward crises of varied degrees. A new separation, soon to occur, was like the larger one of 1854, which has been reviewed in a previous chapter. The effect of that separation continued to ripple through the Meetings farther west, threatening and sometimes causing lesser separations.

In Plainfield Quarterly Meeting, this earth-trembling under the faith was felt. The conservative element prepared a "testimony" in which the ancient faith and practice of Friends was set forth. The Quarterly Meeting was divided on it and a separation resulted whereby two sets of representatives and two reports came to Western Yearly Meeting in 1877, each presuming to be Plainfield Quarterly Meeting. This dilemma, as presented to the Yearly Meeting, was a pattern repeated in other separations.[28]

Most problems brought before a Friends deliberative body are of a kind that allows more than two alternatives. By postponing action an answer, unseen at first, can be found in continued seeking and worship. Such is the way of Quaker corporate responsibility. It is a course which requires time, patience, and goodwill. The success of this method has been attested many times in Friends history and has

---

[28] Willard Heiss, *A Brief History of Western Yearly Meeting of Conservative Friends and the Separation of 1877;* 1963.

made a difficult question the opening to better thinking and a deeper fellowship through the corporate approach. The outcome is not based upon voting, leaving a victorious majority and a defeated minority, for minorities have often been proved by time to be right and majorities wrong. The hope in this method is for unity on a deeper level. In practice, Friends have not always been able to follow this ideal.

The issue that faced Western Yearly Meeting in 1877 seemed to offer but two alternatives, though with time and patience some compromise might presumably have been worked out. Which was the real Plainfield Quarterly Meeting? Viewed in the light of historical trends this separation of the Conservatives of Western Yearly Meeting in 1877 probably could not have been avoided just as similar separations in other Meetings could not. Too much had occurred in the drift of Friends into the newer evangelical ways leading to programmed meetings, singing, revival meetings, and spontaneous religious exercises. The wave could hardly be rolled back. For those who were rooted in the ancient ways, with emphasis on inwardness and a mutual responsibility for ministry in worship, there seemed to be no other course.

When the problem in Plainfield Quarterly Meeting came to the Yearly Meeting there were deep concerns, but the Meeting decided in favor of the evangelical body. Different terminologies distinguished the two bodies. *Progressives* and *Conservatives* came to be used. A visiting Friend from England on this occasion refers to the former as "liberals." His story of the concern felt over the separation from the Yearly Meeting is perhaps as nearly objective as any we can find. Walter Robson had visited several Yearly Meetings during 1877 and sensed the trend, of which this was one expression. This quotation is from his journal.

> The report of the Com. about the two reports from Plainfield Q.M. deciding in favor of the liberal one, was read & a very painful touching scene followed. Robert Hodson, a dear old Friend, rose & said, — he felt he & his party had no longer any rights or privileges among us & he invited all, young & old who desired with him to maintain Friends principles in their purity, to withdraw to another place, where they might form a Yearly Meeting. Several earnest appeals were made that they might not separate especially [by] the Clerk, Barnabas Hobbs . . . but it

was of no use & 99 men were counted leaving . . . the house. Meanwhile a very similar scene was enacted the other side of the shutters [in the women's Yearly Meeting]. It was *very very* sad.[29]

Though this separation was relatively small it divided Meetings within the Yearly Meeting. At first there were two Quarterly Meetings in the Conservative Yearly Meeting, Plainfield and White Lick. At Sugar Grove Meeting, south of Plainfield, the Conservatives were in the majority. The question of property was ultimately resolved with the Sugar Grove buildings going to the Conservatives and interest in the Plainfield grounds relinquished to the Progressives.

There was a certain measure of extension by the Conservative Yearly Meeting. This included a Meeting at Laura in Ohio near Ludlow Falls and one in Wilmington, Ohio. In 1890 these, with Jericho in eastern Indiana, were constituted a Quarterly Meeting. Some other Meetings were established, but the Yearly Meeting declined in strength and in 1962 ended as a Yearly Meeting, leaving one independent Meeting existing at that time.

### WILMINGTON YEARLY MEETING SET OFF

Like the American expansion in general, the Quaker movement, on its frontier margins, was overextending itself. It was thinning out and into vast expanses of territory. If the Quaker fellowship was to survive, Friends must catch up with Friends and soul with body!

While the race westward continued, another development was taking place in areas not so far west. Settlements were becoming accustomed to their new circumstances. Many earlier Friends came to an area to stay. Joined by other Friends, settlements became communities; and at the creative heart of the Quaker community was the Meeting. Gains were being assessed and consolidated, though in half-intentional ways.

Individuals and families that had been on the move settled and came into the rediscovery of the Quaker fellowship. Meetings were becoming aware of new Meetings that grew like clusters around them as the community of Meetings became Quarterly Meetings. It was like cellular division, with Meeting setting off Meeting and Quarterly Meeting following Quarterly Meeting.

---

[29] Robson papers, Haverford College library.

The history of Wilmington Yearly Meeting is one illustration of this growth and of the conserving of gains.[30] Though Ohio Yearly Meeting had set off Indiana Yearly Meeting, and the latter had established Western Yearly Meeting, there was a Meeting-to-Meeting lineage by which both of the Yearly Meetings in Indiana might be credited to Miami Valley Friends as the parents of all.

The settlements of Friends which later expanded, constituting Wilmington Yearly Meeting, are the oldest north and west of the Ohio River when dated from the settlement of the Thomas Beals family before 1800.

The course, by Quarterly Meetings, ran from Miami, 1809, to West Branch, 1812, to Fairfield, 1815, to Whitewater, 1817, to Blue River, 1819 — these constituting Indiana Yearly Meeting when it was established in 1821.

It was like giving due historical credit when in 1892 the Quarterly Meetings in southwestern Ohio (by this time including Center, 1827) were recognized by Indiana as Wilmington Yearly Meeting. Shortly afterward, in 1898, Friendsville Quarterly Meeting in Tennessee was transferred from North Carolina Yearly Meeting to Wilmington. In this recognition by Indiana Yearly Meeting it was as if children were honoring their parentage. There was, however, nothing gratuitous in the setting off of Wilmington Yearly Meeting. The Meetings of that area had come into a group awareness as distances under slow and difficult travel called for a center that would be more convenient. Most of the Meetings were within Clinton County.

Some Meetings within the Wilmington area had been at one time or another under four Yearly Meetings — Baltimore, North Carolina, Ohio, and Indiana. Now a realignment placed them within a logical one-ness. As early as 1868 the possibility of a Yearly Meeting for that area had been presented to Indiana and was denied. In 1873 the possibility of alternating sessions between Richmond and Wilmington had been requested and refused. Finally in 1890 the request was granted and Wilmington Yearly Meeting was set off. As was usually true, other Yearly Meetings had been consulted and had concurred in

[30] C. Clayton Terrell, *Quaker Migration to Southwest Ohio*, 1967.
Elmer Howard Brown, Jr., "A History of Wilmington Yearly Meeting of the Religious Society of Friends." An unpublished Master of Arts thesis, the College of Religion, Butler University; Wilmington College library.

the action and at the opening session of the new Yearly Meeting representatives were present from nearly all American Yearly Meetings.

Wilmington Yearly Meeting has had a remarkable unity and a spirit of cooperation in the wider services of all Friends in America and the world. Its history in its separate identity is relatively short, but as viewed within the history of Baltimore, Ohio, and Indiana Yearly Meetings to the present its constituent Quarterly Meetings are about one hundred fifty years old.[81]

### CENTRAL YEARLY MEETING SEPARATION

Though the Five Years Meeting, formed in 1902, was the major development of strength within Western Quakerism it was not without its testings. It had been brought together under an impulse toward unity, but it was constituted of diverse elements that had grown apart in expressions of faith and in certain practices. It became a center for the reintegration of Friends, though from the outset it was threatened with defections and separations. Larger separations will be considered later.

The first separation based on opposition to the Five Years Meeting had occurred in 1902 when a very small number in North Carolina withdrew and formed the Conservative Yearly Meeting of that area. The first separation from the Five Year Meeting in the Midwest, stating as its reason dissatisfaction "with conditions prevailing in the Five Years Meeting," was in Westfield Monthly Meeting of Western Yearly Meeting in 1924. The separated members together with a few from nearby Meetings organized themselves as Union Monthly Meeting. A similar development elsewhere in the area resulted in the formation of a Quarterly Meeting. Other separations occurred in small numbers in eastern Indiana, resulting in a second Quarterly Meeting. These two bodies united in 1926 to form Central Yearly Meeting.

Starting with five hundred members in two Quarterly Meetings, the new Yearly Meeting reached its maximum about 1937 with nearly nine hundred members constituting four Quarterly Meetings. At this writing the Yearly Meeting reports three Quarterly Meetings with about five hundred members, the same as at its beginning forty years

---

[81] The part which Wilmington College played in the rise of Wilmington Yearly Meeting is told in Chapter IX, "Education and Schools."

earlier. The increase in membership in the earlier years appears to have come, in the main, through the addition of member Meetings from other local separations. The Yearly Meeting has had Meetings in at least six states — Indiana, Iowa, Michigan, Washington, Arkansas, and Kansas.

That the Yearly Meeting, in its separation, was concerned for purity of the faith, as viewed by its members, is given abundant evidence in the minutes. In 1939 the Yearly Meeting epistle stated, "We deplore the growing tendency to bring together all who bear the name of Friends in a great fraternity, with little regard to the spiritual basis of unity." What the Yearly Meeting thought was the basis of unity is added in the epistle of 1941. "We take our firm stand on the position that there is no fatherhood of God in the Scriptural sense apart from the new birth through faith in the shed blood of Jesus Christ, accompanied with repentance and forsaking of sin." In 1949 their discipline was amended to state that "sanctification is subsequent to regeneration, and is the second definite work of grace which is for all who have been born again. . . . It is the eradication of the sinful or carnal nature . . . by the baptism of the Holy Ghost."[32]

The mission work of the Yearly Meeting has been centered chiefly in Bolivia and a close correspondence has been carried on between the Yearly Meeting and the mission field.

In 1941 Central Yearly Meeting expressed a concern "at this critical time [for] . . . young men who are of military age . . . [and to] do all within our power to give our full moral support . . . to preserve the tender conscience and spiritual life of our conscientious objectors. The basis must be scriptural grounds." A committee was appointed with whom their young men could confer "if they so desire." Among the promises expected from a new member, as stated in 1955, was "to abstain from any voluntary encouragement or support of war, or belonging to the army *by choice*" (italics added).

Their discipline, as of 1960, related the peace testimony to the franchise in this manner: "If one votes for another to be President whose duties include the declarations of war if the occasions arise, he cannot consistently decline military service when the President calls on him." They relieved the dilemma somewhat by adding in a

---

[32] Everett L. Cattell, *The Spirit of Holiness,* William B. Eerdmans Publishing Co., 1963, presents views of the doctrine of holiness.

minute, "We take the position that Friends exercise this franchise, if they so desire."

In 1961 they approved sending epistles to London Yearly Meeting and to New Zealand. They held regular epistolary correspondence with Ohio Yearly Meeting, and with Kansas and Oregon after the latter two withdrew from the Five Years Meeting. They later corresponded with Rocky Mountain Yearly Meeting.

They maintained interest in Christian Education in the local Meetings, being watchful over the kind of literature used. Daily Vacation Bible School was a regular summer project for several years.

Central to, though independent of, the Yearly Meeting was the Union Bible Seminary at Westfield, of which William M. Smith was the leading Friend. Indeed, he was at the center of the separation and might well be referred to as the founder of Central Yearly Meeting.

### INDIANA — A NEW QUAKER CENTER

The development of Friends settlements into Meetings and Yearly Meetings in the Indiana area presents a wide range of diversities, but also a solid core of Quaker witness. At the heart of the Indiana development was a cluster of Quaker personalities in whom the blend of evangelical zeal and social concern was evident. They represented the spirit of Elizabeth Fry, the deep concerns of John Woolman, the legislative interests of John Bright, and the spiritual ardor of the "Valiant Sixty," and at the same time were Friends of the new frontier.

Timothy Nicholson, Rhoda Coffin, Allen Jay, and Barnabas Hobbs are but a few of those who rekindled the life of Friends in Indiana as the third Quaker century evolved. Timothy Nicholson, as a member of the Indiana Board of State Charities, pressed relentlessly for penal reform and for enlightened treatment of the mentally ill and the retarded.[33] In this period Friends were not simply being fashioned by the times; they were changing the social conditions, and non-Friends in the leadership of the state were made keenly aware of it. William Nicholson, brother of Timothy Nicholson, was the first clerk of Kansas Yearly Meeting, holding that office for several years, and was influential in the development of California Yearly Meeting.

Though not residents of Indiana, two Quaker women of the Mid-

---

[33] Walter C. Woodward, *Timothy Nicholson: Master Quaker,* the Nicholson Press, 1927. This volume is an excellent review of an important formative period in Indiana.

west were exemplars of evangelical zeal and social reformation. Elizabeth L. Comstock, called the Elizabeth Fry of America, visited prisons, advocated new and corrective methods within these institutions, and at the same time worked for the conversion of prisoners. She played a major role in service to freedmen after the Civil War, from Michigan to Kansas.[34] Laura Haviland was also a zealous worker for escaped slaves of the Underground Railroad and later for freedmen.

Friends of Indiana had spread at this time into several states of the Union, had created a complex of Meetings at the heart of the nation, had hosted in the formation of the Five Years Meeting, and had helped in making Indiana a center of midwestern Quakerism.

## NOTE

At this time structural changes in several Yearly Meetings are being made. The pattern of Quarterly Meetings is being changed to "Regional" areas, embracing a larger number of Meetings. The superstructures of the Yearly Meetings are also being greatly altered in California, Indiana, and Western Yearly Meetings. Some others are reviewing their need for change.

---

[34] *Life and Letters of Elizabeth L. Comstock,* compiled by C. Hare; London and Philadelphia, 1895.

# Chapter 4

## HICKSITE FRIENDS IN THE MIDWEST

From the great separation at Mt. Pleasant, Ohio, in 1828, tremors ran through the Ohio Meetings and into Indiana, resulting in smaller separations.

The Ohio Yearly Meeting (Hicksite), near the same in numbers as the Orthodox body, was concentrated in eastern Ohio. Existing records indicate that in 1836 there were five Quarterly Meetings in the Hicksite Yearly Meeting which met alternately for several years at Mt. Pleasant and Salem. Their numbers eventually decreased until in 1918 only two Quarterly Meetings reported, and in 1920 the Yearly Meeting was laid down.

### Indiana Yearly Meeting

The separations in Indiana, following that of Ohio, were not large enough to disrupt Indiana Yearly Meeting (Gurneyite). Three Quarterly Meetings experienced some separations, and the separated portions of Whitewater, Miami, and Blue River constituted Indiana

Yearly Meeting (Hicksite).[1] The new Yearly Meeting experienced some growth as new Meetings to the north, and as far west as Iowa and Nebraska, were established. Of those to the north, Clear Creek in Putnam County, Illinois, became one of the stronger centers.[2]

## MEETINGS IN IOWA

In 1855 and 1856, Hicksite Friends from Virginia settled in Henry County, Iowa. Their first meetings were held in a schoolhouse. There were able leaders among them and very soon they felt the need for an established Monthly Meeting. In a request to Fairfax Quarterly Meeting in Virginia they expressed a sense of their "painful situation in being deprived of an opportunity of attending religious meetings of Friends" such as they had known.

Fairfax Quarterly Meeting in reply stated their "feeling of deep sympathy with our absent brethren and sisters in their remote and tried situation." A committee was appointed to open the Monthly Meeting as requested. They came bringing books and a register for membership statistics and in December 1856 established Prairie Grove Monthly Meeting. Since the schoolhouse was not available for the holding of midweek meetings, Fairfax Quarterly Meeting and Prairie Grove Monthly Meeting shared in the expense of erecting a meetinghouse.

Somewhat later another settlement was made in Muscatine County and Wapinonoc Monthly Meeting was established in 1866. The two Monthly Meetings were united in Prairie Grove Quarterly Meeting, under Baltimore Yearly Meeting.

The Meetings were active in the philanthropic work of peace, temperance, prison reform, women's rights, and helping Negroes and Indians. In 1893 there were about four hundred members, but by 1912 there were fewer than two hundred in three Meetings, and they were widely scattered.

Louis T. Jones evaluates their life, as he reviewed it, in 1914:[3]

---

[1] *Friends Miami Monthly Meeting Centennial*, Waynesville, Ohio, 1903. Presents the development of Friends Meetings before and after the separation of 1828.
Paper, by E. Hicks Trueblood, "A Historical Sketch of Blue River Monthly Meeting" [Indiana]; 1815-1895.
[2] *Minutes*, Illinois Yearly Meeting, 1875-1967.
[3] Louis T. Jones, *The Quakers of Iowa*, the State Historical Society, Iowa City, 1914; Part III, Ch. II, "The Hicksite Friends in Iowa."

. . . these Friends few though they are in numbers, may be said
to have more nearly preserved the true characteristics of the
primitive Quaker than have the other sects going by that name . . .
with the possible exception of the Springville settlement of
Conservative Friends in Linn County.

This distant Meeting to the far west, under Baltimore, with the
scattered situation of Blue River Quarterly Meeting in Indiana and
Illinois, and with the new Meetings to the north, suggested the need
for a new alignment along geographical lines. In response to a request for a new Yearly Meeting, a joint committee of Indiana and
Baltimore Yearly Meetings was appointed to consider the question.
The committee reported favorably and in 1875 Illinois Yearly Meeting (Hicksite) was set off jointly, consisting of Blue River and
Prairie Grove Quarterly Meetings, with Jonathan W. Plummer as
clerk. The spirit of Indiana Yearly Meeting and all Hicksite bodies
is well exemplified in the new Yearly Meeting.

## ILLINOIS YEARLY MEETING

The establishment of the Yearly Meeting brought new life as
plans were made and followed through for visitations of new Friends
settlements and scattered families to the west. Hicksite Friends, having
been given the "Northern Superintendency" for Indian work by the
United States Government in 1869, found some new opportunities for
nourishing small settlements of Friends in Nebraska.[4]

The Yearly Meeting sent a memorial to Congress on the position
of Illinois Yearly Meeting regarding peace and arbitration, and also
wrote the Illinois legislature presenting their testimony against capital
punishment. Efforts were started at once to collect funds for a new
Yearly Meetinghouse and Friends gave evidence of accepting seriously
this responsibility as a Yearly Meeting of Friends.

In keeping with the common practice of Friends of that period,
separate Yearly Meetings were established for men and women, but
by 1887 the Women's Meetings received a suggestion from men Friends
to consider the propriety of holding all sessions of Illinois Yearly
Meeting jointly in the future. Much feeling was expressed both for
and against the proposed move. The proposal was accepted though

---

[4] See Chapter 10, "Quakers and Indians."

"there was not entire unity in making the change." Many Hicksite and Gurneyite Yearly Meetings made similar moves during the latter part of the nineteeth century, uniting men's and women's Meetings.

By 1887 there were Illinois Yearly Meeting committees to deal with literature, Indian affairs, gambling and kindred vices, peace and arbitration, prison affairs, and temperance. Their responsibilities reveal a wide range of interest. In some cases, their statements of faith show a close likeness to those of Orthodox bodies in the West. About fifty years earlier Elias Hicks had said regarding the Scriptures:

> I have always endeavored sincerely to place them in their true place and station, but never dare exalt them above what they themselves declare; and as no spring can rise higher than its fountain so likewise the Scriptures can only direct to the fountain from which they originated — the spirit of truth. . . .

The Minutes of Exercise in the first sessions of Illinois Yearly Meeting stated that in the meeting for worship "the power of prayer was felt to solemnize and prepare for this expression of our views of the doctrines of the Gospel of Christ, and its converting grace for the redemption of sinners from the wiles of sin." Two years later the minutes said: "Christ we accept as the Son of God, having all power from the Father. As God is a spirit, his son must be spiritual, like begetting like. . . . Christ was sent as the Savior of men, and as a Savior seeks entrance to the soul of each accountable human being." In 1887 they distinguished between "creed" and "doctrine," adding that "no greater mistake in regard to our profession can be made, than for one to say we have no doctrine." Referring to the "doctrine of Jesus . . . [that] God is a spirit and they that worship Him must worship Him in spirit and in truth," they then add that this "became a fundamental doctrine of the Society of Friends."

The reports on State of Society followed the way of most Friends Meetings, by answers to the Queries. The answers indicated concern for plain and honest speech, Bible reading, education for all children, and punctuality in meeting obligations in business. They discouraged tale-bearing, the use of liquor and tobacco, all forms of gambling, lotteries, and the taking of oaths. These replies are about the same as those given in meetings of other branches of Friends of the period.

Though in 1891 the Friends in Illinois reported "no schools under our care," they endorsed compulsory education for public schools and gave special attention to the religious education of their own children. A First Day School Association was formed and became a significant part not only of their Yearly Meeting but also that of the Friends General Conference organized later.

They gave attention to the ministry (nonpastoral), and in 1895 ministers were "advised not to neglect any opportunity for meditation, for storing the mind with ideas; to seek from time to time during the week for divine qualification to properly fulfill the ministerial duty." Close counsel of the elders with the ministers was encouraged. The Yearly Meeting in 1908 was concerned for "bearing of faithful testimony to a free gospel ministry." It was granted that paid ministers were often inspired, and the Yearly Meeting was hesitant to call them "hirelings."

Illinois Friends were solicitous of better relationships between the Hicksite and other branches of Friends, and in a statement, "To All Who Claim the Title of Friends," in 1885 referred to the "unhallowed separation." They left open a door of hope "looking into the form of worship, life, conduct, and conversation of these separated members." They found "in the essential of testimony and worship such agreement that the view is warranted in a sustained trust and hope, that under the drawing of Divine love, the scattered flocks will, each hearing the voice of the Good Shepherd, gather and be united in one fold." They expressed "to all who go under the name of Friends a desire, and a trusting that we feel a forming preparation for such oneness in spirit that will more and more tend to oneness in faith and testimony. . . . "

In 1892 a joint committee was appointed, representing the Hicksite Friends and those of the Orthodox persuasion, then in session as a Conference (later becoming in 1902 the Five Years Meeting), to represent the Society of Friends in the Columbia Exposition, shortly to be opened at Chicago. Jonathan W. Plummer was appointed chairman from the Hicksites and Calvin W. Pritchard from the Orthodox. A parallel joint committee of women Friends was also appointed.

The conference of Orthodox Friends (mainly Gurneyites), meeting then at Indianapolis, found considerable difficulty in following through on this opportunity in the World's Fair. They doubted whether Friends could be consistently represented in a world congress of religions, Christian and non-Christian, though the purpose was announced as "uniting religion against all irreligion." To fail in appointing a committee, however, would leave the representation of Friends to the Hicksites, and they felt this would give "a wrong impression to non-Friends."[5]

The joint committee was appointed, but a minute from Illinois Yearly Meeting, in 1893, states that

> we found our Friends of the Orthodox branch on the Central Committee hampered by frequent objections from their membership, to union with our branch of Friends in this work, and believing we could each do better work alone, we separated in goodwill, and each formed a committee of its own membership for separate action.

The response of the Hicksite body to the Congress of Religions shows a view in contrast to that of the Orthodox body:

> Out of the great gathering representing the principal religions of the world, non-Christian as well as Christian, we hope to see an influence which will change the long time bitterness and separation between those who desire a common good, to a degree of sympathy and fellowship that will allow them to cooperate in future efforts under the Fatherhood of God, that will leave all minds freer to recognize whatever is true in the faith of others and whatever is unessential in their own.

The Hicksite Friends Yearly Meetings on the North American continent came to be seven in number: Philadelphia, New York, Genesee (Canada), Ohio, Illinois, Indiana, and Baltimore. Ohio Yearly Meeting (Hicksite) was discontinued in 1920. Certain cooperative activities led these Yearly Meetings toward a closer fellowship. The first of these was the First-Day School General Conference, formed in 1868. In 1881 the Friends Union for Philanthropic Labor was organized, following lines of work similar to that of the present-day American Friends Service Committee. In 1893 the Friends Religious Conference grew out of the World's Congress of Religions, held in that same year. A concern for schools and colleges brought together in 1894 the Friends Education Conference. These cooperative

---

[5] *Minutes,* Conference on Unity (Orthodox), 1892. Pages 24, 25, and 313 present the Orthodox response.

agencies later were associated within the General Conference of Friends.

Illinois Yearly Meeting seems to have made the main effort toward formation of the General Conference of Friends, consisting of seven Hicksite Yearly Meetings. In 1879 their minute states:

> We are therefore united in proposing for the consideration of the several Yearly Meetings that once in five years or oftener a general conference be held . . . for the consideration of . . . Indian policy; arbitration in all its branches; capital punishment; prison reform; intemperance; compulsory education, and cognate subjects.

The Yearly Meeting desired "that the Conference may in the beginning be prohibited by its own action and by the action of the Yearly Meetings . . . from any consideration of doctrinal subjects, disciplinary provisions, or the internal affairs of any Yearly Meeting." The General Conference began officially in 1902, the same year in which the Five Years Meeting was formed. It has become a biennial Meeting with very large attendance, held until recently on the seashore at Cape May, New Jersey. The name of Jonathan W. Plummer, first clerk of Illinois Yearly Meeting, looms large in the history of the General Conference. He has been referred to as the "father of the General Conference," which established a lectureship in his name in 1961.

Illinois Yearly Meeting now consists of Blue River and Fox Valley (Chicago) Quarterly Meetings and Northern Half-Yearly Meeting. The membership has generally ranged somewhat over a thousand members.

## FAITH AND PRACTICE TODAY

Lawrence McK. Miller, one of the present-day Hicksite writers, summarizes their fellowship in these words:

> First, there was the conviction that the authority of the Inner Light or Christ Within was central for Quakers and that it was possible for the same Spirit that was revealed in the Scriptures to be revealed in the lives of contemporary men and women. These Friends contended that God had written on the tablet of the human heart His divine law. Salvation was a constant and repeated spiritual process of renewal. The unit of spiritual value

was the individual human spirit. Therefore, these Friends rejected the restrictions of Christocentric orthodoxy while at the same time claiming an allegiance to Jesus Christ.

Secondly, Hicksite Friends had a strong allegiance to the traditional form of Quaker worship, based on expectant waiting for divine guidance. In those areas of the country where the new ideas of pastoral leadership for a meeting and of programmed services were being introduced, Hicksite Friends championed a liberal theological approach along with the conservation of the orthodox manner of worship. In respect to this holding to the traditional form of worship, they were in unity with the Conservative Friends, although they were separated from these Friends in terms of religious thought.[6]

During this period they gave evidence of a tolerant spirit toward other branches beyond that which Orthodox Friends of the Midwest were able to achieve. Their sense of Christian responsibility on social problems was both deep in concern and inclusive in scope. In more recent years they have been in the forefront when all Friends have cooperated in the social issues of their day.

## NOTES

Family names of Friends moving to Indiana include the following (for a more nearly complete list, with points of origin and settlements, see Weeks, *op. cit.,* p. 272-280): Albertson, Barker, Beard, Beeson, Benbow, Binford, Blair, Bogue, Bundy, Coffin, Cook, Cosand, Davis, Dixon, Draper, Elliott, Farlow, Fellow, Frazier, Gordon, Hall, Haugh, Henly, Hinshaw, Hodson, Hubbard, Jessop, Jordan, Julian, Kendal, Lamb, Marshall, Moffit, Moon, Morris, Newby, Newson, Nicholson, Nixon, Overman, Perisho, Pritchard, Puckett, Sanders, Stalker, Stuart, Symons, Tomlinson, Trueblood, Unthank, White, Wilson, and Woodward.

Judge Taft, referred to on page 97, was Alphonso Taft, father of President William Howard Taft.

[6] *American Quakers Today,* edited by Edwin B. Bronner; a Friends World Committee publication, 1966; p. 43-57.

# Chapter 5

## ACROSS THE MISSISSIPPI – IOWA SETTLEMENTS

Farther, farther west the wagons rolled. Their only foreknown boundary was the mighty Mississippi, whose basin extended from the Appalachians to the Rocky Mountains, gathering into its southward flow the waters of half a continent.

Now began the second stage of the great migrations and the fulfillment of continental America. The first stage followed the Ordinance of 1787, opening the Northwest Territory as far west as the Mississippi River. In that period many Ohio and Indiana Quakers had settled. The second stage began with the Louisiana Purchase from the French in 1803, opening the lands beyond the great river and extending the new nation toward the Pacific coast.

The endless wagon trains, accompanied by herds of cattle, moved over Illinois, crossed the Mississippi, and occupied the rich farm lands of Iowa Territory. At a point near Peoria, Illinois, 1,743 wagons were counted in a single month. Between 1850 and 1860 the population of Iowa increased from roughly 192,000 to 675,000. This annual average of about 48,000 quickly filled the borderland areas and moved farther inland.

Within this great stream the little Quaker caravans and the single wagons must have seemed, to Friends on the move, to be small indeed, but in Quaker history they were very significant. Two hundred miles from the western border of Indiana Yearly Meeting a new Quaker stronghold would develop, becoming Iowa Yearly Meeting of Friends. As previous chapters have indicated, there were some Friends settlements in Illinois of which those in Putnam and Vermilion counties were the larger. There were some Quaker families sprinkled across the state, and some of these later nourished Meetings, but Illinois had no concentration of Friends such as those of Ohio and Indiana. This second stage of Quaker migration overleaped, in the main, the great rich farm lands of Illinois.

In 1835, eleven years before Iowa was admitted as a state, the first Quaker family settled in the southeastern tip of the territory. Isaac Pidgeon with his wife and seven children drove an ox team from South Carolina to Rushville, Illinois, to the home of his sister and family, covering the long distance in fifty-two days. Leaving his family temporarily at Rushville, he pressed on to Iowa, locating at a point near the present Salem. He harvested prairie hay to feed the cattle he would bring from Illinois, then returned to Rushville and brought his family to their new home. Theirs was probably the first Quaker cabin west of the Mississippi.[1]

Shortly after, Aaron Street came, returned to Indiana, and brought his family. Isaac Pidgeon and Aaron Street were determined to found a Quaker community in Iowa, and Salem soon became a center and gateway for more migrating Friends. A third Friend, Peter Boyer, joined them in staking out the town site of Salem. This was the fourth Salem founded by the Street family. In 1837 a caravan of nine Quaker families moved from Williamsburg, Indiana, to the new Salem community in Iowa.

By what routes and methods of travel did these early settlers come, cross the great river, and make their way beyond? Friends were by no means the first ones. Enterprising people who preceded them had made the first roads, though with only the tracks of their

---

[1] Louis T. Jones, *The Quakers of Iowa*, the State Historical Society of Iowa, published 1914. An excellent account of the Friends in Iowa.

wagon wheels. There were probably military roads created by preceding wars. Ferries had been established over the Mississippi River, though in the dead of winter wagons and herds crossed on the ice. Some Friends came by boat down the Ohio River and up the Mississippi. They brought limited supplies, depended on wild game, and when food ran low they sent one of their number back to Illinois for supplies.

Meeting for worship near Salem was started in the home of Henry W. Jay, and in 1838 the first Monthly Meeting was established by Vermilion Quarterly Meeting of Indiana Yearly Meeting. The members of the committee appointed by Vermilion Quarterly Meeting to set off the new Meeting were Abraham Holaday, Thomas Ruebottom, Jeremiah H. Siler, Henry Pickard, and Achsah Newlin. The following year the first meetinghouse west of the Mississippi was erected near Salem. Meetings were formed as the Quaker population moved out northward and westward from southeastern Iowa, and other immigrants crossed the river farther north.

The travel letters of the English Friend Robert Lindsey, on his visit with Benjamin Seebohm in 1850, are very revealing as to the rapid spreading of Meetings and the grim circumstances on the frontier. Accustomed to the climate of England, they could hardly have chosen a worse season to visit Friends Meetings in Iowa. It was the dead of winter, with "20 [degrees] below zero and a wind blowing," during part of their travels. They drove in a carriage, presumably from the Adrian Friends settlement in Michigan, over Illinois, crossed on the ice of the Mississippi and arrived at the home of Joseph D. Hoag at East Grove, five miles from Salem.[2]

Distant Friends travelling "in the love of the gospel" were a great boon to isolated Friends on the frontier. Joseph and Amos Hoag arranged to escort Robert Lindsey and Benjamin Seebohm in their circuit of visitation. They started north, meeting Friends families, stopping at Mt. Pleasant, then driving several miles farther north to Iowa City. From there they turned a few miles east to the home of Laurie Tatum, then drove west to Hammers Settlement near Newton in Jasper County, where a few Friends families from Tennessee had settled. Here they held a meeting with Friends. Travelling in

---

[2] *Ibid.*, Part I, Ch. VI. In 1858 Sarah Lindsey accompanied Robert Lindsey on a second visit.

weather well below zero and sleeping in cabins that were far from windproof, they found it hard to keep warm. With a breakdown of their carriage and inability to find hospitality at some places along the road, they had a rough experience of Iowa winter weather.

From Hammers Settlement to "Friends on the Three Rivers" they reached the "most distant and most westerly meeting of Friends on the continent." Twelve Friends were accommodated overnight in one room of the Joseph Carey cabin. There were two beds for four persons and the rest, wrapped in buffalo hides, slept on the floor. Passing through the Dutch community of Pella they visited Spring Creek and Richland settlements and Pleasant Plain Monthly Meeting (established in 1842), finally returning to Salem.

Here they attended Monthly Meeting, which was conducted in a "weighty manner" somewhat typical of the times. Certificates of membership for a family with fourteen children from Virginia were received. The family had come in two wagons, over 1,500 miles in two months. After further visitation of Meetings in the area, the English Friends returned home, having left evidence of the loving concern of English Friends for those in the expanding settlements of frontier America.

One year later William Evans of Philadelphia Yearly Meeting visited some of the Friends' settlements in Iowa. He wrote, "The residences of the settlers in this place [the Oakley settlement], scattered over prairie land, are chiefly log buildings, the settlement being several miles in extent."[3] Later, Friends invaded counties farther north and by 1855, having settled in the northernmost county of Winneshiek, requested Monthly Meeting status. The official Meetings of Friends now ranged from extreme south to north across eastern Iowa.

### BIRTH OF THE YEARLY MEETING

In 1848 the first Quarterly Meeting was set off at Salem, followed in 1852 by the establishment of Pleasant Plain Quarterly Meeting. In 1858 Red Cedar (formerly Oakley) Quarterly Meeting (now Bangor) had been set off by Indiana Yearly Meeting. Friends were now beginning to feel the need for a Yearly Meeting of their own area. The concern arose in Red Cedar Quarterly Meeting as indicated in a

---

[3] *Ibid.*, p. 68.

An early scene at the Iowa Yearly Meeting House in Oskaloosa

John Henry Douglas

Jonathan Plummer

minute of 1858, at which time "it was concluded to appoint a joint committee of men and women Friends, to meet and confer with similar committees from the other Quarterly Meetings, and take the whole subject in all its bearings into serious consideration."[4]

The other Quarterly Meetings concurred in the request and suggested that the Yearly Meeting be held in the Oskaloosa area in Mahaska County. A request was forwarded to Indiana Yearly Meeting in 1859 which in reply appointed a committee to visit the Iowa Quarterly Meetings and local Meetings and report back to the Yearly Meeting. Twelve members of the committee were able to make the visit and the committee reported in the minutes of 1860:

> Our Friends in Iowa received us with much kindness, and assisted us in travelling from place to place. . . . We found large and respectable bodies of Friends at Red Cedar, Bangor, South River, Pleasant Plain and Salem Quarterly Meetings, and entered into much sympathy with them in their situations, and also in regard to their proposition, concerning which we found a united sentiment in each meeting.

Indiana Yearly Meeting granted the request and suggested that the opening session of Iowa Yearly Meeting be held no earlier than 1863 or no later than 1865, allowing time for arrangements. The first session was held in September 1863 at Spring Creek near Oskaloosa. A roughly constructed shed to serve as the meetinghouse for the first gathering was built; it was large enough to seat seven hundred fifty men Friends, while the nearby meetinghouse of Spring Creek served for the women's Meeting. Thirty years later, in 1893, the men's and women's Yearly Meeting sessions were united.

### A BRANCH OF THE UNDERGROUND RAILROAD

Friends having fled from slave territory had settled just across the border on free soil in eastern and southwestern Ohio, in southern Indiana, and in southeastern Iowa. Being very near to the border lands between slave and free territory, Iowa Friends found opportunity for a new attack on the evil and were not long in responding to the opportunity.[5]

---

[4] *Ibid.*, Part I, Ch. IX.
[5] *Ibid.*, Part III, Ch. I.

Salem, only twenty-five miles from the Missouri line, soon became a busy station on the Underground Railroad line that led from Missouri northward to Canada. By whatever means, slaves in northern Missouri heard of the "broad brimmed" people in Iowa and understood that if they could get to the Quaker settlements they would be assisted toward freedom. This led to work with fugitive slaves similar to that of Levi Coffin in Indiana. The Quakers became ingenious in their secret piloting and hiding of runaway slaves.

Slave hunters from Missouri became so frustrated in their search, and then so furious in their anger, that they threatened to destroy the community of Salem. Once when they captured some fugitives and started back to Missouri they were faced with some Quakers, unarmed but determined, who refused to let them pass unless they could prove that these people of color were indeed escaped slaves. The Missourians could do nothing but turn back to Salem for a court session. Their only evidence of the identity of the Negroes was *their* word, and this was not acceptable evidence in court. Quakers were counsel for the Negroes, and the community was almost wholly made up of antislavery people. Proof by the slave-hunters was practically impossible and the fugitives were freed.

Soon after this incident a large band of Missourians rode into Salem in search of fugitive slaves. Upon hearing of their coming the Friends sent the slaves into the wilderness of brush and trees until the danger was past. The band of men came determined to search every "nigger-stealing house," and were readily admitted to the Quaker homes only to find nothing. Having no immediate evidence against Salem residents they rode away. There are many stories of the area and the period very similar to those told by Levi Coffin of his work in Indiana and Ohio.

As in North Carolina, the two testimonies — that against slavery and that against violence — came to the test. John Brown of Kansas, violently antislavery in his sentiments, came to Springdale in Cedar County, Iowa. He knew of the Quakers and their hatred of slavery. He was given a limited and cautious welcome, but spent a winter in the area where he and his band practiced, more or less in secret, the tactics of what would now be called guerrilla warfare. The secret could not be easily kept when military drill was observed by the citizens.

As much as Friends believed in freeing slaves they were adamant in their opposition to violence as a method. This brought Springdale Monthly Meeting to a clear statement of their position on the issue, but not until the John Brown band had left and made an attack on the arsenal at Harpers Ferry with the intention of securing arms. The statement of the Monthly Meeting said in part:

> While we believe that our principles of peace were never dearer to most of our members than now, we feel it to be a cause of deep regret that those engaged in the late, deplorable outbreak at Harpers Ferry, have been entertained & otherwise encouraged by some of our members.
>
> While brought under a deep concern we desire to establish a forgiving feeling toward those [Quakers] who may have been overtaken in weakness & would tenderly admonish all to an increased watchfulness in the precepts of our Redeemer.[6]

John Brown had made another kind of inroad on the Quaker fold by enticing two boys, Edwin and Barclay Coppoc, from Quaker families, to join him in his violent schemes. Edwin Coppoc, two years before, had been disowned for defection from the Quaker faith. He was captured in the Harpers Ferry attack and hanged by the United States government along with John Brown and others. Barclay Coppoc escaped and, as a fugitive from law, returned to his home in Cedar County. What he had done called for action by the Meeting. The committee calling on him found him unrepentant and he was disowned. The peace testimony against violence ran deep in the Quaker tradition and held firm before, through, and after the Civil War.

### ABOLITION SEPARATION IN IOWA

In a previous chapter the controversy and separation of 1843 in Indiana Yearly Meeting over the question of abolition was presented. It should be remembered that at this time Indiana Yearly Meeting included the Meetings and Quarterly Meetings in Iowa Territory. The controversy in Iowa followed much the same line of argument as in Indiana and resulted in similar, though smaller, separations.[7]

The committee appointed by London Yearly Meeting for re-

---

[6] *Ibid.*, Part IV, Ch. I; p. 196.
[7] *Ibid.*, Part III, Ch. I; the abolition separation.

storing unity stopped first in Richmond and then came on to the western areas of Indiana Yearly Meeting. William Forster of the London committee referred to the Iowa settlements around Salem as "the most remote point of our travels." He wrote of meeting in a "log house in the open prairie . . . pretty well filled with new settlers and their children; such a lot of babies as I have never before seen in so small a Meeting."

All Friends of the area were presumably antislavery in sentiment but, as in Indiana, were not agreed on the methods to be pursued. Here also some Friends withdrew, forming another Meeting of Anti-Slavery Friends and uniting with the new Indiana Yearly Meeting of Anti-Slavery Friends, centered at Newport, Indiana.

By 1845, when the London committee came, about fifty of the Iowa separatists had been dealt with for "detraction" and some had been disowned. Here in their meeting at Salem with the London committee there was a sense of "the precious solemnity which covered the Meeting," as expressed by one Iowa Friend, after which the subject of the visit was introduced by George Stacey, clerk of London Yearly Meeting. "Accept, we beseech you," the London communication in part read, "our earnest and affectionate entreaty that you will relinquish your separate meetings . . . and again assemble for the public worship of Almighty God with those with whom you have been accustomed thus to meet."

The Anti-Slavery Meeting gave a clear reply on their position, referring to "the course of London Yearly Meeting, and your course as a committee, as very extraordinary. That without ever entering into an impartial examination of the causes that led to the difficulty . . . you enter into judgment, and require us to return, without an effort to remove the causes of the difficulty that separates us."

The committee also attended the original Salem Monthly Meeting which prepared a minute expressing appreciation for "our beloved Friend William Foster [Forster], a minister with his brethren . . . all from England in the prosecution of their visit . . . whose company and labor of Gospel love . . . have been satisfactory & edifying."

A final effort by the separated Friends was made with the London committee to achieve an understanding of their position; the committee, however, insisted they had not come to adjudicate over the rightness or the wrongness of the two sides but to urge the separatists to reunite with the other Meetings. The committee, who had seemed to the Iowa group high-handed and demanding, left for Indiana, having failed to repair that which only time could heal. The Anti-Slavery Meeting finally declined and ended as members died or moved, while a few rejoined the original Meetings.

## EXTENSION SERVICE FOR FREEDMEN

When Lincoln's Proclamation of Emancipation came, Friends of Iowa gradually turned to helping the freedmen. Combining their efforts with Ohio, Indiana, and Western Yearly Meetings they collected money and clothing in large amounts, and also established schools. Different areas were assigned to the Yearly Meetings in this large cooperative effort. Missouri and Kansas were assigned to Iowa as their responsibility. Isaac T. Gibson of Salem was appointed General Agent, and in the 1866 sessions of Iowa Yearly Meeting an excellent report on schools for freedmen, with Quaker teachers, was made, together with length of terms and enrollment. The figures are of sufficient significance that they are given in some detail.

> In Missouri at Weston, eight months (length of term), two teachers, 127 enrolled; at St. Joseph, eight months, two teachers, 350 enrolled; at Sedalia, four and one-half months, one teacher, 140 enrolled; at Columbia, five months, one teacher, 70 enrolled; at Springfield, eight months, two teachers, 450 enrolled; at Mexico [Missouri], five months, one teacher, 60 enrolled; in Kansas: at Atchison, six months, two teachers, 160 enrolled.[8]

Including their First Day Bible Schools, Friends of Iowa were ministering to more than two thousand ex-slaves, and their children.

### Expansion of the Yearly Meeting

This was an era of expansion and dispersion of Friends, from the Alleghenies to the Pacific coast, as reflected in the 1887 statement of John Henry Douglas, the first Superintendent of Iowa Yearly Meeting. He reported

> . . . churches in Wisconsin, Iowa, Minnesota, Dakota Territory, Nebraska, Oregon, Washington Territory, California and Texas,

---

[8] *Minutes,* Iowa Yearly Meeting, 1865, p. 35; 1866, p. 17, 18.

and individuals scattered in the great northwest . . . [having] about one hundred churches, with an average membership of one hundred . . . [and] about one hundred and forty ministers; some fifty of these in active work [located pastors or evangelists].[9]

All of these were under Iowa Yearly Meeting. With the expansion of Meetings came also an increase in new members. During the four years of service by John Henry Douglas as superintendent of Iowa Yearly Meeting there were 7,430 conversions reported, with 2,595 brought into membership. This increase brought forcibly to the attention of the Yearly Meeting the need for more adequate pastoral care.

In 1880 the first move toward a pastoral arrangement, whereby converts could be cared for, had been brought before the Yearly Meeting. The proposed action recognized "the right of meetings . . . to invite ministers or other Friends whom the Lord had qualified for that service to reside and labor among them" with partial or entire support to be provided. The Yearly Meeting was not ready for the step and the proposal was not approved.

In 1886 the Yearly Meeting again considered the issue and officially adopted the pastoral system, as reflected in the following minute.

> That it is advisable for each particular meeting to have a regular ministry; and that meetings be encouraged to call and support ministers . . . as pastors. . . .
> That the Evangelistic Committee of Iowa Yearly Meeting be authorized to provide as far as possible for the supply of ministers and workers . . . in meetings desiring such help. . . .[10]

They added that the action was taken because of "the deplorable fact that many individuals brought to Christ through the labors of our evangelists have been left almost immediately to themselves, and in many cases have fallen away. . . . Our pastoral oversight has not kept pace with our evangelistic ingathering." By 1889 there were fifty-one located pastors with fifteen being given full-time support. The pastoral system was now official, and a new level of questions on pastoral qualifications would follow, along with definite changes in the manner of conducting meetings for worship.

---

[9] *Minutes*, Iowa Yearly Meeting, 1887, p. 13, 14.
[10] *Minutes*, Iowa Yearly Meeting, 1886, p. 13.

## THE CONSERVATIVE SEPARATION AND DEVELOPMENT

The evangelical wave that swept through the Midwest into Iowa, issuing finally in the pastoral system, had not come without serious concern and opposition by many Friends who believed it to be a complete departure from traditional Quakerism. It seemed to them wholly foreign to the tested and trusted ways that had characterized Friends Meetings until that time.

What the conservative Friends of the Yearly Meeting witnessed around them seemed like a return to that from which early Friends had revolted. On the other hand, to the evangelical Friends this surge of evangelistic outreach was like a return to the vigorous preaching and ingathering of George Fox and his contemporaries in which they saw "a great people to be gathered" and set out to "gather" them. Evangelical Friends were impatient with simply conserving past forms and methods.

### The Wilburite Friends of Iowa

The tensions which led toward the separation in Iowa Yearly Meeting might be said to have started in the early 1850's.[11] Two Hampton brothers, followed shortly by Joseph Edgerton, Francis Williams, Jesse North, William P. Deweese, and William P. Bedell, most of them from Ohio, settled near the present-day Springville in Linn County. They were joined by Caleb Gregg, a minister who shortly became a central personality in the new Meeting formed under Red Cedar Monthly Meeting and who expressed himself as favoring the views of John Wilbur. He was "dealt with" for his views and in the end this led to a separation in the Quarterly Meeting in 1854, the same year of the Wilbur separation in Ohio.

Around 1860 there was a Wilburite settlement in Keokuk County. Among the families of the settlement were those of Jeremiah Stanley, Benjamin Bates, and Evan Smith. Other Meetings developed and soon Hickory Grove Quarterly Meeting was formed, under Ohio Yearly Meeting (Wilburite) Friends, including Red Cedar, Whittier, and the Meeting in Keokuk County. The main achievement of Wilburite Friends in the area was the establishment of Scattergood Boarding School.[12] It continued until 1913, but after being closed

---

[11] Jones, op. cit., Part III, Ch. III.
[12] See Chapter 9, "Education and Schools."

for several years was reopened, first as a hostel for German refugees and later as a secondary school.

## The New Conservative Development

Though with nearly identical beliefs, the Wilburite and the Conservative Friends of Iowa are not to be confused. They had their distinct historical lines arising from two different separations. The Wilburites, as we have seen in a previous chapter, arose from the separation occurring first in New England in 1845 and then in Ohio in 1854. Friends Meetings were established in Iowa under Ohio Yearly Meeting (Wilburite) Friends. They had their district identity as a Quarterly Meeting in Iowa before the Conservative separation in Iowa took place.

The first rift preceding the Iowa Conservative separation occurred in Bear Creek Monthly Meeting in 1867. The evangelical wave had been coming to its crest for several years, but not until that date had open opposition developed. Stacy Bevan and John Bond, ministers carrying minutes from Bangor and Honey Creek Meetings, had stopped at Bear Creek on their way to visit Friends in Kansas. Here they held a meeting of an evangelical nature. Stacy Bevan's account presents some of the aspects of that experience.

> Many hearts were reached and all broken up, which was followed by sighs and sobs and prayers, confessions and great joy for sins pardoned and burdens rolled off, and precious fellowship of the redeemed. But, alas, some of the dear old Friends mistook this outbreak of the power of God for excitement and wild fire and tried to close the meeting, but we kept cool and held the strings, and closed the meeting orderly.[13]

Such was the explanation by Stacy Bevan, but to those for whom the older tradition was precious this was indeed a definite break from it. By 1872 there had been some concern in Iowa Yearly Meeting for the revivals over which the Yearly Meeting had little control. A committee was appointed to have oversight of these "general meetings" and seek to make them constructive.

In 1877 the tension at Bear Creek came to a crisis and the conservative group withdrew, formed a separate organization which took on the proportions of a Quarterly Meeting as some other separations

---

[13] Jones, op. cit., p. 164.

in Bear Creek Quarterly Meeting took place. The two groups sent reports and appointed representatives to Yearly Meeting as Bear Creek Quarterly Meeting. Joel Bean, the presiding clerk, stated that neither report could be received until it was determined which one was valid. The problem was referred to the representatives who decided in favor of the evangelical body.

This brought Friends directly to the point of separation. Stanley Pumphrey and Walter Robson, in attendance as visitors from England, visited Bear Creek Friends and, as told in the diary of Robson, "begged them not to complete the separation. . . . The poor dear Friends took our labours very kindly. . . . They replied that they had not left us but we were leaving them. . . . The command had gone out to them, to come out and be separate."[14] The Yearly Meeting appointed a committee to attempt a reconciliation.

All efforts failed and in the sessions of 1877, according to the Robson account, "when we had broken up Yearly Meeting this afternoon and were all in the yard outside a Friend from Bear Creek called out from a top window" that they had rented a city hall and invited all who sympathized with them to meet there. They prepared a statement of their position on faith and practice and on September 7, 1877, set up Iowa Yearly Meeting of (Conservative) Friends.

Soon other sympathetic separations within Meetings occurred and two new Quarterly Meetings were formed: Salem in Henry County and Springdale in Cedar County, including some West Branch Friends. These with the Bear Creek separatists formed the new Conservative Yearly Meeting.

The Wilburite separation in Iowa had its beginning earlier, in 1853, one year before the separation in Ohio, while Iowa Friends Meetings were within Indiana Yearly Meeting. The earlier separation in New England in 1845 had required Indiana Yearly Meeting to choose between the two groups in New England and they had recognized the larger Gurneyite body. Some Friends in Iowa held with the smaller Wilburite group and this led to a small separation in Red Cedar Monthly Meeting and Salem Quarterly Meeting in Iowa.

For several years Wilburite and Conservative Meetings existed

---

[14] Robson *Journal*, Haverford College library.

in very close proximity to each other. Though holding the same views they had separate histories and for a time held their separate identities, though in all friendliness and love. On a First Day morning the Friends of the two bodies often met each other on their way to their respective meetings, those from West Branch going to Springville and those of Springville to West Branch, a distance of about two miles. The distinction has now ceased to exist.

### NORWEGIAN FRIENDS IN IOWA

Fiction could hardly create a more exciting story of spiritual adventure than the history of Quakerism coming to Norway and Norwegian Friends coming to Iowa. John Frederick Hanson's *Light and Shade From the Land of the Midnight Sun* has given wide circulation of the story.

Enoch Jacobson, born in 1790 at Stavanger, Norway, appears to have been the first Friend of that country. As a young man in his teens he went to sea without the consent of his parents. The privateer on which he sailed was captured by the British and taken to a harbor in Scotland where he was imprisoned. In a letter to a friend he told of seeing one of Robert Barclay's books, supplied by British Friends, and hungered to know more "about the secret workings of the Almighty."

His letter came into the hands of Friends, who sent more literature to the men on the prison ship. With other prisoners, he wrote, "We began to hold silent meetings before the Lord, previous to our knowing anything of the manner in which Friends hold their meetings." When later released and returned to their own land, four of the men continued their meeting for worship, a few others joining them.

In 1818 Stephen Grellet and William Allen visited them. It was a turning point in the life of these new Friends. British Friends carefully nurtured the group, writing "to the King of Sweden and Norway" setting forth the principles of Friends and easing the way of this group which had met some persecution at the hands of the state church. Thomas Shillitoe was another English visitor to Norway in 1822.

Kleng Peerson, "who held more or less with Friends," came to America from Norway in 1821 looking over the prospects. On his return home he kindled interest in America, with its "freedom from religious persecution" and the openings to settlers. Freedom from persecution by the Lutherans played a large part in drawing them toward Friends in America.

Many Norwegians migrated to America. Our concern in these pages is with those who came to Iowa.[15] The first Norwegian Friends settlement in Iowa was in Lee County in 1840, in the southeastern tip of Iowa Territory. Some of their members joined the Mormons who for a time had settled in that area. Others moved farther north, near Salem, and established Sugar Creek Friends Meeting. They were destined finally to settle much farther north and west in Marshall County, near Le Grand, with Sugar Creek finally dying. One of their families had gone to Le Grand in 1858 and had sent urgent invitations to the others, who came shortly after them.

At first this new community attempted fellowship with the Le Grand Friends Meeting, but the language barrier made it impossible. They established their own "Indulged Meeting" under Le Grand and named it Stavanger for their city in Norway. As a result of a visit to Norway by Lindley Murray Hoag in 1853 a community in the valley of Roldal, high in the mountains, was discovered. They were Quakers in principle though never having heard the name. They formed a Meeting under Stavanger Friends, but military demands and the pressure and persecution by the Lutheran Church caused about fifty of them to migrate to America. They came by ship to Quebec and finally to Le Grand in 1869, swelling the little Norwegian community to considerable size.

They did not enjoy the ways of Iowa Yearly Meeting and in 1885 affiliated with Conservative Friends. In 1891 they established a Friends Boarding School which prospered for some years but finally was closed. They later changed to the pastoral system and, though they are independent, Iowa Yearly Meeting furnishes pastoral leadership for them. Culturally they have been largely absorbed by their American environment during their four generations at Le Grand.

In 1914, Louis T. Jones summarized his view of the bodies of Friends in Iowa in these words:

> . . . while a persistent spirit of conservatism has led the smaller

---

[15] Jones, *op. cit.*, Part III, Ch. VI.

body of Orthodox Friends in Iowa into . . . decline, a growing disregard for its original tenets now threatens to leave the larger Yearly Meeting little that is distinctive in character. . . . Is there not somewhere between these two extremes a happy medium, which would be advantageous to both? It is possible that the rising generation in both sects . . . may find sufficient common ground on which to reunite. Indeed the trend of events would seem to point in that direction.[16]

His words have proved truly prophetic in his call to "the rising generation." Friends of Iowa are not primarily concerned with re-uniting in some structural sense. More important are the fellowship and the mutual confidence that have grown, witnessing to Friends everywhere what love, persistently practiced, can do.

Friends have probably experienced no more tensions and separations than have most Christian bodies. To Quakers these disturbances may feel worse because they seem to contradict the reputation of Friends as a peace-loving body. Contention and separation in political affairs are generally viewed as in the nature of things, to be taken in stride. But differences in religious views are generally taken more seriously, for religious faith generally is considered a matter of life-and-death importance to those who are involved.

A slight defection here or there is often seen as a potential disaster to the religious body and must be stopped before it is too late. Hence, at times, the rush to stop a rift has only deepened and widened it. Had they been left to themselves, some of these disagreements might conceivably have disappeared. The ancient Query, still read in most Friends Meetings today, seems to suggest immediate attention: "When differences arise do you make earnest effort to end them speedily?" Not all differences were crucial, for some kinds of disagreements were signs of growth. But seen in the context of history on the frontier, and with the issues involved, most separations of Friends appear to have been inevitable.

---

[16] *Ibid.*, p. 183.

# Chapter 6

## ON THE GREAT PLAINS –
## KANSAS AND NEBRASKA

One has not seen America in its natural magnificence until he has seen it in three dimensions — not only that of the heights of the Rocky Mountains and the depths of the Grand Canyon, but also the alluring distances on the Great Plains.

If one doubts the peculiar spell that the plains can cast on the spirit of a traveller let him, in the spring, drive on the turnpike from the northeast corner of Kansas southwest to Wichita and the Oklahoma line beyond. The treeless hills roll on every side like the waves of an ocean. The shadows of clouds on a sunny day move across the hills, giving the impression of a restless sea. This wide-sweeping area has been referred to as the "grand prairie ocean," with caravans of prairie schooners "making port."[1] If the traveller turns west at any point on this southwest highway and follows one of the straight, long roads to the Colorado line he will find this "sea" levelling out into a great "calm" as the flat lands spread toward the Rockies.

[1] Walter Prescott Webb, *The Great Plains;* Ginn and Co., 1931.

John Noble, the painter, reared in Kansas, later painted seascapes on the coast of Brittany. He carried the spirit of his plains experience into his art. Of it he said, "I believe it taught me to understand the sea. . . . It was at this time that some of my fellow artists began to speak of the way I was painting the sea . . . as no one else had painted it."[2]

As on the sea, so on these plains there was no permanent stopping place for the schooners with their migrating families. But long before the schooner era of the nineteenth century, Spanish and French expeditions moved across the plains and gave the present Kansas a recorded history dating back to the midsixteenth century. Parts of Kansas have been under six flags — English, French, Spanish, Mexican, Texan, and the U. S. A. Coronado's Spanish expedition is said to have crossed the Arkansas River in 1541 near the site of the present Dodge City. In 1593 another Spanish venture was made in search of "Quivira," a legendary prairie Utopia or Atlantis, but the shining walls of Quivira were never found.

Such a venture would not be reported to the Spanish throne as complete failure and the chronicler was equal to his assignment with a tall story, rarely exceeded!

> The cornstalks were as tall as those of New Spain and in some places even taller. The land was so fertile that even though the corn had just been harvested, there was a second crop about six inches high, without other cultivation or preparation of the soil than pulling up the grass and making some holes in which the corn was planted. There were many beans and some calabashes, and plum trees between the planted fields. These were not irrigated fields, but depend on seasonal rains, which, as we learned, must be very regular in that land [sic!].[3]

By contrast, Pike's expedition in the early 1800's found the plains of Kansas to have but a limited value to the American nation. For Pike and his contemporary explorers this was the "Great American Desert."[4]

Contrary to all reports, Quivira was finally found, not as a spe-

---

[2] *Ibid.*, p. 488, 489; from the *American Magazine*, August 1927, p. 34ff.

[3] William Frank Zornow, *Kansas: A History of the Jayhawk State.* Copyright 1957 by the University of Oklahoma Press. P. 26.

[4] Webb, *op. cit.*, p. 155ff.

cific site, but as a home for immigrants who turned a desert into the "breadbasket of the nation." The gold of Quivira can be seen today in early June as waves of ripened wheat suggest another kind of sea on the plains.

## NEW FRONTIER CONDITIONS

Running from north to south and following roughly the eastern boundaries of the Dakotas, Nebraska, and Kansas is a broad timberline. On the east side, with the heavier rainfall, trees generally thrive. On the west the more arid area begins with few trees, except those along rivers and creeks. The timberline is therefore the "cabin line," log cabins being the usual structure in the early days of homes to the east and sod houses common to those on the west. Eastern Kansas is more like Missouri and Iowa in the average rainfall and in timber; but farther to the west the more arid plains begin, including about three-fourths of the state.

In natural resources of rainfall, trees, and soil, migrating Friends would not find a great difference in moving from Ohio to Indiana and Iowa. In those states a farmer could, without changing his methods of cultivation, get similar results in corn, wheat, and other crops. On the Great Plains new and untested ways were required.[5]

These facts of nature rose like a barrier that threw back the first wave of immigrants. Their wagons going west sometimes carried signs saying "Kansas or Bust" and a returning wagon would occasionally carry a sign saying "Busted." It took three waves of immigrants before the would-be settlers learned fully how to coax a living from the soil. Changing wild sweeps of prairie land to cattle ranges, and then to cultivated farms, exacted a high price of those who conquered the plains.

Here was a new kind of conquest, a confronting of enemies where tools rather than weapons were required. The first and essential tool was the sod-breaker. Its plowshare ran four to six inches below the surface covering of buffalo grass and its sweeping mouldboard laid the soil over in long ribbonlike layers held together by the grass roots. These were cut into squares or rectangles and laid in a kind of earth masonry to form the walls of a pioneer house. Along creeks and

---

[5] *Ibid.*, p. 366-374.

rivers enough timber could be found to make a roof, which was then covered with several layers of sod.

The Kansas Quaker farmer, along with his neighbors, found that he could not plant his crops in the usual way, on a level plowed field. There was too much wind that eroded the smooth fields. He must leave some stubble as a rough surface and plant his corn in deep furrows to be filled in as the young stalks grew. This gave his corn rootage below the dry surface when rains failed. A plow with mould-boards on each side, called the lister, was an early answer to this dry-farming need. (*Dry farming* means cultivation with only scanty moisture.) Furrows and ridges were then levelled as the growing corn was cultivated. Newer farming tools and methods have followed that early battle with the weather and the soil.

The strong wind that threatened the plowed fields was harnessed by the windmill (common also in the East) which drew abundant supplies of water from deep and never-failing sources. Springs and streams were not required for life on the plains. The earliest fuel for cooking food and for warmth was the sun-dried manure of buffaloes and cows, commonly called "cow chips" or, facetiously, "prairie coal." The coming of corn crops furnished cobs for fire, and with the development of railroads coal from the East became available.

It is important to have this background of early plains life in order to understand the circumstances that surrounded Quaker immigrants and their neighbors. No other Quaker settlements faced conditions like those of the Kansas-Nebraska area. Others had not required so much imagination and ingenuity for building a viable family life and an economic future. That these pioneers succeeded has abundant evidence in the Kansas of today, with homes and comforts second to none.

The caravan trains and the single wagons rolled across these tree-less prairies in large numbers. During 1865, from May to November 4,472 wagons were counted passing through Council Grove.

## KANSAS QUAKER SETTLEMENTS

Concern for Indians led the first Friends to Kansas. In the 1830's the Shawnee Indians were forced by the government to accept a treaty whereby they were moved from Ohio to a new reservation in what is now the northeast corner of Kansas. They had implored Friends not to forget them. In 1836 the Shawnee Mission, with a boarding school and a meetinghouse, was established by Friends in that area.[6]

Not only their concern for the Indians, but also their antislavery sentiment, helped to bring the Quaker migrations to Kansas. In 1820 the Missouri Compromise provided that slavery should be excluded from the Louisiana Purchase north of latitude 36° 30' with the exception of the state of Missouri. This would have made Kansas free territory. But the Missouri Compromise was repealed in 1854 by the Kansas-Nebraska Act, which left the question of slavery to be settled by vote of the people in any state coming into the Union from the Kansas-Nebraska territory.

The Dred Scott decision of the Supreme Court in 1857 added fuel to the fiery spirit of the northern antislavery leaders. Among other provisions, the decision "held that no Negro slave or descendant of a slave could be a citizen of the United States" and that "Congress had no right to prohibit slavery in the territories and that the Missouri Compromise had been null and void from the day of its enactment."[7]

This decision shifted the issue from argument to the battleline. Whether Kansas was to be free became a focal question for the nation. On that decision hung the future of other states yet to be carved out of the Louisiana Territory. Proslavery and antislavery groups moved into the new territory, and the conflicts that came in the wake of the mass migrations gave the emerging state a reputation as "Bleeding Kansas." From the New England and other northern states settlers came to live and vote for freedom. Within these migrations the Quakers also came.

Probably the first Friend who came with the intention of making his home in Kansas was George M. Harvey; he came in 1854, the year that Kansas was opened as a territory under the provision of the Kansas-Nebraska Act. He was followed shortly by Samuel D. and Henry Harvey, Ira Hadley, and Joel Hiatt. In that year William

---

[6] Rayner W. Kelsey, *Friends and the Indians,* published by Associated Executive Committee of Friends on Indian Affairs, 1917; Ch. VII.
See also Ch. X, "Quakers and Western Indians," in *Quakers on the American Frontier.*
[7] John A. Krout, *United States to 1865;* College Outline Series, Barnes and Noble, Inc., New York (sixth edition), p. 124-129.

H. Coffin, Eli Wilson, and Benajah W. Hiatt met at Indiana Yearly Meeting and determined upon a visit to Kansas. By railroad, by stage, and by boat up the Missouri River from St. Louis they came to Westport, the present Kansas City.[8]

Stopping at the Shawnee Mission they secured supplies, staked out claims, and went back to Indiana for their families. Returning to Kansas the next year they established on Stranger Creek a settlement later known as Springdale. Living in the timbered area of eastern Kansas, they built cabins, split rails for fencing, broke sod, and planted crops.

In 1856 the first Friends Meeting was held in the cabin of Benajah Hiatt with at least seven families. They wrote to Whitewater and Milford Monthly Meetings in Indiana Yearly Meeting, suggesting an "established meeting," to be attached to Whitewater.

> Dear Friends:
>
> We, the undersigned members of the Society of Friends, and nearly all members of the above meetings and residents of Kansas Territory, feeling the need of your Christian care and oversight, and wishing to more fully enjoy the privileges of Religious Organization, have unitedly come to the conclusion to propose that an established meeting may be set up and held at some point near Stranger Creek, in Kansas, as may be most convenient, if in the judgment of Friends such a movement might seem best for the advancement of the cause of truth.
>
> We number at present in this locality nine families of Friends comprising fifty members . . . meeting together for worship on first days near two years.
>
> We have also part of the time kept up a school for our children . . . attended by an average of near twenty scholars; all of which have been taught by competent Friends.[9]

Whitewater Quarterly Meeting approved the establishment of this body as Kansas Preparative Meeting. A committee to visit and consider setting off the new Meeting was appointed. This and other Meetings in the area were set off in 1862 by Indiana Yearly Meeting as Kansas Quarterly Meeting.

---

[8] Rufus M. Jones, *Later Periods of Quakerism II,* Macmillan and Co., Ltd., London, 1921; Ch. XXI. The migration of Friends to Iowa and Kansas.

[9] Sheldon G. Jackson, *A Short History of Kansas Yearly Meeting;* Day Print Shop, Wichita, 1946; p. 35.

To the southwest of the settlement another one was forming at Cottonwood, a few miles west of the present Emporia; it laid the basis for the setting off of Cottonwood Quarterly Meeting.

Within a period of twelve years 2,600 Friends settled in Kansas and spread not only to the Cottonwood settlement but also to the southeastern corner of Kansas in Cherokee County and, following the Civil War, into southwestern Missouri in Jasper County. Meetings which were formed in this area were included in Spring River Quarterly Meeting, established in 1869.[10]

### THE YEARLY MEETING ESTABLISHED

Friends of Kansas began to feel the need for a separate Yearly Meeting and made request for it to Indiana Yearly Meeting. In 1869 Indiana Yearly Meeting considered the request.

> By the reports from Kansas, Cottonwood and Spring River Quarterly Meetings it appears that they are united in requesting the establishment of a Yearly Meeting to be located . . . at or near Lawrence to be called Kansas Yearly Meeting of Friends.

A committee appointed by Indiana Yearly Meeting visited the Kansas Meetings and reported favorably in 1870. Their relation with other Friends Yearly Meetings was indicated in this minute of Indiana Yearly Meeting:

> It is the judgment of this meeting that Kansas Yearly Meeting be opened at the time and place proposed, in the year 1872, *provided the consent of the Yearly Meetings with which we correspond be obtained thereto* [italics added].[11]

Consent was given by the other Yearly Meetings, including London and Dublin. Kansas Yearly Meeting opened according to plan in 1872 at Lawrence, Kansas, with William Nicholson as clerk.[12]

A perspective of views and concerns of the Yearly Meeting, as it was launched into history, can be seen, in part, in the reports of the Quarterly Meetings. These were based on the Queries, as those of other Yearly Meetings had been for more than a century. Both questions and answers were nearly the same in all branches of the

---

[10] "The Newman Collection," memoirs of several Kansas Friends, assembled by Herman Newman; original in Kansas State Historical Library, Topeka, Kansas.

[11] *Minutes,* 1870; Indiana Yearly Meeting.

[12] Jackson, *op. cit.,* Ch. VI.

Society of Friends at the midpoint of the nineteenth century. Some of these replies would soon be outdated as important changes took place.

For many years Friends of all Yearly Meetings had urged faithfulness in attendance at First Day and midweek meetings for worship. Laxness in attendance at midweek meeting, generally held in the morning of Fourth or Fifth Day, was common to most Meetings. This was a matter of continuing concern. Even though weak in attendance, their midweek meetings were held for many years by the faithful few.

In Kansas, where wheat was the main crop, attendance at midweek meeting held an unusual degree of economic risk at harvesttime. The labor of an entire year was represented in the ripened fields of wheat. Rain, hail, or fire might come suddenly, destroying it all. This did not deter many Quaker farmers who left their reaping machinery idle in the field for a few hours while they attended midday meeting. Today, in most Meetings the midday gathering has changed to evening prayer meetings, with a small attendance generally.

The plainness of speech (use of *thee* and *thou*) and the strictures favoring distinctive Quaker clothing were changing in the late nineteenth century. Disownments for infraction of the discipline were lessening and finally ceased except in unusual cases.

Though the objection to "ministers' wages" as practiced in the pastoral system later gave way, the charter from the State of Kansas under which Kansas Yearly Meeting operates states that the Yearly Meeting was organized to promote the fellowship and the religious education of the Religious Society of Friends in Kansas among those called Quakers that *do not hire pastors or sing hymns* (italics added)!

By 1882, when a Committee on Pastoral and Evangelistic Work was organized, a systematic attempt was made to meet needs by supplying leadership. By 1889 the first general superintendent for this work was appointed. The first pastor reported in Kansas Yearly Meeting was mentioned in 1886.

The "unnecessary use of intoxicating liquors" changed to an emphasis on total abstinence. In Kansas this was a major accent in all social reform. Kansas enjoyed for many years her temperance reputation as the driest state in the Union.

The witness "against bearing arms" gradually gave way in large part, but a changing witness as to responsibility in peacemaking followed in the wake of the First World War, chiefly under the American Friends Service Committee. The experience of Kansas Quakers in the changing peace witness was hardly different from that of most Western Yearly Meetings.

### "Bleeding Kansas" — Political Turmoil

As we see the new Yearly Meeting starting on its way it is well to review more fully some background problems which faced Friends at the beginning. Those opening years for Friends on the prairie were crucial and formative. We should see the context of life in which Quaker communities were formed.[13] The developments that marked the Friends of midwestern America in general, and those of Kansas in particular, are not understandable apart from the environment, material and social, in which they lived. Sometimes the attitudes of non-Friends in this conflict situation set Friends apart, in contrast to the religiously blest militancy of their neighbors.

How often guns and Bibles have been associated, if not confused, as weapons in common! John Brown is depicted in the mural in the state capitol at Topeka with a gun in one hand and a Bible in the other calling his followers into the battle. "New bands of immigrants coming to Kansas were bringing rifles, and money was being solicited in the East to arm settlers. These rifles were known as 'Beecher's Bibles', because Henry Ward Beecher's congregation had raised money to give each member of the Wabaunsee colony a rifle and a Bible." Boxes marked "Bibles" were suspected of containing guns.[14]

Almost from the first the conflict between proslavery and anti-slavery forces was a disturbing element. Quakers "bled" with "bleeding Kansas." Border ruffians from Missouri conducted raids on anti-slavery settlements in an attempt to frighten them and discourage further migrations of Friends and their antislavery neighbors. John Brown and his band, referred to in the chapter on Iowa, responded with similar violence on the antislavery side.

As Friends moved into troubled Kansas other Friends were with them in spirit. John Greenleaf Whittier wrote from his New En-

---

[13] Jones, *op. cit.*, Ch. XXI.
[14] Zornow, *op. cit.*, p. 72.

gland home "The Kansas Emigrants," from which the following lines are taken:

> We cross the prairies as of old
> The pilgrims crossed the sea,
> To make the West, as they the East,
> The homeland of the free!
>
> We go to rear a wall of men
> On freedom's southern line,
> And plant beside the cotton tree
> The rugged northern pine!
>
> .    .    .    .    .
>
> Upbearing, like the Ark of old,
> The Bible in our van,
> We go to test the truth of God
> Against the fraud of man.

There was a spirit in the Quaker movement to Kansas similar to that of the antislavery Friends earlier in the southern states. Theirs was a kind of quiet crusade, moving unarmed, bearing only the weapons of the spirit. In 1855, skirmishes between the proslavery and the antislavery forces resulted in the death of Thomas W. Barber. This inspired Whittier to pen these lines, "The Burial of Barber":

> Bear him comrades to his grave;
> Never over one more brave
> Shall the prairie grasses weep,
> In the ages yet to come,
> When the millions in our room,
> What we sow in tears, shall reap.
>
> .    .    .    .    .
>
> Well to suffer is divine;
> Pass the watchword down the line,
> Pass the countersign: "Endure."
> Not to him who rashly dares,
> But to him who nobly bears,
> Is the victor's garland sure.

An attack was made on the Friends Shawnee Mission in 1856.

The following is taken from the account in the minutes of Indiana Yearly Meeting.

> One day in August several children were taken out of school by their parents who gave as the reason, that they feared an attack on the mission. . . . The day following the removal of those children . . . a posse of eighteen armed men rode into the mission dooryard. They had thrown down the fence and made their way through the farm to the barn. There they had found all the horses harnessed ready for work in the field. They cut the harness in pieces and threw it on the ground, put saddles on the horses, and led them out with the ones they were riding. The Superintendent went out to remonstrate with them, and to entreat them to leave one horse that he might go to Westport . . . to bring a doctor for his wife who was then lying sick in the house. He was cursed and abused by the man who called him a "nigger stealer" and the leader, pointing a gun in his face, ordered him to leave, or, said he, "this is only the beginning of what you may look for!"[15]

Undaunted, Friends opened the school again the next year. William H. Coffin gives an account of his own experiences in a threatened raid.

> My wife was in the house with our four little children and knew nothing about it and I said nothing. We could expect no favour from such a body of men, composed, as they were, of the worst description of *border men of the Jesse James type,* and I had little confidence or expectation that a hurried rally of the neighbours would succeed in stopping them, organized as they were. I do not think that I was afraid at that time, being young and excitable, but my education was such *I could not, with conscience, kill a man;* but when I got to reasoning with myself about my duty in the protection of my family, my faith gave way. I had an *excellent doubled-barrelled gun,* and I took it outdoors and loaded it heavily with buckshot. It was near bedtime, my wife and children soon went to sleep, and I barred the door and set my gun handy, and made up my mind I would shoot any man or set of men that undertook to break it. A cabin, built as they were of logs at that time, made a pretty good fort; but I could get no sleep, having laid down with my clothes on. Finally, towards

---

[15] *Minutes,* Indiana Yearly Meeting, 1857.

midnight I got up, wife and children peacefully sleeping, *drew the loads from my gun* and put it away; and then, *on my knees, I* told the Lord all about it and *asked his protection;* and so, casting all my care upon Him, I felt easy, went to bed, was soon asleep, and slept until sun-up the next morning. . . .[16]

As was usual with Friends, they exercised their responsibilities as citizens by way of the franchise. They had come to Kansas to vote for freedom. Despite the dangers involved they of the new settlements went to Leavenworth to cast their votes. Here is an account by one of them of that experience.

A great many Missourians had come over from Platte county and were congregated in the streets. For some reason, they concluded to let the free-state men cast their votes, and then break up the poll. In the afternoon, when I had just voted, as James Wilson came next to me he was collared by an armed man and thrown to one side; and then a large body of men, armed with guns, revolvers and bowie-knives, knocked in the window at the voting place, captured and carried off the ballot box, and beat nearly to death one of the judges, Wetherald by name, a worthy young man and a member of our Society, living in the city. The free-state men were utterly overpowered by numbers and made *no resistance,* which was the very *best thing, under the circumstances,* to have done.

Rival constitutions were written and the fate of the state on the slavery question was in doubt for several years. The coming of the Civil War drew attention to the larger conflict, and in 1861 Kansas was admitted to the Union as a free state.

## Years of Expansion and Testing

Further expansion of Friends settlements led them toward western Kansas and ultimately into eastern Colorado and into Texas and Oklahoma. In this period of Quaker expansion new settlements appeared and disappeared under the hazards of frontier conditions.

An example of Quaker colonizing with its risks and failures was one led by John Franklin Moore, brother of Joseph Moore of North Carolina and Indiana fame. About twelve Indiana families settled in Stevens County south of Hugoton, near the Oklahoma border.

---

[16] Jones, *op. cit.,* p. 848-850.

They named their new settlement Lafayette, for the Indiana city, favorite of John Moore.[17]

Lumber was brought one hundred miles by wagons from Garden City. Here John Moore erected a building that served as a store, a post office, a schoolroom, and a meeting room on the lower floor, with an office for Dr. Furnas and with living quarters upstairs. A Day School and a Sunday School were taught by Lydia Ann Wilson. John Moore and Lydia Ann Wilson were married here.

The little settlement could not succeed in the hard times that came with drouth, hot winds, and grasshoppers in the summer and with freezing winds of the winter. Crops failed and in one very severe winter their cattle froze on the range. The settlement was disbanded, and for several years one lone building with the name *Lafayette* on it stood in a kind of grandeur on the flat, far-sweeping prairie which the little Quaker community was not prepared to conquer.

The succeeding waves of immigrants learned from the preceding ones in large-scale trial-and-error experiences, the errors often being very costly.

There were, during these times, boom periods in the state, and booming by boasting was common. Enterprising promoters were making the most of it. Boom towns were planned and promoted with extravagant promises to the unwary Easterners. A Kansas historian writes of the period in these words:

> The boomers of the early period seemed to be trying to establish towns on the corners of every section in the eastern townships. In the later period they moved into western Kansas, and, in addition to promoting towns, engaged in some of the riotous quarrels over the selection of county seats . . . brought about by town promoters who sold lots to citizens on the promise that their town would certainly be selected as the county seat. . . .[18]

Quakers were doubtless caught in the promotional schemes that represented half-truths. When the full truth was known by experi-

---

[17] From an account written by Ellen Moore, sister of John, and loaned by his daughter, Edna Moore Ellis.

[18] Charles C. Howes, *This Place Called Kansas*. Copyright 1952 by the University of Oklahoma Press. P. 45.

ence, and not by rumor, later immigrants developed the treasures of the plain and formed stable communities, making Kansas an important part of the national economy, but the state was won by hard work, ingenuity, and raw courage.

Turbulent Kansas! The state was born in conflict and the years immediately following were, like her weather, unpredictable. "Kansas does nothing with moderation" is a recurring comment of her historians. A kind of fiery independence and individualism threw into history some very unusual persons. One of the best known, following a course of extra-legal behavior, was Carrie Nation (non-Friend) of Medicine Lodge, with her hatchet. She was a one-woman crusade against the liquor interest.

In 1899 she started her smashing march on evil in Kiowa. In 1900 she proceeded to Wichita and with stones and hatchet started the reduction of the Carey Hotel saloon. When arrested and thrown into jail she cried, "Never mind, you put me in here a cub, but I will go out a roaring lion and I will make all hell howl!"[19] When she was released she continued her crusade elsewhere. Though lawless in her method, she attacked the lawless contradiction of saloons in a prohibition state.

William Allen White, Kansas sage and editor of the *Emporia Gazette,* wrote an editorial entitled "Hurrah for Carrie." In it he said, "At first the Gazette was against Carrie Nation. She seemed to be going at it wrong end to. But events justify her. She is right. . . . She has aroused the law-abiding people of Kansas to the disgrace of lawbreaking — partly by the example of her own lawlessness."

Along with the general opposition around them to the liquor interests, Friends majored in the temperance cause. They had their own strong personalities leading in this work. Mary Sibbitt, a Friend and known to many as Aunt Mollie, was referred to by her contemporary temperance workers as "the Kansas cyclone." Along with her effective speaking she was gentle in spirit while firm in conviction of the rightness of her cause. During World War I, because of her interest in soldiers in transit, she was referred to as "the mother of the cookie jar."

The heroic advances of Kansas Quaker communities were made

---

[19] Emory Lindquist, *Kansas: A Centennial Portrait;* reprint from the *Kansas Historical Quarterly,* Topeka, 1961, p. 12.

against a background of natural adversities. Late 1859 to early 1861 was the "year of thirteen months" when no rain fell. A snow in the winter did not compensate for the loss. The "ground broke open in great cracks . . . and a burning hot wind in July and August [1860] withered everything before it . . . wells, springs and streams dried up." Added to this was an invasion of grasshoppers. Some Friends had stored pumpkins and corn and subsisted on these alone.

Several times Kansas Friends turned to the East for aid. London, Philadelphia, Ohio, Indiana, and Iowa came to their rescue in this period that had brought many of them near to starvation. At this time many Friends returned to the East. William Coffin and Ansel Rogers gave leadership to relief activities. They travelled through the Quaker settlements, holding meetings and surveying the needs. They secured seed wheat from Iowa and Ohio Friends and distributed supplies of food sent to stricken Quaker families. William Coffin wrote of their experiences, as the grim realities were realized.

> I well recollect we sat in silence for a while, our friend (Ansel Rogers) opened the Bible and read the 37th Psalm, with its precious promises, and our faith laid hold on that one which had so many times before sustained us in time of war and deep distress and raids, in which we had found perfect protection and few losses. "Trust in the Lord and do good and verily thou shalt be fed." Our friend [Ansel Rogers] then offered to raise $500 and deposit [it] in the bank at Leavenworth City, to be drawn on by a committee to be appointed by our monthly meeting, to render aid among our members where needed. This was done, but in a very short time with no solicitation by our committee, I received quite a sum of money from Thomas Kimber Sen., donated by Philadelphia Friends and also Marshall Dickinson and Co., New York Friends and others. We received also a large amount of supplies from Ohio Friends, shipped free, of cornmeal and flour, and our committee formed a general depot for such supplies in Leavenworth City, and to Friends neighborhoods afar off, sent orders so they could send their ox-teams and get them. In our own neighborhood we kept a depot with our friend Ansel Rogers as dispenser, and all who especially needed were amply supplied.[20]

---

[20] A letter from William Coffin to Herman Newman, in the Newman Collection, Kansas State Historical Library.

How precious has been the fellowship of Friends in time of need! Though living a century later they can well have a sense of historic gratitude for those of former years. Friends of London, Philadelphia, and other Yearly Meetings often helped in financing new meetinghouses and schools in Kansas, as well as coming to the rescue in a time of peril. As in the first century of Quaker history when Friends responded with help for those in prison, so they again united their resources for a time of distress, and the Meeting for Sufferings took on its ancient glory and meaning.

Visiting ministers often attracted large gatherings of Friends and others. In many instances there was no building large enough to accommodate the attenders. In a timbered country such as those of eastern states, meetings were sometimes held under the trees. Here on the Kansas plains little shade was available. In one instance a cornstalk meetinghouse was erected in anticipation of visiting ministers. This consisted of a framework of upright timbers with wires drawn around them and bundles of cornstalks leaning against the enclosure to serve as a wall. A few branches of trees, with prairie grass covering the whole enclosure, constituted a roof. This structure protected them from wind and sun.

### THE CONSERVATIVE SEPARATION

As in Ohio, Indiana, and Iowa Yearly Meetings, the move toward evangelical methods and the pastoral system led to a separation. The reasons for the separation, the same as those related in the Yearly Meetings to the east, need not be repeated here. The conservatives were led by Cyrus W. Harvey. He had attended Earlham College and came to the Spring River area of Kansas Yearly Meeting in 1867. Feeling a sense of outrage at the evangelical-pastoral developments in Kansas Yearly Meeting he visited widely among the Meetings urging opposition to the trend.

In 1879 the conservatives of Spring River Quarterly Meeting withdrew and set up a Quarterly Meeting of their own. They sent a report and representatives to Kansas Yearly Meeting that year, and the Yearly Meeting was faced with two sets of reports and representatives, both claiming to be Spring River Quarterly Meeting. When the Yearly Meeting recognized the evangelical body the conservatives formed their own Yearly Meeting from separatist groups in areas throughout Kansas Yearly Meeting. For ten years Cyrus Harvey edited the *Western Friend* and maintained a continuing attack on the course of evangelical pastoralism. In 1929 the Yearly Meeting was discontinued and the remnants were added to Iowa Conservative Yearly Meeting.

*Two Major Centers Develop*

The development of Meetings and Quarterly Meetings in Kansas Yearly Meeting cannot be fully given here. The story of two main settlements must suffice. Shortly after the turn of the twentieth century it became evident that the Yearly Meeting had developed around two main centers, Wichita and Haviland.

Wichita was publicized as the "Peerless Prince of the Prairie." It also laid claim to the distinction of the "Athens of the West" as nine different colleges were at one time either planned or in the building. Among these was the Quaker dream of John Bright University, which never rose higher than the foundations. Friends University, the successor to that effort, will be presented in a later chapter. The course of Wichita was from cow town to boom town and almost to ghost town, then back again in a slower, gradual development to her present status as a metropolis on the plains.[21]

A Friends Meeting was started there in 1878, and the first meetinghouse was erected in 1887. In 1899 a separate congregation was organized at Friends University. It has maintained for years a membership of 1,000 or more. The Yearly Meeting sessions were, from 1872 to 1897, held at Lawrence. After 1897 they were held alternately at Lawrence and Wichita. Since 1925 all have been held at Wichita.

Friends University and the cluster of Meetings in the Wichita area have made this a center of Yearly Meeting interests. The offices of the Yearly Meeting are located there. University Friends Meeting, the largest in the Yearly Meeting, carries a heavy responsibility for the annual sessions. There is a close relationship between the local Meeting and Friends University.

One hundred miles to the west of Wichita another settlement developed.[22] In 1884 Benjamin H. Albertson, Lindley Pitts, Jabez

---

[21] Juliet Reeve, *Friends University — The Growth of an Idea;* Wichita Eagle Press, 1948, p. 3-9.

[22] Weston F. Cox, *The Community of Haviland, Kansas;* Friends Bible College Press, 1966.

Hall, and James Gulley came from Indiana. They left their families at Rose Hill, near Wichita, and travelled on to the present site of Haviland. They plowed small plots, erected shanties, and then brought their families from Rose Hill. Ira and Riley Woodward and Isaac and Martha Woodard and their families came to the new settlement near this time.

In 1885 a Sunday School was organized, a sod meetinghouse was built, and meetings were held in it until 1893, when the Meeting moved to their new academy building. In 1905 a separate meetinghouse was built; it was used until 1963, when the present beautiful and useful building was erected.

In 1885 the Meeting was set off by Rose Hill as Liberty Monthly Meeting. The name was soon changed to Haviland Monthly Meeting when the new settlement chose the name honoring Laura Haviland, who was prominent in antislavery work.

Soon a number of Meetings were established in the surrounding territory and Haviland Quarterly Meeting was set off by Kansas Yearly Meeting. With the Friends academy as a central attraction the Haviland community grew in both size and influence.

Mary Albertson Hockett, daughter of Benjamin Albertson, has reported from memory the surveying of land and the beginnings of home life in the Haviland area during the later years of the 1800's.

Perhaps no other Kansas Quaker settlements faced more hazards than did that at Haviland. In the autumn of 1885 a great prairie fire swept the plains from Dodge City to Pratt County with a great loss of property. Sod houses provided a protection which lumber structures could not. In the year 1886 the great blizzard and the freezing winds again proved the importance of the sod house as protection. During this year many cattle were frozen. In 1887 the grasshopper invasion destroyed all crops and green foliage, leaving a bare land in its wake.

As if these were not enough to test the mettle of the pioneers, the cattlemen who resented the fenced areas of the farmer started a rumor that Indians were on the warpath. Some settlers left the area, but most of them stayed. The report was based on a simple movement of Indians from one locality to another.

One heroine of these early years was Dr. Mary Knapp Bennett, who "was doctor, nurse, cook and comforter. She pulled teeth, set bones, treated wounds and delivered 1500 babies." She was indeed a true horse-and-buggy doctor travelling far and wide, day and night, over the Kansas prairie.

The stories of frontier days may seem to indicate, to those who do not know the brighter aspects of Kansas, that the Quaker settlements had nothing but trouble. This would be a misrepresentation of their experiences. They had their prosperous years when crops flourished and good homes were built. Many of the hazards of the early day have disappeared. As land was cultivated, prairie fires were ended and the grasshopper menace was greatly reduced. Even the occasional drouth is met by dry-farming methods that conserve moisture. Kansans have learned how to meet the unevenness of their weather and to hedge against hazards.

The Friends Bible College in Haviland has been a focus of Friends interests. A later chapter will present its history.

From 1872 to 1910 the membership of Kansas Yearly Meeting grew from over 2,600 to more than 12,000. Since then there has been a general decline (common to other Yearly Meetings) to fewer than 8,200 as of 1964. Why the decline? Sheldon G. Jackson, Kansas Quaker historian, suggests that it is due to the passing of the revival period, the movement farther westward by Kansas Friends, and the shift from rural to urban centers in which members have joined other Christian churches or ceased attending anywhere. Whatever the explanation, the causes are similar to those of Friends elsewhere in western America.[23]

An active program of church extension has been started in recent years, resulting in the establishment of one or more new Meetings per year for more than a decade.

In Kansas Yearly Meeting there are now seventeen Quarterly Meetings having eighty-eight Meetings in five states — Kansas, Colorado, Oklahoma, Missouri, and Texas — occupying an area nearly 1,000 miles in extent.

### On Northern Plains — The Nebraska Frontier

The history of Friends on the Great Plains is by no means an

---

[23] Jackson, *op. cit.,* p. 89.

unbroken series of success stories. In their failures, whether or not of their own making, there is something to be learned. In some cases these stories appear almost like "successful failures" as qualities of life with a spiritual significance rise from experiences in those communities that sprang up with promise and then vanished. These experiences should not be allowed to fade from Quaker history. Some of the history of Friends in Nebraska exemplifies this type of life.

The physical background of soil and climate in Nebraska is nearly the same as that of Kansas. Indeed, the Great Plains from Canada to Texas are alike in those respects. The hazards of prairie fires, eroding winds, occasional drouths, and grasshoppers, along with or following years of abundance, were common to all.

This was the prairie frontier! It would require more than invading frontiersmen with their caravans of covered wagons — indeed, it would take more than settlements — to conquer these plains. The frontier would be won, but not by the device of a flag flown over its great sweep, nor by stakes driven for boundaries, nor by legal documents, called deeds, in the county courthouses. This frontier needed tillers of the soil as well as cattle rangers. Those who would win must have homemaking instincts and purposes of a spiritual kind. To hold and truly own this land, immigrants had to stick with it until its secrets were unlocked and they could stand upon it as true victors.

It required more than a half-century of trial and error by pioneering groups to make claims into homesteads. A new set of rules for a land unlike those farther east must be made. There was little or no advance information on weather and rainfall on the plains. There were only rumors, generally exaggerated, spread by ill-informed migrants. The prairie areas could be known only by living on them.

Nebraska came into the Union as a state in 1867, but not out of a political turmoil such as had marked the history of Kansas only a few years earlier. The plains were open and calling, and immigrants were coming. The earliest Friends to respond were probably Hicksites arriving about 1869, when President Grant asked Friends to oversee the work with Indians on the Great Plains and divided the area into superintendencies. Hicksite Friends had been given the northern superintendency and Samuel M. Janney came to Omaha by government appointment as Superintendent for Indian Affairs in the area.[24]

Other agents serving under Samuel Janney, for each of the Indian tribes, constituted a small beginning of Quakers in the area. Samuel Janney called together Friends and interested persons in what might be called the first Quaker Meeting in Nebraska. Names of Hicksite Friends during these first few years included Jacob M. Troth, George Truman, William Coffin, Barclay Jones, William Shotwell, Jacob Webster, William Burgess, Isaiah Lightner, Asa Janney, Albert Green, Edward Painter, Howard White, and Thomas Lightfoot.[25] By 1877 a request for a Monthly Meeting at Genoa was approved by Prairie Grove Quarterly Meeting (mainly in Iowa). This was the first Monthly Meeting of Friends in Nebraska.

In 1869, Orthodox Friends also made their advent into the state.[26] They came in covered wagons from Pleasant Plain Meeting in Iowa to make homesteads in northeastern Nebraska. By 1881 a meeting for worship and a Preparative Meeting were established by Pleasant Plain Meeting. In the next year Spring Bank was set off by Pleasant Plain and in 1883 was transferred to Greenville Quarterly Meeting in Iowa. In 1892 the Meetings of the area were set off from Greenville as Spring Bank Quarterly Meeting.

With no concern for state boundaries, Friends of northern Nebraska included South Dakota in their evangelistic efforts and sometime later developed Meetings and established Mt. Vernon Quarterly Meeting in that area. Judging from the names of Friends, their postal addresses, and reports in the *Nebraska Friend*, there were no fewer than five Meetings in that Quarterly Meeting in the early years following the establishment of Nebraska Yearly Meeting. Other Meetings were established in the northwest area of Nebraska by the new Quarterly Meeting.

Friends had also settled in southeastern Nebraska and became a Preparative Meeting under Bear Creek Meeting, Iowa. Five families from Salem Meeting in Iowa later settled in the adjoining county of Saline. These two settlements united in asking Pleasant View

---

[24] Kelsey, *op. cit.*, p. 187ff.

[25] *Ibid.*, p. 190, names of Hicksite Friends serving as agents.

[26] "The Crosbie Papers," memoirs of Milo and Julia M. Crosbie, 1927. See also J. Evelyn Mott, "History of Friends in Nebraska"; thesis for the Master of Arts degree, Haverford College, 1927.

Quarterly Meeting of Kansas Yearly Meeting (Washington County, Kansas) for an established Monthly Meeting.

Herbert J. Mott, who had a background of mixed Quaker-Methodist heritage, came to Furnas County in southwest Nebraska in 1889 and soon became the leading Friend in the entire Nebraska area.[27] He had become uncomfortable with Methodist doctrines and rejoined Friends, his older heritage. While on a business trip to Dundy County he was persuaded by a local newspaper editor to preach to a community gathering. He accepted reluctantly but found that the response was so great he could hardly leave what he had started.

As a result of Mott's efforts, Hiawatha Friends Meeting was established the next year, 1889, by Ackworth Quarterly Meeting in Iowa, and within the year Hiawatha Quarterly Meeting was set off. Within three years from its establishment the Quarterly Meeting, which had been established *without a birthright Friend in its membership,* had eight Monthly Meetings, composed of twenty-two Preparative Meetings, with eight hundred members! People came from several miles to attend, and from these non-Friends the Friends Meetings were created. In their view, to have a church was to have a pastor leading it. They were religious people without leadership and at once they united around the first minister coming into the new community.

John Henry Douglas, the superintendent of Iowa Yearly Meeting, came to Hiawatha when the Quarterly Meeting was established and "rejoiced that now Friends had become established in each of the four corners of Nebraska." He had a great concern that in some way these scattered groups of Friends might become acquainted and united. He predicted "that before many years Friends would become established in central Nebraska and that some time there would be a Yearly Meeting."

Hiawatha Friends Academy was opened in 1890. Schools established on the prairie frontier contemplated the production of leadership. In the second year of the academy forty students joined Friends. A two-story building was erected with classrooms on the second floor and a large room for the Meeting on the lower floor. The

---

[27] Herbert J. Mott, *Nebraska Central College, The Early Days,* 8p. (undated).

local community of non-Friends helped to build and support the academy.

In this period of "boom and bust," new projects blossomed quickly and quite often died nearly as fast. No sooner had the academy started on its promising way than a period of drouth began. Herbert Mott now turned to activities of relief. Many people did not have enough seed to plant the following year. He visited Friends in New England, New York, and Philadelphia, raised nearly $2,000, and received many barrels of clothing. A worse drouth followed in 1894 when about three-fourths of the Friends of this section moved away. By 1898 only four Meetings out of the original number remained. The academy was closed never to open again, the remaining members being unable to support it. Those who left the community had moved to eight different states as far east as North Carolina and as far north and west as Alaska.

Friends had settled and developed Meetings in the four corners of Nebraska and in South Dakota, and would soon develop others in the area of Denver, Colorado. Here was a perimeter of Meetings, but with no center, no focal point or organization, to draw them together into a common fellowship. They were hundreds of miles apart in a time when transportation was inadequate for the great distances.

Herbert Mott sensed the need that must be met if these scattered Meetings were to have a future. He felt that "the successful home missionary must be a good evangelist," but that he also must be "efficient as a teacher of truth . . . as an organizer . . . as a good pastor." He was certain that "competent pastoral leadership is indispensable."

## Development From Rim to Center

There were two major concerns that turned the attention of leading Friends to central Nebraska. One was the need to develop a central-area body to "fill in" the larger area itself. The perimeter of Meetings could hardly be brought into a working fellowship without such a development. The central eastern part of the state was more promising physically than the areas on the rim. Nebraska Friends needed a strong, attractive central body.

There were a few Friends starting settlements in the central area. One of the first was near Clarks and another at Alda. Small though this trend was, it helped to develop the idea of a central focus. The trend increased and by 1898 there were nine Meetings in the Platte valley area, and Platte Valley Quarterly Meeting had been established. It was estimated that ninety percent of the membership in the Nebraska area had no Friends background. In 1899 the newly established journal, the *Nebraska Friend,* reflected:

> Belonging to two yearly meetings, we practically have none. The great distance to either Lawrence, Kansas, or Oskaloosa, Iowa, practically debars the larger number of our people from all the privileges of Yearly Meeting, summer school, etc. Our churches, belonging to six different Quarterly Meetings are so divided, not in heart, but in association, that we do not know one another . . . our educational interests demand instant attention . . . we must guard against the mistake that Friends . . . have made of scattering their strength by trying to maintain several weak, poorly located institutions where one could do the work easily and well . . . . We do not want a Yearly Meeting [for Nebraska] yet. We are not ready for it.

## Birth of a Prairie College

A committee met in 1898 to face the issue, and "with a great reach of faith that almost startled ourselves, it was unanimously determined to establish a school of the prophets."

Not feeling ready to request a Yearly Meeting status, they formed the Nebraska Church and Educational Association of Friends. This being in lieu of a Yearly Meeting it was provided that

> if a Yearly Meeting should be formed . . . the Association would end. . . . [T]he Association in no way interferes with any relation hitherto existing between Monthly, Quarterly or Yearly Meeting. It does not supplant, but supplements. It is in full unity with both Iowa and Kansas Yearly Meetings. . . . It will submit reports to both Yearly Meetings.

Meetings in Nebraska were invited to join the Association, whose functions were like those of a Yearly Meeting. Annual sessions were held and an encouraging attendance gave promise of support for the plan, the first annual meeting being held in 1899.

The Association felt providentially led in determining the site for the school and in the purchase of property. In 1885 the Methodist Church had erected a very adequate building on a section of land adjoining Central City. Drouth and resulting hard times had led them to abandon the school, and a local businessman, James Stephens (non-Friend), had purchased the land and the building, holding them for some worthy use. Arrangements were made for the transfer of property to the Association. The building, which had deteriorated during nonoccupancy, was redecorated and placed in good condition. It was rededicated in 1899 and in the fall of that year was opened as Nebraska Central College.

There was a Friends college in Central City before there was a Friends Meeting! That fact was not overlooked and a meetinghouse was started in the same year with only one Friends family in the city. A series of meetings in the new building attracted overflow attendance. The building was dedicated the year the college opened. A membership of one hundred, including a few birthright members, had resulted and a Monthly Meeting was established — all within one year.

Evangelical work in Nebraska, with its amazing response, had spread like a prairie fire and had delivered to the responsibility of Friends more than they could carry. Their efforts to meet the needs were heroic, as faith continually leaped beyond sight with a high measure of hope.

What was happening on this "blazing" frontier did not escape the attention of Friends farther east. Rufus M. Jones, editor of the *American Friend* (then edited at Philadelphia), had written on Friends in Nebraska:[28]

> The reason for the expansion of Quakerism in these newer regions is that those who have gone with it believed in it with all their souls, and believed that it has a message suited to the needs of the people to whom they carried it. They did not stop to question or quibble, and they were not afraid of risking their truth in new soil or under new conditions. They sowed their truth broadcast and trusted the Lord, and the harvest has come and is still coming.

[28] The *American Friend*, Vol. VI, No. 28, p. 652.

Herbert Mott, editor of the *Nebraska Friend,* reprinted the editorial by Rufus Jones and added, "We thank God for the *American Friend* and its gifted, cultured, consecrated editor, and hope that every Friends family in Nebraska may subscribe for the *American Friend."*

Although a so-called "school of the prophets" was a major concern in the establishment of the school at Central City, it was by no means the total concern. As was common in Quaker school practices in the West, grammar school and high school grades were included and, for the first year, one year of college. This changed in the years ahead until the grammar school was dropped and later the academy, leaving a four-year liberal arts college.

The school was now established and a local constituency of concerned Friends had developed at Central City. Some families of Friends began to move from outlying Meetings to Central City to place their children in the school. People of the community (non-Friends) had given financial support to the school and the Meeting at Central City. Dormitories were soon erected and the school was well on its way.

### THE PRAIRIE YEARLY MEETING

The Nebraska Church and Educational Association had prepared the way for the next move — the establishing of a Yearly Meeting. Was there sufficient core strength for sustaining a Yearly Meeting with its college at the center?

In no other Yearly Meeting, it can be safely said, would a Yearly Meeting and a school be more interdependent than in Nebraska. Here came the test of faith as these Friends viewed it. They must rise together or the movement would retreat and face defeat. There seemed to be no halfway point.

Iowa Yearly Meeting and Kansas Yearly Meeting each had its own college and could hardly be expected to support another. Iowa, which had become involved more than Kansas in the Nebraska development, was too far away to understand and hold warm fellowship with distant Nebraska Meetings. Either Nebraska Friends must create and sustain their own identity or end in failure.

Again the *Nebraska Friend* raised a pertinent question: "Shall we adopt and give names to orphan meetings as they knock at our door and then leave them alone to live or die; or shall we be a real mother church. . . ? " The editorial saw the danger of a course in which "Quakerism of Nebraska will be composed of scattering, poorly located, selfish, half-dependent, half-starved meetings."[29]

These Friends were sure that the nonpastoral type of Meetings could not live on the frontiers of Nebraska. They had observed the conservative tensions and the separation in Kansas Yearly Meeting and felt that this amply demonstrated that view. The *Nebraska Friend* had written editorially that in Kansas the conservative Friends were

> trying to reproduce in Kansas the type of Quakerism that obtained in Indiana a quarter of a century ago. These dear Friends have made two mistakes: they are seemingly unconscious of the fact that twenty-five years have passed, or that they are in Kansas. There can be but very little growth in spirituality or members under such conditions. The successful soul-winners in Nebraska and Kansas are the men and women who can and do adapt themselves to the field in which they labor and the age in which they live.[30]

The Nebraska Church and Educational Association meeting in 1906 came to the unanimous decision to request the establishment of Nebraska Yearly Meeting. They had canvassed their constituency and reported that all Monthly Meetings were favorable, despite the sense of responsibility it laid upon them.

In 1902 the Five Years Meeting of Friends had been organized, composed of all pastoral Yearly Meetings, with the exception of Ohio Yearly Meeting. The request by Nebraska Friends in 1906 came through Iowa Yearly Meeting to the Five Years Meeting sessions of 1907. Now, for the first time, a superior body had been created to assume the responsibility. The Five Years Meeting approved and appointed a committee to open the new Yearly Meeting in 1908.[31]

The Yearly Meeting began with seven Quarterly Meetings composed of thirty-four Monthly Meetings having members in three states. Paonia, on the western slope of the Rocky Mountains in Colorado, had requested Quarterly Meeting status, and represented the Friends

---

[29] The *Nebraska Friend,* Vol. 1, No. 6, p. 41.
[30] *Ibid.,* No. 9, p. 65.
[31] *Minutes,* Five Years Meeting, 1908.

most remote from Central City. Denver Quarterly Meeting had joined the Association in 1905.

Friends living in the older communities of the Atlantic coastal region, and those of London, Dublin, and other areas of the world, can readily sense the greatly different circumstances in which western American Friends colonies were formed and developed, especially those on the Great Plains. Compact communities of the East, with less movement and more stable weather and climatic conditions, would develop and retain more conservative and traditional practices.

Friends on the western frontiers adapted to their conditions. It was a case of adapt or die. In adapting they had retained an element of their heritage in the evangelical sense of mission so clearly observable in the first half-century of Quakerism.

## Weather-Tested Friends

The course of the Nebraska Yearly Meeting in the decades following its organization is very much like that of Kansas Friends. Years of drouth and prosperity followed alternately. In those years, Friends learned the ways of wind and weather and largely mastered the proper methods of dry farming and hedging their resources against the uncertain years.

During the depression years of the 1930's, experienced everywhere in America, there was also a long period of drouth which resulted in the so-called "dust bowl." Many areas of western Nebraska, Kansas, and South Dakota were caught in swirling clouds of dust which sometimes obscured the sun at midday. Complete farms were eroded and for a few years no crops were raised. The grasshoppers ate every green blade and leaf until only a barren desert was left of what had once been good farms.

Caspar and Elizabeth Hanson of South Dakota, who stayed through the long grim period, living, along with their few neighbors, on government relief checks, reported that not a spear of green could be seen anywhere, and the hope that the rains might come "next year" became a deferred hope. But the rains finally came and the desert blossomed again.

In the midtwentieth century new methods and implements for farming have been developed and many small family-owned farms have been absorbed in vast acreages, often owned by landlords in urban centers and operated by renters or hired personnel. This has changed the entire Midwest, but has especially affected home and economic life on the plains. Moving to urban centers for industrial employment has had a depleting effect on many rural churches. New Meetings now are being developed in urban centers. There are yet many family-owned and -operated farms, but their numbers have been greatly reduced.

The struggle to retain Nebraska Central College reflects these changing conditions. The college fought a heroic battle against great odds as the supporting base gave way. For these later years of service one cannot pay too high a tribute to Ora W. Carrell as president, the trustees of the college, and the loyal Friends who sacrificed to maintain it. In 1952 the college closed, uniting its resources and records with William Penn College at Oskaloosa, Iowa, in 1961.

Though the college has ceased operation, its significance is not to be appraised by its closed doors but by the lives of those who went through its doors while they were open. That procession of young Friends has moved into many areas of the Society of Friends and bears witness to the valor of its saints on the prairie who gave more than hard-earned money. They gave themselves in heroism rarely matched elsewhere among Friends.[32]

---

[32] The separation of Rocky Mountain Yearly Meeting is told in Chapter 12.

# Chapter 7

## TO THE NEW NORTHWEST –
## ON HISTORIC TRAILS

For the intrepid invaders of the continent there would be no place "where the trails run out and stop." Primeval forests with their jungles of undergrowth, broad rivers, and vast plains had not stopped them. Would the Rocky Mountains, along with the High Sierra and Cascade ranges, prove impregnable?

Viewed in the longer context of history the westbound migrants seem only to have paused at the foothills, as if to catch their second breath, then moved on and up until they stood on the roof of a new world as had Balboa three centuries before. He had crossed the isthmus connecting two continents and had seen the vast Pacific. They had crossed a continent and moved into the valleys of abundance in the Northwest with its luxuriant growth. For the Friends who came later this was a second "Canaan," far richer than the valley of the Jordan which their religious forebears had seen from the hills of Moab.

There were stages in this conquest of the American continent. First of all was that of the Indians. Centuries before Columbus and other explorers touched the Atlantic shores, the Indians had developed a vast network of trails. These probably extended from shore to shore. There is evidence that a measure of commerce had linked many of the tribes in a common economic interest, in a trading of their few and simple products.

The white explorers were not without help in their advancing frontier. The Indians were safe guides over well-known trails when surveying parties charted the West. The Indians doubtless saved them from long and costly probings of mountain ranges in the search for passes to the coast. How often the Indians were paid with trinkets while unwittingly losing their homes and hunting grounds to the people who would finally prove to be their despoilers! That is another story on the stained pages of American history.

Who indeed were the pioneers? Whether Kipling was thinking of Indians or of the first white explorers, he raised a question of priority in his poem, "The Explorer." He had come from India enroute to England by way of San Francisco and the American continent in 1889. What he saw in the new moving drama appealed to his poetic insight.

> Well I know who'll take the credit — all the clever chaps that followed —
> Came, a dozen men together — never knew my desert fears;
> Tracked me by the camps I'd quitted, used the water-holes I'd hollowed.
> They'll go back and do the talking. *They'll* be called the Pioneers![1]

Spanish and English explorers earlier had plied the seas on the coast and merely by the fact of their presence in the area had laid claim to the land they occupied. In the northwest inland area the Hudson Bay Company was not only a commercial enterprise in the British empire but also had become the political authority of the area. Rooted in the British tradition, yet largely independent from London control, they had brought a stable sense of law and order to the area.[2]

---

[1] *Rudyard Kipling Verse,* Inclusive Edition, 1885-1918; Doubleday Page and Company, 1925.

[2] Dorothy O. Johansen and Charles M. Gates; *Empire of the Columbia,* Harper & Row, 1957; p. 99ff.

In 1803 Thomas Jefferson proposed the opening of trading centers on the Indian frontier and the exploration of the sources of the Missouri River with a view to following "the best water communication which offered itself from thence to the Pacific Ocean." Such was the dim picture in the minds of the most informed government leaders of the day.

By 1843, the Oregon Trail was opened and migrations to Oregon had developed into considerable numbers. This famous trail, after uniting the Omaha and Fort Leavenworth branches, followed the Platte River through the Nebraska area and had proceeded through the "South Pass" of the mountains to Fort Hall, north of the Great Salt Lake. Here it split. The California branch veered southwest, following the Humboldt River to Sacramento. The Oregon branch followed in general the Snake River valley to its confluence with the Columbia River and then down the river to the coast.

In 1842 a provisional government of the Oregon Territory under the Americans had been formed and soon afterward the wagon trains began to roll in larger numbers from the Great Plains to the new Northwest.

American expansionists became heady with the wine of adventure and national aggrandizement. Political and economic interests ran strong, and, as the migrations increased, the whole course of the westward movement became known as the fulfillment of the "manifest destiny" of the nation. The tide of movement took on religious overtones, as if it were the will of God! This was expressed in a report on the Territory of Oregon. "This movement goes on with predestined certainty, and the unerring precision of the great works of eternal Providence, rather than as an act of feeble man."

## Oregon Quakers Arrive

Not until this emotionally toned wave of migration had reached its crest did Friends come in significant numbers.[3] Why were not the Quakers satisfied with the well-watered central areas of America? Why must they tempt fate on the Great Plains, called by many of that period the Great American Desert? Why, having settled there, did they at once seek out new trails through the most difficult barriers

---

[3] Ralph K. Beebe, *A Garden of the Lord,* a history of Oregon Yearly Meeting of Friends Church; The Barclay Press, 1968.

of a continent, over arid plains and rugged mountains greater than any of the Appalachian chain?

Among the heroic stories of migrating Friends is that of Hannah Stanton. As the family was coming by wagon over the Oregon Trail her husband became ill and died. She buried him somewhere along the trail and continued with her children over a six-month period before arriving in Oregon. The main stream of Friends came later, generally by the railroad, completed in 1869, across the entire continent.

Coming early on a visit to Oregon Friends, Robert and Sarah Lindsey of England had carried the Quaker-evangelical contagion to many areas of the world—Africa, Australia, New Zealand, Nova Scotia, Canada, and the Yearly Meetings of America. The value of their visits, and those of other Friends who followed them, could hardly be overestimated at a time when the visiting Friend was the only live current running through the isolated Quaker families on the frontier. The spiritual influence of English Quakerism in that period runs clearly through all of the western settlements and Meetings of Friends. The Lindseys were leaders and exemplars, and their diaries are important sources of information on early frontier conditions among Friends.

Probably the first Friends gathering in Oregon was held with the Lindseys in Salem in 1859, the year in which Oregon was admitted to the Union as a free state.[4] At a public meeting held in the Salem courthouse their audience included the Governor, a Justice of the State Supreme Court, and other officials. Robert Lindsey explained the Quaker custom of a silent waiting, and then out of the silence spoke on "vital Christianity, Jesus Christ being held forth as the chief corner-stone, elect and precious." They also preached in courthouses at Eugene, Oregon City, Hillsboro, and Portland. In courtrooms filled to overflowing with non-Friends, Robert Lindsey found opportunity for his concern "to preach the unsearchable riches of Christ." In Portland they found six people connected with Friends. During their three months' visit in the Oregon and Washington areas they found eighteen Friends dispersed throughout the territory.

The evangelical strain evident in the ministry of the English Friends continued in the years following. In 1860 and again in 1873,

---

[4] Robert and Lela Morrill, "The History of Friends in Oregon"; typed, 1938.

Mary B. Pinkham, an American Friend, came preaching and visiting. "I see a monthly meeting of Friends in this valley, a quarterly meeting, and I think a yearly meeting," she proclaimed, with a prophetic hope. Other Friends visiting in "the love of the Gospel" were John Scott, Sarah Morrison, and the much-travelled Friend, Abel Bond, from Cottonwood Quarterly Meeting in Kansas.

In the history of Oregon Yearly Meeting the name of William Hobson looms large. He is generally referred to as the founder of the Yearly Meeting. He was born in North Carolina in 1820 and married Sarah Tulbert in 1844; in 1847 they, with their two children, crossed the Alleghenies to Indiana. He came to Iowa in 1851; there he located on Honey Creek in Marshall County as a member of what is now Bangor Meeting, later moving near New Providence. He entered fully into the work of Friends, felt the call to visit those living farther west, and in 1870 made his first trip to the west coast.

The transcontinental railroad having been completed, he came by train to California, visiting his brothers near San Jose. By boat, by stage, and on foot he made his way north from San Jose to Oregon. Having heard good reports of the country in southeastern Washington, he went by boat and train from Portland to Walla Walla. He was greatly impressed with its possibilities for settlement. He had not yet seen the Chehalem valley on this trip, and Walla Walla might well have been his selected site as a center for Friends had he not, on a second visit to that area, "discovered that a disastrous freeze had wiped out the peach crop. This was too much like Iowa for Hobson, who was more horticulturalist than farmer. He visited the Chehalem valley a second time, after giving up the Walla Walla country, then decided the Newberg area met his needs."[5]

Hobson spent a month in the area of Salem, Oregon, before returing to Iowa. His concern for a Quaker settlement in Oregon deepened into a sense of mission.

> I have felt it my duty to find out what I well could about this country, that I might be able to tell of it correctly, and I continue to believe that some good Friends ought to emigrate and commence settlements in several places . . . and help build up good settlements that may exert a happy influence upon many in these

[5] Personal letter from Myron Goldsmith, June 20, 1968.

countries. . . . I feel satisfied now and have peace of mind as having thus far performed a duty for the sake of many.

Quaker women ministers played an important part as Friends came to Oregon. Thomas and Mary B. Pinkham (a minister) were liberated by Iowa Yearly Meeting for a second visit to the coast. Coming near the same time from Kansas were Nathan and Elizabeth White and Rebecca Clawson, the latter a woman of great power in the ministry.

In 1875 William Hobson[6] made his second and decisive trip to Oregon, bringing with him John S. Bond and the families of David and Margaret Wood and Perry C. and Hannah Hadley. William Hobson made his headquarters at the home of Nathan and Elizabeth White.

> In 1874-1875 Rebecca Clawson was holding appointed meetings at various places in Salem. Sometimes she spoke to the convicts at the State Penitentiary, and at the close of one such service a prisoner came forward desiring to speak with her. He had known something of Friends, and was attracted by the Quaker bonnet. He told Rebecca Clawson the sad story of his imprisonment, and pleaded with her to visit his sorrowing wife and children, still living upon the farm in the Chehalem Valley. . . .
>
> It developed that the lonely wife on the farm at West Chehalem was related to William Hobson. . . . The story of the woman's affliction, with subsequent news of her illness, led him to visit her in her home. This visit was made in Eleventh month, 1875, and before that month was out, William Hobson had decided to buy the tract of 320 acres upon which the woman was living. The sale was arranged within a few days, and thus began the permanent settlement of Friends in the vicinity of Newberg.[7]

Now William Hobson could say, "The selection is made. A settlement has already begun to form. . . . Some are on their way to this place and many more have their thoughts this way." He saw in the new beginning for Friends in Oregon the "rearing of a light that will shine far into the world."

---

[6] Myron D. Goldsmith, "William Hobson and the Founding of Quakerism in the Pacific Northwest"; a Ph.D. thesis, 1962.

[7] *The Northwest Friend*, Vol. XXXIX, No. 5 (July 1959), p. 9.

## SETTLEMENTS BECOME MEETINGS

This site would later blossom into Newberg and become the center for a new Yearly Meeting. The little Chehalem settlement began holding meetings in the home of William Clemmens, later known as the Woodward place (the home of Ezra H. and Amanda Woodward). Now the Meeting and First Day School alternated between the Clemmens and the Hobson homes. At the Hobson home the people often met in a grove of trees.

William Hobson went back to Iowa that year, sold his property, and returned in 1876 with his family to the new permanent home in the Chehalem valley. He had also persuaded other recruits, and the little settlement began to grow. One year later the attendance at Chehalem had grown to seventy. It was time to provide more room. David and Margaret Wood had built a commodious home and invited the Meeting to use a large upper room. In 1877 these Friends requested Monthly Meeting status from Honey Creek Quarterly Meeting in Iowa. The latter entered the following minute on their records.

> At Honey Creek Quarterly Meeting of Friends, held in Hardin County, Iowa, Fourth month 6, 1878:
>
> A request is received from Friends of Chehalem Valley, Yamhill County, Oregon, asking for the establishment of a monthly meeting at that place, to be held on the first Seventh-day in each month, and to be known by the name of Chehalem Monthly Meeting. This request was considered, and the meeting united in granting it, and establishes the monthly meeting accordingly, and hereby authorizes the said Friends to open and hold a monthly meeting on the first Seventh-day in each month thereafter, consecutively.
>
> Copied from the minutes of Honey Creek Quarterly Meeting Friends, held in Hardin County, Iowa, on the 6th of Fourth month, 1878, and signed by direction thereof.
>
> Edward Taylor,<br>Jane H. Blair,<br>Clerks.

This was the first Monthly Meeting on the coast, though San Jose, in California, had earlier been made a Preparative Meeting. In only sixteen more years Oregon Yearly Meeting would be set off. Though Newberg was the first Monthly Meeting, a meeting held at Dayton in the home of Nathan and Elizabeth White in 1875 may be said to have been the beginning of the first regular meetings of Friends in Oregon.

From the visit of the Lindseys onward a warm evangelical spirit pervaded Oregon Friends as it had the Yearly Meetings from which they came. In 1878-1879 a revival movement broke out in the Chehalem (Newberg) Meeting with no visiting minister in the community. It grew out of a "reading meeting." Such meetings were common since the early days of North Carolina Friends who convened to read tracts. These tracts generally were written to feed the spiritual life of Friends. Reading from the Bible was central to reading from all other literature. Sometimes these meetings had taken a turn which led to First Day Schools or, as they are generally now called, Sunday Schools, and heralded the present programs of Christian Education.

In other cases the reading meetings broadened into meetings for hearing visiting Friends or for common inspiration in the spiritual life. These "general meetings" in some instances became preaching meetings and in turn developed into revival meetings. When a reading meeting at Newberg became a revival meeting the idea was by no means new. Revival meetings during this period were common among Methodists and other churches and resulted in considerable growth as converts became members. Friends were not without examples on every side.

In the 1870's the addition of converts and the coming of new Friends gave abundant evidence that they had arrived to stay and to build a firm future. Those settling in the 1880's added the core strength of old Quaker stock from eastern Meetings and gave an assurance of permanence. The Chehalem (Newberg) valley settlement moved toward its destined place at the center of future Oregon Quakerism.

Illustrative of the migrations in this second period of settlements was the coming in 1880 of Ezra H. and Amanda Woodward with Jesse and Mary Edwards and their families from the Mooresville area of Indiana.[8] Travel by train was, by that year, the generally

---

[8] Elizabeth H. Emerson, *Walter C. Woodward, Friend on the Frontier* (private printing, 1952), portrays in personal experience the migration of a Friends family, and the beginning of a Quaker community.

accepted method over long distances. The rail had largely replaced the trail. Walter C. Woodward, then but two years old, became later the secretary of the Five Years Meeting and the editor of the *American Friend*. Writing as editor from the recorded memory of his parents he gave a moving picture of their trip to Oregon, which was typical of travel at that time. "They provided their own bedding [on the train], cooked their own meals . . . and when they wanted exercise, they hopped off the train on an upgrade and trotted along the right of way. They had time to see the country and enjoy their altogether new experience."

The terminus of the Union Pacific Railroad, then but eleven years old, was San Francisco. The rest of the trip by the Woodward-Edwards party was by boat, up the coast. Jesse Edwards, in 1883, laid out the town of Newberg and Ezra Woodward purchased the *Graphic* (the local newspaper) and the Clemmens home where the first Friends Meeting had been held. The new area had been named Newberg in 1869, a concession to the postmaster whose home in Bavaria had a similar spelling.

The deeds to the lots in the new town forbade the manufacture, sale, or use of intoxicating liquors. With a strong Quaker group and the local newspaper in the hands of a Friend, the Quakerization of the community was well-nigh complete. The non-Friends neighbors sometimes felt the restrictions.

Amanda Woodward, in the fiftieth anniversary number of the *Graphic,* told of a neighbor who came to their home on a Sunday wanting to borrow a gun for hunting. Disgruntled with the Quaker restraints he said, "It used to be here that we could all pile into a big wagon on Sunday morning and go visiting and have a big dinner and a horse race, and a dance, and if there happened to be a preacher around we'd have a sermon. Now if we go anywhere we don't find anybody at home. They all go to church since the Quakers came."

To accommodate the enlarged Quaker community more room was required and in 1880 the first Friends meetinghouse in Oregon was erected. In 1886, the name of Chehalem Meeting was changed to Newberg. The next year Alder Monthly Meeting on the eastern border of the state was established. Another Monthly Meeting also in the extreme eastern area was established near Ontario with a settlement of Friends started by William P. Samms from Geneva,

Kansas. With the establishment of new meetings, Newberg Friends requested from Iowa Yearly Meeting the setting off of Newberg Quarterly Meeting.

In the 1880's and the 1890's, several new Meetings were started in the Northwest: Middleton, Rock Lake, Marion, Dundee, Salem, Springbrook, Portland, Upper Dry Creek, and East Chehalem. Some of these Meetings were later discontinued. A new Quarterly Meeting was in the making when Salem Monthly Meeting was organized in 1891 "subordinate to Newberg Quarterly Meeting." In the same year Iowa Yearly Meeting was requested to set off Salem Quarterly Meeting, including Salem and Marion.

### Meetings Become a Yearly Meeting

Being far from the parent Yearly Meeting in Iowa, Oregon Friends felt the need for a Yearly Meeting of their own. In 1891 Iowa Yearly Meeting approved their request in the following minute.

> A request was presented from the Friends residing in Oregon, comprising the two quarterly meetings of Newberg and Salem, asking that a yearly meeting be established at Newberg, Ore., in Sixth month, 1892, and to be known as Oregon Yearly Meeting.
>
> This meeting, without a dissenting voice, unites in granting the request, and with the approbation of other yearly meetings, the meeting will be opened at the time suggested in the request.
>
> Iowa Yearly Meeting of Friends, held from 8th to the 15th of Ninth month, 1891.
>
> Stephen M. Hadley, Clerk

It required an additional year to get the "approbation of other Yearly Meetings" that were in correspondence with Iowa Yearly Meeting, and the new Yearly Meeting was duly opened "in Sixth month, 1893."

Whereas the Lindseys had found eighteen families in Oregon thirty-four years before, there were now almost a thousand members. The first clerks of the Yearly Meeting were Thomas Newlin, presiding clerk, and Jane E. Blair, recording clerk. John Henry Douglas had been a moving spirit in the development of Friends Meetings in Oregon and was named head of the Evangelistic and Church Extension Board. Lines of interest considered and planned for the new Yearly Meeting included home and foreign missions, First Day Schools, peace and arbitration, Christian Endeavor for the youth, temperance, and education.

The new revivalism was evident in the reports on evangelism and extension. The pastoral system was definitely accepted and plans for evangelists and pastors were discussed. John Henry Douglas spoke "with no uncertain sound, and committed himself most unqualifiedly to the pastoral system." The pioneer spirit prevailed, lending itself to the work of developing new Meetings. The membership during the first year increased by four hundred, one-half coming by request, the rest representing new Friends settlers.

William Hobson, like a Quaker Moses, had stood on the summit of a Chehalem mountain and viewed his "Jordan Valley." But, like Moses, he was not able to see the fulfillment. He had died in 1891, two years before the organization of the Yearly Meeting. There is also a fitting parallel with George Fox, who, over two centuries before, had stood on Pendle Hill and had seen "a great people to be gathered." Now Oregon Friends had "gathered" a people in rapidly growing numbers and the valleys of abundance were answering to their labors. The first stage of Quaker conquest in the new Northwest had been achieved.

### EXTENSION IN IDAHO

The Snake River running across southern Idaho turns north and becomes a part of the boundary line between Oregon and Idaho. In general the Oregon Trail followed this valley to its confluence with the Columbia River. Oregon immigrants following this trail would have found little to attract them in the arid wastes of the sagebrush country of southern Idaho. Not until a system of irrigation was developed did this desert begin to blossom. That accounts for the relatively late settlements of Friends in the area.[9]

Kansas furnished more Idaho settlers than did any other Yearly Meeting. Despite the earlier forbidding prospects, a Quaker family from North Branch, Kansas, settled in the Boise area in 1896; they were followed by other families, and a Monthly Meeting was estab-

---

[9] Ronald Gene Stansell, "Fifty Years of Friends in Idaho," thesis in the Program of Intensified Studies, George Fox College, 1965.
Beebe, *op. cit.,* p. 37ff.

lished in 1898. Kansas Yearly Meeting then carried responsibility for this new development, but in the following year turned the care of Friends Meetings there to Oregon Yearly Meeting.

In 1863, Idaho had been made a territory and, in 1890, was admitted to the Union as a state. It was not until 1910 that the first irrigated crops were raised. For a few years before this, many inhabitants of "The Bench," as the area was called, had made their living by working on lakes, dams, and canals that would later bring an abundance of water from the Snake River.

The spiritual tone and the direction of Friends Meetings on the frontier were largely influenced by one or more strong personalities who gave leadership to them. In Idaho the leading Friend was Anson Cox.[10] Born in 1844, he had been reared in the silent-meeting tradition of Friends, was converted in a Methodist revival meeting, but retained his membership with Friends. Like many other Friends of the time he had made several moves. While living in Indiana he had visited Kansas Friends in Gospel ministry in 1879 and, in 1883, moved with his family to north-central Texas. He later served for a time as pastor of the Scotts Mill Meeting in Oregon and then moved to southern Idaho, where he continued in pastoral ministry. Here he was a key personality in the extension work of Idaho Friends.

In 1906 three Monthly Meetings in the Boise valley were set off as a Quarterly Meeting, and by 1910 there were seven "preaching points" under the existing Monthly Meetings, with a membership of four hundred. These members, for the most part, had come from Kansas, Iowa, Indiana, and Ohio, and some had moved back from the Willamette valley in Oregon. When irrigation came in, the price of land was raised, thereby slowing the rate of immigration. Converts gave the Meetings added strength.

Mountain View Meeting, later named Greenleaf in honor of John Greenleaf Whittier, soon became a strong center, as the Friends academy was established. William Brown, born in Indiana and later educated at Penn College (Iowa), became a central figure in the Greenleaf settlement. The first meeting was held in his home. In 1906 the Greenleaf meetinghouse was built. By the next year there were thirteen Quaker families at Greenleaf.

---

[10] *Memoir of Anson Cox;* published by the Greenleaf Friends church, Greenleaf, Idaho.

As in most frontier settlements, the evangelistic emphasis was strong and extension work resulted in the establishment of new Friends Meetings. Young people were enlisted in the work under the organization of the Christian Workers League in 1928 and within ten years the five Meetings had grown to ten and the membership from about eight hundred to fourteen hundred.

This work led also to the camping program whereby spiritual retreats inspired and trained young people for the work of ministry in church extension. In 1930-1931, Boise valley Friends built Quaker Hill, a campground-retreat center, and a program for several age groups was started. Partially because of geographic convenience, Oregon Yearly Meeting has six retreat centers in a large program of worship and training for all ages; in 1965 it reported 1,550 in attendance.

Friends were not the first of the church groups coming to southern Idaho. The Disciples, the Church of the Brethren, the Methodists, and others were there in the Boise area, but the Friends soon became the strongest church group. In some cases cooperation with other churches led to joint work for a time. Friends were, in various ways, related to cooperative work of the Free Methodists, the Nazarenes, the Pilgrim Holiness, and the Salvation Army. In 1936 they united with the Idaho Holiness Association.

These connections tell much about the kind of religious attitude and expression of Friends and their ecumenical trend. In one Meeting, Homedale, a unique dual membership arrangement was worked out whereby members could belong to the Meeting and retain their church membership elsewhere.

There are now fourteen Meetings with over 1,500 members comprising two Quarterly Meetings, Boise and Greenleaf, in the Idaho area. Oregon Yearly Meeting now has eight Quarterly Meetings composed of forty-seven Monthly Meetings in three states — Oregon, Washington, and Idaho — with a membership of about six thousand.

William Hobson's vision of a great people to be gathered into a Yearly Meeting has been fulfilled!

# Chapter 8

## ON THE PACIFIC RIM –
## TO FABLED CALIFORNIA

The western frontier was vanishing at the turn of the century. The new America now lay over 3,000 miles from coast to coast.[1] The great Pacific had done what vast plains and rugged mountain ranges could not do. It had stopped the *avant-garde* of the westward conquest. This far and no farther! There was a finality about this new barrier, a barrier that would stay the American conquest for another half-century, until the new age of speed and space would overleap land and sea, adding Alaska and Hawaii, first as territories, then as states.

California was a prize to be won early, assuring not only the western boundary but also all territory between the Atlantic and the Pacific. The nation was now continentwide. The areas not-so-far west could wait and be filled in later with states yet to be born. After California was admitted to the Union seventeen new states, from West

---

[1] Earl Pomeroy, *The Pacific Slope;* Alfred A. Knopf, 1965. A history of the political background and the geographic influences.

Virginia to Washington, were added, the last ones being Arizona and New Mexico in 1912.

Not only the scope of the territory, but also the speed with which the nation came to its new geographic boundaries, seems in historical retrospect all but incredible. Only sixty-one years before California was admitted to the Union as a state in 1850, the first Congress under the Constitution had assembled and George Washington had taken the oath of office as the first President of the United States of America. The American nation did not simply evolve or grow into its stature; it all but exploded into existence.

The old frontier was vanishing and a new frontier was coming with the twentieth century. While yet heady with the new wine of conquest the nation must now enter a period of assessing gains, filling in the annexed territories, establishing law and order, and determining legislative responsibilities on a regional basis, in a long period of self-development.

The character of the United States in both home and foreign policy would be affected by the spirit of expansionism for years ahead. Size, speed, and independence would mark the country with a kind of uniqueness, puzzling if not exasperating to the longer-established nations of the Old World. America would find and refine her soul as she turned from the outwardness of the old frontier to the inwardness of the new and, ultimately, to her new responsibilities as a world neighbor. Here was frontier enough to evoke the best and the worst during the creative disturbances that would all but convulse the country as she settled into her character as a nation.

### FRIENDS AND THE CALIFORNIA LURE[2]

If this was an explosive experience for the nation it was one also for Friends. Within one lifetime some Friends could well have been born in Nantucket and moved to the Carolinas, then to Ohio, to Indiana, to Iowa, to the Great Plains, and finally to California or Oregon. One might be not far from the truth to say, figuratively, that at least one generation of Friends was born in the covered wagon.

For more than a century after the migrations from the East and the South to the West began, a new branch of the Society of Friends

---

[2] David C. LeShana, *Friends in California,* Barclay Press, 1969.

was in motion with the rest of their moving neighbors. They would hardly turn and look back until the final barrier of the sea ended their trails westward. Though in the historical sweep of events this seems true, it would present an imbalance of historical facts to leave that impression as the only one.

There was at the same time a strong tie between the moving Quakers and the settled Quakers, between those moving on the trails to Oregon and California and those of the established Meetings in North Carolina, Ohio, and elsewhere. So firm was this tie that no Meeting would be established without action of a founding Meeting farther east. As stated earlier, no Yearly Meeting would be established (until much later) without consultation with all other Yearly Meetings, including London. This tie was not primarily structural, but like that of an organism. There was always a kind of homesickness on the Quaker frontier — the "parents" had in some way been left behind!

In 1849, California had caught the attention of the world when the gold rush brought thousands to the area. In 1848, gold had been discovered by an explorer. A wave of excitement followed, bringing hapless adventurers in search of quick riches, from the North and South Americas and from Europe. There were a few Quakers who, presumably, felt the lure of gold more than the love of God drawing them! But they were few indeed. It is probable that adventure and the search for an exotic land brought the first Friends who, not having primarily a religious interest, wrote little or nothing about their experiences as Friends.

There were exceptions to those who came chasing the rainbow of gold. William Sherman, an Ohio Friend, came in 1849, settled into business and ranching, and became prominent in the life of San Francisco. Two friends from England, John and Thomas Bevan, established a drug business in the same area.

Whatever the motives impelling them, a few families of Friends had settled in northern California when in 1859-1860 Robert and Sarah Lindsey of London Yearly Meeting arrived. This was the third and last journey for Robert Lindsey, the inveterate traveller, and the first and only visit by Sarah Lindsey to America. Before completing this journey they visited Friends in Australia, the Sandwich Islands (Hawaii), and Africa. Their contribution to the early life of Friends on the American frontier was of considerable importance. They were generally on the frontier very shortly after the first Friends families had settled.

The Lindseys, not always favorably impressed with the spiritual condition of the isolated families of Friends on the Pacific coast, called the few available Friends together for meetings as the way opened. They also held occasional public meetings in courthouses or available public buildings. Sarah Lindsey, not only a woman minister but also a Quaker, was a special attraction. She seems not to have enjoyed such popularity. She confided to her journal that "none but those who have been placed in such situations can understand fully what a cross it is for a woman to be made a spectacle to a congregation by sitting upon a raised seat without a female companion in places where only men are in the practice of exercising the gift of preaching or praying in public." These visiting Friends were also invited to hold public meetings in other churches of the region and generally received a warm welcome.

Their impression of Quakerism in California as of 1860 was less than encouraging. They had visited nearly every Friends family in the state and had found many of them discouraged and homesick. One Friend, of Manchester, England, was tired of his venture and longed for the home he had left. Another Friend, from Ireland, was trying to accumulate enough money to make his way back. The first Friends had more or less filtered through to California and in their settlements lacked strength because of isolation.

In 1861 Joel and Hannah Bean held meetings in San Francisco, in the home of William Sherman. Abel Bond of Kansas visited in the San Jose area, preaching and distributing tracts. During the winter of 1865-1866 he stayed in the Hobson (brother of William Hobson) home and helped to construct the first Friends meetinghouse at San Jose, the first in California. In 1873 San Jose Friends Preparative Meeting was set off by Honey Creek Quarterly Meeting of Iowa Yearly Meeting. James Conney was the first clerk and his wife, Jane M. F. Conney, served the Meeting as the first Friends pastor in California.

It was not until the decades of 1880 and 1890 that Quakers began to arrive in California in sufficient numbers to establish settlements. Generally they were farmers, but there were exceptions. In 1873 Lawson and Lucinda Hollingsworth came from Indiana to the

Pasadena area and opened a grocery. Their son, Doctor H. T. Hollingsworth, later became mayor of Los Angeles. Another Friend, Micajah D. Johnson, served near the same time as treasurer of the city. From Pelham and Niagara Falls, Canada, other Friends came, followed by scores, forming a new Quaker community on the coast.

By 1881, meetings were held in the home of Adonijah Gregory. More Friends came from Iowa and Kansas and in 1883 a building was purchased for use as a meetinghouse. In 1884 Pasadena was established as a Monthly Meeting under Springdale Quarterly Meeting of Iowa Yearly Meeting. Not far from this settlement another was being made at El Modena by a group of Friends from Lawrence, Kansas, and in 1886 were established as Earlham Monthly Meeting of Friends by Hesper Quarterly Meeting of Kansas Yearly Meeting. The name was later changed to El Modena. In 1887 "Pasadena and Earlham [El Modena] Monthly Meetings united in requesting the organization of a Quarterly Meeting and the same was established by the concurrent action of Iowa and Kansas Yearly Meetings in Eleventh month, 1887."

Friends were now arriving in considerable numbers and Meetings were established at Ramona, Wildomar, Alamitos, and Long Beach, and in 1894 at Berkeley.

Friends of southern California were blest with good leadership. William V. Coffin, experienced in Indian work, Dr. William Nicholson, formerly clerk of Kansas Yearly Meeting, and Jeremiah A. Grinnell, having an organizing skill, were among the leading Friends of the area.

### WHITTIER — FROM DREAM TO REALITY

Aquilla H. Pickering is credited with planning the colony to be known as Whittier. As a Chicago businessman he visited the Pacific coast in 1887 and after surveying widely the available areas, selected the site of present-day Whittier. The business features in this development present a rather long and hazardous adventure. It is sufficient here to report the formation of the Pickering Land and Water Company. The names of Friends in this enterprise indicate who the leaders were in the formation of what would become the chief center of California Quakerism: Jonathan Bailey, president; Hervey Lindley, secretary-treasurer; Aquilla Pickering, John Painter, Eleazer Andrews, Dr. Fordyce Grinnell, Edward Newlin, and Milton Lindley.[3]

This company purchased extensive acreage and the development of a new colony was under way. What was the right name for such a colony? The name *Quaker Town* would not do — "the worst town in Indiana is called that." Micajah D. Johnson is credited with the suggestion of the name *Whittier* in honor of the Quaker poet. There was some precedent for this in Iowa, where a town carried that name and a school at Salem, Iowa, had been named Whittier. The external markings of their city must be Quaker; so the two main streets were Philadelphia (east-west) and Greenleaf (north-south). Other streets were also given Quaker names.

The name was not chosen without correspondence with John Greenleaf Whittier and the presentation to him of a choice double lot. Giving his consent and concern for the new colony as a "Quaker City," he wrote:

> I use that term in no sectarian sense, for I see good in all denominations, and hope that all will be represented in the settlement. I trust that its Quakerism will be of the old, practical kind, "diligent in business and serving the Lord," not wasting its strength in spasmodic emotions, not relying on creed and dogma, but upon faithful obedience to the voice of God in the soul.[4]

Whittier, the poet, had become somewhat suspected by midwest evangelical Friends of holding too-liberal views. In a letter to Friends he assured them he was "neither a Unitarian nor a Universalist." He added his hope for the high moral level of the new Whittier community.

> I cannot doubt that care will be taken that the dreadful evil of intemperance shall not be permitted to fasten itself upon the young settlement, and that in *sobriety, industry, large charity,* active benevolence, and educational privilege, it may prove an example worthy of general imitation, and fulfill the fond anticipation of its Founders.

---

[3] Charles W. Cooper, *Whittier Independent College in California;* The Ward Ritchie Press, 1967; includes history of Friends in the Whittier area.
[4] *Ibid.,* p. 15.

The most cherished of the Whittier blessings on the new colony was expressed in his poem:

> Dear Town, for whom the flowers are born,
> Stars shine and happy songbirds sing,
>     What can my evening give thy morn,
>     My winter to thy spring?
> A life not void of pure intent
> With small desert of praise or blame;
> The life I felt, the good I meant,
> I leave thee with my name.[5]

The birth pains of this new Quaker colony would last for the remainder of the nineteenth century and into the twentieth. Not even the boom-and-bust period of the Great Plains exceeded that of California. The new city was launched on its way with great acclaim. By Christmas of 1887 the "magic little city of Whittier" claimed eight hundred inhabitants with a bakery, a drugstore, a post office, a livery stable, a general store, a boarding house, a hotel, a bank, a newspaper —*and twelve real-estate offices!* Friends were coming by train-car loads. Railroads were booming their own future by attracting people with low fares. Competing railroads enticing immigrants at one time reduced the fare from Chicago to Los Angeles to one dollar. Publicity was blazoned in the headlines: "Whittier! Whittier!! Whittier !!! Queen of the Foothills and Crown of the San Gabriel Valley." "Whittier is the coming place. It will dwarf Monrovia and eclipse Pasadena. Nothing can stop it! The Quakers are coming from all over the United States." Quakers have never moved quite as fast as those reports suggested; but Americans on the frontier were not known for understatement and the sparing of adjectives!

This was, in some measure, due to the expansionist era in which regional rivalries brought out claims and counterclaims and in which promoters excelled with extravagant language. The measure of "bust" was in direct proportion, generally, to the amount of "boom" and advance promises made. Inflation was followed by deflation, and great plans collapsed on the drawing boards.

A new era of slow but solid accomplishment would come and make Whittier the substantial Quaker center it is today. These sharp

---

[5] T. Eugene Coffin, *Living Waters Flow West;* private printing (1957?), p. 34.

curves upward and downward in California history were not wholly
of California making. The nation itself was in the throes of economic
maturing, and panics were common.

The *Christian Worker* of Chicago cautioned in 1888, "A poor
man had better look well before he leaps into California." In one
period more people left Whittier than came to it though some returned later. Others came later in larger numbers as southern California moved through the period of frontier development and settled
into a new and stable era.

Friends may have suffered less from deflationary times than did
many others. Washington Hadley had come to Whittier and established a branch of the Bank of America. He was a solid businessman
of sound judgment and helped to tide many persons and projects
through difficult days.

One aspect of Friends life that helped them to keep a level of
spiritual health in the boom days was the ability to laugh at themselves. Many of the exaggerations of the period were appropriated in
the facetious banter to be found in their correspondence with Friends
farther east. Texas has now replaced California as the state of tall
stories, but stories then were tall enough. One California Friend
wrote, "When your letter came [from the East] I was on a ladder
in my back yard gathering tomatoes." There were humorous stories
of fifty-pound sweet potatoes and other vegetables in proportion.
Jonathan Bailey certified one presumed exaggeration by sending,
collect, a pumpkin weighing nearly two hundred pounds to a doubting
Friend in Western Yearly Meeting.

Further certification of California fruitfulness can be checked
with the journal of Robert Lindsey, written twenty years earlier.
English people have generally been known for understatement. "The
accounts we hear of the unusual fruitfulness of California would
be deemed fabulous, if they were not well authenticated. Two hundred
bushels of potatoes have been produced from one acre, some weighing
six pounds each. Onions so large as to cover a dessert plate, water-
melons weighing sixty pounds, and pumpkins two hundred pounds
each." Californians may do what they will with this story — doubt
it, top it, or leave it! Whatever the facts were at that time, California
has been rightly known for its fruit and garden products when
adequate water resources are applied to the good soil.

## The Yearly Meeting Formed

Though the hazards that attend new ventures in an unknown area had not passed, Friends of southern California began to consolidate their gains, drawing together in the usual Quaker sense-of-kind. The first general conference of Friends in the area was called in 1892, immediately preceding the sessions of Pasadena Quarterly Meeting. The question was raised as to whether the time had come for requesting a Yearly Meeting for California. Again the spirit of good humor as well as enthusiasm was expressed by William Coffin in his call to attend. "If you have bought a piece of ground come to the conference and go to see it afterward; if you have bought five yoke of oxen prove them by driving them to the conference; if you have married a wife come to the conference on your wedding tour and bring your wife with you." Friends came! They tented during the conference on the grounds of Long Beach.

A second conference the next year at Long Beach advanced the concern for a Yearly Meeting and a petition was forwarded to both Iowa and Kansas Yearly Meetings. Iowa deferred action on the request for one year. Friendly rivalry as to where the Yearly Meeting should convene was settled as Pasadena changed her request, favoring Whittier instead of Long Beach.

After the usual conferring with other Yearly Meetings the request was approved by Iowa, with Kansas cooperating, the opening sessions to be held at Whittier in 1895. Concern of American Friends for the approval of London Yearly Meeting and the concern of London for the establishing of American Yearly Meetings are indicated in the actions taken by London in 1894. The request was placed before London Yearly Meeting by way of a postscript to the Iowa epistle, which stated that

> the request from Pasadena Quarterly Meeting for the establishment of California Yearly Meeting, to be opened at Whittier, California, in Third Month, 1895, having been considered for one year, was granted, and, with the approval of other Yearly Meetings, will be opened, as requested.

To this request London Yearly Meeting (1894) recorded:

> This Meeting desires further information than it possesses on the circumstances of Friends in the district of California, and

the reasons that have led to the setting up of this new Yearly Meeting. It therefore asks the Meeting for Sufferings to inquire into the facts of the case and report to us next year.

In the following year the minutes state:

> The report from the Meeting for Sufferings in response to our Minutes of last year on the subject of . . . the establishment of the new Yearly Meeting of California, has been received. . . . We desire to recognize California Yearly Meeting, and we appoint . . . Friends as correspondents. . . . We have received and read an epistle from California Yearly Meeting held in Third Month this year. . . . "

This recognition was after the fact. The new Yearly Meeting had been established before the report of the Meeting for Sufferings was considered. Doubtless the approval of London Yearly Meeting was wanted, but it was not assumed to be a requisite for the formal opening of California Yearly Meeting.

The Yearly Meeting was opened as planned, at Whittier in March 1895. Credentials for forty-three Friends from seven Yearly Meetings were read. John D. Mills of Kansas and Cyrus Beede of Iowa headed their respective delegations from the establishing Yearly Meetings. Only one month before, "Pasadena Quarterly Meeting, with the approval of the parent Yearly Meeting [Iowa] established Whittier Quarterly Meeting. This enabled them to qualify for a Yearly Meeting with two Quarterly Meetings." This represents a hurried procedure, unlike the usual method, though similar to the action taken in the formation of Oregon Yearly Meeting.

The Yearly Meeting opened with a few more than 1,200 members in two Quarterly Meetings. There seems to have been an oversupply of ministers and representatives, each feeling an obligation to speak in a meeting overexercised by visitors. The Yearly Meeting adopted the *Christian Workman* as its official Yearly Meeting periodical, at the same time commending the *American Friend,* started only the year before. The meeting was held in the upstairs of the new college building. The preface to the minutes of this year paid tribute to the beginnings, thirty years earlier, of Quakerism in California with the visits of Robert and Sarah Lindsey and later of Mary B. Pinkham, John Scott, William Hobson, Sarah Morrison, and Abel Bond.

In the interest of noting some of the leading Friends from other Yearly Meetings during this period, the names of representatives to attend the opening of California Yearly Meeting are listed: New England: George A. and Jennie W. Crossman; North Carolina: John W. and Mary C. Woody; New York: Albert K. and Eliza P. Smiley; Ohio: Jacob and Phila A. Baker; Indiana: Allen Jay and Mary H. Goodard; Western: Franklin and Mary Moon Meredith; Iowa: Cyrus Beede, L. Maria Deane, John F. Hanson, Mary T. Thomas, and John Y. Hoover; Kansas: John D. Mills, Hannah E. Sleeper, and Margaret B. Smith; Wilmington: Jesse Hawkins and Clara Todhunter; Oregon: John Henry Douglas, Elwood Scott, and Mary E. K. Edwards.

Whittier Quarterly Meeting, which had been swept into the new Yearly Meeting organization, had evolved from the settlements of the Whittier area. In May 1887, the first Friends meeting in Whittier had been held in the home of Jonathan and Rebecca Bailey. Absalom Rosenberger in a historical sketch says:

> This was the real beginning of the Friends Church in Whittier. In December of that year Whittier Monthly Meeting was opened by direction of Pasadena Quarterly Meeting, under the jurisdiction of Iowa Yearly Meeting of Friends and approved by Kansas Yearly Meeting. By the end of that year the Meeting had called Dr. Elias Jessup as their first pastor.

It is well to note the type of leadership exemplified by Elias Jessup, who was, among other leaders, destined to play a large part in Quaker history on the Pacific coast. Hoosier-born and schooled at Earlham College, he first taught Negro freedmen in Missouri, then studied and practiced medicine in Iowa, where he served in the state senate and ran for governor. He migrated to Oregon, served in its state senate, and helped found its Quaker college. Then, feeling a call to the ministry, he came to Whittier.

The preface to the Yearly Meeting minutes of 1895 states that

> Friends Meetings are also held in San Francisco, College Park near San Jose,[6] Los Angeles City, and in Colusa County. But

---

[6] LeShana, *op. cit.,* Ch. 6, relates fully the controversy that centered around San Jose Meeting. A letter from Joel Bean to Rufus M. Jones reviews the controversy. See Appendices, the section entitled "Papers and Letters."

with the exception of Los Angeles, the Friends composing these meetings are members of other Yearly Meetings and they are therefore not under the authority of California Yearly Meeting.

At this time the Conservative Friends, few in number, began holding meetings in the Pasadena area, at first in the home of William P. Evans. In 1894 they built a meetinghouse and a Monthly Meeting was established under Hickory Grove Quarterly Meeting of Iowa (Conservative).

Fifty years after the gold rush of 1849 and the advent of a few Quaker families to central California, a Yearly Meeting had been established and the future of Friends in California was assured with its main strength in the southern part of the state. California presents quite as much of an amalgam of races, nationalities, religious sects, and secular interests in its large population as does its counterpart, New York, on the east coast. The latter has been roughly four hundred years in the making while California, in the main, has developed in less than a century.

During the three-fourths of a century, California Yearly Meeting, in the earlier stages, increased numerically by immigrations of Friends from states farther east, especially from Iowa and Kansas. In later years the numerical increase has come largely from Friends who retired to California and from non-Friends families who have come in all but tidal waves of immigration. The Friends church nearby has offered a spiritual home for parents and children and the membership has thereby been affected by non-Friends heritage. The Friends community church has been a new fact within recent Friends history in western America and, though not confined entirely to the west coast, has been developed most largely in California Yearly Meeting.

Distance from other Yearly Meetings has naturally resulted in a separate program of missionary and other outreach activities. The program of the Five Years Meeting has not, until very recent years, enlisted close cooperation by California Yearly Meeting. A reorganization of the Five Years Meeting (now Friends United Meeting) has brought the full range of member Yearly Meetings closer together; and there is a new united impact in which California is very much in evidence.

The experience of California Yearly Meeting raises into focus a relatively unique aspect of ecumenical relations for Friends. The contribution of California Friends to this present-day development will be seen more clearly in the years immediately ahead.

The Yearly Meeting has been very active in church extension. The Men's Movement has put financial strength into the erecting of new church buildings in the fast-growing communities. In the statistics of 1964, eight new churches are listed in as many new areas between 1950 and 1963, with a combined membership of over one thousand. The Yearly Meeting has been alert to the facts of population growth, and the giving for outreach has been multiplied year by year. The Yearly Meeting has worked cooperatively with the Friends United Meeting in the work of extension whereby a pastoral Meeting was opened at Phoenix, Arizona. Pacific Yearly Meeting is also involved in that area, with a nonpastoral Meeting in Phoenix and with Friends in Tucson.

---

The geographic aspect of Western Quaker history had ended. The great Pacific lifted its forbidding barrier. The territorial lure had gone. Within about one century, travel had changed from trail to road to rail, and soon to skyway. New frontiers phased in as the older ones phased out. It is now time to ask, "What happened to Friends of the American frontier as they hurried to occupy new lands?" Viewed from that point in history, what would be next as new chapters of Quaker life were being written? The following pages will raise these questions in turn.

NOTE

At this time structural changes in several Yearly Meetings are being made. The pattern of Quarterly Meetings is being changed to "Regional" areas, embracing a larger number of Meetings. The superstructures of the Yearly Meetings are also being greatly altered in California, Indiana, and Western Yearly Meetings. Some others are reviewing their need for change.

# Chapter 9

## QUAKER EDUCATION AND SCHOOLS

As Friends opened elementary schools, levelled them upward into secondary standing, and ultimately established colleges they were exemplifying their peace witness. They were beating swords into pen points, for their only weapon was the pen and their target the mind.

The development of Quaker education was a parallel current with that of religion; it was a part of the same stream. Neither could have existed without the other — not for long. Outwardly and historically this is seen in the meetinghouse and the schoolhouse sitting side by side. Linked together, religion and education were mutually strengthened, whereby the Quaker stream of life was deepened and broadened.

Education was the handmaiden of religion, but the time would come when this dominance would be challenged and the relationship between them would be reviewed. The issue would never be fully resolved but would evolve with new questions and fresh insights.

Back of the development of schools on the frontier were the heritage and the example of Friends in the older settlements of the

New England and Philadelphia areas and those farther back, in England. George Fox had set the example by the establishing of two schools as early as 1668, and three years later there were fifteen Friends boarding schools in England. In 1690, London Yearly Meeting lent strength to the movement by urging Monthly and Quarterly Meetings to establish schools and advising against the training of Friends children by non-Friends.

Overlapping in time were the schools established by Friends in eastern America.[1] In 1689 a school was established by Friends of Philadelphia. The school was chartered by William Penn in 1701 and still exists as the William Penn Charter School. By 1746 Philadelphia Yearly Meeting, following the course of London, advised the Monthly Meetings "to encourage and assist each other in the settlements and support of schools," supplied with teachers "careful in the wisdom of God and a spirit of meekness, gradually to bring them [the pupils] to a knowledge of their duty to God and one another." A Query was prepared by Philadelphia Yearly Meeting to be answered by the Monthly Meetings. "Are there schools established for the education of our youth under the care of teachers in membership with us and superintended by committees appointed in the Monthly or Preparative Meetings?" By 1750 there were forty schools in America under the care of Monthly Meetings and by 1800 sixty-five or seventy are listed.

The Yearly Meetings of the east coast are still predominant in the number of schools under Friends care, or Meeting-related, at both elementary and secondary levels. Only in the number of church-related colleges do Friends in the West predominate.

There were four logical stages in the development of schools by American Friends. In the first stage were the elementary schools, appearing chiefly in the seventeenth and eighteenth centuries. In the second stage were the academies and the boarding schools (secondary level) appearing in the East mainly in the first half of the nineteenth century and in the West chiefly in the latter half of the century. In the third stage were the colleges. In the fourth stage two types of schools have appeared — centers for adult studies, such as that of Pendle Hill (1930) offering no degrees and requiring none for attenders though beamed to the graduate level of studies; and a degree-

---

[1] The full list of Friends schools cannot be given here. Information can be secured from the Friends Education Council, Philadelphia, Pa.

granting institution on the graduate level, the Earlham School of Religion (1960).

## ELEMENTARY SCHOOLS AND THE FOURTH "R"

For frontier Friends, education did not consist simply of the three *r's*, but *four* — religion, reading, 'riting, and 'rithmetic — *and in that order!* Education must be God-oriented. Reading meant primarily ability to read the Bible and secondarily to read the tracts or other literature prepared by Friends of Philadelphia, New England, and England, and circulated by visiting Friends.

Elementary schools in all of the southern and western Yearly Meetings were similar in their development. They often started in Friends homes and then were moved to buildings erected for that purpose, generally located very near the Friends meetinghouses. Teachers were required to be those "in membership with the Society," and a "guarded education" included compliance with traditions in the "simplicity" of dress and speech (the use of *thee* and *thou*).

### Schools of Southern Friends

Records on the educational work of southern Friends for the earlier period are very scarce.[2] Friends had tried to provide education for their children in homes and in meetinghouses before they were able or inspired to construct separate buildings.

The following minute indicates an interest by no means new to Friends of that year.

> 1716 . ye . 30 . th day . of . ye . 4 . th month . at . a . quarterly . meeting . at . Little River . . . . friends . are . advised . to . be . diligent . and . careful . in . scholling . of . their children . and . if . their . be . any . poore . friends . that . be . in . unity . have . children . and . not . able . then . that . friends . belonging . to . ye . meeting . with . them . do . by . assisting . of . them . bring . up . their . children . to . neasaery . learning.

A Query in the minutes fourteen years later indicated not only a continuing interest in education but also its effect on written expression.

---

[2] Zora Klain, *Quaker Contribution to Education in North Carolina,* 1925; University of Pennsylvania. The chief resource for this chapter on southern Quaker education.

Are the necessities of the poor among you relieved, are they advised and assisted in such employment as they are capable of, and is care taken for the education of their children, are there any children among you growing up without any education?

To supply the materials for religious education Friends naturally looked to their own writers, as is shown in a minute of 1743 advising those responsible for the schools " . . . to Send to Boston to have George Fox's Primmers reprinted, . . . to Collect out of those primmers Such apart of them as Shall be suitable for young persons that are just entering upon Learning. . . . "

This brief sampling from pages of Fox's *Primmers* gives some insight into the content of studies of that time.

Instructions For Right Spelling and Plain Directions for Reading and Writing True English With several delightful things very Useful and Necessary, both for Young and Old, to Read and Learn. . . . The several sorts of Letters. Alphabet in German type; in Roman small, capital and italics. Double letters and consonants . . . The child's Lesson (moral and religious instructions) . . . Proper Names in Scripture divided into Syllables and the Signification of them in English; together with other memorable passages, mentioned in Scripture . . . The Significance of the seven Arts. Rhetoric . . . Astronomy . . . the Law of Distribution of the Stars. Geometry . . . measuring of the Earth. Music . . . The Muses Art . . . Arithmetic. . . .

The Friends schools were established for Friends children, but in many cases they included non-Friends children of the communities. Minutes and Queries show the concern of Friends to aid children of poor homes.

This was a do-it-yourself era in Friends history, reflected in the schoolroom no less than in the building of a cabin or in the hammering out of farm tools and kitchen utensils. As cabin schools started Friends on the long way toward Quaker colleges the statement by James A. Garfield illustrates the spirit of that period: "Give me a log hut, with only a simple bench, Mark Hopkins on one end and I on the other, and you may have all the buildings, apparatus and libraries without him."[3]

---

[3] From an address to Williams College alumni, December 28, 1871.

Friends of southern states were in the business of education before the state assumed responsibility for general education. The change
toward inclusion of non-Friends children and the employment of
non-Friends teachers lessened the control of Friends, until in 1831 it
was reported that "there is not a school in the limits of the Yearly
Meeting [North Carolina] that is under the care of a monthly or
preparative Meeting. The teachers of Friends children are mostly
not members of our Society and all schools are in a mixed state."

The experiences of Friends in southern states are reflected in
the educational developments in the Northwest Territory.

## Schools Beyond the Ohio River

The schools of Indiana will suffice to depict the early concerns
and experience of Friends beyond the Ohio River in frontier elementary education. It should be noted that in all other Yearly Meetings formed during the westward movement, schools were conducted
from the time of their first settlements. Not many names of schools
are available, nor even the numbers, but it may be assumed that in
the earlier stages they were almost as numerous as the Meetings,
whether held in cabin homes, in meetinghouses, or in buildings constructed for school purposes.

One of their earliest cooperative endeavors after erecting family
cabins was the felling of trees and the hewing of them into shape for
the walls and the roofs of meetinghouses. In many cases the meetinghouses served double duty as schools. In other cases family cabins
housed the first schools. Soon schoolhouses were built by the joint
labor of the men. The first ones were simple indeed. Often there
was no wooden floor, only the tightly packed soil. Windows, if any,
were covered by greased paper that allowed only a subdued light. In
the typical very early schoolhouse the room was heated by an open
fire in the center with a pole extending through a hole in the roof,
hopefully to attract the smoke upwards. Fireplaces were installed in
later buildings. The benches were made of split logs with no backs.
Desks, in the earlier structures, were often placed along the walls;
there the students could stand and study or write.

The first Friends school of record in Indiana was opened at
Whitewater (Richmond) in 1811-1812 under a standing committee
whose duty it was "to care for schools." When the first log meeting-

house was vacated in favor of a new brick building this school appears to have continued in the old log meetinghouse until about 1836, after which the school continued elsewhere as Friends Academy. The academy was first taught by Isaac Hiatt. He was followed by Barnabas C. Hobbs, William Haughton, Hiram Hadley, Erastus Test, and Cyrus W. Hodgin.

Frame buildings were erected as sawmills made lumber available. Then came benches with backs and also desks at which two or three pupils sat. The teacher on his platform reigned supreme and with a kind of authority highly questioned if not discarded in the schools of today.

In the earlier days the rod was not spared if needed. This was displayed in full sight of the pupils and doubtless held a silent discipline over the naughty ones. Though Quakers in the earlier days resorted to such discipline they were among the first to put it aside. One method commonly used was to send the misbehaving child home with a note to his parents who, after administering such discipline or counsel as they might choose, brought the child back to school where he made due apology. Later disciplinary procedure moved beyond the "no lickin, no larnin" idea and rested on moral persuasion.

Meetings were closely tied to the school through the school committee, one of great importance in the practice of Friends. In many cases the committee was required to meet and to make regular visits to the school, where members questioned the pupils informally.

Gradually the elementary schools added higher branches. The curriculum depended, in part, on what the teacher was prepared to teach. In some cases Latin, Greek, or natural philosophy might be taught to the older or more able pupils. The curriculum was limited only by the knowledge of the teacher, but always the "four r's" were basic. The Bible was sometimes used as a textbook. It was generally read daily by the teacher or a pupil, and passages were memorized as a part of schoolwork. In the school conducted under White Lick Quarterly Meeting it was required that the teacher and the pupils "cease from all literary pursuits, once every day and gather into silence" in which the Bible was read.

The breakthrough of learning on every level, then and now, always meets with the resistance of settled ideas. Barnabas C. Hobbs wrote of the "dear old saints" who feared the teaching of geography that the earth was round. They were convinced that Scripture taught the flat earth. Even this early newer scholarship was being both felt and feared in the evolving history of Friends schools. It would later appear in sharper form on the higher levels of learning.

The influence of Eastern Friends was felt in frontier education. Professor Thomas Chase of Haverford College lectured at both Philadelphia and Iowa Yearly Meetings, and his address, printed in 1868, was preserved and quoted in Western [Indiana] Yearly Meeting. In it he had said:

> There is danger from unsanctified mental activity and undevout science, but these cannot be met and conquered by ignorance . . . we must be armed with the weapons of knowledge . . . for sound learning and true science are the inseparable allies of religion. . . . It becomes us to provide Schools, whose teachers are not mere *pretenders,* conceited *quacks,* but devout and earnest persons who trace all truth to its divine source, who recognize in all history the guiding hand of Providence and to whom the heavens and the earth, the land and the sea, the whole animal, vegetable, and mineral creation, "declare the Glory of God and show His handiwork."

The time came when more non-Friends were admitted and some of the traditions were adjusted to meet the conditions. On this change the White Lick School made the provision that

> both teacher and pupils (particularly those who are members of the religious Society of Friends) observe plainness of apparel and endeavor to habituate themselves to using the plain grammatical Scripture language [*thee* and *thou*]. Those who are admitted as pupils and not members of said Society are not required to observe this rule any further than their principles or the wish of their parents or guardians will admit.

There were three types of schools. First, those supported and operated under a Friends Meeting which paid the teachers; the subscription schools, in which the teachers were paid a determined amount by the parents for each child; and the third was a combination of the two. A term seldom exceeded twelve weeks and not all of the children in a family attended at the same time. This was in some cases due to inability to pay for all of them, also due in part to the need for older children to help with the farm work during certain seasons. Sometimes a school would hold both winter and summer terms.

In later years the religious emphasis changed somewhat in some of the schools. Until late in the nineteenth century the Query asked by Indiana Yearly Meeting read, "Are schools encouraged for the education of our youth under the tuition of teachers *in membership with us?*" (italics added). Meetings seem to have replied always in the affirmative. In 1867, in Western Yearly Meeting, the Committee on Education presented a different Query, "Are the Committees careful to employ religiously *concerned* Teachers?" (italics added). The reply, in many instances, was "Committees are careful to employ religiously *inclined* Teachers" (italics added). This change in the requirement for teachers indicates an increase of "mixed" schools, with a lessened emphasis on "teachers in membership."

In selection of teachers the Friends testimony on the equality of the sexes was evident. They had to face the objection of non-Friends parents that "wimmin ain't fittin to be teachers." Earlier Friends schools did not often appoint women teachers, but this may well have been due to the hard work involved in running the school. Wood had to be carried and the teacher had to be janitor and grounds-keeper as well. That this imbalance between men and women teachers was overcome is shown in the report of Indiana Yearly Meeting in 1850 when ninety-one men and one hundred and six women teachers were reported.[4]

It is fitting to pay special tribute to Barnabas C. Hobbs, who served in many educational capacities, as teacher and principal in elementary schools, then in academies, and later as the first president of Earlham College. From 1868 to 1871 he was State Superintendent of Public Instruction for Indiana. He prepared readers to be used in four grades of Friends elementary schools. This was a great advance beyond the earliest of Friends schools in which the only books were whatever the families might have accumulated. Later books by non-Friends did not meet the Quaker ideals and Barnabas C. Hobbs responded to the need for readers "free from popular sentiments which conflict with their [Friends'] views concerning civil government, Christian philosophy, and Christian courtesy. . . . "

---

[4] Ethel Hittle McDaniel, *The Contribution of the Society of Friends to Education in Indiana;* published by Indiana Historical Society, 1939.

Schoolbooks published by eastern Friends were also used. The following simple poem, in *The Select Reader No. 1,* published by the Tract Association of Philadelphia, illustrates the combined teaching of virtue and reading. Amusing to us, it may have been effective in the lives of little Quakers who had to memorize it.

THE LAZY BOY

'Tis royal fun, cried lazy Ned,
To coast upon my fine new sled,
And beat the other boys;
But then I cannot bear to climb
The slippery hill, for every time
It more and more annoys.

So while his school mates glided by,
And gladly tugged uphill, to try
Another merry race,
Too indolent to share their plays,
He was compelled to stand and gaze,
While shivering in his place.

Thus he would never take the pains
To seek the prize that labor gains,
Until the time had passed;
For all his life, he dreaded still
The silly bugbear of a hill,
And died a dunce at last.

There is no record of the number of Friends elementary schools in Indiana, except that given in 1850 when ninety-six schools were reported in Indiana Yearly Meeting. When added to the nearly thirty academies established after 1850, which generally included some elementary grades, the number of Friends schools existing in Indiana at one time or another between 1810 and 1900 may have been well over one hundred twenty-five. Many of them were established far in advance of the public school system and helped to set the standards.

It was difficult for Friends to witness the decline of these schools as some of them became public schools and others closed their doors. When their future looked dark Joseph John Mills, in 1884, said, "Let the Society of Friends put the education of its children entirely out of its own hands . . . for twenty years, and at the end of that time there will be found very few boys and girls playing on the streets of Quakerdom." If viewed statistically one might question the fulfillment of his prophecy, but that Friends lost much in this transition can hardly be questioned.

Except for the larger number of schools in Indiana, the history of education in other frontier Yearly Meetings is nearly the same. Physical conditions in the form of buildings varied. In Ohio, Indiana, and Iowa adequate timber made possible the building of cabin structures for homes, meetings, and schools. In Kansas and Nebraska sod and dugout schoolhouses were common.

The coming in of public schools with the vanishing of Friends elementary schools took a similar course in all Yearly Meetings. How many hundreds of Friends schools may have existed at one time or another in all southern and western Yearly Meetings is not known.

As the twentieth century dawned, a great formative period was passing into history. "Guarded education" of the earlier tradition was fading. If Quaker education was to be "guarded" from that time on it would have to be under a different discipline. The old "guards," those that kept Friends marked in the sight of their neighbors as a "peculiar" people, were down. A new and confusing time lay ahead. The following pages on Quaker education of the secondary and college levels will trace this development further.

### The Era of Quaker Academies

Before the coming of standardization in education there was no clear line between elementary and secondary schools, or between secondary and college level. The terms *school, academy,* and *college* were somewhat ambiguous. Yet there was a differentiation along broad, general lines. The elementary schools of Friends were based mainly on the "four r's," as indicated above. In some instances the higher-level courses were added and the schooling offered began to take on the character of secondary education.[5]

---

[5] Rufus M. Jones, *Later Periods of Quakerism II,* Macmillan and Co., London. Ch. XVII, "Friends in Education," p. 705-710 lists Friends secondary schools.

*A Souvenir of Friends Schools,* reprinted from *Western Work,* Oskaloosa, Iowa [near 1900]. Brief accounts of all Friends colleges and several academies of the period together with short biographical notes on the presidents of the colleges.

William J. Reagan, *A Venture in Quaker Education at Oakwood School;* private printing, 1968.

Barnabas C. Hobbs

Walter and Emma Malone

**Hartland Academy, Iowa**

This is typical of many of the academies established in Quaker communities across the Midwest

As the elementary grades were dropped, with the coming in of public schools, more secondary courses were added to some schools and, in general, the term *academy* was usually adopted — sometimes called seminary, boarding school, or high school. In the later stages of secondary school development the academies became standardized as four-year schools from which students were graduated with diplomas, prepared to enter college.

Whereas an elementary school in the earlier days had been located near a supporting Meeting, the secondary level school was generally supported by one or more Quarterly Meetings. The growth of Quaker settlements, better roads, and the close association of Friends in Quarterly Meetings made the new cooperative support possible. The value of this period of secondary education can hardly be over-appraised. The academies prepared many teachers for the public schools which had, for the most part, absorbed the Friends elementary grades. They also equipped leaders for the local communities and Meetings and prepared many students to enter colleges and universities.

There were at one time or another during the nineteenth century at least sixty-five schools classed as academies, boarding schools, seminaries, or high schools under the care or influence of Friends or Friends Meetings from North Carolina to the west coast. Many of them had courses on both the elementary and the secondary level. Howard Brinton reports that at least ten academies existed in North Carolina in 1885, and names Belvedere Academy (1834) and Woodland Academy (1876). New Garden Boarding School (1837), later becoming Guilford College, also offered the secondary level of courses.[6]

It is impossible to include a statement regarding all of the academies in the respective areas. Those presented here represent typical circumstances and developments.

*Tennessee*

The Friendsville community in Blount County, Tennessee, claims the distinction of being "the only Quaker town left in the South today." Certainly it has the only Friends academy still existing in the South, giving it a unique place among Friends.[7]

Within the settlements of Friends in the Lost Creek and New

---

[6] Howard H. Brinton, *Quaker Education in Theory and Practice;* Pendle Hill Pamphlet No. 9, 1940; p. 47.
[7] From literature supplied by Friendsville Academy.

Hope Quarterly Meetings of Tennessee, Newbury (Newberry) Friends
Meeting was established in 1803 by North Carolina Yearly Meeting.

In 1857 two schools were established; one for boys, known as
the Friendsville Institute; and one for girls, known as the Newberry
Female School. The two schools were later united. Friends in
England, New York, and Philadelphia gave it financial support and
furnished books for its library. Its student body included from the
beginning both Friends and non-Friends of the area. No child was to
be denied education because of lack of funds.

Mass migrations of Friends in the early 1800's, followed by the
Civil War, brought the school near to closing. After the war Friendsville Institute started rebuilding. In 1881 the school was chartered by
the state as Friendsville Academy. The school has gone through some
very difficult times, but with new planning and the including of
interested non-Friends on its board and its supporting constituency
it now has a student body including grades seven to twelve, housed
in some modern buildings and serving young people chiefly from the
southern area. The Friends Meeting nearby, closely cooperating with
the academy, is a member of Friendsville Quarterly Meeting of Wilmington Yearly Meeting.

*Ohio*

Shortly after the setting off of Ohio Yearly Meeting in 1813, concern was expressed for a boarding school for Friends children.[8] Not
until several years later were sufficient funds collected, a site chosen,
and buildings erected at Mt. Pleasant, with the school opening in 1837.
Friends of London and New England Yearly Meetings gave generous
assistance. With the Wilbur-Gurney separation of 1854 the school
passed into the hands of the conservative branch. In 1875 the building
burned and in 1876 the school was moved to Barnesville, Ohio.

As a four-year secondary school under Ohio Yearly Meeting (Conservative), it is making an important contribution not only to the
Conservative branch, but to all Friends.[9] Many young Friends of

---

[8] *Quaker Sesqui-Centennial,* 1812-1962; Ohio Yearly Meeting (Damascus). Gives
a brief review of Friends schools under Ohio Yearly Meeting.

[9] *American Quakers Today,* Edwin B. Bronner, editor; Ch. 5 on Conservative
Friends, by William P. Taber, Jr. A brief reference to Barnesville and Scattergood
Friends schools.

*Olney,* 1876-1926; a brief history of the Conservative Friends School at Barnesville,
Ohio.

every branch have graduated, prepared for entering college. Former students of "Olney," as the school is affectionately known, have served the Society of Friends in their home Meetings and communities and in many areas of the world.

In 1857 Friends Boarding School at Damascus was opened by Ohio Yearly Meeting (Gurneyite) for Friends children of the area. By 1876 it included eight elementary grades, plus four years of high school and a two-year normal school for training teachers. Many leading Friends of Ohio Yearly Meeting were educated in the school. In 1910, because of insufficient funds for a successful operation, it was leased to the township school board, to which it was finally sold, West Branch High School being its present-day successor.

Raisin Valley Seminary near Adrian, Michigan, was opened in 1850 under Adrian Quarterly Meeting within New York Yearly Meeting. In 1869 the Quarterly Meeting was transferred to Ohio Yearly Meeting. Besides the usual curriculum of elementary and secondary levels it offered varied courses, paralleling roughly those of Damascus Academy. With the coming in of public schools its attendance dropped, and with decreased financial support it closed in 1908.

Though the Friends Bible Institute and Training School of Cleveland, Ohio, founded in 1892, was not classed as an academy it served, in general, the young people of that age and older. Established and directed for twenty-six years by Walter and Emma Malone, it produced a large number of ministers and missionaries. Among the latter are Esther Baird, missionary to India; Arthur and Edna Chilson and Willis Hotchkiss, who helped to found the Friends Mission in Kenya (1902); Jefferson and Helen Ford, who served several years in Africa; Carson and Vercia Cox, serving in China; and later Clifton and Betty Robinson in India.

In 1937 the name was changed to Cleveland Bible College. After a succession of presidents following the resignation of Walter and Emma Malone in 1918, their son-in-law, Byron Osborn, came to the helm in 1951. It was under his leadership that the institution became Malone College, moving to Canton, Ohio.

*Indiana*

With the establishing of Indiana Yearly Meeting in 1821 and

with the growth of settlements across the state, more than twenty academies were established in Indiana at one time or another, chiefly in the latter half of the nineteenth century.[10] Among the earliest and most influential was Bloomingdale, started in 1846 as an "Agricultural Manual Labor School" with practical physical labor on the farm, along with the classroom studies. Among the best known and the last to close were Spiceland Academy (1870-1922); Central at Plainfield (Western Yearly Meeting, 1881-1919); Fairmount (1885-1923); and Vermillion in Illinois (Western Yearly Meeting, 1874-1932).[11]

Spiceland Academy drew major support from tuition paid by the state. When this was discontinued the school was weakened and finally closed. A similar support by the local township undergirded Fairmount Academy. When this was withdrawn desperate efforts were made to continue, but the school was finally closed, the last of the Friends academies in Indiana.

Blue River Academy in southern Indiana illustrates the development of an elementary school into an academy. As early as 1815 the first school was started in the meetinghouse a few miles northwest of Salem. For a few years it was moved short distances as new buildings were constructed. In 1860 a frame building was erected and Blue River Academy was founded. From this area and through this school came men and women of prominence in the educational and church leadership of Friends in the West. As in the case of most Friends colleges, Earlham College grew out of the secondary-level — Friends Boarding School (1847). The Friends Academy, established in 1836 in a different location, had preceded it.

The spirit of these vanished schools is caught in some of their statements of purpose.

> We believe that he only is governed in any true sense of the word who governs himself. — *Bloomingdale Academy*
> The government of the school is based upon the idea that manhood is more than scholarship, and that self-respect and self-control, on the part of the student, are important factors in the formation of character. — *Spiceland Academy*

---

[10] McDaniels, *op. cit.*, Ch. V. An excellent review of Quaker education in Indiana.
[11] Opal Thornburg, *Earlham, The Story of a College;* 1847-1962; Earlham College Press, 1963, p. 128.

The object of this institution is to give thorough training of the mental powers, to establish students in habits of self-reliance and industry, to inculcate moral and religious instruction, to assist those who come under its influence in becoming their own masters. — *Fairmount Academy*

Closely related to Indiana Quaker elementary and secondary education is White's Manual Labor Institute. In 1850 Josiah White of Philadelphia left a large sum of money to Indiana Yearly Meeting for the education of poor children, irrespective of race or color. His daughters later added a large gift. Near Wabash over seven hundred acres were purchased and buildings were erected in 1859. In 1883, with government aid, Indian children were also housed and taught in the school. In 1895 the Indian project was abandoned as government established its own schools. Now orphan children and other young people are cared for and educated as wards from counties and juvenile courts. The Institute has done remarkable service. Its classroom studies and its practical training in the school and on the farm have made a well-rounded educational experience in keeping with Friends ideals.

*Iowa*

In 1845 Reuben Dorland came to Salem Friends settlement from Poughkeepsie, New York, and founded Salem Seminary on his own responsibility.[12] By 1851 the student enrollment reached more than two hundred. He had a staff of three teachers and offered courses on both the elementary and the secondary level. His death in 1852 weakened the school, but Salem Monthly Meeting rallied to it and erected a new and more nearly adequate building.

In 1867 the Whittier College Association was formed and in 1868 opened its doors as Whittier College, with John W. Woody as president. The school met with an immediate response in student attendance. In 1874, building facilities were expanded and a campaign for endowment funds was launched. The national panic of 1877 and failing crops put the school in debt and in 1885 the building was destroyed by fire. With characteristic courage Friends again rallied to the cause and in 1887 erected a new building. For years it continued

---

[12] Louis T. Jones, *The Quakers of Iowa;* published by the State Historical Society of Iowa, 1914; Part IV, Ch. V, "Educational Work Among Iowa Friends."

as a Friends academy but closed its doors in 1910. By that time Penn College had started at Oskaloosa and Friends support was divided.

In 1860 Red Cedar Monthly Meeting started a small academy and in 1866 united with the "Independent District" of Springdale in the establishment of Springdale Seminary. The school prospered and Friends continued in their part of its operation until 1877, when they turned its operation to the public school system.

In 1867 Ackworth Academy was established. It continued until 1910, when it ended and the building was remodeled and turned to the use of the local Meeting. West Branch Academy (1867), Lynn Grove Academy (1867), Stanford Seminary (1869), Le Grand Academy (1872), Pleasant Plain Academy (1876), Hartland Academy (1888), and Earlham Academy (1892) were established. These academies belonged, in varying arrangements, to Friends or were controlled by them, but later disappeared. Penn College also had a preparatory department at its beginning, making a total of twelve academies, or their equivalent, in the history of Iowa Yearly Meeting. This was a strong undergirding of the total work of Iowa Friends and a contribution in leadership that helped to give Friends of the state a future.

White's Manual Labor Institute was established when the Meetings of Iowa were yet under Indiana Yearly Meeting, by the same gift. In 1851 over 1,400 acres were bought near Salem, Iowa, for that branch of White's Institute. From the beginning the institute in Iowa had a difficult road. Good renters for the land were hard to find and there was a failure of crops. The panic of 1857 further weakened the school. In 1864 Indiana Yearly Meeting suggested that Iowa Yearly Meeting (formed only the year before) take over the responsibility. The history of the institute is a complex one. The property was leased for some years to the state for a reform school. During another period the government placed Indian children under the care of Friends until they were withdrawn and placed in a government school. For a time a girls' school was maintained. Today Quakerdale Boy's Home near New Providence, Iowa, represents the final development. It is located on good farm land where twenty-two boys (in 1963) were being cared for. The boys attend the New Providence public school and the New Providence Friends Meeting, and work on the farm.[18]

---

[18] *Ibid.*, Part IV, Ch. III.

Scattergood School, near West Branch, Iowa, was opened in 1890 by the Conservative Friends. In 1873 Clarkson Sheppard and George J. Scattergood of Philadelphia visited Conservative Friends of Iowa who at that time belonged to Ohio Yearly Meeting (Conservative). Observing the difficulties of proper education for Friends children, they recommended the establishing of a boarding school in that area. The Conservative boarding school in Ohio was too far away to accommodate many Friends of Iowa.

Some thousands of dollars were raised in Philadelphia for the purpose of purchasing a site and erecting buildings within the area of Hickory Grove Monthly Meeting, in Cedar County. The school was to be under the care of Hickory Grove Quarterly Meeting. In 1890 the school was opened, with a capacity for about fifty children.[14]

In 1931 it was temporarily closed. During the Second World War it was used as a center for European refugees. This was followed by re-opening the school in 1944. The school has been a very significant and creative development along Quaker ways of life and education. A school farm provides involvement of the students in school support. Staff and students form a closely knit community.

Though operated now under the care of Iowa Yearly Meeting (Conservative) it is open to all Friends, making it a contributing center to the life of the Society of Friends. Its courses are college preparatory in academic standards, and its spirit and order are in keeping with the best in Quaker traditions.

## Kansas

Within a period of ninety years, beginning with the opening of Grellet Academy (1878) and extending to the closing of Haviland Academy (1968), there were thirteen academies in the geographic area covered by Kansas Yearly Meeting. Some of these continued only a few years.

As in other Yearly Meetings, the elementary schools opened the way to higher courses. The first elementary school was started in northeastern Kansas in a log building belonging to Benajah Hiatt. His cabin served both as a meetinghouse and as a schoolhouse. The first teacher, V. K. Stanley, described the building.

---

[14] *Ibid.*, Part III, Ch. III, p. 160-162. For later history, see literature from the school.

This primitive school house was built of small logs, not hewn, cut from a grove nearby. The cracks were stopped up with split pieces of timber, commonly called "chinks," and mortar, composed of mud and prairie grass roots. . . . The floor was rough and the roof composed of three-foot boards riven out of oak timber . . . was held on by weight poles such as were commonly used in that day.[15]

That kind of schoolhouse construction was common in northeastern Kansas, where Friends first settled. Groves similar to those of Ohio, Indiana, and Iowa were available. Farther west the level plains begin, trees are few, and sod or dugout schools and meetinghouses were common.

Not all of these schools can be reviewed here, but three of them will illustrate, in a general way, the course of Quaker academies in Kansas Yearly Meeting.

With the opening of Kansas Yearly Meeting in 1872, concern was expressed for the education of Friends children and in 1873 it was proposed that a Yearly Meeting "high school" be established. With this incentive, Walnut Creek Quarterly Meeting opened Grellet Academy (the name honoring Stephen Grellet) in 1878, near Glen Elder Meeting in Mitchell County. William P. Trueblood, a graduate of Earlham College, was the first teacher. His teaching career included other academies and finally Friends University. The Grellet building burned in 1893 and with the coming of a local high school was never rebuilt.

There was a succession of academies in Kansas Yearly Meeting, including one in Texas, one in Colorado (existing for only a few years), and two in Oklahoma. The following paragraphs tell part of the story of North Branch Academy (closed in 1941) and pay tribute to the many teachers and principals of Friends academies in every Yearly Meeting.

There were many men and women Friends whose careers were given almost entirely to Friends academies as principals and teachers. Not all of them can be named here and given due credit, but two of these Friends in addition to William P. Trueblood will serve as ex-

---

[15] Sheldon G. Jackson, *A Short History of Kansas Yearly Meeting of Friends,* Days Printshop, Wichita, Kansas. Ch. XII; quoting from the *Kansas Educator,* Hutchinson, 1905. This chapter also reviews the Friends academies of Kansas.

amples of service to Friends in several Yearly Meetings during a unique period of Quaker secondary education.

Henry H. Townsend, educated in Le Grand Friends Academy in Iowa and in Earlham College, served as principal and teacher in six academies within three Yearly Meetings: Damascus, in Ohio; Le Grand, in Iowa; and four in Kansas — North Branch (in two separate periods), Hesper, Fowler, and Haviland. One of his Quaker students in North Branch Friends Academy, well known among Friends, was Gilbert Bowles, who has written of his appreciation of Henry Townsend and also of his own educational experience. This letter by Gilbert Bowles is given here at some length for what it reveals not only of the service of Quaker teachers and principals, but also of the life of Quaker young people and the condition of farm life which tested deeply the devotion of teachers, students, and Friends supporters.

> I know what drouths meant, when in the eighties I was a boy on a Jewell County, Kansas farm. Vividly, I remember the hope with which in the spring and early summer of 1887 I sowed the oats and planted and cultivated the corn, for my father had promised that if the crops were good that summer I might study the coming winter at Grellet Academy, in Mitchell County, forty miles to the south. Although wheat and oats failed, there was still hope until early July, when hot southwest winds withered and scorched the corn. All was gone, save the possibility of an autumn crop of turnips, on which we largely lived the following winter. We did not suffer physical hunger, but keen is the memory of the intellectual and spiritual hunger of those summer and autumn days when with other farmers' sons I worked at building the roadbed of the Rock Island Railway line which that year was put through northern Kansas.
>
> The winter brought to me no study at Grellet Academy. Instead there was eager evening reading of a country teacher's books while husking corn in southern Nebraska where a gracious rain had fallen, and ten days snatched from wood cutting to attend a district school. Another summer on the farm, a month at the country Normal and a year's teaching in a country school.
>
> When two years had passed by Henry H. Townsend came into my life at the call of neighbor farmer Friends who through vision, courage and faith transformed the local meetinghouse into two school rooms, partitioned with curtains, and in early October, 1889, opened Northbranch Academy, four miles from our home.

Henry H. Townsend was the first Principal, with Anna R. Townsend as Assistant. For four happy, creative years they were my teachers. As often as I recall those days, my sense of gratitude deepens. I owe much to other teachers, but that was the period of most of my important life decisions, and of the awakening and shaping of abiding life interests.

Within that period at Northbranch Academy, my previous decision for Christ was vitalized, strengthened and steadied. Meager as was our supply of books, I learned to choose, to use and to appreciate the best available literature. The little volumes of Alden's Encyclopedia, purchased with admission fees to our literary exhibition, meant as much to me then as does the Brittanica now. My zeal for a short course at a business college, with its beautiful penmanship and promise of an early salaried position, was shaped by Henry Townsend into a decision to finish the four years course at Northbranch Academy. That decision now appears to have been a watershed between two distinct life courses. The personal appeal of a visiting evangelist to become his associate was, under the guidance of my friend and teacher, seen as a new incentive for more thorough preparation for a life of Christian service.

After an opening word at one morning worship period, our Principal sat quietly for an hour or more while the students, all save one or two, without urging or anticipation, knelt one after another and under the evident guidance of the Spirit of God offered vocal prayer. No emotional pressure, but an atmosphere in which repentance and dedication could find expression. We knew that morning that we had touched laws and forces in the Universe as real and tangible as those to which our teacher introduced us when he opened for us the doorways into physics, chemistry and astronomy. Even a brief course in geology under Henry Townsend, with references to the Genesis story of "Creation," helped to give to me an attitude of reverence and a sense of unity in the presence of all truth. When later studies and life contacts brought me face to face with modern thought problems in relation to the things of the Spirit, I was not afraid in any part of God's world.

Within these four years at Northbranch Academy, came other important life experiences. In the early stages of my peace education came Irene B. Hester's Essay on War, the writing of my first essay on peace, stimulated by Hemmenway's "Daily Remem-brance", a precious book discovered in the Meeting Library, and the first great lecture on peace by Dr. Benjamin F. Trueblood on the European Outlook for War and Peace.

The awakening of lifelong interest in foreign missions came within that period, not directly through H. H. Townsend, but I was in a world in which I could be guided through one more crisis period by his friendship and wisdom toward purposeful and constructive preparation for life work. Forced for financial reasons to teach in the spring term of the third year, it was my teacher friend who strengthened my decision to complete two single term courses while working on the farm that summer, and through his cooperation I was able to finish with my class the next spring.

I do not yet know how much I owe to Henry Townsend for keeping before me through the four years at the academy, and through the following year while teaching, the value and the possibility of attending one of the Friends' Colleges, a dream which then seemed to me almost as distant as a journey to the Holy Land. So far as I can judge, Penn College and all of its meaning for my later life came because Henry H. Townsend was my teacher and my friend.[16]

Frank H. Clark, another Friend whose career was in the administration of Friends academies, started teaching at High Point, North Carolina, where he was the principal of the Colored Industrial School near the end of the nineteenth century. He served as principal of Friends academies in six states. After teaching in North Carolina he served as principal at North Branch, Kansas; Vermilion Grove, Illinois; Whittier Academy at Salem, Iowa; Haviland, Kansas; and Friendswood, Texas. To each of these he brought new life and strength.[17]

Haviland Friends Academy was opened in 1892 with Albert F. Styles as principal. Shortly after, a two-story building which served both the school and the Meeting was erected. The Meeting had, to this time, met in a sod building. The academy, offering the usual elementary and secondary courses, soon dropped the preparative department and followed the usual standardized high school forms, giving diplomas upon graduation, preparing the graduates to enter

---

[16] From a personal letter by Gilbert Bowles, loaned by Gertrude Townsend Kershner, daughter of Henry and Anna Townsend.

[17] Information given by Evelyn Clark, daughter of Frank H. Clark.

college. The continued operation of the academy to its close in 1968
can be almost wholly attributed to the establishing of the Bible Training School (now Friends Bible College), of which it was a department.[18]

Friends Bible College at Haviland, established in 1917, was unique
within the educational organization of Friends, offering both secondary and college level courses. It was established as the Kansas Central
Bible Training School, to which a two-year junior college course was
added. Scott Clark was the principal and the moving spirit in the
beginning of the school. In 1930 the present name was given the
institution. Later a four-year program leading to the Bachelor of Arts
and the Bachelor of Science degrees was provided. The academy was
accredited by the Kansas State Department of Education and the Bible
College by the Accrediting Association of Bible Colleges, of which
it is a member. Besides the formal courses leading to a degree, special
provisions are made for training in Pastoral Studies, Religious Education, and Bible. A Christian Workers Certificate is offered for
"special services" courses.

Friends Bible College offers "a Bible-based philosophy of education" and "each degree candidate is required to complete a minimum
of thirty hours in Bible and Theology." In addition to the emphasis
on Bible study the school states one of its purposes in the following
words:

> It is a primary aim of the faculty to help each student ac-
> cept Christ as his personal Saviour. The student is urged to make
> the Bible the foundation for his philosophy of life. He is en-
> couraged to consecrate his life to Christ for that incoming of the
> Holy Spirit without which fullest service to God is impossible.
> Friends Bible College is concerned that its graduates be
> happy, well-adjusted, a stable element in society, capable construc-
> tive workers, and witnesses to the saving grace of our Lord.[19]

The Friends Bible College carries in its curriculum the usual
college courses in English, mathematics, social science, physical
science, two foreign languages, commercial subjects, home economics,

---

[18] Weston F. Cox, "The Community of Haviland, Kansas," thesis for a seminar in
American Civilization, Wichita State University, 1966, reviews the background of the
community and the development of the Friends Academy and Friends Bible College.
[19] Friends Bible College Bulletin, 1966-1967; p. 17.

industrial arts, Bible, music, and health education. It maintains an athletic program as well as an interschool program in music and speech. It is a continuing example of "guarded" education on the college level.

It has among its alumni many ministers, missionaries, teachers, farmers, and professional people, and has woven a spiritual fiber into the life and work of Kansas Yearly Meeting while contributing to leadership elsewhere among Friends.

Grellet, North Branch, and Haviland are but examples of Friends academies in Kansas whose educational service of nearly a century was crucial to the survival and the development of Quakerism on the Great Plains.

## Oregon and California

There was not the need for academies at the end of the nineteenth century as there had been a few decades earlier. Both Oregon and California Yearly Meetings came into existence in the later period, more than twenty years after Kansas Yearly Meeting and over seventy years after Indiana Yearly Meeting. The place filled by the academies was, by 1890-1900, beginning to be filled by public high schools. The history of Friends on the west coast, though coming somewhat later, overlapped the era, and the concern for the higher courses in education led to the founding of a few academies.

In 1883, after the starting of the first district school at Chehalem (Newberg), the Monthly Meeting appointed a committee, raised funds, erected a building, and, in 1885, opened Pacific Academy with Dr. H. J. Minthorne as principal. His famous nephew, Herbert Hoover, later to become President of the United States, was in the first class. Dr. Elias Jessup, who later helped in the establishing of Whittier College, gave leadership to the drive for funds. As with most other Friends academies, the school included at the beginning some elementary courses but eventually moved to the secondary level entirely. The academy later was changed to college level with the establishing of Pacific College in 1890.[20]

The first catalogue of 1886 stated that the courses required five

---

[20] Ralph K. Beebe, *A Garden of the Lord,* a history of Oregon Yearly Meeting of the Friends church; the Barclay Press, 1968. For statement on Pacific Academy, p. 124-125. For Greenleaf Academy (Idaho), p. 160-162.

years for completion, two of those years to be on the elementary level. The attitude of Friends of the period is reflected in a statement of the school regarding moral standards.

> Since immoral and sinful practices are incompatible with the highest mental and physical development, no one is desired as a student who is not willing to abstain therefrom. . . . [S]ome amusements, while not considered sinful by some, are calculated to distract the minds of students from their studies, they are also strictly excluded from the pastimes or recreations of students while attending the Academy.

These restrictions were very much the same for all academies of Friends.

Friends Polytechnic Institute was started at Salem, Oregon, in 1892 but closed four years later. It was not the first time that Friends gave to their schools names that promised more than the institutions could fulfill at the time. Another school of some influence among Friends, but independent, was Portland Bible Institute, of which Edward Mott was the head for several years.

*Idaho*

With the development of Friends settlements in Idaho and their addition to Oregon Yearly Meeting, Greenleaf Academy was established in 1908. With a class of sixteen, five of them non-Friends, including a Catholic, the school was on its way, at a time when most Friends academies elsewhere were declining. Helping the school at its beginning were Isaac and Carol Beals, also William Brown from Iowa. Edwin McGrew, later prominent in educational circles as president of Pacific and Penn colleges, was on the establishing committee. Emmett Gulley, later president of Pacific College, was a member of the first graduating class. Serving as a teacher of the academy for the longest period of the time was Frank D. Roberts.

Greenleaf Academy, like the three other present-day Friends secondary schools of the West — Barnesville, Scattergood, and Friendsville — is an obvious denial that Friends schools of that level must necessarily close because of competing high schools, though their maintenance may be difficult. Rather than declining, Greenleaf Academy has increased in the number of students and in the addition of buildings and equipment.

## Whittier, in California

The economic conditions of early California settlements explain largely the rough road of Whittier Friends Academy on its way (from 1888 to 1900) to becoming Whittier College. Charles W. Cooper, Whittier historian, writes of the three stages in the development of Whittier Academy, describing them as the "three academies," the first two failing for economic reasons — the first academy of 1888; the second of 1889— and the third, of 1891, which evolved by 1900 as Whittier College. From the beginning the dream-word *college* was used when as yet no college existed.[21]

These "three academies" conducted both primary and secondary schools. John Chawner, who had taught in Bloomingdale Academy in Indiana and in Penn Academy in Iowa, and Dr. William V. Coffin, who had been his pupil at Bloomingdale, Indiana, merit special recognition for their heroic work during the early years. Each had served as principal. Difficult as were those years, the academy gave focus to the new Whittier community and finally gave to California a strong college.

The two Quaker academies on the west coast have made a unique contribution to the administration of the national government. Herbert Hoover was a student in the first class of Pacific Academy at Newberg, Oregon, and Lou Henry, who later became his wife, was a member of the first class in Whittier Academy. After their graduation from Stanford University, they were married and in 1928 Herbert Hoover was elected President of the United States, at which time he was a member of the Friends Meeting at Newberg, Oregon.

In 1890 a training school for Christian workers was started in Whittier; it moved later to Huntington Park. Doctrinal disputes in the Huntington Park Meeting led to a separation of the school with independent status, though it was still under the management of individual Friends. It took a "fundamentalist" position as opposed to what its leaders thought was "modernist" within California Yearly Meeting. Eventually it changed the name of Training School for Christian Workers to Pacific Bible College, now located in Azusa, California.

---

[21] Charles W. Cooper, *Whittier Independent College of California;* the Ward Ritchie Press, 1967; p. 27-38.

*Schools for Negroes*

As late as 1917 the Board of Education of the Five Years Meeting reported that there were six schools for Negroes under the care of Friends.[22] One of these was at High Point, North Carolina, under the care of New York Yearly Meeting, with over a hundred pupils and employing Negro teachers. Thirty-five of the pupils were doing secondary schoolwork. The school had a farm and trades were taught. New England and North Carolina Friends were also assisting with the school. Under Indiana Yearly Meeting, Southland Institute near Helena, Arkansas, had about three hundred fifty pupils, of whom thirty were in the high school department.

Two schools were under Philadelphia Friends, one at Cheney near Philadelphia and one at Christiansburg in Virginia. Two were under Hicksite Friends at Aiken and near Charleston, South Carolina.

The Bureau of Education in the Department of the Interior was quoted by the Five Years Meeting Board of Education as saying that "no religious group has surpassed the Friends, either in financial contribution or personal endeavor for the education of the Negroes." These and other schools for Negroes indicate the way by which Friends have initiated educational work which ultimately passed into other hands.

### FROM ACADEMIES TO COLLEGES

Rufus M. Jones caught well the spirit of the early era of Friends education on the frontier.

> The founders and early Quaker teachers were not preparing their pupils for college; they were preparing them for life, and they were resolved to have the work honestly done. The culture was somewhat plain and severe, but after all it was genuine *culture*. It formed and beautified character, and it fitted well for life and service. The recipients of it did not know a vast number of things, but they knew a few essential things almost perfectly, and they learned to love the things that are excellent.[23]

Now a new day has dawned. The passing of Friends academies

---

[22] Minutes, Five Years Meeting, 1917. See Epilogue for further references to Friends and interracial issues.

[23] Rufus M. Jones, *Later Periods of Quakerism II;* Macmillan and Co., Ltd., London; p. 684.

completed a phase of Quaker corporate life which the closing of their elementary schools had started. The Quaker colony-type settlements were being merged into the community. From this time on non-Friends influences became a significant element as the new inclusive communities were formed. The fellowship of Quaker youth with other young people during the week led to a refashioning of church loyalties. The relationships of children and young people often determined where they went for their church-related life. In the meantime the Friends Meetings in the West had become more like the local churches of other religious bodies.

There was a threefold aspect to the development of Friends education on the college level among Western Friends. This must be seen both in the context of the times in general and in the new development among Friends in particular. The older emphasis on a "guarded education" was reemphasized, but along different lines. Whereas the outward peculiarities of speech and dress had been accented, the purity of the faith now became the main issue.

First of all, the new scholarship, with its challenge to many traditional modes of thought, was disturbing every educational institution, both those of Friends and those of other churches. This tide seemed to threaten the very foundations of faith, and battle lines were drawn, in many cases, between the advocates and the opponents of the "new thought." The battle words *higher criticism* and *evolution* were sounded across the areas where Friends colleges existed and church-college relationships felt the tremors of that impact. Later the deeper search for meanings within statements of faith came, but at the earlier stages the issues were often seen in black and white. The deepening of a well-rooted faith would not come without some measure of disturbance. There were doubtless many Friends whose insights caught the deeper meaning of those turbulent days and helped to steady both church and school.

A second aspect was the development and the final acceptance of the pastoral system. This introduced a new element into the church-college relationship. As indicated in another chapter, the movement which became a "system" started in the 1870's, became generally accepted in the 1880's, and was generally approved in the 1890's by the Yearly Meetings into which it came. By 1900 it definitely affected the policy of Friends colleges.

More definitely affected were the colleges established during the 1890's. These included Friends University, Pacific College, Whittier College, and later, Nebraska Central College. The need for pastoral leadership was a definite concern of Friends and their Meetings during that period. Failure to produce pastoral leadership was considered by many leading Friends as partial failure in the purpose of colleges.

Those two influences accented the third aspect — the respective responsibilities of both church and school in a church-related college. That school and church each carried responsibilities not wholly alike was recognized, but the exact relationship between the two was not clear. To church leaders it appeared that a college *established by* the church should be *responsible to* the church, producing leadership for it. To the educator, concerned for the integrity of free inquiry, no ulterior purpose, however worthy its ideals, should divert the educational method. Education must be education! At the same time Friends educators were deeply concerned for leadership in Friends Meetings, for indeed the colleges suffered in large measure for lack of it. But they believed that education must not be narrowly channeled to any one purpose.

True education, so they felt, must accept hazards. Predetermination as to what kind of person, with his beliefs and attitudes, must come out of the college was in their minds *educational heresy*. To the orthodox churchmen the producing of even one graduate whose faith and attitude were changed to unorthodox positions was a *religious heresy* for which the church college should, in some measure, be held responsible.

For church and school this has been a perennial problem. The tension which this created could lead either to a breaking point or could become a tension of growth in which church and school would find strength, each from the other. In some instances the gap widened between college and church while in others there was a growing understanding which would be to the advantage of both.

### Guilford College
Because the development toward the higher level of education, in the areas with which this chapter is concerned, began in North Carolina it is well to see the birth and the growth of the idea in that area of Friends history from which the chain of Quaker colleges,

established in most Friends Yearly Meetings westward, had their rise.[24]

In North Carolina Friends history there was one Friends school that came to stay! Starting as New Garden Friends Boarding School, chartered in 1833 and opened in 1837, it survived the acid test of the Civil War and emerged in 1889 as Guilford College. It has a long and heroic record. The school became a center that attracted a supporting constituency of Friends who in turn became a solid, concerned community.

It started with the reading of a Friends Query. In the Yearly Meeting sessions of 1830 Jeremiah Hubbard was at the clerk's table, reading answers given by the Monthly Meetings to the Queries. One of these asked " . . . and do those who have children endeavor to train them up in the principles of our religious profession, to reading the Holy Scriptures, and use the necessary restraints for their preservation?"[25]

The answers to that Query troubled these Friends and led to the appointing of a committee. Visiting Friends from other Yearly Meetings were invited to join them — William Evans from Philadelphia, Jonathan Taylor from Ohio, and James Hadley from Indiana. The committee reported that a school was needed and a second and larger committee was named to consider a specific plan. They were now getting under way, and in the sessions of 1831 a subscription of funds was started.

Though the committee gave a broad base to this new institution-to-be, it required two heroic figures in the Yearly Meeting to see it through. Nathan Hunt, whose father, William, was a first cousin of John Woolman, was a patriarch and a commanding personality of the Yearly Meeting. With him was Jeremiah Hubbard, a pioneering educator, whose little red brick schoolhouse was nearby.

Knowing the need for Friends teachers in the schools around them, this committee wisely advised starting a normal school. Meetings were asked to select their strongest prospects for a teaching ministry, persons who might become students in a boarding school. Again we see the basic religious concern contained in one sentence that prefaced the plan for a school:

---

[24] Dorothy Lloyd Gilbert (Thorne), *Guilford, A Quaker College;* private printing, 1937.
[25] *Ibid.,* p. 11.

And we believe that the Christian and literary education of our children consistent with the simplicity of our religious profession [is] of very deep interest if not of paramount importance in supporting the various testimonies that we profess to bear to the world, and even to the very existence and continuance of our Society.[26]

Friends from northern Yearly Meetings responded to their pleas for help, and by 1837 the school was opened. Migrations to the West were well under way at this time, threatening the future of Quakerism in North Carolina. The restraints were powerless to stop the erosion in the Yearly Meeting. That may well have been one incentive for this action in strengthening Quaker leadership.

Friends were united and well seasoned in the wisdom and the faith of their Quaker forebears. Visiting Friends had come from England, Ireland, and areas of the North under a concern of ministry. These visitors were concerned not only over slavery but also over the spiritual life and educational opportunities of Friends.

In the New Garden Meeting, Jeremiah Hubbard's voice must have come like the thunder of doom to the assembled body of Friends in a meeting for worship that was not only silent but was also marked by sleepers: "Sleep in mercy and ye wake in judgment." He was among those who would not let Friends go to sleep on education. His little brick schoolhouse nearby helped to plant the idea that blossomed into New Garden Friends Boarding School.

Dougan and Asenath Clark were appointed as the first superintendents of the school as it opened at New Garden in 1837. The school was the first coeducational institution in the South. This was a witness not only to the educational interest of Friends but also to their testimony on the equality of the sexes. If there were to be Women's Meetings as well as intelligent homemakers there must be education for girls. Though non-Friends schools were beginning during this period in North Carolina, the Friends school carried this distinctive witness. Much of western Quaker history owes a special debt to the center and the school that became Guilford College.

Among the "tall" men of North Carolina Quaker history was Nereus Mendenhall. He came to the New Garden Boarding School well equipped for teaching and for the stellar administrative work he

---

[26] *Ibid.*, p. 14.

did before and through the Civil War. He had the instincts of a scholar, studying because he loved learning. He was educated in three fields: medicine, engineering, and education. He had completed a four years' course in two years in Haverford College, with honors. His life was also related to educational work in the state outside of Friends circles. It was not alone his educational attainments that gave him height and strength. He had the spiritual qualities of love for his work and a heroism that held the school open during the bitter years before and during the Civil War.

When war clouds were gathering and the storm threatened, Nereus Mendenhall packed his goods and sent them to the station for a westward move, as had thousands of other Friends. One might draw a parallel with the experience of Elijah. It was as if he heard the "still small voice" within asking, "What doest thou here, Nereus?" He knew that at this crucial moment he belonged at New Garden Friends School. The goods were returned to his home and he took his place in the history of the Yearly Meeting and the school for the duration.[27] Largely through his valor the school never closed. Associated with him were other Friends, one of whom was Alethea Coffin, mother of Addison. She served as matron. She had earlier gone to Indiana, walking half the way, and returned on horseback in 1833 to New Garden.

English and Philadelphia Friends gave support to the school, both in money and in books. These were in short supply during the war when there were not enough copies of one textbook to supply each student. Nereus Mendenhall could teach without books, important as they were. Lack of writing paper and school tablets led to writing examinations and tests on slates. Perhaps more difficult even than book and paper work was finding food for the school. The war left Friends and their neighbors generally destitute. New Garden Boarding School was one light on the spiritual horizon, a light that had all but been extinguished.

Under the Baltimore Association, formed to aid North Carolina Friends during the reconstruction period, Joseph Moore, a teacher in Earlham College, came to survey, plan, and bring help to Friends, particularly for their educational needs. He travelled over the Yearly

---

[27] *Ibid.,* p. 100, 101.

Meeting, advising, organizing, and securing help for Friends schools which through the war had become almost nonexistent. The record of those few years of reconstruction is impressive. More than forty Friends schools were established by the Baltimore Association, teachers were trained to head them, and buildings were erected or equipped as schoolhouses. Allen Jay of Indiana followed Joseph Moore in the period of reconstruction, helping Meetings as well as schools toward a new stability.[28]

At last the great day came and Guilford College was born in 1889 with Louis Lyndon Hobbs as president. The first name suggested for the institution was King College in honor of Francis T. King of Baltimore, who had headed the reconstruction work under the Baltimore Association. But he declined the honor. The name *Guilford* was then chosen — for the county in which the school was located.

Lyndon Hobbs was succeeded by Thomas Newlin, who had served as dean and as head of the new Bible department, and had also served as president of Pacific College, vice-president of Wilmington (Ohio) College, president of Whittier College, and vice-president and dean of Guilford College. After his resignation in 1917, a small executive committee consisting of Howard H. Brinton, Lyndon Hobbs, and Alma T. Edwards directed the college for one year.

In 1918 Raymond Binford, professor of biology, was appointed president. His purpose is well stated in his own words:

> Since the [First] World War new movements have arisen. The human mind is satiated with analytical facts. It is demanding a new synthesis. It is demanding of the scholar not that he supply new analytical data, but that he put the thing back together and make it work. In response to this demand many efforts at correlation have been made.

In 1934 Raymond Binford resigned after a very significant period in which the core strength of Guilford had been advanced.

Successor in the presidency was Clyde A. Milner. He had come to the college in 1930 and became head of the department of philosophy. When he retired in 1966 after thirty-two years he had been the

---

[28] Stephen B. Weeks, *Southern Quakers and Slavery;* The Johns Hopkins Press, 1896, p. 308-321; describes the work of the Baltimore Association.

fourth president within seventy-eight years—a record of presidential tenure of unusual length among Friends colleges.

As Grimsley Hobbs, fifth president, came to the helm of Guilford College from the Earlham College faculty in 1966, he represented a family line of presidential calibre. His great-grandfather, Nereus Mendenhall, was the first principal of New Garden Friends Boarding School and his grandfather, Lyndon Hobbs, was the first president of Guilford College.

It is appropriate to quote the well-chosen words of Dorothy Gilbert Thorne in the closing paragraphs of her *Guilford: A Quaker College*. Referring to the first century of the college she states that the road is long which leads back to 1837,

> when Victoria ascended the English throne, when a financial panic swept over the United States, when Emerson delivered the address, "The American Scholar," at Cambridge, when Joseph John Gurney travelled in America, New Garden Boarding School first opened. The travelers along this road have been many; yet those who come up the path which leads from New Garden Boarding School in 1837 to Guilford College in 1937 have a steady gait. They walk in faith and in determination. They bring with them the hundreds of children to whom they have taught "whatsoever things were civil and useful in the creation." They believe in peace, equality, freedom — they are Quakers. They are confident that their tradition translates as well today as it did a century ago.[29]

Having traced at some length the unfolding of higher education among Friends in North Carolina, we shall take shorter glimpses of the colleges in the areas farther west.

### Earlham College

Of the schools with which this history of Friends is concerned, New Garden Boarding School in North Carolina was the first on the secondary level among those later to become colleges. The Friends Boarding School at Richmond, Indiana, was opened ten years later. The Civil War greatly disrupted educational progress in the southern states and it was not until 1889 that Guilford College could be chartered. Earlham College, changing to college status thirty years earlier,

---

[29] Gilbert, *op. cit.*, p. 316.

in 1859, thereby became the first college established within the Yearly Meetings of Friends under consideration in this chapter.[30]

There were two main reasons for changing from secondary to college-level work. The need for preparing teachers for secondary schools was evident. If Friends did not train their young people they would be trained in other colleges and perhaps be lost to Friends. Nor did Friends Boarding School want to be simply a preparatory school for colleges run by other churches or by the state. A college was the next logical step in the fulfillment of educational responsibility.

The introduction of this first college among western Friends was not easily made. The words *college* and *degrees* evoked opposition from many Indiana Friends. Degrees were to be granted "without unnecessary form and ceremony." During the change care was required in the choice of words as the college idea was eased into acceptance by Friends. The first degrees were granted in 1862 (referred to earlier as "legal certificates") and Superintendent Barnabas C. Hobbs became president in 1867.

In 1878 it was proposed that Western and Ohio Yearly Meetings join Indiana Yearly Meeting; but Ohio declined, and in 1880 ownership of the school came into the hands of Indiana and Western. Joseph Moore, teacher of natural sciences, studied at Harvard University (1859-1861). During his teaching career and his fifteen years as president, following Barnabas C. Hobbs, the name of Joseph Moore became one revered in Earlham history.

In the administrative succession of Joseph John Mills, Robert L. Kelly, David M. Edwards, William C. Dennis, Thomas E. Jones, and Landrum R. Bolling, Earlham College has deepened and broadened its life and service, becoming a first-rate college of liberal arts, church-related without undue control by the church. That course has not been easy, as questions on student regulations and academic freedom in the realm of political, economic, and racial issues have been faced with resulting tensions. In the main these have been tensions of growth, giving the college its particular identity as a Friends institution.

During the past two decades under the administration of Thomas E. Jones and Landrum R. Bolling new buildings, modern equipment,

---

[30] Opal Thornburg, *Earlham, The Story of the College,* Earlham College Press, 1963.

development of an extension program with the University of Indiana, research projects, practical programs for training of industrial personnel of the area, and foreign study programs have made a new dimension in the service of the college.

The spirit of Earlham is well summarized in the words of President Landrum Bolling:

> Every responsible college or university, must warn its students that they are engaged in dangerous pursuits, that those pursuits may upset them, that old ideas may tumble into the dust before their eyes, and that the new idea may prove unsound as well. They must be helped to see that it is the process of searching, the skill in searching, the commitment to searching which are at the center of the educational adventure. And they must be helped to discover that it is only by coming to know the truth that men can be made free.[31]

## Wilmington College

A major reason for the setting off of Wilmington Yearly Meeting from Indiana Yearly Meeting (1892) was Wilmington College, which had been established twenty-one years earlier.

In 1870 Friends of the area had purchased the unfinished structure of what had started as Franklin College under the Christian Church. In 1871 it was dedicated and opened as Wilmington College. Indiana Friends then had two colleges, with Indiana and Western Yearly Meetings sharing in Earlham College. The interest of Friends in the Wilmington area naturally turned toward the college in their midst. It would be difficult for Indiana Yearly Meeting to hold equal interest in two colleges, and the concern of Indiana Friends was turning toward Earlham. Shortly after being set off, Wilmington Yearly Meeting took over major control of the college bearing its name.

As in other Friends colleges of the western areas, the concern for religious leadership was an important motive. John Henry Douglas, a leading evangelical Friend of the period, helped in the raising of funds. Jonathan Bailey, who later played a prominent part in the development of Whittier College in California, was a leading supporter.

As was the case with other Friends colleges, the secondary-level courses constituted the main courses of the college at the beginning.

---

[31] *Ibid.*, from **Bolling** inaugural address, p. 406.

But a few years later these were dropped and the higher-level studies, expanded and strengthened, led to the four years' liberal arts program. Oscar Boyd, long associated with the college as teacher and dean, indicates four phases in its development. The first phase emphasized the classical studies; the second, the development of the sciences; the third phase accented teacher training. The fourth phase, as viewed a few years later, gave the college a balanced curriculum of liberal arts and a life-integrated program. Under the presidency of S. Arthur Watson the college was accredited by the North Central Association of Schools and Colleges. The foundation and the scope of the college were strengthened and the way was opened for the creative years following.[32]

During the administration of Samuel Marble an integrated program of work-study was introduced and the college moved into a creative period in which higher learning and daily labor were linked in a common educational experience. With the cooperation of an industrial firm a "split-shift system" was developed which aided the student financially, but which was primarily aimed at his understanding of the business world. The program also offered to industry a measure of understanding of the purposes of the college and the direction in which higher education was moving. Mind and hand were united in a common corporate experience of the students simultaneously with a new world outlook.

What began during that period has been expanded in the present period of Wilmington College whereby responsibility in national and world affairs has been awakened in a life-integrating program of education.

James Read brought to the presidency important experience on the level of the United Nations programs. This experience is reflected in the expanding vision of responsible Quaker education. The development of Peace Corps training is but one expression of this concern. The farm owned by the college offers opportunity for an agricultural-educational integration, but it also offers an opportunity for training in Peace Corps work.

---

[32] As president of three Friends colleges (Wilmington, Friends University, and William Penn), Arthur Watson helped each of the colleges to achieve accreditation under the North Central Association.
Oscar F. Boyd, "The History of Wilmington College"; typed.

*William Penn College*[33]

In 1860 Iowa Yearly Meeting Boarding School was started beside the Spring Creek meetinghouse two or three miles northeast of Oskaloosa. In 1863 the building burned and Iowa Yearly Meeting appointed a large committee (in 1866) to review the "educational wants of the members." In 1867 the Iowa Union College Association of Friends was formed.

Meanwhile Thorndyke Institute, directly north of Oskaloosa, had been started by Henry and Anna Thorndyke, prominent Friends of New England.

The two schools were merged in the new plan and a site bordering Oskaloosa on the north was chosen. In 1871 a building was started and in the fall of 1872 the new school was opened. During the year the name was approved and Penn College opened in the fall of 1873 with John W. Woody as president. Friends of Philadelphia generously supported the new venture for several years following.

The course of Penn College has not been smooth, chiefly because of financial difficulties. After accumulating an endowment, substantial for that time, the college lost most of it in failure to face economic realities and to adjust accordingly. There was a succession of short-term administrations during which a holding operation was essentially the policy. The great depression of the early 1930's and the coming of the Second World War brought it near to failure.

A period of experimentation was followed somewhat later by an upturn in the progress of the college. When S. Arthur Watson, who had been president of Wilmington College and Friends University, came to the presidency the lost accreditation by the North Central Association of Schools and Colleges was regained. He had accomplished accreditation in all three colleges of which he had been president. New buildings were erected, faculty and library were strengthened, and an increased attendance gave the college a new beginning.

What was started during his administration was continued as Duane Moon became president. The increased enrollment, the erection of new buildings, and the continued strengthening of the faculty have placed the institution on a level hardly conceivable a few decades earlier.

[33] Louis T. Jones, *op. cit.*, p. 247-250.

The present state of the college would not be possible but for the loyal support of Friends of Iowa Yearly Meeting, the alumni, and the Oskaloosa community when only faith, evoking loyalty and sacrifice of a high order, kept the doors of the college open. As a policy of reconstruction and recovery was adopted, the name was changed to William Penn College.

Some of the same problems which have marked the life of all Friends colleges have been faced, particularly in its church-related experiences. On the whole there has been through the years a strong church influence without undue church control in the policies of the college. William Penn College has taken on a new stature among Friends institutions.[34]

*Friends University*

In the history of Friends University a larger history of Friends and their experiences in the booming era on the Great Plains is revealed. The college was born during a turbulent era of expansion with inflation followed by panic, deflation, and recovery. It was a time of great dreams and of plans that often grew beyond reality, but out of the times a stable college came.[35]

In their plans for education, Kansas Friends reflected the boom years on the Great Plains frontier. Wichita heralded herself as "The Peerless Princess of the Plains," and also added to her prospective glory the title, "The Athens of the West." At this period there were, at one time, nine colleges under plan or being constructed in Wichita. Methodists, Baptists, Presbyterians, Lutherans, Congregationalists, Disciples, and Catholics — all had planned colleges and some had started buildings that were never completed. The Congregationalists succeeded in establishing a college that was later to become Wichita University.

Most of these plans for colleges were made during the 1880's and collapsed in the 1890's. Among these was that of some Friends who, independent of Kansas Yearly Meeting, organized in 1887 and made plans for John Bright University. Land was acquired, foundations were laid, and the first story was being built when the con-

---

[34] At this writing a history of William Penn College is being prepared by S. Arthur Watson.

[35] Juliet Reeve, *Friends University, the Growth of an Idea;* Wichita Eagle Press, 1948.

struction stopped, because of lack of funds, and was never finished. But that was not the end of the Quaker dream. It would finally be realized through unforeseen circumstances.

The Christian Church (Disciples) near the end of the century and in memory of the martyred President, had erected Garfield University not far from the site of John Bright University. Its doors were opened with great promise in an unfinished building flanked by two dormitories. By 1893 its doors were closed and the property was offered for sale. In the meantime Kansas Yearly Meeting had seriously discussed the establishment of a college. At this juncture James M. Davis, a wealthy Quaker businessman and alumnus of Penn College, saw in the property and in the concern of Kansas Yearly Meeting what he felt was an opportunity for Friends on both local and national levels. He was a great-grandson of Nathan Hunt, who had helped to establish Guilford College. Whether the Guilford stories about college beginnings in North Carolina stirred his imagination we cannot know. He purchased the Garfield buildings and offered them to Friends.

Despite the objections of Kansas Yearly Meeting and of Friends of the Philadelphia area he insisted that the new institution should be called Friends University, with the hope that it might move beyond college status to become a school worthy of the greater name. It has never fulfilled that part of his ambition. It is today a college of liberal arts. The terms by which it was given to Friends will not allow the changing of the name.

In the meantime Iowa Yearly Meeting and Penn College had invited Kansas Yearly Meeting to share in joint responsibility for the college at Oskaloosa. For a short while Kansas Friends were named to the Penn College board, but the hope of Iowa Friends for a united control did not develop.

Kansas Yearly Meeting accepted the gift from James M. Davis and in 1898 Friends University opened with fifty-three students, only twelve of college level, the others being in the preparatory (secondary) school. These few were in a building large enough to accommodate at least 1,700, the number that had been enrolled at one time in Garfield University. On the broad plains the giant structure of five stories with Gothic towers loomed against the prairie sky. It was said by the local newspaper to be the largest college building under one roof in the United States at that time.

Edmund Stanley, the first president, had attended a Friends academy near Lafayette, Indiana, and had taught a freedman's school at Carthage, Tennessee. When the Ku Klux Klan warned him to leave he refused, and the school was burned. Learning that armed men were guarding him, he left, not approving of armed protection. In 1894 he had been elected Superintendent of Public Instruction for the State of Kansas. He and two of his successors in the presidency of Friends University, W. O. Mendenhall and David M. Edwards, were graduates of Penn College. Under the administration of W. O. Mendenhall the school moved into the ongoing program of a good Friends college. David M. Edwards and W. A. Young sustained that level in their administrations. Under S. Arthur Watson accreditation of the college was regained. Under presidents Lloyd Cressman, Lowell Roberts, and Roy Ray new advances were made, studies in purpose and policy evaluations were reviewed, and a future course was determined.

Though the school never became a university it became a college worthy of the name. Increased enrollment, new buildings, added endowment, and accreditation in the North Central Association of Schools and Colleges has made it a firm institution.

*George Fox College*

Pacific Academy, established at Newberg, Oregon, in 1885, became Pacific College six years later with Thomas Newlin as the first president.[36] The purpose that inspired the academy continued in the college. This was stated in the first catalogue of 1891.

> It is the aim of the college to offer to young men and women the benefits of a liberal Christian education. Its courses of study are arranged to give that broad culture which should be the possession of every intelligent man and woman. The founders recognize the great importance of religious training and the work of the class room is not merely consistent with Christianity, but decidedly Christian in its character. It is the fond hope of the management that Pacific College shall send out many Christian teachers, ministers and missionaries.

That hope has been fulfilled very substantially.

---

[36] Beebe, *op. cit.*, p. 125-162.
Elizabeth H. Emerson, *Walter C. Woodward, Friend on the Frontier;* private printing, 1952; p. 51-83, a personal experience of the earlier days of the college.
*Remembering Seventy-five Years;* an anniversary brochure.

The main problem that came to Pacific College as a church-owned institution was due not only to the influences indicated above, affecting all colleges, but also the parallel tensions that developed between Oregon Yearly Meeting and the Five Years Meeting regarding questions of faith and practice. The details of that period cannot be given here. The questions that were raised between the Yearly Meeting and the college were, in the main, of the same kind as those appearing between the Yearly Meeting and the Five Years Meeting. Unlike some other Friends colleges which, during similar times of tension, moved further from the Yearly Meeting to which they were related, Pacific College came further under the guidance of the Yearly Meeting and a period of harmony followed the coalescing of interests.

The college had early been committed to the orthodox position. In 1897 the board of managers "resolved, that no teaching, either by teacher or text book, should be permitted in Pacific College that in anyway discredits the authenticity of any portion of the Bible . . . that in all Bible teaching its truth is to be admitted without question." In 1910 the "inspiration of the Holy Scriptures" was reaffirmed with the addition that the "teaching and work shall be in harmony with that of the great body of the Friends Church in America, as exemplified in Penn and Earlham Colleges and others in like standing." In 1920 the policy stated that "instruction and standards of Pacific College shall be in harmony with the Gospel of Jesus Christ, as held by Friends and as set forth in the Richmond Declaration of Faith."

Confusion, due to the name *Pacific* being used by other institutions on the coast, led to changing of the name to George Fox College. A statement of faith, following the lines indicated above, is included in a present-day catalogue of the college. The purpose of the college includes the belief

> that the future of civilization rests in the minds and hearts of serious youth, motivated by their Christian faith . . . highly educated to meet the challenges of our changing society. George Fox College is founded on the tenet that only through Christianity can solutions be found to the problems of our complex world . . . humanitarian service and evangelism are upheld as worthy ideals, not only in the so-called professional church vocations, but in every calling.

Though the position held by George Fox College was not wholly unique among Friends educational institutions, it has been particularly characterized by the attempt to link the evangelical faith with higher education. The resulting tensions between church and college have, at times, run deep.

It was during this very exacting period that Levi T. Pennington came to the presidency of the college. His was the longest tenure (1911-1941) in the college's history. During his thirty years of administration the strain was great, but despite the difficulties considerable endowment was raised, the curriculum was standardized and strengthened, and the basic structure of the college was laid. Tribute to his life of over ninety years, one-third of which was given to the college, has been marked outwardly by a beautiful hall, dedicated to Levi T. and Rebecca Pennington.

In some respects difficulties were greater under the administration of Emmett Gulley, who succeeded Levi Pennington as president. These two administrations represented heroic service whose benefits would be later realized.

The presidency of Milo C. Ross has helped to fulfill the troubled dream that lay at the heart of the history of the college. A coalescing of Yearly Meeting and college interests has taken place. Milo Ross came to his administrative work from successful years as a minister in Oregon Yearly Meeting and as a church extension leader. Financial support for the school has been substantial, the student enrollment has been greatly increased, and the facing of new problems in a new era is evident.

An excerpt from the report of the president in 1965 brings a fresh focus and insight.

> The issues assail the conservative Christian college in daily temptations as the church exerts dominance . . . the number of youth desiring an education increases by the year . . . . The moral obligation to provide the best for our youth weighs heavily upon us, and the exploding world of knowledge leaves a mandate that is irresistible.

### Whittier College

Like a chain of islands, Quaker centers now lie across America. Nearly all of them are clustered around a school or a college. As in an archipelago, their educational institutions are connected beneath the surface like several island-peaks of one mountain range, and though different in their visible forms they rise out of the same spiritual heritage.

The last of the colleges established in the nineteenth century was Whittier.[37] Even before the concern for a Yearly Meeting arose, the plans for a Quaker college were made by Friends who promoted the establishment of the Quaker colony. As in other Friends schools, the term *college* was used prematurely, representing a hope later to be fulfilled. In 1891 a third attempt at establishing an academy succeeded, resulting in the beginning of Whittier as a college in 1900 with Charles E. Tebbetts as the first president. Chief credit for the success of the third attempt must be given to the organizing genius of Dr. William V. Coffin and the business insight of Washington Hadley, whose services spanned the years of the academy and the beginnings of the college.

Thomas Newlin, who had been president of Pacific College, became the second president of Whittier. Replying to charges of unorthodoxy he stated in his annual report:

> Education is the real work of the church . . . this includes evangelism and missionary work. . . . In college our students are taught and encouraged to analyze, compare, and dissect . . . animals, plants, rocks, theorems, philosophy, literature and creeds. . . . And the ultimate vindication of truth must rest on the findings of the human heart and mind in one's own experience. . . .

The direction of the college seems to have been set for that period and for the future.

A new stage for Whittier was introduced in the 1920's by Walter Dexter, president, and Hershel Coffin, dean. They developed "the Whittier Idea" in which the college would be "functional," integrating the student's life with his courses. The perspective, lost in specialization, must someway be restored in the college curriculum. This effort set the college on an important course, difficult if not impossible to achieve, but one which would not be fully abandoned. As late as 1946 the "Principles of Organization" sought to "organize the curriculum around the college objectives instead of around more conventional

---

[37] Charles W. Cooper, *op. cit.;* the complete history of the college.

departmental goals . . . *to break down the traditional departmental lines* within the fields of knowledge." That idea haunts the minds of many educators everywhere and is reflected in the programs of some other Friends colleges.

An important service was added with the merging of the Broadoaks Kindergarten Training School at Pasadena — a center for laboratory child research and teacher training.

Tension between the college and the community over certain social issues developed, particularly during the two world wars. At this point the trend among Friends regarding their testimonies is illustrated in a way by no means peculiar to Whittier. Under the pressure to cooperate with the war effort some faculty members resigned along with W. O. Mendenhall, the president. Despite the peculiar pressures of wartime the college has retained an interest in the area of peacemaking through conferences and courses offered. In the face of anticommunist hysteria the college has held to a constructive approach to international tensions. The Copenhagen Campus, in Denmark, is one dimension of international responsibility maintained by Whittier College.

As in all Friends colleges, there are alumni who have become distinguished in their respective fields. The most widely known of Whittier graduates is Richard M. Nixon, a member of East Whittier Friends Meeting, who has experienced a succession of political responsibilities. He was elected to Congress, to the Senate, and to the Vice-Presidency, and, in 1969, became the thirty-seventh President of the United States.

Paul Smith was the first president of the college from the faculty ranks. His administration has helped to bring Whittier College to the fulfillment of its role as a Quaker-community type of school, though it is an independent institution. It has become a high-level college within the educational life of southern California. Overlooking the Pacific Ocean, the college carries a broad dimension of concern in keeping with its Quaker heritage.

### Malone College

The latest of the Friends colleges to be established in the Midwest was Malone College, under Ohio Yearly Meeting, at Canton, Ohio. The evolving of the college from the Friends Bible Institute and Training School at Cleveland, established in 1892, is indicated earlier.[38]

After the turn of the twentieth century Ohio Yearly Meeting became concerned to establish a college, quite apart from the then-existing schools — Raisin Valley Seminary, Damascus Academy, and the Friends Bible Training School. A strong board of trustees was appointed and subscriptions started toward buying a property. Feeling the financial weight of their existing schools, the project was abandoned until the Bible Training School of Cleveland was forced to sell its property and move because of a new highway under construction.[39]

The story of that move with its seeming miracles is quite exciting, but too long to relate here. Byron L. Osborn, principal of the Training School at that time, carried the exacting responsibilities whereby the school came to Canton, Ohio, and was chartered and opened as Malone College in 1957. Byron Osborn continued as its first president from 1957 to 1960, when he retired from active work in the Yearly Meeting.

In 1960 Everett L. Cattell became president. He had carried executive responsibility for the mission work in India for twenty years, and had been for much of that time a member of executive bodies in the ecumenical levels of Christian missions in that country. As a missionary statesman, he was by no means unfamiliar with administrative responsibilities as he came to the presidency of Malone College.

The college, at this writing, has observed the seventy-fifth anniversary of its beginning in 1892. Ohio Yearly Meeting at last has a liberal arts college, accredited by the North Central Association of Schools and Colleges, with a student body of 1,200 — including Catholics, Jews and a wide range of Protestants and others — and a full-time faculty of forty-three. In addition there are ten assistants, and a number of visiting lecturers are brought in annually. This represents a remarkable growth in its brief history.

The college catalogue of 1967-68 defines its character and purpose as a liberal arts college, offering

---

[38] Walter R. Williams, *The Rich Heritage of Quakerism;* William B. Eerdmans Publishing Co., 1962, p. 227, 228.
[39] *Quaker Sesqui-Centennial,* 1962.

> an informed and disciplined reflection in the major areas of man's learning . . . functions of the mind, such as judgment, analytical and problem-solving thinking, understanding of human behavior . . . and the means to make learning a life-long process . . . and the arts of communication.
>
> Malone is Christian in its commitment and, at the same time endeavors to be completely fair to students who may not share this conviction . . . Bible courses are required . . . the faculty is held responsible for a fair and full presentation of the range of possible interpretations . . . lecturers are invited to campus representing many persuasions, religious and political, with which students should be acquainted. . . .

The Yearly Meeting is giving excellent support to the college as a new day dawns for Ohio Yearly Meeting. The Yearly Meeting has turned from isolation in relation to other Friends bodies. Evidence of this is the part which Ohio plays in the development of the Evangelical Friends Alliance (to be considered later) and in the appointment of official representation to the Friends World Conference in 1967.

### Adult Education

In the development of Friends educational ventures there has emerged a fourth stage directed, in the main, to post-college studies. These have taken different forms. In some cases, both in England and in America, summer schools for adults have been held. Centers have also been developed with permanent, year-around, administrative staffs and with lectures on various aspects of Quaker life and thought. Woodbrooke in England and Pendle Hill near Philadelphia have become important centers to which Friends and others from various countries have come to lecture or to study. These institutions neither require degrees for enrollment nor give any for courses taken. They serve as an integrative influence for the Society of Friends on both national and world levels.

Quaker educational institutions of the West are greatly indebted to those of the East, from which the initial incentives came and under whose cooperation and training Quaker teachers and administrators were supplied.

## Graduate Level Training
*The Earlham School of Religion*

In this fourth stage of Friends educational development the Earlham School of Religion was founded in 1960 at Richmond, Indiana, under a board of advisers drawn from nearly all Yearly Meetings of Friends in America.

From the beginning of Friends secondary schools and colleges in the pastoral area there has been a concern for the training of ministers. The colleges have responded with courses or with departments of religion or Bible.

The Earlham School of Religion, developed on the graduate (seminary) level, has recognized the wide scope of pastoral needs, both for the established work of the pastoral Meetings and for new ministries by which the church seeks to penetrate and serve the community. Under Wilmer A. Cooper as the first dean of the Earlham School of Religion an expanding interest has developed, considerable financial support has been secured, and the enrollment has grown. There is an assurance of a new, varied, and extended service by the school. The purpose and program may be summarized from its own statements.

> The Earlham School of Religion is a Quaker graduate school for the education and training of men and women for the Christian ministry. It is the first such school on the seminary level to be established by Friends in their 300 year history. It began in 1960 within the administrative framework of Earlham College. As it develops its own identity and grows in strength it is becoming increasingly independent with a separate faculty, and administrative and financial structure. Its objective is to serve the leadership needs of Friends as well as students of other persuasions who are drawn to the school by the character of its program.

> The School of Religion is without apology a Friends (Quaker) graduate school. This means that it is grounded in the religious experience of Biblical religion and Christian faith. Its approach is not narrow, sectarian or creedal, but it is clearly committed to the historic Quaker emphasis upon the oneness of the Jesus of history and the Christ within. We hold that Christ is present, that he guides and directs, and that his will can be known and obeyed.

> At the same time Quakers emphasize a community of faith

in which every member is a responsible and participating member. This is both a worshipping and [a] caring fellowship of those committed to one another in Christ; it is also a witnessing fellowship of mission and service to others.

The School of Religion offers a program of academic and field study leading to either of two degrees: the Bachelor of Divinity or Master of Arts in Religion. The three-year B. D. program is designed for students preparing for pastoral ministry, including preparation in preaching, pastoral counseling, religious education, group work, and community service. The M. A. program prepares students for a variety of non-pastoral ministries: teaching religion, directing retreat-renewal centers, industrial and campus ministry, international service, and secretaries of Friends Meetings.[40]

Closely associated with Wilmer A. Cooper in the initial stages of development were Landrum R. Bolling, D. Elton Trueblood, and Thomas E. Jones. Alexander C. Purdy, who had recently retired as Dean and Hosmer Professor of New Testament at Hartford Theological Seminary, shared his counsel from his years of important experience and for five years served as professor of New Testament in the Earlham School of Religion.

At last Friends have a graduate school offering the equivalent of a theological seminary, but seeking to retain and enhance the values and spirit of the Quaker movement. It attempts to be alive to our present-day world and to be creative in the preparation of a ministry to meet the needs.

As the second decade opens, the administration is alert to the rapid changes taking place and is ready to adjust to new elements in educational structures and to new needs of the church and of the community.

---

[40] Brochure by the Earlham School of Religion.

# Chapter 10

## QUAKERS AND INDIANS

The record of friendly relations between Quakers and Indians is a classic within American history. It glows against a dark background of white aggrandizement, fraud, and violence by which the Indians were deprived of their homes and hunting grounds and were pushed back, year by year, into the uncoveted badlands of the continent. It is remarkable that despite the invading despoilers the Indians were relatively peaceful. Their response to the goodwill of the Quakers and their friends of other religious bodies belies their reputation of being basically warlike. When they were hostile it was probably because of fear and for self-defense.

Friends first arrived in the New World in 1656,[1] and in 1682, the same year that Penn arrived in America, George Fox wrote

An Epistle to all Planters, and Such Who are Transplanting Themselves into Foreign Plantations in America. . . . And into

[1] Rayner W. Kelsey, *Friends and the Indians, 1655-1917;* New Era Printing Co., 1917; p. 22. This volume by Kelsey is the main source of information presented in this chapter.

all places where you do outwardly live and settle, invite all the
Indians and their Kings, and have Meetings with them. . . .

Best known of the Quaker-Indian relations is that of William
Penn and early Pennsylvania. Penn came to the New World as a
convinced Quaker. His statesmanship and peace policy were rooted
in the Quaker traditions. One year before his advent in the province
he wrote to the Indians with whom he would later be associated.

> My Friends: There is a great God and power that hath made
> the world and all things therein, to whom you and I and all
> people owe their being and well-being, to whom you and I must
> one day give an account for all that we do in the world. This
> great God hath written his law in our hearts, by which we are
> commanded to live and help and do good to one another.[2]

In 1682 Penn arrived and in the following years purchased land
from the Indians "creek by creek." Three years later he wrote that
he had made "seven purchases from the Indians and in pay and
presents" had paid them "at least twelve hundred pounds."

In 1683 the famous treaty of Shackamaxon was written in a meeting of Penn with the Indians. "This," says Voltaire, "was the only
treaty between these people and the Christians, that was not ratified
by an oath, and that was never broken." Of this treaty Penn wrote,
"When the Purchase was agreed, great Promises passed between us,
of Kindness and good Neighborhood and that the Indians and English
must live in Love as long as the Sun gave Light." The Indians replied
that "many Governors had been in the River, but that no Governor
had come himself to live and stay here before; and now having such
an one that had treated them well, they should never do him or his
any wrong."[3]

From that time onward the Indians of many tribes requested
Friends to be present when treaties were made with their white
neighbors or with the government. They had learned by sad experiences how treaties were written to deprive them of their rights and
how readily white men broke their promises. The Quakers could not
forestall all misfortunes that came upon the Indians but they could be
"a friend in court" in dealing with the government.

---

[2] *Ibid.*, p. 24, 25.
[3] *Ibid.*, p. 63.

A century after Penn's "holy experiment" a message was sent from a confederation of chiefs in 1793 "to the Commissioners of the United States" reviewing the grievances of the Indians and including what was to the Indians a basic issue, that "the king of England never did, nor ever had any right to give you our country . . . we have never made any agreement with the king, nor with any other nation. . . . We consider ourselves free to make any bargain or cession of lands whenever and to whomever we please."

So long as William Penn was in control, and his peace policy was in effect, good relations with the Indians of Pennsylvania were maintained. By 1756 the Scots and the Irish who had settled in the area became impatient of Penn's peace policy. Officials of the colonial government changed and non-Friends were elected to the Assembly. William Penn's sons defected from the Quaker faith, and the stage was set for a bloody conflict.

When war broke between the French and the English the Indians aligned themselves with the French. In 1756 the Governor and the Council of Pennsylvania declared war on the Indians and offered bounties for Indian scalps (sic!). This complete reversal of policy led Friends to resign from official positions rather than to be identified with war. The peace policy which had lasted for seventy-five years had come to an end.

That the change in policy, followed by years of bitter warfare, did not alienate the Indians from the Quakers is shown in a message from the Indians following a visit by two Friends in 1773.

> We think that as we two brothers, the Quakers and the Dela-wares, were brought up together as the children of one man, it is our Saviour's will we should be of one religion. . . . Now you have come and opened the road. . . . We are poor and weak, and not able to judge for ourselves, and when we think of our poor children it makes us sorry; we hope you will instruct us in the right way, both in things of this life as well as the world to come.[4]

In one sense the "holy experiment" of Penn had failed. But as seen on the larger stage of history it was the only policy that could succeed, and its light would never go out!

---

[4] *Ibid.*, p. 33, 34.

From the Quaker view all war was wrong, and war against the Indians was especially reprehensible. But would violence *in defense* of innocent Indians be justified? In one instance, at least, a distinction was made. Some frontiersmen, incensed over Indian raids, had murdered a small Indian group and then started toward Philadelphia to attack some Christian Moravian Indians. To some young warm-blooded Friends this presented a peculiar test of their peace principles. Should they remain aloof or take up weapons in defense of this Indian group? This led some of them to join the militia. Though the belligerent frontiersmen were turned back by persuasion, the defection from the Quaker peace stand was obvious, and this did not pass without serious examination by the Monthly Meeting of Friends. The issue was on the borderline between a police type of action and war itself. Whatever moral predicament it may have presented, the basic concern of Friends was not changed.[5]

Beneath all testimonies of Friends was belief in the essential oneness of humanity under one God. This was a stubborn root that would not give way, and its main expression was in the Quaker peace witness. This peace principle could not stand as a dogma, adequate for every exigency that might arise, but it could and did hold firmly as a way of life. Being creative and unyielding, it kept Friends prepared for opportunities to demonstrate the way of peace in crucial moments of history.

The quintessence of this Quaker spirit is to be seen in John Woolman, perhaps more than in any other Friend. When the colonies and the Indians were at war he penetrated the frontier to visit the Indians. In his journal he recorded his spiritual preparation for that journey:

> Love was the first motion and thence a concern arose to spend some time with the Indians, that I might feel and understand their life and the spirit they live in, if haply I might receive some instruction from them, or they be in any degree helped forward by my following the leadings of truth among them.[6]

In that spirit he visited and spoke to them. It is hardly surprising

---

[5] Rufus M. Jones, *The Quakers in the American Colonies;* Macmillan and Co., Ltd., 1923; p. 506, 507.
[6] *Ibid.,* p. 405.

that following a meeting with them an Indian was heard to say of Woolman's conversation, "I love to feel where words come from."

In the early period Friends visited the Indians under *individual* concern. Other Christian denominations preceded Friends in their *corporate* "missions" to the Indians. Catholics, Congregationalists, and Moravians had gone preaching the Gospel. Friends early had expressed doubts about the success of preaching. William Savery wrote in 1794 about his doubt on "what influence it has had on their manners and morals. . . . They have heard of Jesus Christ through their missionary, and have been taught to sing psalms and hymns in their own soft, engaging language," but he feared it was "in word only." Friends too had preached, but they soon sensed the need for practical service. It was not until the midnineteenth century that individual concerns moved toward corporate action of a practical mission type.[7]

It is not possible to record here the entire range of Quaker services with Indians, but these are largely exemplified in their work, mainly with the Shawnees in the Midwest during the nineteenth century.

Before going into the history of this service with the Shawnees it is well to take a closer view of Indian habits of thought and life. Theodore Hetzel, authority on Quaker-Indian history, depicts the sense of oneness which the Indian felt with the earth. The world of nature was an essential part of his life. He communed with it and through it held a mystical relationship with the Great Spirit.

> Indians did live in a remarkably harmonious relationship with nature, so it may be worth our while to consider what they may be able to teach us. We may help them to a higher standard of living and to a longer life expectancy, while they may help us to "learn at last to shape a civilization in harmony with the earth." Indians have learned a respect for nature — a sense of awe, wonder, joy and reverence that we should emulate.[8]

For the so-called civilization of our time the Indian offers a lesson and, to those of insight, suggests a warning — the earth does not belong simply to man, but man also belongs to the earth! He must learn the laws by which the earth and its resources were created and are sustained. Only then can man be sure that it will

[7] Kelsey, *op. cit.,* p. 36.
[8] Theodore Hetzel, "We Can Learn from the American Indians"; reprint from the *Friends Journal,* Jan. 15, 1963.

sustain him and his race in the centuries ahead. Hetzel quotes Joseph Wood Krutch: "The thing which is missing is love, some feeling for, as well as understanding of, the inclusive community of rocks and soils, plants and animals, of which we are a part."[9] Not having discovered this, man despoils the earth, erodes it, devastates its resources, and cuts across the longer cycle of life by which one generation serves those that follow.

It requires little imagination for us to see the difficulties that came when two cultures, so diverse in background and social habits, met each other, one of them holding power over the other. The Indian world with its natural life and its hunting economy knew nothing of the world presented in the conquest by the whites. The Indians knew of no written treaties, only oral agreements which must be mutually trusted in order that they might live. They had developed habits of honesty with one another, shown especially in their ways of hunting and trapping. If an Indian found an animal in a trap not his own, he hung the prey on a tree or bush nearby and reset the trap for his neighbor. The Indians of far northeastern Canada, those of Alaska in the far Northwest, and the Shawnees of midland America held this practice of honesty and good sportsmanship in common.

Those are but a few of the aspects of Indian life that help one to understand the nature of the intercultural impact within which Quakers tried to serve. Friends were a go-between when understanding was needed, and they stood in defense of the weaker side when white and Indian interests clashed.

In one instance the Indians had invited Friends to attend a treaty meeting with representatives of the United States government. It was well attended by both whites and Indians. Having been influenced by the mission work of non-Friends churches the Indians on that occasion wanted to start the meeting with the singing of hymns, an experience unfamiliar to Friends. The Quaker representatives acceded to their wish. Of this experience William Savery wrote:

" . . . they appeared very devout, and I thought that the melody and softness of their voices in the Indian language, and the sweetness and harmony that attended, exceeded by far anything of the

---

[9] *Ibid.*, same page.

kind I have ever heard among the white people. Being in the midst of the woods, the satisfaction of hearing these poor, un-tutored people sing with every appearance of devotion their Mak-er's praise, and the serious attention they paid to what was de-livered to them, conspired to make it a solemn meeting, long to be remembered by me.[10]

In 1794 a war between the United States government and certain tribes of Indians ended and a treaty was signed at Greenville, in Ohio Territory, the following year. Friends of Philadelphia, distressed with bloodshed and feeling a deep sympathy for the Indians, sent a letter of friendship together with some presents as symbols of friendship. General Anthony Wayne, representing the government at this treaty meeting, read the letter and addressed the Indians.

> Younger Brothers — I have received a letter from your friends, the people called Quakers, with a message to all the nations [tribes] here assembled. The Quakers are a people whom I much love and esteem for their goodness of heart and sincere love of peace with all nations. Listen then to their voices, and let them sink deep into your hearts. . . . [T]heir present, you see is small, but being designed with the benevolent view of promoting the happiness and peace of mankind, it becomes of important value. They wish it to be considered merely as a token of regard for you, and a testimony of their brotherly affection and kind remem-brance of you.[11]

Whether General Wayne misused the Quaker message and pres-ents to ease the way for a treaty favoring the United States, we perhaps cannot know. At any rate, the Indians knew by the presents and the message that the trusted Quakers remembered them.

In this treaty the boundaries of the Indian reservation were care-fully described. It was provided that they could sell to no one except the United States government. That provision was intended to fore-stall sharp-practicing white frontiersmen from making fraudulent ar-rangements with the Indians. It thereby kept future Indian land deals in government hands.

---

[10] Kelsey, *op. cit.,* p. 34, 35.

[11] Henry Harvey, *History of the Shawnee Indians;* Ephraim Morgan and Sons, Cincinnati, Ohio, 1855; p. 119. For more information on Friends and Indians in the Ohio-Indiana area see Harvey.

## THE MIDWEST STORY

The Friends of Baltimore had become concerned for Indians of this area as early as 1795. A farm was opened by Friends on the Wabash River southwest of present-day Fort Wayne (Indiana) in the early 1800's. By example and by training the Quakers helped the Indians to change from a hunting economy to that of agriculture. Corn, cattle, and hogs were raised on the Quaker farm and the men were encouraged to do the heavy farm work while the women were taught spinning, weaving, knitting, and homemaking. The change was very slow, but the new way of life was emerging with a measure of success. With the rise of what might today be called "red power" (opposing all white customs) under Chief Tecumseh and his brother "The Prophet," the mission was closed.

The more significant and enduring service of Friends was in the present Wapakoneta area of Ohio. In 1811 Friends erected a grist-mill on the Auglaise River and later acquired a sawmill by which food and lumber could be made available to the Indians. The British-American War of 1812 interrupted the work. In 1815 the Indians asked Friends to return and the government gave its approval. Ohio Yearly Meeting, formed two years before, appointed a committee on Indian work and joined Baltimore Yearly Meeting in the work at Wapakoneta. The kind of practical work which had been started on the Wabash was now continued on the Auglaise River. Indians were trained in agricultural life and their women were helped in the arts of homemaking.

Friends of Indiana later united with Baltimore and Ohio Yearly Meetings in the work at Wapakoneta. They established a school and opened a program of agricultural training. The old hunting economy was giving way with every move westward and the clearing of timber for farms. The Indians showed adeptness to the new life, learned to plant extensively and to raise cattle and hogs. Some of them made sufficient progress that they owned and operated their own farms successfully.

Perhaps the most prominent, though not the first, Quaker leader among the Shawnees of this area was Henry Harvey. He came to the mission in 1830 and left an excellent record. He brought to his work a depth of the understanding and fellow-feeling which had marked the service of his predecessors in that area. Preceding him was Isaac Harvey, whose work was especially marked by his sympathy and courage. Under very unusual and testing circumstances he was able to help break the hold of witchcraft on the Indian community. It is a story worth remembering and is well told by Henry Harvey.[12]

An Indian was ill with what Isaac Harvey presumed to be "pulmonary consumption." Upon one occasion when visiting him with food and medicine he found him prostrate on the floor, his back slashed by a knife. The Indian "prophet" was present and acknowledged that he had inflicted the wounds to extract the evil spirit which a witch had conveyed to him.

A few hours later an Indian woman, with her child, rapped on Harvey's door crying, "They kill-ee me; they kill-ee me!" She had been charged with the witchery that caused the Indian's illness. With the help of a neighbor, Harvey hid her for a day with the intention of finally sending her secretly to a Quaker settlement some distance away. The council of Indian chiefs was meeting at the time and one of them, Chief We-as-se-cah, came to Harvey to relate the story and tell their decision to put her to death as a witch. He suspected Harvey of concealing the woman and offered to intervene on her behalf if Harvey would present her to them, hoping that the council of chiefs would grant a pardon.

Meeting with the council, Isaac Harvey was convinced that they would not relent and offered his own life as a substitute for hers, indicating that he was unarmed and entirely at their mercy. This caused considerable stir, some of the Indians becoming hostile. At this point Chief We-as-se-cah came forward, calling Harvey his friend, and offered his own life for that of the "Qua-kee-lee" friend. One by one the members of the council of chiefs gave in and, coming to Harvey, acknowledged him as their friend and agreed to pardon the woman. This one case may well have ended their practice of killing witches. The woman charged with witchery was Polly Butler, daughter of General Richard Butler by a Shawnee wife.

Though there was increasing evidence of the ability of the Indians to develop an agricultural economy, they were again forced to move. Under the pressure of white frontiersmen, treaties were broken and the Indians' land was taken by the government, though with some

---

[12] *Ibid.*, p. 169-183.

financial provisions made for their removal to Indian territory, in the area of present-day Kansas. This was a heartbreaking experience for many of the Shawnee Indians who had prospered with their farming and homebuilding in Ohio.

The Indians, unacquainted with the white men's ways of doing business, often got into debt. This fact, coupled with sharp dealings by white traders, led to claims against them. Removing them from the Ohio area involved both government and Indians in arranging for payment of debts and in facing unjust claims. Great promises were again made by government representatives as to the conditions by which they would be settled in their new territory.

Late in the fall of 1832 the majority of the Shawnees left for their new lands on the Kansas River. The journey of nearly eight hundred miles was long and arduous. They arrived in December with many of them cold, hungry, and ill. Money promised to them was slow in coming. The erection of buildings and the starting of new farm life was slow and painful. By the summer of 1833 the remainder of the Shawnees were removed.

Their farewell to the Quakers of Ohio-Indiana was heartrending. They wept bitterly as they said good-bye.

> We have been brothers together with you the Quakers for a long time. You took us by the hand and you held us fast. We have held you fast too. And although we are going far away from you, we do not want you to forsake us. . . . Through all we have found that by holding to the Friends we have done best, so we hope always to be in your hands.

Henry Harvey writes of this move:

> They were poorly fitted out for this journey, at that late season of the year . . . all ages and classes, from a hundred years old . . . to the infant not two days old — all had to leave at the bidding of the white man; sick or well, prepared or unprepared, this people — who were once a free people — had now to obey their masters . . . a stronger power has them under its control . . . all they can do is to plead for mercy, in their present unsettled and ruined condition.[18]

---

[18] *Ibid.*, p. 231. Frederick B. Tolles, *Nonviolent Contact: The Quakers and the Indians;* from the "Proceedings of the American Philosophical Society," Vol. 107, No. 2, p. 93-101.

In less than three years Indiana Yearly Meeting sent a deputation of three Friends to visit the Shawnees in their new location in Kansas Territory, having the endorsement of Baltimore and Ohio Yearly Meetings and with a letter of introduction by Lewis Cass, the Secretary of War, under whose department the care of Indians was placed. Friends found the Shawnees clearing timber, building homes, planting corn, and developing small herds of cattle and hogs. How warm the greeting which Friends received!

### Quaker Service Under the Government

The work of Friends with Indians moved into the spotlight of national attention in 1869 when President-elect Ulysses S. Grant turned to Friends for supervision of Indian work on the Great Plains.[14] The light kindled by William Penn had not gone out! Not only did the Indians retain it in their lore and feeling for Friends; the government also recognized it, and Penn's policy was thereby vindicated, nearly two hundred years later.

The Indian wars of the 1850's and the 1860's had been costly in blood, hatred, and money. The war policy was obviously failing. It was estimated that in the Cheyenne War of 1864 the cost of every Indian killed was a million dollars. General Sherman had said that "fifty Indians could checkmate three thousand soldiers." Against that background of bloodletting, the way of Friends appeared sensible and workable. Rayner Kelsey summarizes it well.

> The missionary and philanthropic efforts of Philadelphia Yearly Meeting (Orthodox) for the Allegheny Senecas of New York, the largely successful effort of the various eastern Yearly Meetings (Liberal) to protect the Seneca Nation in its landed rights and the succeeding philanthropic efforts for the Senecas at Cattaraugus; the missionary efforts of the various Yearly Meetings (Orthodox) among the western Indians, as exemplified by the mission establishment among the Shawnees in Kansas and one carried on among the Kaws of the same state by Western Yearly Meeting for several years following 1863; the frequent pilgrimages of individual Friends among the Indians for religious or philanthropic service; the proverbial and outstanding friendly attitude

---

[14] Kelsey, *op. cit.*, Ch. VIII.

of the Indians toward Friends; — all of these things united to emphasize the contrast between the Friendly method and the war method of dealing with the natives.[15]

Some Friends had been called into Indian service under President Lincoln and their work was well known. In 1867 the *Weekly Chronicle* of Washington, D. C., made a suggestion.

> The treaties made by Wm. Penn were always respected by both parties, and the peaceful sect of which he was a distinguished member have been traditional friends of the aborigines, and always kindly regarded by them. We have often thought that if the Society of Friends, who so successfully colonized and civilized the Senecas in western New York, and with such judgment and benevolence managed their affairs with the Government, could be induced to take charge of the subject of colonizing the Indian territory, and instructing the Indians, they might prepare them for the inevitable future.[16]

In 1869, under the suggestion of Iowa Yearly Meeting, a conference of Orthodox Friends was held at Baltimore and a deputation was sent to interview President-elect Grant. Friends of other bodies had also been busy in urging reforms in Indian affairs. In February 1869 identical letters were sent by the office of General Grant to all Friends' groups that had expressed concern.[17]

> *Headquarters Army of the United States,*
> *Washington, D. C.,* February 15, 1869
>
> Sir: General Grant, the President elect, desirous of inaugurating some policy to protect the Indians in their just rights and enforce integrity in the administration of their affairs, as well as to improve their general condition, and appreciating fully the friendship and interest which your Society has ever maintained in their behalf, directs me to request that you will send him a list of names, members of your Society, whom your Society will endorse as suitable persons for Indian agents.
>
> Also, to assure you that any attempt which may or can be made by your Society for the improvement, education, and Christianization of the Indians under such agencies will receive from

---

[15] *Ibid.,* p. 162, 163.
[16] *Ibid.,* p. 165.
[17] *Ibid.,* p. 168ff, gives the account of Grant's arrangement with Friends.

him, as President, all the encouragement and protection which the laws of the United States will warrant him in giving.

Very respectfully, your obedient servant
(Signed) E. S. Parker
*Brev. Brig. Gen., U.S.A. and A.D.C.*

Friends now were working with Indians *under government appointment.* The Associated Executive Committee of Friends on Indian Affairs (including all branches or bodies concerned) was organized in 1869. The Northern Superintendency, including roughly the present state of Nebraska, was assigned to Hicksite supervision and the Central Superintendency, including Kansas and Oklahoma Territory, was placed under the care of Gurneyite Friends.

By December 6 of that year, President Grant in his first message to Congress made the following report:

> I have attempted a new policy toward these wards of the nation. . . . The Society of Friends is well known as having succeeded in living in peace with the Indians in the early settlement of Pennsylvania, while their white neighbors of other sects in other sections were constantly embroiled. They are also known for their opposition to all strife, violence, and war, and are generally noted for their strict integrity and fair dealings. These considerations induced me to give the management of a few reservations of Indians to them and to throw the burden of the selection of agents upon the Society itself. The result has proven most satisfactory.

These two superintendencies were headed and staffed by Quakers, and a new kind of "holy experiment" was under way. Could Friends with their background of personal service meet the requirements of statesmanship under government control? They were destined to render a large and important service, but also to discover how far they could and could not go when the government held the final word on policies.

For one decade (1869-1879) they had a relatively free hand in directing the work. Upon the inauguration of President Hayes a deputation of Friends interviewed him on the prospects of their assignment under government. Despite his assurance that their work would be continued there came a change in the administrative attitude at Washington. The new Commissioner of Indian Affairs was unfriendly to the work of Friends. Several agencies were taken from Friends' supervision and in 1879 Friends, finding the relationship with government intolerable, resigned from their supervisory responsibilities.[18]

## THE CONTINUING SERVICE

This did not end the service of Friends with the Indians. Some schools were retained as their responsibility and they also supplied many teachers for government schools. Having worked under government they now were free to pursue their opportunities in such ways as were open to them. Now the Associated Executive Committee of Friends for Indian Affairs started on a new chapter of service. Both the Gurneyite and the Hicksite Friends had educated Indian children, trained the adult men in the methods of farming, helped the women in homemaking and child care. The closing of their relationship with government did not represent failure any more than did the ending of the work of Penn.

Again more Indians were moved, this time to Oklahoma Territory, and a new kind of service, religiously motivated and oriented, was started as "mission" stations which continue to the present day. The method of Friends in their work has been well expressed — to find what good things the Indians want to do and help them do it. The purpose underlying all is both spiritual and physical. The spirit is that of trying to understand them and work *with them*.

The struggle of the Indians *against* the government ended in the 1880's.[19] The contest was unequal. Today there are about 500,000 Indians living as involuntary wards of the government. Whether to maintain cultural identity of Indians or to assume — and therefore move in the direction of — cultural integration with the white population is one of the principal and continuing questions that have sometimes made for an uncertain policy of government.

In 1929 Herbert Hoover, as President of the United States, appointed Charles J. Rhodes and J. Henry Scattergood, his fellow

---

[18] Historians are not agreed on the success of this service of Friends under government control. That there were failures is quite clear. Policies of the government made the Quaker administration difficult in many cases. See Bibliography in Appendices, *i.e.,* Richardson and Tatum.

[19] *Ibid.,* p. 196-199; reports the end of the work under government.

Quakers, as Commissioner and Assistant Commissioner respectively. Considerable progress was made in increased appropriations from Congress for the welfare and the education of Indians. Many day schools were founded and boarding schools were subsidized. The loss of Indian lands was slowed down, and a program of service was centered in the Indian community and its culture.

An American-Indian conference held in 1961, involving ninety tribes and bands, stated their view on the issue:

> . . . we, the Indian People, must be governed by principles in a democratic manner with a right to choose our way of life. Since our Indian culture is threatened by presumption of being absorbed by the American society, we believe we have the responsibility of preserving our precious heritage. We believe that the Indians must provide the adjustment and thus *freely advance with dignity to a better life.*

Friends have never ended their work for and with the Indians although government policies have changed and the Indians have been moved from reservation to reservation. Friends have tried to adjust to the new conditions and their service has taken diverse forms.

*Rough Rocks Mission*

Friends of Rocky Mountain Yearly Meeting now maintain a mission at Rough Rocks in Arizona.[20] It is evangelical in spirit and method and at the same time is practical in its service with the Navajo Indians. Classes in Navajo and English are conducted. Bibles in the Navajo language have been distributed and Bible classes are conducted using the two languages. New buildings with educational and dormitory facilities have been erected. A meetinghouse for worship and evangelistic effort has been erected. Small phonographs with Bible and other recordings in Navajo have been placed in homes. Sick persons are taken to doctors or to the hospital. Vacation Bible schools and "released time" classes are held. Children from a nearby government school attend some classes.

Centered in evangelical interest, yet serving the outward physical needs of the Navajos, this work has the depth and dimensions of earlier Friends work in the midwest areas of a hundred years ago, but with improved facilities and techniques.

---

[20] *Minutes* of the Yearly Meeting.

*American Friends Service Committee*

This committee is working in a dozen areas of the country, and many non-Friends organizations are assisting. The committee is working on Indian reservations and in off-reservation centers in cities where Indians need help in adjusting to city life. Teaching arts and crafts, camping, starting small home industries, and even publishing a tribal newspaper are among the activities the American Friends Service Committee has helped and encouraged. As legislation on behalf of Indian welfare has come before the Congress of the United States the Friends Committee on National Legislation has been active, from its headquarters in Washington, D. C., urging justice and relief for the scattered Indian tribes.

*The Friends Committee on National Legislation*

Continuous attention to interests of Indians has been given by this committee on the legislative front in Washington, D. C. It has encouraged hearings before Congressional committees and has brought prominent and knowledgeable Friends to testify on the injustices to and the needs of Indians. This work has been in the line of concern of William Penn and the unending service of Friends for these first Americans whose hunting grounds and homes have been claimed, to a large extent, by Congressional action.

*All-Friends Committee*

With the removal of Indians from New York, Pennsylvania, Kansas, and other areas to Oklahoma Territory, the Associated Executive Committee of Friends for Indian Affairs (representing all Friends) centered its work in Oklahoma. This work has combined church, educational, relief, and social service activities which are now conducted in four Meetings or centers — the Kickapoo Friends Center, the Hominy Friends Meeting (Osage Indians), the Wyandotte Friends Meeting (several tribes), and Council House Friends (chiefly Seneca and Cayuga tribes from New York).

Though these centers are within the pastoral Friends tradition they are flexible in their approach and at times hold unprogrammed meetings. The pastoral form most needed is that of community leadership, helping Indians overcome their reluctance to be involved in community affairs, in voting, and in general acceptance of health and social agencies.

# Chapter 11

## THE CENTURY OF CHANGE

It required a century and a continentwide frontier to form three-fourths of the Society of Friends in America into a branch with its present pastoral system.[1] At the turn of the twentieth century Yearly Meetings (Gurneyite) on the east coast as well as those of the western areas included pastoral Meetings. Of the eastern Yearly Meetings, North Carolina, New England, and New York, in the main, became pastoral. Baltimore Yearly Meeting held mainly to the older tradition. The Philadelphia Meetings have always been nonpastoral.

The pastoral Meetings later became "programmed," having an order of procedure in the meetings for worship, whereas those of the older tradition were "open," meeting on the basis of silent waiting and having no paid leadership. There are now many Meetings combining certain features of each with an informal approach to their meetings for worship.

Although the pastoral system took final form during the last

---

[1] *Minutes* of the several Yearly Meetings have been the chief resources for this chapter.

three decades of the nineteenth century, the forces which slowly shaped it cover roughly a hundred years. In the year 1800, Friends families were beginning to settle in the great Northwest Territory. By 1900 there were seven Gurneyite Yearly Meetings west of the Alleghenies which, with four on the east coast and one in Canada, constituted the Five Years Meeting (1902). In the same year seven Hicksite Yearly Meetings, including those of the East and the West, were brought together in the organization of the Friends General Conference. Wilburite Yearly Meetings, together with certain separated bodies of the last part of the nineteenth century, constituted the Conservative Friends who, though in close unity in faith and practice, formed no overall organization but were aware of their common faith and practice and developed a sense of fellowship.* Of the evangelical-pastoral Yearly Meetings in the West, Ohio alone remained outside the Five Years Meeting. No branch of Friends offered a replica of the first generation of midseventeenth-century Quaker Meetings. Changes had occurred in all of them, east and west.[2]

### As the Pastoral System Evolved

There have been four emphases in the history of the Quaker movement — inwardness of life, especially observed in the meeting for worship; shepherding of the Quaker flock, as a pastoral responsibility; outreach in winning other people to the faith; and service and reform activities.

Though these four aspects have marked Friends history, they have never had equal accent in any later period or in any branch. At times one or more of these emphases have been largely eclipsed. During the quietistic period, following the rise of the Quaker movement, the emphasis was on inwardness, whereas pastoral responsibility consisted mainly in enforcing the rules of outward behavior, keeping the Society deeply marked by traditional habits of thought, and holding to uniformity in the externals of the Quaker community.

In that period the evangelical aspect (to use a later term) had waned but not ceased. There were visiting Friends such as William

---

[2] D. Elton Trueblood, *The Paradox of the Quaker Ministry;* the 1960 Quaker Lecture, Indiana Yearly Meeting. And *The People Called Quakers;* Harper & Row, New York, 1966. These references give background and scope on the pastoral ministry.
* See Appendix 5 for the "Family Tree" of American Yearly Meetings.

**First Friends Meeting, Indianapolis**
Interior scene of a contemporary pastoral meeting for worship

Rufus M. Jones

Savery who helped to keep the spirit of outreach alive. It is not strange that in the reaction which later struck Friends this element would, in some areas, become the chief accent, almost to the exclusion of the others. The evangelical wave came in with such force that many Friends were marked by another extreme in which silent worship was almost lost in the fervor of preaching, and the pastoral function was second to the "winning of souls." Reform activities often became limited chiefly to temperance.

The pastoral system came into existence primarily through the evangelical door. Friends in leadership of the Yearly Meetings saw some of the extremes within this trend and tried to stem the tide, but with only moderate success. Leaders available for special help in the local Meetings were, for the most part, visiting evangelists. Sometimes they were called back to a Meeting where a revival had brought in new prospects for membership, and were asked to teach rather than preach. They were expected to teach the Christian faith as interpreted by Friends and, as a pastoral function, help to establish the faith of the converts.

The development of the pastoral trend as seen in the minutes of Indiana Yearly Meeting is typical of other Yearly Meetings of that period. In their sessions of 1880 the Meeting of Ministers and Elders recommended to the Yearly Meeting the appointment of a committee of concern because of "a deep exercise in reference to the needs of some of our Meetings, and the failure to reap the full advantages that should have been derived from evangelistic work. . . . " The committee was given the responsibility of general oversight of the Meetings, the "promulgation of the gospel," and supplying the needs of Meetings that lacked ministry.

In 1881 the committee reported on the situation in the Yearly Meeting. There were one hundred thirty-seven meetings for worship, consisting of more than 16,000 members. Could Friends hold to the ancient line of universal ministry in the Meeting and at the same time arrange special help by a proper placing of ministers? There were two hundred acknowledged ministers in the Yearly Meeting, unevenly settled among the several Meetings. One may read in the lines and perhaps between the lines the issue they faced: Dare they help in *placing* ministers as well as *acknowledging* their call to the ministry? Their minute was carefully guarded:

It has been our desire to encourage the gifts of the membership, and not so fully to supply them with acknowledged ministers
as to lessen in any degree the responsibility resting upon the
membership, and leading them to neglect the gifts entrusted to
them.

The traditional way was weakening and the new was coming
toward birth. The Yearly Meeting was not yet ready to regularize
or systemize pastoral work. To move in that direction would mean
something lost from the Quaker tradition, as Friends then viewed
it, though also something gained in help to the Meetings.

Ministers of that period were not in full-time service. They were
also farmers, teachers, or businessmen, or were in other lines of work.
They were available to be moved from one Meeting to another only
insofar as each could for a short while leave his business of making
a living. Moving the residence of a minister permanently in order
to fill a need could not be easily arranged.

The committee was also concerned about the emotional, ephemeral
nature of evangelistic work in some Meetings. Friends were uneasy
about the trend of uncontrolled evangelical efforts and were striving
earnestly to stabilize the Meetings. At the same time they witnessed
the work of other Christian churches around them which were attracting Quaker young people into attendance and membership. Their
report of 1881 continued in these words:

> We do not believe that the idea which prevails in the Chris-
> tian community is a correct one, that each church must be under
> the specific care of a priest, rector, pastor or settled minister. We
> do not think it apostolic, and believe that it tends to destroy the
> priesthood of the believers, and to set up a human head upon
> whom the members increasingly rely, and thus neglect the duties
> which devolve upon them. Still, we believe pastoral care and
> visitation is necessary, and that our elders are especially appointed
> for that work; hence it has been our desire to encourage them in
> a careful and systematic work for the oversight and care of the
> flock, and not only elders, but many others, both men and women,
> whom God has called to the service, and who, by its exercise
> gradually develop the gift.

The committee labored earnestly with its dilemma and tried, as
the minute shows, to encourage elders in their pastoral responsibilities.

How many responded and with what measure of success is not known, but it was clear that they did not meet the need.

The moving of a minister from residence in one Meeting to another under some kind of financial arrangement savored of a "hireling ministry." This was a truly feared prospect in the minds of conservative Friends, though in a few instances this had proved helpful and the committee had to acknowledge it.

Then came another step. The ministers of the Yearly Meeting were called together to discuss the problem. Beyond the main intention of the committee this meeting was a move toward recognizing the ministers *as a class,* giving them a sense of special responsibility.

In 1886 one hundred forty revivals were held in Indiana Yearly Meeting, with 3,600 conversions and nearly 2,000 seeking membership. The concern to conserve these gains had not lessened. A report quoted from the New Testament exhorting elders not to be "lords over God's heritage, but examples to the flock" acknowledged that some are called to be "pastors and teachers," these pastors not necessarily being elders. The Yearly Meeting was asked to "take some step to assist in supplying this need for more pastoral work in our Meetings." By 1889 fifty-two Meetings were under pastoral care with ministers in full-time pastoral work.

The report in 1902 states that the "pastoral question is still claiming much attention [and] may be adjusted that all our Meetings may be blest with a consecrated, capable and spiritually-minded ministry, one that is largely *free from business pursuits"* (italics added). By this year (in which the Five Years Meeting was organized), the practice of calling ministers into full-time service was well established. It would be disputed, but the system was in to stay. It had been generally and officially blest by most of the Yearly Meetings.

Was it truly a "system" that existed in 1902, or was this a case of pastors without a system? Within thirty years pastoralism had all but erupted into existence, though it had evolved slowly from the preceding years. Now came the question of improving it, making it effective in the work it was supposed to accomplish, and training men and women for it. These and attending questions would be faced.

## NONPASTORAL FRIENDS VIEW THE CHANGE

The coming in of pastoralism was not without considerable

shock to Friends of the nonpastoral persuasion. When it was learned that the Meeting at Pasadena, California, employed a pastor and that the meetinghouse had a steeple and an organ it was felt that some of the changes "strike at the life" of the Society of Friends.

In 1886 the *Friends Review* (Philadelphia) wrote on the indefiniteness of the pastoral question.[3] It recognized that Friends opened the pastoral trend in supporting their travelling ministers. Though the *Review* saw "preaching for gain to be unchristian," it asserted that

> church extension, the work of spreading the Gospel, and the edification of the body, ought never to be allowed to suffer for the want of money. Those who, called and qualified of the Lord, are rightly taken from secular business to labor spiritually in the harvest field, ought to be cared for, in carnal things, by their brethren.

The *Review* then adds this question, "Can we go farther than this now?" This by no means indicated that the *Friends Review* favored pastoralism in the Midwest, but it raised the question of pastoral needs that confronted every Friends Meeting. It left doubt as to whether there was a clear way by which Friends could meet them satisfactorily.

At this period tensions were not merely between East and West. There were Friends in the Philadelphia area who felt that uniting the *Friends Review,* of the nonpastoral persuasion, with the *Christian Worker,* of the pastoral view, to form the *American Friend* in 1894 had all but sold the Quaker birthright. One disturbed Friend wrote to Rufus M. Jones, the editor:

> It can no longer be disguised that the [*Friends*] *Review* has surrendered the last phase of attachment to the principles which many of us hold dear, and that the publication in its present form is to be used as the organ of the western agitators who have wrecked the Society of Friends in all places where they have obtained a foothold. Also that it is indicative of a design to seek to engraft upon Philadelphia Yearly Meeting the methods which have practically blotted out the existence of the Society of Friends in most parts of America. . . . I wish to enter my solemn protest against this entire proceeding. . . . I don't feel that I can be a

---

[3] *Friends Review,* Vol. XL, No. 18, Dec. 2, 1886, p. 280-283.

subscriber to the consolidated periodical, and I wish my name taken off the subscription list.

He referred to these Friends as "agitators," "schemers," and "parasites," yet did "not want to be uncharitable"[4] (sic!).

A humorous aspect of the hypersensitive reaction to the pastoral development appears in the *Friends Review* and is repeated in the *Friends Intelligencer and Journal* in 1887. Pastoral Friends of the West had found difficulty in furnishing an adequate living for the families of pastors and had suggested the need for a man or "a strong and earnest woman, without a family." In this possibility the two Quaker journals of Philadelphia reflected what was felt to be another serious deviation looming. "Is it not supposable, that some meetings might make it a condition that their pastor should not marry? There, at some distance, looms up the idea of celibacy of the priesthood; which is well known . . . in the Roman Catholic church."

It should be noted, from the standpoint of present-day practices, that the terms *pastoral* and *nonpastoral* are not wholly accurate. The differentiation in terms might instead be *programmed* and *unprogrammed* — those having an "order of service" in the meeting for worship and those meeting on the basis of silence or the open meeting. A Meeting without an employed pastor may, and often does, lay the pastoral responsibility on all of the members. Likewise in a pastoral Meeting the pastor is expected to assist the other members of the Meeting in sharing the responsibility.

The pastoral system was all but inevitable. There was no longer the question of whether Friends should try to meet pastoral needs, but rather the question of how to meet them.

Richard Henry Thomas of Baltimore was one of the more able opponents of the "one-man method," as he called it. In 1895 he wrote:

> Nothing would be less in accord with my desires than to introduce the "Arch Street [Philadelphia] ideal of the ministry", as exemplified by Arch Street Meeting, throughout our Society. But this is certainly not the true alternative to the Iowa ideal [under concern at that time], which is simply destructive of Quakerism. There is life in it, but it is on lines absolutely inconsistent, it seems to me, with the apostolic freedom we should

---

[4] *Papers* of Rufus M. Jones, Haverford College library.

strive to live in. Is a middle position tenable? We want neither, but something different from both, but not *between* them — although with full life, power, flexibility, adaptability and with a 19th Century message.[5]

This was less than specific as to an alternative. Benjamin True-blood, a leading Friend of that period, was an exponent of what he called the "New Quakerism." He viewed the break with pastoralism by early Friends as being against "the extreme formalism and empty professionalism of that day." He viewed the idea of Quakerism being "primitive Christianity revived" as referring to the "life and religious activity of the first century, *not its forms*"[6] (italics added). He believed that "Quakerism itself became formal in the dark century of 'quietism'. It has now broken from that shell — free!" Though he does not here directly commend the pastoral way he seems to approve the new freedom of the period.

We can hardly pass on from this question without noting the thinking of Rufus M. Jones, who in 1907 wrote on the subject of pastoralism.

> In a very few years these successful evangelists were all settled as pastors. The temptation to take this short-cut to a solution of the task of shepherding the people was undoubtedly great. But it was just as certainly a blunder. A great moment had come in the history of our Society . . . everything turned on meeting it with clear insight and fore-vision. It was not time to catch up a system which is a doubtful blessing in the other churches and fix a poor imitation of it on our Society. But the false step was taken and we are suffering from it today.[7]

It was easier to suggest "clear insight and fore-vision" and to call the course taken a "blunder" than to suggest a clear alternative. After-the-fact judgments offered little help.

The pastoral system became a permanent form. The situation, as Friends viewed it, was crucial. Change or die! Meet the problem of pastoral needs or fade out of existence as Friends Meetings! Many Friends Meetings did not change and most of these ultimately closed.

---

[5] *Papers* of Rufus M. Jones, Haverford College library.

[6] Views of Benjamin F. Trueblood on the future of Friends may be read in the *American Friend,* Vol. II, No. 24 (June 13, 1895), p. 574.

[7] *Papers* of Rufus M. Jones, Haverford College library.

There were, of course, important exceptions in the Hicksite and Conservative bodies of the West, as related in other chapters. It is doubtful whether many of the present-day institutions of Friends in the West — their schools and colleges — would exist today if the pastoral system had not been adopted.

The pastoral method of today does not rest solely upon the accidents of history but upon the needs to which it ministers, now. Friends of this persuasion are not apologetic for they believe that the conditions and needs to which it speaks require it and, far from forsaking it, they are concerned to make it more effective in its ministry to the total needs of the individual and of his community. They represent one new and creative expression within the varied forms of the Society of Friends. They are not looking backward as if to some lost Eden, but forward; and they welcome the interest of all Friends in their way of life. They are sure that they have preserved certain aspects of the Quaker heritage like that of the "Valiant Sixty."

It could be questioned whether the terms *programmed* and *unprogrammed* (as descriptive of the meeting for worship) are sufficiently clear. They are the terms most commonly used by Friends. The term *program* suggests an unvariable form, such as that of a musical or other similar occasion. Many meetings are very flexible, not only having periods of silence but welcoming participation by the attenders. The terms *ordered* and *open* to characterize meetings for worship might offer additional meaning.

### The Changing and the Permanent

While some innovations and changes were being made there were other elements of the Quaker heritage that remained, in principle, unchanged. A brief review of these aspects of pastoral Meetings, the new and the old, reveals the emerging Quaker image of the frontier.

### Music

As in other persons, so in Quakers, there was a strain of music. The feeling for melody, rhythm, and harmony would generally find expression one way or another. Singing was, in part, an escape from dull labor and boredom. The harder the labor and the more unrelieved the hours of toil, the greater the hunger for relaxing and inspiring song. The outward circumstances had much to do not only with the *need* to sing but also with *what* was sung. The words and tunes would likely suggest escape from labor to a time of rest, or depict ordinary life in a strain of satisfying emotional release. On the frontier this was often expressed in ballads or folk songs, and these in turn were sometimes reflected in the tunes and words of religious expression.

Tunes from the ballads and folk songs were, in some instances, the same as those used in religious meetings. One example of this appropriation of tunes comes from a song of the plains.

> O the hinges are of leather
>    and the windows have no blasts,
> While the clapboard lets
>    the howling blizzard in,
> And I hear a hungry coyote
>    come stealing through the grass
> To my little old sod shanty
>    on the plain.

On the farm and in the kitchen this song was sung during the week and the tune was sung again in Sunday worship with other words of religious experience. The outlet for this spirit of music was found in farm and home, and sometimes in the public school where, on occasions, parents met with teachers and children in songfests. It was not far from the schoolhouse to the meetinghouse and the spirit of song did not naturally end when children came to meeting where the "creaturely activity" of music was frowned upon. Furthermore, those who attended First Day meetings were not all of Quaker background, and the traditions of silence seemed strange to them.

Not far from the Quaker meetinghouses were other Christian churches where singing was an essential part of worship. It was common practice in these neighboring churches for an individual to start a familiar song with others joining in singing. Freedom of individual leading in ministry was generally accepted by Friends, but the "interruption" of worship by song was not. Sometimes when an individual worshiper started singing in a Quaker meeting some Friends would join in it and others would leave the room in protest.

**Lynville Christian Endeavor Society**
Note the musical instruments

Nathan and Esther Frame

Dougan Clark

The main move toward congregational singing came through the First Day School (Sunday School), where singing by children was permitted. The common treadle organ was allowed in many Sunday Schools long before music in the meeting for worship was tolerated. When the first singing was permitted in the meeting for worship it was informal, and *without an instrument.* The next crucial decision was whether to allow the organ or the piano in the meeting for worship. In Iowa, as in some other areas, there were some awkward but humorous situations in which organs were moved in and out of the room for worship according to the views of the person or committee holding responsibility. There was some alternating between tuning fork and organ until ultimately the organ or piano came in to stay as a part of the meeting for worship.

Another influence on the Friends Meeting was the spirited singing in the evangelical movement. Around Friends Meetings, Methodist, Baptist, and other churches were conducting evangelistic meetings in which lively singing was an attraction, next to the sermon itself. Friends young people attended these gatherings and found an outlet for their pent-up feelings. The restraints of the Quaker meeting seemed to them antiquated and unnatural.

In 1873 Western Yearly Meeting, still holding the traditional line, stated that the "use of music being almost inseparable from its abuse [desires that] Friends may not deviate from our established practice on the subject." The question of sincerity arose as Friends were asked to sing "other men's words," and in 1880 Western Yearly Meeting reminded Friends that "we should avoid singing falsehoods, or hymns the sentiments of which do not express our standing or experience in Christian life." This insight suggested the dangers then (and now) of singing words which one might never use in thoughtful discourse.[8]

Years later the programmed meeting for worship became fixed in the practice of pastoral Friends and music came to be a permanent element in it. By 1965 a report of the Music Committee of Oregon

---

[8] Margaret Hadley Weesner, "A Survey of the Status of Music in Western Yearly Meeting Local Meetings of the Society of Friends," a thesis presented to the Division of Graduate Instruction, Butler University, 1963.

Ida Mae Miller writes a column in *Quaker Life,* "Music for Meeting," which offers help and encouragement for better music and a spiritual interpretation of its contribution to worship.

Yearly Meeting stated that "next to the ministry of the Word, we believe the ministry of music to be the most important part of a church service."

The move has been not only from no music to music of varied kinds, but also to *better* music. Interest in music has not been confined to any one branch of Friends, though only in the pastoral Meetings has it been incorporated in the meeting for worship. In many programmed-type Meetings silent periods and music are both included, and Friends of the unprogrammed Meetings enjoy music and singing on occasions other than that of the meeting for worship.

*Business Meetings*

Another aspect of early Quaker practice which was retained was the method of making decisions in business meetings. Voting on business issues was seldom practiced during this period of change. From that time to the present, Friends of all areas, with exceptions, made decisions on "the sense of the Meeting," being unwilling to take action if a reasonable objection should be raised.

*Women in Ministry*

The testimony on equality of women in ministry and in the work of the church was maintained. There seems never to have been any official discrimination against women ministers, and many women Friends have served as evangelists and pastors. As early as 1893 Lida Romick served as one of the first pastors in Oregon Yearly Meeting. In the earlier period Sarah Lindsey of London Yearly Meeting had helped, doubtless, to demonstrate the effectiveness of women ministers, though pastoralism was not an issue at that time. Following her came women Friends whose effective labors were obvious from the very beginnings of Western Meetings. Esther Frame was a woman minister of great power and was welcomed among Friends Meetings.

Perhaps Mary Moon Meredith was the most widely known of women Friends ministers of the evangelical bodies. She was of queenly bearing, well educated for her time and gifted as a speaker. She was invited to pulpits of many Christian churches at a time when opposition by non-Friends to women ministers was very strong. She broke through those barriers of opposition in the churches of North Carolina, preached in the log meetinghouses of Indiana and in the sod meetinghouses of Kansas, and was a representative at the opening of California Yearly Meeting where she was accepted as a visiting minister. Though firm in her evangelical views she never indulged in controversy or divisiveness. Many women Friends ministers have followed in her train, serving in many Meetings as evangelists and pastors.[9]

## Young Friends and Christian Education

There were three main aspects of the Friends Meeting of this period: the meeting for worship, the First Day School (sometimes called Scripture School and later Sunday School), and the fellowship of Young Friends.

Earlier meetings were held for the reading of tracts, which were generally circulated by visiting Friends. These meetings ultimately took two directions. Some of them evolved into "prayer meetings" and, in some cases, opened the way for revival meetings. Others took an educational direction, becoming Scripture Schools and ultimately Sunday Schools. These in turn led to programs of Christian Education as departments in the local Meetings, in Yearly Meetings, and, ultimately, in the present-day Friends United Meeting.

Though the main body of attenders was made up of young children and youths, the Sunday School evolved with an educational program for the entire age range. Young people of teen age and older became associated in a second organization generally called Christian Endeavor. This was not of Quaker origin, but was the organization for young people in other Christian churches, crossing denominational lines. It proved to be one of the ecumenical links that led to interchurch fellowship locally and nationally.

It was mainly through young Friends, led generally by young adults, that the evangelical wave came among Friends with the pressure for change. It was also through the younger people, in general, and Christian Endeavor in particular, that the idea and the inspiration for foreign missions came into some of the Yearly Meetings. The interdenominational programs of the young peoples' meetings spread and inspired the concern. The Christian Endeavor bodies within California Yearly Meeting, for instance, were especially active

---

[9] Lela Gordon Chance, *Repentant Rebel;* Vantage Press, 1969. Personal experiences of a Quaker woman minister-pastor, in both home and church responsibilities.

in starting missions and supporting missionary personnel. In most Meetings, Christian Endeavor has been, in later years, replaced by Young Friends associations; and these are often related to one another across Yearly Meeting lines. The Friends United Meeting maintains a Young Friends department, and the Young Friends of North America has representatives from all branches.

*Quaker Camps and Retreat Centers*

It was concern for Young Friends that led originally to the summer camp programs and to the erection of buildings and accommodations for them. This development has come rapidly within recent decades until nearly every Yearly Meeting within the scope of this history has at least one campground of its own. Oregon Yearly Meeting has several. Those bodies of Friends which do not own campgrounds and buildings often use those of other religious bodies. These Quaker campsites now are located on the hills, in the mountains, and at the shore of the Pacific under Oregon and California Yearly Meetings; on a mountain crest under Rocky Mountain Yearly Meeting; on the plains of Kansas, on the rolling hills in Iowa, on lakes of Indiana and Ohio, on a lake of North Carolina, and on the coast of Maine.

The summer programs which began as Young Friends projects have now been expanded to include children and older Friends as well. They are generally conducted in the interest of worship, fellowship, recreation, peace work, interracial concerns, Christian education, and mission and service activities. They attract a large attendance and have become a major part of Yearly Meeting programs. Centers of the American Friends Service Committee hold conferences and family camps with programs of social concern. "Quakerism in the Summer" is an important aspect of a year-around program in these areas.

*Retirement Homes*

One of the latest developments in present-day Yearly Meetings of Friends is that of retirement homes. Among pastoral Friends there was an urgent need to care for aging leaders who had served with small compensation and faced their later years without adequate financial security. The pastoral system required this added provision for its ministers, missionaries, and others. The longer-view responsibility was late in coming.

In the main it was not until near the 1960's that Friends awakened sufficiently to begin planning and building retirement homes and financing entrance for those who needed help. The need has not yet been met adequately, because of the high cost of maintaining the homes, but the idea of caring for their aged members has stirred Friends to fulfilling their responsibilities.

Nearly all Yearly Meetings from North Carolina to Oregon and California have either built homes or have them definitely planned or under construction. Some of them provide total care, including dining rooms, apartment kitchenettes, health centers, and hospital care. Others provide cottages where self-care makes for a relaxed retirement among other persons of similar background. The great need is for funds whereby aging persons can be financed in the new retirement centers. The residents generally include not only ministers and missionaries but also other Friends and some non-Friends.

*Temperance Concerns*

The peace witness is given more extended consideration elsewhere in these pages. Though war seemed remote at the beginning of the twentieth century, certain other evils within the community called for immediate attention. As stated previously, the migrations westward included lawless elements as well as people with religious motivation. The "wild west" was, in many areas, truly wild. Many individuals escaped from law in the East to anonymity in the West, where law and order were not yet established.

Chief of the evils was the immoderate use of liquor. Somewhat earlier, Friends, like other citizens, considered liquor to have certain medicinal qualities. Levi Coffin had alcoholic beverages in his store at Newport (Fountain City, Indiana) and purchase was by prescription from a Quaker doctor. This kept less scrupulous dealers from handling it. This did not lessen Quaker concern over the misuse of liquors, and it shortly led to the emphasis on total abstinence. In the temperance cause there was little or no distinction between the views of Gurneyites, Hicksites, and Wilburites.[10]

Of the prevalent "corruptions" of this period liquor was the chief one. Liquor-as-medicine came to be opposed completely as an evil

---

[10] It appears that during this frontier period no other testimony claimed more universal support by Friends of all branches than that of opposition to the liquor industry.

and no other moral battle claimed more of a united concern of Friends in every Yearly Meeting of every branch, especially in the West. The *Friends Intelligencer and Journal* (Philadelphia), representing the views of Hicksite Friends, proclaimed against both liquor and tobacco.

The city of Newberg, Oregon, had been laid out by Friends, and deeds to property included the prohibition of sale or use of alcoholic beverages. Friends of Whittier were adamant on the subject. Whittier must be dry! Friends women of Whittier drove out one saloon by what we would call today a "knit-in." They simply sat in the saloon, knitting and sewing. The would-be customers were embarrassed by the presence of the women and the saloon had to close. Carrie Nation, though not a Quaker, was a heroine of Kansas drys; Friends women rallied to the temperance cause, though with less militancy.

With all the aplomb of a veteran reformer-orator, a young Friend in Whittier College who won first place in an intercollegiate contest included these words in his oration: "Our fathers struck the shackles from four million slaves. It is for us, the inheritors of their glory, and I trust of their noble patriotism, to rise in the strength of our young Christian manhood and deliver our beloved country from the pernicious despotism of the liquor traffic." Such were the idealism and the optimism of Quaker youth!

*Intra-Quaker Tensions*

As the nineteenth century ended there were two trends among Friends. On the one hand was the new scholarship creating deeper tensions. On the other was the move toward unity. Orthodox Friends for some time had been concerned about their fragmentation and the accompanying deviations from common practices.

Certain conferences with limited representation relating to peace, education, Indians, and freedmen had been held from time to time and represented the integrative movements of Friends bodies. The Peace Association of Friends had been organized in 1867. In 1869 the Associated Executive Committee of Friends for Indian Affairs brought the branches of Friends into a cooperative venture within the administration of the Federal government. The *Friends Review* (Philadelphia) and the *Christian Worker* (Chicago), representing two rather distinct emphases, were united in 1894 in the *American Friend*. Common points of view on peace, temperance, and certain social issues were held. Added to these was the rising interest in missionary activity among Orthodox Friends.

These, in some measure, transcended the major division between Friends of pastoral and open Meetings. There was a kind of home-sickness for the earlier unity of the Society of Friends, and despite the differences, deeply felt, there was a yet deeper feeling for oneness.

At the same time the intellectual climate was changing both in London Yearly Meeting and in the American Yearly Meetings. Nor was the new mood confined to Friends. Every Christian church was feeling the impact of new thought, especially in relation to their educational institutions. A new tide was moving in and ancient moorings were under test. In London Yearly Meeting the issues introduced by the new scholarship were faced in a historic conference at Manchester in 1895. The tensions were sufficiently met to avoid a separation. In America the strain was too great to prevent some divisions.

The religious controversies of the period centered around Biblical interpretations. *Higher criticism* was a main battle term of the period. The term *criticism* itself was not widely understood. It suggested to many people the concept of faultfinding, the idea of man sitting in judgment upon the eternal Word, whereas the Biblical scholar used it in the sense of examination and discernment in light of the context of the times and the ideas in which the Scriptures were written. To most Christians — among them many Friends — it seemed that the very foundations of faith were being questioned. Attitudes of literal versus liberal interpretations were created. The Darwinian idea of an evolutionary type of creation suggested to many people a tension between science and religion. These issues have been referred to in the chapter on education. We can do no more here than indicate something of the disturbance it caused among Friends.

Besides the general climate of change within which the life of Friends was cast, there were the continued deviations of practice from the historic Quaker norm. As early as 1836 Elisha Bates of Ohio Yearly Meeting had been baptized and was disowned for it. The idea, based on what was believed to be a literal interpretation of the New Testament, persisted and in 1885 David B. Updegraff of Ohio Yearly Meeting was baptized by immersion. He was thereafter a representative of that view and had influence upon many Friends.

He had little trouble finding passages in the New Testament which seemed to him to fortify his position.

Closely associated with David B. Updegraff was Dougan Clark, a professor in Earlham College. A statement by Dougan Clark in the *Christian Worker* had prophesied that Friends would one day adopt water baptism. During Ohio Yearly Meeting sessions of 1894, at a memorial service for David B. Updegraff, whose death had occurred shortly before, Dougan Clark, along with some others, was baptized by "pouring." A more complete account of this is given in the letter of Walter Malone, printed in the appendices of this book.

Ohio Yearly Meeting endeavored to follow the older, settled position of Friends. The Representative Meeting in 1883 had prepared and submitted to the Yearly Meeting a statement reaffirming the spiritual nature of baptism and communion, adding that "no one should be received, acknowledged, or retained in the position of Minister or Elder among us, who continues to participate in or advocates the necessity of the outward rite of baptism or the supper." Monthly Meetings were to be bound by that rule. The Yearly Meeting, in a later year, decided not to adopt the statement of the representatives, but instead took the position of toleration.

Eight other Yearly Meetings were spurred to close the door on this deviation in their own Meetings and reaffirmed the settled Quaker position. Indiana Yearly Meeting made a declaration almost word for word like that recommended to Ohio Yearly Meeting, adopting it without dissent. To be true to their declaration, this Meeting was required to divest Dougan Clark of his standing as a minister, though not of his membership in the Meeting.[11]

This break from Quaker practice in the adoption of water baptism and outward "communion" seemed to many Friends to be the lowering of the last barrier. And in at least one area of Friends it was felt that little was left of original Quakerism but the name. Could anything be done to stop the spiritual erosion, as viewed by Friends of that day, and in some measure recover the lost ground? The first of the general conferences on unity was called for that purpose.

---

[11] A letter from Walter Malone to Rufus M. Jones gives an account of the public baptism of Dougan Clark (R. M. J. papers, Haverford College library). Papers regarding the controversy in Whitewater Meeting (Indiana) as related to Dougan Clark may be seen in some Friends college libraries.

# Chapter 12

## A NEW ORDER EMERGES –
## THE FIVE YEARS MEETING

To many leading Quakers of the 1880's the changes represented a departure from the first-century heritage and signaled a dissolution of the Society of Friends. The alarm was felt not only from coast to coast in America, but also in the parent body, London Yearly Meeting. Could the trend be stopped and the earlier unity restored?

From time to time conferences relating to specific problems such as peace, work for freedmen, and administration of Indian affairs had been held by Friends, but none had been concerned with the nature and the structure of the Society of Friends as such. The question was widely recognized. Was it not time to face the crisis and do some definitive thinking and writing on the essentials of Quaker faith and practice?

### The General Conferences on Unity

The time was ripe for such a meeting and the call in 1886, by Indiana Yearly Meeting, to all other Yearly Meetings "in correspondence with us" received a wide response. In 1887 the first general conference of the Gurneyite-Orthodox bodies was held at Richmond, Indiana. Representatives came from all Yearly Meetings of this branch of Friends in America and from London and Dublin Yearly Meetings.[1]

Although the pastoral system was one of the controversial issues, it had, by the 1880's, become generally accepted if not endorsed by most of the Yearly Meetings represented in the conference. The most immediate issue was that of water baptism and outward communion, as advocated by David B. Updegraff; but his attempt to bring a discussion of the question to the conference was immediately and firmly suppressed. The conference stated that the question had been answered by the entire history of Friends and that the Quaker position was already clearly stated in existing Yearly Meeting disciplines. The subject was disposed of by quoting and adopting a minute of Indiana Yearly Meeting as the action of the conference. "We believe it to be inconsistent for anyone to be acknowledged or retained in the position of Minister or Elder among us who continues to participate in or to teach the necessity of the outward rite of Baptism or the Supper." This was short of disownment of those who accepted the rites.

Having established firmly its position on that question the conference moved to its major concern: "Is it desirable that all Yearly Meetings of Friends in the world should adopt one declaration of Christian Doctrine?" The answer came readily, for such a statement would speak to the main purpose for which the conference was called. A committee was appointed and its report containing the statement of faith covering all major topics of faith and practice was approved. Joseph Bevan Braithwaite of London Yearly Meeting, one of the most influential members of that committee, has been credited with responsibility for the content of the document. The turn toward the orthodox-evangelical position of Friends had earlier been encouraged by Friends from London Yearly Meeting and now the trend was climaxed by what has come to be called the Richmond Declaration of Faith. By this time a new turn in London Yearly

---

[1] *Proceedings of the General Conference of Friends,* for 1887, 1892, and 1897, with minutes and stenographic reports, are available in many Friends college libraries.

Meeting was taking place, with a more liberal emphasis emerging.

Definitive statements on religious faith generally open the way to division. Writing and approving of this common statement of faith allayed but did not ultimately resolve the questions it raised. Questions had become issues, deep running, and what was temporarily expedient and apparently uniting became the source of tensions and further separations. The main questions, as understood by the conference, had been raised, but they would be raised again, with varying answers.

Despite the sensitive attitudes the conference had exposed Friends to Friends in a face-to-face meeting and had stated something in common. They all knew that in some deeper and historic sense they belonged together. Before the conference adjourned it was agreed that Friends should meet again at five-year intervals. The conferences which followed in 1892 and 1897 developed more awareness of the nature of the diverse views and practices of Friends and, in some measure, led to a closer fellowship. The possibility of cooperative undertakings led to proposing a permanent organization of Yearly Meetings.

The conference of 1892, meeting in Indianapolis, considered Friends literature, meetings for worship as related to the pastoral and unprogrammed forms, church government, and the history and nature of the Society of Friends. There were both exponents and opponents of the pastoral system and all had a full opportunity to speak. The discussions did not end in complete unity, but points of view were generally exposed and understood. The pastoral system as a settled way had to be accepted, while being open to criticism and correction. The conference adjourned

> with a lively sense of the brotherly kindness and courtesy which have marked the deliberations of the Conference, and with heartfelt prayers for the blessing of the Lord our God upon our beloved Society and upon all the members of its widely extended organization, and for the extension of His kingdom throughout all the world.

The conference of 1897, also meeting in Indianapolis, moved much farther toward a united organization which would have a discipline in common and some measure of legislative authority. A communication from Indiana Yearly Meeting requested "the approaching conference to consider whether the time has not come to advise the Yearly Meetings to confer delegated powers upon the conference, so that, in the future its conclusions shall be binding on all the Yearly Meetings that unite in granting such authority." A similar request from Kansas Yearly Meeting "affirms its position taken in 1887 and 1892 favoring a general conference with legislative powers and a uniform discipline for all the Yearly Meetings." Wilmington Yearly Meeting asked the conference "to formulate some plan of union or federation . . . and submit the same to the various Yearly Meetings for their ratification." A similar request came from Western Yearly Meeting.

The conference approved the move toward union and a common discipline, and appointed a committee with representatives from the constituent Yearly Meetings to present a plan. The conference believed that "such a union of our Yearly Meetings would tend to protect them from common dangers and strengthen their joint participation in Christian work." The committee was asked to include a uniform discipline and submit it to the Yearly Meetings for their approval.

When the fourth conference convened in 1902 at Indianapolis the committee on union and a uniform discipline made its report, presenting not only the new discipline but also favorable action by New England, New York, Baltimore, North Carolina, Wilmington, Indiana, Western, Iowa, Kansas, California, and Oregon Yearly Meetings. (Canada Yearly Meeting came in later.) The Five Years Meeting, which opened the next morning in its first session, had awaiting it a "common Declaration of Faith, Constitution of Government and Rules of Discipline of the general body of Friends in America."

Philadelphia and Ohio Yearly Meetings did not unite with the Five Years Meeting, but for distinctly different reasons. The pastoral-evangelical development seemed alien to Quakerism as viewed in Philadelphia. On the other hand, Ohio Yearly Meeting feared what was thought to be a liberal trend emanating chiefly from the East and also being expressed by many of the leaders of the Five Years Meeting. The voice of the *American Friend* and the discussions of the conferences did not have the ring or tone of the evangelical faith as seen by Ohio. There may have been also the fear that the issue of water baptism and the outward communion would be brought to the fore and bring a tension within the Yearly Meeting as well as within the Five Years Meeting.

Whether, in view of the firm action taken by the general conference of 1887 on the subject of water baptism and the Lord's Supper, Ohio Yearly Meeting could have been admitted into membership without a separation in the Yearly Meeting is a question that history raises but cannot answer. To admit Ohio Yearly Meeting into membership would have raised the issue decisively. The Richmond Declaration of Faith was utterly clear on the outward rites and would, presumably, have forced a difficult decision by both Ohio Yearly Meeting and the Five Years Meeting.

Even so, in many sessions of the Five Years Meeting from that day to the present, Ohio and Philadelphia Yearly Meetings have been extended invitations into membership. They have been invited also to send fraternal representatives to the Five Years Meeting. Philadelphia has generally responded with appointed attenders. Those attending from Ohio have generally come out of personal interest and friendliness.

## The Five Years Meeting Organized

"The Five Years Meeting of Friends in America, the purest and most temperamental and intractable democracy in the world!" It was a moment of truth-in-humor for Walter C. Woodward when in 1917 he penned those lines as the first full-time secretary-editor for the Five Years Meeting of Friends. He had put his hand to the plow and there was no looking back. He saw the size and the complexity which the first stages of the undertaking presented as he held the dual role of secretary to the Five Years Meeting and editor of the *American Friend*.

The Five Years Meeting was all but impossible and at the same time a necessity. So much had happened that the possibility of a working unity might have seemed, to a practical observer, quite remote; but the way of the Spirit runs deep and dares the impossible. If the roots call for something the branches must respond. Nothing is ultimately impossible except that which ought not to be, and time has more than justified the dream and the cost by which the Five

Years Meeting (Friends United Meeting), has come to be and is still becoming![2]

There was a longing, a lure toward oneness, in the scattered and fragmented Society of Friends in western America. Quakers held a common spiritual ancestry. Surely separatism was not the answer for those whose existence sprang from a common dynamic source. The changes from earlier Quaker traditions seemed to many Friends to deny first-century Quakerism even while that heritage was claimed and praised. No area or branch had retained a pure example of George Fox Quakerism.

The concerns of the first Five Years Meeting sessions are indicated by the boards and the committees named or adopted in 1902. Those appointed were the Boards on Evangelism and Church Extension, Education, Legislation (concerned with public issues), and Condition and Welfare of the Negroes. Existing agencies adopted as channels of service were the American Friends Board of Foreign Missions (an independent association), the Associated Executive Committee of Friends for Indian Affairs (including all Friends), and the Peace Association of Friends in America (including representation of Orthodox Friends bodies). The *American Friend,* then edited and published in Philadelphia by an independent association, was approved as the channel of communication for the Five Years Meeting.

There were some very difficult problems to be faced by this new working body of Friends. One was the great geographic distances. Only a few representatives could cross mountains and plains for annual or occasional meetings and for the sessions that would be held every five years. Would their common concern be strong enough and imaginative enough to hold distant bodies together in fellowship?

There were also diverse economic backgrounds. These differences were evident in the financing of the new united venture. A few Meetings represented the business and professional life of large towns and cities. These were accustomed to an economy of fixed incomes, salaries, and budgets, whereas the vast majority of the Meetings were rural. For rural Meetings monthly checks of specified amounts were little known. Their members faced the hazards of wind and weather and of small or large crops with a resultant wide fluctuation of living

---

[2] The account of the formation and development of the Five Years Meeting has been taken almost wholly from the minutes of that body.

standards. Though money was an essential in buying and selling, much of the livelihood of the farmer came from farm to dinner table in amounts uncomputed in dollar values. Much of early farm life was of a hand-to-mouth kind of economy. To people of the rural areas the city-business-professional life seemed soft and expensive. The budget required for operation of a national program appeared to be simply overhead expense. The gap between city and rural economy made for misunderstanding and ill-supported programs.

By the 1960's these two worlds were measurably merged. Friends moving into the cities and those living in the rural areas became more urban-minded. Farmers now patronize the supermarkets quite as regularly as do their city cousins. The farmer has always been required to be a businessman, but now he is often a bigger businessman, needing and having more know-how than many city business people. The western American economy is now more fully integrated and has entered a new day. Friends have been a part of the economic development, as is reflected in the financial history of the Five Years Meeting.

Another problem at the beginning was the growing spirit of independence. The Quakerism of the first two centuries of Friends was marked by its cohesiveness within the local Meetings and the Yearly Meetings. It was not individualistic. If anything, it was too demanding on individual thought and behavior. That spirit was challenged by the environment on the American frontier which presented quite a contrast to the inherited Quaker ideal. On the frontier a fierce independence developed in the onrush of adventure and enterprise. Isolation meant insulation as the currents that held people together in common loyalties were weakened. The frontier required self-sufficiency in a catch-as-catch-can game of exploration and exploitation of opportunity, and a new sense of independence within the conditions of isolation was a logical result.

In a previous chapter tensions which appeared in the educational work of Friends have been presented. The same questions arose in the general conferences and in the Five Years Meeting almost from the beginning, although there was an air of tolerance and flexibility in the period from 1887 onward while the new integration of Yearly Meetings was under way. There had to be some kind of workable agreement if there was to be an identifiable body possessing some

Quaker substance as well as the Quaker name. An element of expediency was necessary if the new move was not to be broken up in its first few years. No one wanted to contemplate such an experience, and unwelcome ideas were, in some cases, tolerated rather than approved.

### Doctrinal Tensions

Not in the writing of the declaration of faith, but in the interpretation of it, came the test of the new body of Friends. Were they truly united or had they only agreed or conceded on the hastily written words in the interest of holding together, trusting that time would strengthen the roots of fellowship and turn disagreements into tensions of growth?

A part of their hope lay in the work pile which the new Five Years Meeting had ordered for itself. Under Edmund Stanley of Kansas Yearly Meeting as the first clerk, the Five Years Meeting moved with a measure of confidence in the services which it assumed, and appointments were made accordingly.

The history of the Five Years Meeting may be viewed in three stages or levels of its development. The first, from 1902 to 1917, was a period of developing self-awareness as an official body. The first two sessions, those of 1902 and 1907, continued the discussions that had marked the preceding general conferences, and delineated more clearly the areas of cooperation and outreach that were now becoming departments of the Five Years Meeting. The organizational structure was shaping into a logical and functional order, and the need for an employed staff in a national headquarters was now evident.

At the same time the question of doctrine was threatening. By 1912 the Five Years Meeting realized the depth of the division. It was this which ran like a faultline under the new association and now and then sent tremors across it. The sessions of 1912 were the most crucial of that period. Some representatives came wondering whether the structure would hold together. The question revolved around the interpretation of the Richmond Declaration of Faith and the Letter of George Fox to the Governor of Barbados. Following the early aversion of Friends regarding creeds, a sentence in the Declaration of Faith had been approved stating that it was not to be regarded as constituting a creed. To some Friends this was a Quakerly position, but to others it seemed like doubting the statements they had approved.

The request that this sentence be stricken from the statement of faith failed by a narrow margin in the 1912 sessions, but that did not end the question. Ten years later the words were stricken.

*Toward a Firm Structure*

Despite the difficulties relating to doctrine, the meeting of 1912 was at the same time an occasion of advance in the organization of the Five Years Meeting and the unifying of program. A commission on "The Efficiency of the Five Years Meeting" had done its work well and brought in a comprehensive report. In harmony with the guide lines presented by the commission, specific areas of work were approved and boards and committees were appointed in the fields of Evangelism and Church Extension, Missions, Legislation and Temperance, Education, Peace, Condition and Welfare of the Negroes, Indians, Social Service, Young People's Activities, Bible Schools, and Publications (including the *American Friend*). Evincing interest in the interchurch movement (later known as the ecumenical movement), a small Board on Federation of Churches was appointed. An Executive Committee of the Five Years Meeting was formed, having one representative from each Board and representing each Yearly Meeting.

The outline of work was wide in scope and needed periodic meetings of the boards and an employed staff if it was to be successfully advanced. This would require finances and time in which to evolve and implement a working program. Correspondence of board and committee members across continentwide distances was important, but it was only a beginning toward the working arrangement that evolved over fifty years later.

The Five Years Meeting approved the opening of a central office at Richmond, Indiana, the appointment of a General Secretary and assistants, and, if funds could be found, employees for the work of the Bible School and Young Friends boards.

By the time of the 1917 sessions, office space in downtown Richmond had been rented and Walter C. Woodward had been employed as General Secretary and editor of the *American Friend,* with Ruthanna M. Simms as assistant. Walter Woodward, a historian and professor in Earlham College, had his earlier background in newspaper publishing in Newberg, Oregon. By 1919 a residence in downtown Richmond was purchased as headquarters for the small staff, including those of the Mission Board and the Publication Board, with the beginnings of a bookstore.

The first stage of Five Years Meeting history (fifteen years) also marked the beginning of the second stage, 1917 to 1950. The organization now had a home and a small staff of full-time workers. This was the beginning of a period which would be marked by continuing tension and some separations, but the longer view would not call it a failure. Indeed, when the superstructure was under test the foundations were being strengthened. It was more like the storm-lashed tree whose roots adjust to the stress.

### WITHDRAWAL OF YEARLY MEETINGS

The intra-Quaker tensions of the period suggest another aspect of the peace testimony. Within limits, controversy is not wholly bad. It can be creative and often is found to be when reviewed across a longer span of time. Likewise, separations are not necessarily wrong. Sometimes they seem necessary, as in the cases within the Five Years Meeting. They can occur within a spirit of mutual understanding and consent.

Differences of views, as expressed between bodies of Friends, can be expressed frankly yet not bitterly. In the main this was true in the actions minuted during the separations of Oregon and Kansas Yearly Meetings from the Five Years Meeting.[3]

### Oregon Yearly Meeting

Established in 1893, Oregon Yearly Meeting had been invited three years later by Kansas Yearly Meeting "to cooperate in a union of all the American Yearly Meetings . . . that would enable all Friends to give a united sentiment at all times on moral, civil and religious reforms." Oregon Yearly Meeting agreed and in 1897 sent representatives to the third general conference of Friends.[4]

The omission of the phrase saying that the Richmond Declara-

---

[3] The history of their withdrawal by the three Yearly Meetings has been taken from their minutes and from those of the Five Years Meeting for that period.

[4] Ralph K. Beebe, *A Garden of the Lord,* a history of Oregon Yearly Meeting; The Barclay Press, 1968. Pages 50-55 present the tensions and the separation.

ation of Faith and the Letter of George Fox to the Governor of Barbados was *not to be construed as a creed* by no means resolved the conflict of ideas. The interpretations and implementation of those statements revealed how far apart bodies of Friends had drifted during the nineteenth century and later. The tensions between the two general views came to the breaking point first in Oregon Yearly Meeting.

The awakening to the disparity of views was continuous and cumulative, as reflected in the minutes of the Yearly Meeting and the Five Years Meeting and in the *American Friend*. In the sessions of Oregon Yearly Meeting of 1919 the issue came to a focus. With a conciliatory note recognizing "the many problems which would naturally come" to Five Years Meeting boards, the Yearly Meeting thought it would be well to insert a question in application blanks for candidates to the mission field to ascertain whether or not the applicant was thoroughly orthodox in faith and experience.

The Yearly Meeting also stated that as the "Board of Publications is publishing the *American Friend,* and the Bible School periodicals and papers . . . the Boards heretofore mentioned must cease to publish anything in any of their publications not in harmony with the doctrinal standards" as stated in the Declaration of Faith and the Letter of George Fox to the Governor of Barbados. Propositions coming from a Monthly Meeting and a Quarterly Meeting asking that the Yearly Meeting withdraw from the Five Years Meeting were directed to the Quarterly Meetings for their action, to be reported to the Yearly Meeting in 1920.

Though the Yearly Meeting in 1920 was not united on whether to withdraw from or remain in the Five Years Meeting, resolutions were approved and directed to be sent to the General Secretary of the Five Years Meeting. The objections centered on publications, though including other departments. The final resolution stated:

> We demand on the part of all our Boards and Publication Staffs that they review the requirements to which the Five Years Meeting has pledged itself, and conform thereto . . . and to no other. It is therefore understood that if these conditions are not remedied by the next Five Years Meeting in the reorganization of its various Boards, Oregon Yearly Meeting will feel at liberty to withdraw should it so elect.

The Yearly Meeting in 1922, immediately preceding the Five Years Meeting sessions, "united in the belief that Oregon Yearly Meeting at this time should request the Five Years Meeting to go on record as accepting these related documents as the officially authorized Declaration of Faith of the Five Years Meeting of Friends in America."

In response the Five Years Meeting recognized "with profound sorrow that there is in the world today a great drift of religious unsettlement, unconcern and unbelief" and reaffirmed the statements of faith, but stated that "our Christian faith involves more than the adoption and profession of written statements," and asserted that "loyalty and devotion to a living Christ and in an inward experience of His spiritual presence and power in the soul" is the ultimate test of faith.

The Five Years Meeting agreed that "since the clause which was adopted ten years ago stating that these declarations of faith are not to be regarded as constituting a creed . . . has been widely misunderstood in at least two directions" *that clause should be eliminated.* This seemed to satisfy all of the representatives. John Henry Barlow, attending from London Yearly Meeting, voiced his "thankfulness at the manifestation of harmony he was witnessing among American Friends."

By 1924 Oregon Yearly Meeting felt that though the statements of faith had been made official they had not been implemented in the Five Years Meeting and set the year 1926 as the date at which the Yearly Meeting would withdraw if leadership and policies of the Five Years Meeting had not been adjusted to what the Yearly Meeting believed to be the proper interpretation of the official statements.

The General Secretary and the Executive Committee of the Five Years Meeting had not ignored the concerns of Oregon Yearly Meeting. But they had to recognize the whole Five Years Meeting membership and the views of other Yearly Meetings as well. A statement of 1926 indicates not only the attitude of the Executive Committee for that year but also the effort at reconciliation for this period of stress. A committee had been appointed to confer with a similar committee of Oregon Yearly Meeting, and the Executive Committee expressed the "hope that nothing may occur which will be allowed in the slightest degree to diminish a feeling of unity between Friends in different parts of the Five Years Meeting or to jeopardize that vital spiritual union between each individual Christian and Christ himself."

This did not relax the tension, and in 1926 Oregon Yearly Meeting "in keeping with its action of 1924" declared that it "does now cease to cooperate with its [Five Years Meeting's] departments of work and to send delegates to its sessions." The door was left slightly ajar by adding, " . . . until the Five Years Meeting assumes responsibility for such leadership as indicated by its action in 1922, and through such a leadership creates a basis for confidence, unity, and cooperation, satisfactory to Oregon Yearly Meeting."

A substitute proposition was presented in the Yearly Meeting suggesting that the Five Years Meeting become less authoritative and legislative and come "more nearly to the place of a body for conference and cooperation, and give more autonomy to the Yearly Meetings in the planning and carrying out of their work both at home and abroad." This was not accepted and the first significant separation from the Five Years Meeting occurred within the first quarter-century of its existence.

*Kansas Yearly Meeting*

The separation of Kansas Yearly Meeting from the Five Years Meeting need not be told in detail for it was similar to that of Oregon Yearly Meeting. The same doctrinal interests and the same objection to publications of the Five Years Meeting were stated. One objection was somewhat more accented by Kansas than by Oregon Friends, specifically as to persons sent to the mission field; but the line of controversy was broad.

In 1930 Kansas Yearly Meeting received "communications from eleven Quarterly Meetings, a summary of which [was] read and referred to the representatives." The representatives recommended that the Yearly Meeting withdraw all financial support from all boards of the Five Years Meeting at the close of the fiscal year, March 31, 1931; that final action on complete withdrawal be deferred for future action. The Mission Board of the Yearly Meeting was asked to make a survey for a possible mission field of its own.

None of the Yearly Meeting sessions during these years passed without discussion formally or informally on relationships with the

Five Years Meeting. One year before the 1935 sessions of the Five Years Meeting another large Quarterly Meeting urged withdrawal, but the Yearly Meeting disapproved complete severance and a token delegation was appointed to attend the Five Years Meeting sessions. In the meantime financial support had also been reduced to a token payment.

Despite the growing urge coming from the Quarterly Meetings the Yearly Meeting in 1936 recommended "that no [further] change be made at this time in our relationship to the Five Years Meeting."

In 1937 the pressure to withdraw had not been eased. The minority within the Yearly Meeting, which favored membership in the Five Years Meeting, yielded and Kansas Yearly Meeting withdrew from the Five Years Meeting. This very significant and strong minority, especially in the Wichita area, felt that the separation was a sad mistake.

### Rocky Mountain Yearly Meeting

Nearly twenty years after the separation of Kansas Yearly Meeting a third separation occurred in the withdrawal of the main body of Nebraska Yearly Meeting and the formation of the Rocky Mountain Yearly Meeting of Friends, centered mainly in Colorado. This left Nebraska Yearly Meeting a very small body. The reasons for this action were practically the same as those of Oregon and Kansas Yearly Meetings, with one additional objection — membership of the Five Years Meeting in the World Council of Churches and the National Council of Churches.

These objections and the requests for dissociation from the two Councils were presented to the Five Years Meeting. The Executive Committee in 1954 received a request from Nebraska Yearly Meeting asking that, in all printed publicity relating to Five Years Meeting membership in the Councils, "Nebraska Yearly Meeting be recognized as dissociated from the World and National Councils." The Executive Committee consulted the two Councils and were informed that "membership is by the Five Years Meeting rather than the Yearly Meeting and that they saw no clear way to make this exception." The question was again discussed by the Executive Committee in 1955.

In 1956 a letter from the General Secretary on behalf of the Five

Years Meeting of 1955 to Nebraska Yearly Meeting stated that the Five Years Meeting did not approve some statements by some persons connected with the Councils, but "that membership of the Five Years Meeting in these Councils results in values which should be preserved, and . . . that, for the present our membership be continued." The Five Years Meeting expressed "our respect and love for Nebraska Yearly Meeting Friends and our respect for their point of view."

In 1956 the representatives of Nebraska Yearly Meeting recommended and the Yearly Meeting approved the setting off of a new body to be known as Rocky Mountain Yearly Meeting of Friends, with the local Meetings electing in which of the two Yearly Meetings they should hold membership. With a minimum of conflict the separation took place.

In 1957 the Nebraska Yearly Meeting met, reviewed the choices of local meetings, recommended property arrangements, and then divided into separate Yearly Meetings for their respective business sessions. Twenty-one of the twenty-seven Meetings elected to join Rocky Mountain Yearly Meeting, leaving six Meetings to constitute Nebraska Yearly Meeting. Assets from Nebraska Central College were turned to Nebraska Yearly Meeting and those of the Rough Rock Mission in Arizona to Rocky Mountain Yearly Meeting. Records and assets of Nebraska Central College were later turned to William Penn College in Iowa.

## War Resistance and Peacemaking

No other witness of Friends was more firmly and universally held through the first two-and-a-half centuries than that of peace. If a body of Friends dissented from the peace stand they would likely withdraw from the Society of Friends as did the "Free Quakers" during the War of Independence. Many disownments for "going to muster" or participation in war are recorded.

As the country moved toward the Civil War two testimonies of Friends were under test — antislavery and peace. If ever Friends could justify war, surely it would be one fought for liberation of the slaves. Even at this point Friends did not yield their peace stand. Those who had migrated to free territory also held their peace position, though under pressure from the government. In 1862, during the heat of conflict, Ohio Yearly Meeting addressed the President:

To Abraham Lincoln, President of the United States.

The Ohio Yearly Meeting of Friends convened at Mt. Pleasant, Jefferson County Ohio. 9th. month 1862, respectfully represents. — That owing to the present unhappy condition of our Country and the enrollment of names in order to draft therefrom some thousands to be placed in the Army — Many of our members who are now sharing in common with other good Citizens the trials of the times are subject to the still greater trial of having for conscience sake to decline in this particular to obey the authorities of a government under which we enjoy many privileges and blessings and to which we hope ever to be found loyal.

We would briefly call the attention of the President to the fact with which he is no doubt acquainted that our Society has from its rise (a period of more than two hundred Years) borne a testimony against all wars and fightings believing them to be at variance with the pure and peaceable dispensation of the Gospel of Christ — and have constantly under all governments felt constrained to refuse to bear arms or pay an equivalent in lieu thereof — Also to the legislation of various States of this Union in which our members are exempt from military services. And therefore respectfully submit whether there cannot be something done by the authorities of the general government for the relief of all members of our Society not already exempted by State enactments. In conclusion we would express our deep sympathy with the President in the various difficulties which press upon him in this day of sore calamity.

In 1867 the Peace Association of Friends in America was organized following a conference in 1866 called by Ohio Yearly Meeting which drew Friends together from East to West. Friends of the Midwest were very active in its work. John Henry Douglas, a leading evangelical Friend, was appointed its first General Secretary. About 1875 the *Messenger of Peace* began publication. The Peace Association was adopted by the Five Years Meeting as its channel for peace work and later it was absorbed in the peace department of the Five Years Meeting. The *Messenger of Peace* became a section of the *American Friend* and by 1945 ceased as a publication.

A testimony not under continual test is likely to be forgotten. A period of more than fifty years of relative peace came between the close of the Civil War and the beginning of the First World War. In the meantime Quaker settlements were absorbed by the larger communities and the attitudes of some Friends were changed accordingly. The outbreak of World War I revealed how far Quakers had drifted from their ancient peace moorings. Though there was a significant minority that held to the ancient position, most young Friends chose military service. The organization of the American Friends Service Committee in 1917 offered alternative service for conscientious objectors and opened a new day with new thinking on the nature of peace and war. War resistance became, in a significant sense, *peacemaking*.

In the midtwentieth century young Friends serving in the military forces outnumber the conscientious objectors, but the official position of all branches of Friends has been against participation in war. That it became a question for personal decision a century ago is quaintly expressed in a tombstone inscription in the cemetery at Guilford, North Carolina: "William Thomas Parker, Born at Belvidere Perquimans County, N.C., November 21, 1861, Died at High Point, N.C., July 6, 1922, A Life Long Friend but *Never a Pacifist*" (italics added)! Nearby is another tombstone marking the burial site of British and American soldiers killed during the War of Independence and buried in March 1781. Erected by New Garden Friends, it bears the line "Peace and Good Will." This act of goodwill would have been consonant with the Quaker attitude in any period of their history.

In general, deviation from the ancient peace stand was greater in those bodies of Friends in the pastoral traditions, because of changes due largely to isolation and dispersion on the wide frontier. The Second World War further revealed the change, but also opened up new avenues of study and approach to the cause and cure of war.

In recent years Oregon Yearly Meeting may be ahead of other Yearly Meetings in giving attention to their young men of military age. At this time forty-four percent of their young men are conscientious objectors. An Alternative Services Committee of their Peace Board offers counsel and preregisters their C.O.'s. Three volunteers serving in Vietnam as C.O.'s are supported by the student body of George Fox College. Evangelical concern and peace witness are united in these activities of Oregon Yearly Meeting. They are illustrative of similar concerns in other Yearly Meetings.

The Five Years Meeting of 1917 convened in the midst of the First World War, after America had entered the war. A few months after the American Friends Service Committee had been organized the Five Years Meeting asked the Secretary of War to "endorse the request of the American Friends Service Committee that the Friends' reconstruction work, together with other work under the direction of the Committee, be recognized as noncombatant service." The "Message of the Five Years Meeting" written in that session stated:

> This is a solemn hour for us. We and our faith are on trial. We are being tested as never before. We are at the parting of the ways. We shall emerge from this crucible of the world's history, weakened in power and unworthy of spiritual leadership; or we shall rise to the crisis and find through our loyalty to Christ a new vision and increased power for a fresh onward march.

From the Christian Endeavor Society of Whittier Friends Meeting in California came a telegram to the Five Years Meeting saying, "We urge you to do all in your power to have the Friends Reconstruction Unit recognized by the government as noncombatant service. Also that our young men may be discharged from the regular army upon entering the Unit." The responsibility for counselling, publicity, and raising of funds within western Yearly Meetings for this new service fell largely on the Five Years Meeting office. All Friends of every branch were united in this undertaking and soon two units of Quaker young men were in France working in the battle zones, building homes, harvesting crops, giving medical relief, and distributing supplies from American and British Friends. The Friends War Victims Relief Committee of London Yearly Meeting and the American Friends Service Committee were linked in a new peace front more or less paralleling the battle lines.

When the war ended, the question was faced as to a continuing responsibility of Friends during times of peace. Feeling that peace is not simply a space between two wars, but a dynamic way of life, the American Friends Service Committee was continued "to see what love can do" within the tensions and the problems that lead to war. This work of peace*making* would now try to work at the *roots* of violence.

In 1920 an opportunity was offered under the American Relief

Administration, directed by Herbert Hoover, who was a Quaker and a member of Oregon Yearly Meeting. Many Friends from coast to coast were drawn into a child-feeding program in Germany, into meeting famine and disease in Russia, and into other areas of Europe especially. What was started then has since spread to many corners of the earth and with many kinds of services to the spirits, minds, and bodies of people. The Nobel Peace Prize, shared by the Friends Service Council of London and Ireland Yearly Meetings and the American Friends Service Committee in 1947, indicates the acceptance by peoples and nations of the Quaker forms of peacemaking.

Under the heading "Christendom for a Warless World" the Five Years Meeting in session in 1922 addressed a message to all "Fellow Christians and Sister Churches of all Lands," urging "refusal to participate in war, simply and sufficiently because war is by its very nature at variance with the message, the spirit and the life and death of Jesus Christ." The statement also made an appeal for the support of treaties and agencies of governments having to do with arbitration through "international courts of justice [and] a league or association of nations for the preservation of peace. . . ," and stated that "though support of such effort is good, it is not sufficient for the Christian Church. A principle is greater than any or all of its applications."

Friends have worked with other peace churches in the common cause of peacemaking. In 1936 a conference of Brethren, Friends, and Mennonites was held at Bethel College, Newton, Kansas, to consider their respective bases for their peace witness. Out of that conference a Continuation Committee was formed to pursue further their common interests in peace, faith, and action. Robert Balderston represented Friends until his death. This committee has been active for more than thirty years, sponsoring small and large conferences and making joint approaches to government. The activities of the three religious bodies have been similar in some aspects, particularly in the services of relief.

The attitude of Friends in the Second World War had somewhat changed. The First World War caught them almost wholly unprepared. The two decades between the two wars had been a time of awakening not only to the facts and the tragedies of war but also to its cause and cure. The American Friends Service Committee, along with other concerned Quaker groups, had encouraged the creation of centers of understanding within areas of conflict at home and abroad. When the Second World War came there was a place to which to go, a group with which to be identified, a philosophy to be understood, and a broad front of action available to young people.

The ending of the First World War had revealed the futility of military force. "The war to end war" had not ended it and the cause of creative peace appeared more realistic. The public attitude was hardly the same as that of the First World War. War could be seen as "the enemy" even when the answer to it, as a wrong way of solving human problems, was not clear. During this second war period various kinds of alternative services were opened, chiefly that of Civilian Public Service within the United States.[5]

Friends were not silent on the events of the war. When napalm bombs were being dropped on Tokyo, the *American Friend* (representing the Five Years Meeting) called, "Stop this American atrocity!" and continued:

> These words had to be written. In America we have talked too much about the Buchenwald and Dachau concentration camps in Germany to feel that we can, in any comparable measure, be guilty of such atrocities. The evil work of those camps leaves us in a state of amazement and revulsion. Such crimes, we say, are committed only by Germans and Japanese. Yet we are making our own record, at long range.
>
> Certainly we are not directly and personally herding men and women into torture chambers and watching with indifference their slow death. *We are not prepared to look directly upon the work of our hands, but we are prepared to torture — from a distance.* In fact, we *are* doing it. Every day our superforts take not only explosive bombs of the usual sort over Japan, but they also take firebombs, unquenchable jelly fuel, and splatter them over highly congested Japanese cities. General headquarters reports "excellent results."
>
> Excellent Results! In the name of God, what can such words mean! It means that on every raid there are probably hundreds, or perhaps thousands of babies and children that are roasted alive. It means probably that women and children are

---

[5] The Board on Christian Social Concerns of the Friends United Meeting (Richmond) and the American Friends Service Committee (Philadelphia) have full information on this period.

caught in groups by the driving flames which leave seared bodies piled high. It means that we are building up a reputation for wholesale, torturing slaughter. . . . Our condemnation is not against the boys who fly the planes, primarily. These boys are as good and kindly in spirit as are we in civilian life. . . . While Americans may disagree on what should be done to Japan, there would be far greater agreement on what Jesus of Nazareth would say should he walk our paths again. Many of us will continue lauding him, while forgetting what he said.

We can drown that voice in the roar of motors and the thunder of bombs, but we cannot stop it. It is not the voice of an idealist only, it is from the heart of the universe. It is stark realism. Time will catch up with us. The universe will make no exceptions in its retributions. Our judgment is being seared now into our minds and the end is not yet . . . we should yet feel compelled to cry out against the holocaust. America, let us end this orgy of flaming death![6]

Quakers cannot be expected to be expert in how to end a given war, though they have done much to throw light on war itself. They have generally felt that they must hold to their principles of peace, speak out, and try to awaken the conscience of the nation.

Friends peace agencies have moved from the alternative patterns for conscientious objectors as conducted in the two world wars and now emphasize group work independent of governmental arrangements. Alternative service *for individuals* has at the same time been supported. Opposition to conscription and efforts for world order through legislative channels have been accented.

The organization of the Friends Committee on National Legislation in 1943 at Richmond, Indiana, brought yet another intra-Friends agency into action. From the beginning the Society of Friends has been concerned for peace action on the legislative front. One of the most significant Quaker personalities of a century ago was John Bright, member of Parliament and pioneer in constructive legislation for the common people. The legislative work of North Carolina Friends is told in a preceding chapter. The coming of the F.C.N.L. was one present-day fulfillment of early Quaker concern. Raymond Wilson, the first full-time secretary, helped to establish the permanent

---

[6] The *American Friend*, Vol. 52, No. 5, August 26, 1945.

roles of the organization which has proved useful in a two-way influence, bringing to bear upon Congressmen ideas of constructive peace moves as seen by Friends, and also serving as an agency of legislative education for Friends. The Five Years Meeting (F.U.M.) has always supported the Friends Committee on National Legislation.[7]

A center, with a small staff, has been maintained near the United Nations and has kept a close relationship with the members of that important international body; many seminars have been held there, and also in Washington, D. C., on issues of war and peace. These have been sponsored by the Friends United Meeting, by all-Friends groups, and by Yearly Meetings and have brought hundreds of younger and older Friends near to the scenes of Quaker action.

The Peace Association, adopted as a channel of Five Years Meeting service, eventually became the peace department and, uniting with other social concerns, has now expanded into the Board on Christian Social Concerns. Several streams of interests have merged in this department: prison reform, abolition of capital punishment, reforms in penology, laws against child labor, temperance reforms, and, at one time or another, almost the full range of social action. The interrelatedness of all social areas of national and world life is recognized; and the Board, though giving a large share of its attention to international peace, has also been active in the areas of racial relations and economic and political concerns. Racial problems have been especially emphasized in recent years.

The Rural Life Association — independent of the Five Years Meeting but including Friends, Mennonites, Brethren, and others — continued for several years and focussed attention on the economic and spiritual aspects of farm life. All of these concerns and others have flowed into the merging stream of social action. A full-time secretary and assistants now help to guide the Board of Christian Social Concerns.

## MISSION AND SERVICE WORK

*Service and Relief*

Though the missionary movement started among Friends about

---

[7] Many seminars and conferences under F.C.N.L., the A.F.S.C., the Friends United Meeting, and other Friends bodies have been held relating to a full range of social concerns.

one century ago, the service-relief activities began formally among American Friends with the organization of the American Friends Service Committee in 1917 when America entered the First World War. The roots of service and relief reach far back to the very beginnings of the Quaker movement. They started chiefly in relief of persecuted members during the last half of the seventeenth century. The Meeting for Sufferings was organized for the specific purpose which the name implies. Although the body in London Yearly Meeting carrying that name today has become the executive of the Yearly Meeting, the spirit in which it was started continues.

This was the heritage which Friends held as they came to the New World. What was formerly relief of poor or persecuted members came later to include relief of any needy persons. This took special form in wartime. In the Franco-Prussian War, and again in the First World War, British Friends responded to the needs of war victims. The Friends War Victims Relief Committee was joined in service by the American Friends Service Committee as America came into the First World War.[8]

The initial purpose of the American Friends Service Committee was twofold. It provided a constructive opportunity for Quaker conscientious objectors and also relief for those who suffered as the victims of war. When the First World War ended, the American Friends Service Committee continued, as did the Friends War Victims Relief Committee under British and Irish Friends. The latter was succeeded by the Friends Service Council in 1927, representing a union of missionary and service activities. The mission work as a distinct form has receded while the service pattern has increased.

In America these two approaches have been held in distinct patterns and separate organizations, each having its general methods and emphases and following somewhat contrasting courses. The mission work has been concerned with conversions to the Christian faith as interpreted by Friends and with the forming of Friends Meetings on the mission field while at the same time offering practical training in educational, manual, and medical lines. On the other hand the American Friends Service Committee at the beginning held largely

---

[8] Rufus M. Jones, *A Service of Love in War Time;* The Macmillan Co., New York, 1920.

to relief activities within areas of tension. These came later to take the form of cooperative demonstration projects and also centers where the spiritual and intellectual interests of people might find expression.

The service groups have generally avoided the missionary-evangelical approach and have made no attempt to establish Meetings in the areas of their service. However, they have opened the door by which a large number of Meetings have been established, especially on the European continent. The earlier ministry of London Friends and the service of Woodbrooke College near Birmingham, England, have played a major role in this development in Europe.

It is interesting to see the changes taking place as the two streams, "mission" and "service" activities, have come to impinge each on the other. The missionary organizations have moved to a more flexible response, sending out shorter-term workers with specialized training whereas earlier in the movement the acceptance of a call to a mission field was generally considered a lifetime commitment. What was once a mission is becoming an autonomous body of the nationals. On the other hand the American Friends Service Committee at one time was cautious about overstaying in any field of service and stood ready to leave the moment a specific service had been rendered. This was, at times, almost a serve-and-run policy, but now longer-term workers, better prepared as to language and cultural understanding, are being sent. The mission work and the service projects have each taken on some aspects of the other.

Our concern at this point is with the missionary type of outreach.[9] In early Quaker history there was little difference between what are now called the evangelical and the missionary types of outreach. George Fox presented the concern of early Friends when he proclaimed, "I was commanded to turn people to that inward light, spirit and grace by which all might know their salvation." He was pleased to report, in 1654, that "a matter of seventy ministers did the Lord raise up and send abroad out of the North Countries." He saw "the harvest white and the seed of God lying thick on the ground . . . and none to gather it." Those early Quakers were convinced and committed. An artesian power broke through in a day

---

[9] Christina H. Jones, *Amercian Friends in World Missions;* Brethren Publishing House, 1946. This volume is a major source of information on Friends and missions.

Walter C. Woodward

Willis Hotchkiss, Arthur Chilson, and Edgar Hole Embarking for East Africa

Eli and Sybil Jones

characterized by dogmatism and settled traditional forms of religious expression.

By 1660 the early Quaker movement was coming to its crest. Friends began moving under individual concern to many areas of the world. That there was an urgent sense of mission can hardly be doubted though the word and the plan of present-day missions were as yet unknown. Fox could not have known or guessed that his followers three centuries later would divide his message, some of them emphasizing his sense of mission while denying the inward light and others accenting the inward light and omitting the outward mission as demonstrated by him and his Quaker associates. Though there is no example of first-generation Quakerism today, there is a continuing search for the meaning of that great upthrust in the first generation of Quakers.

Friends of the nineteenth century were caught in the spirit of the age. Religious bodies were not immune to the adventure and the enthusiasm attending the age of imperialism. The lure of faraway places was no doubt mixed with personal concern. Daniel Wheeler, in 1833, sailed his own ship to the South Pacific, visited the Sandwich (Hawaiian) Islands, and made contact with the missionaries of other church bodies on the islands.[10] In 1861 Joel and Hannah Bean visited the Sandwich Islands and their contacts with these missions inspired a new interest among Friends in America. Eli and Sybil Jones visited Palestine in 1869 and started a school at Ramallah. By 1871 Samuel Purdie was in Mexico with his printing press and his gospel of the printed word. Under his inspiration schools were soon opened and Indiana Yearly Meeting fostered his work. These beginnings blossomed into Friends missionary enterprises in several areas at home and abroad.

Other religious bodies had awakened earlier and started the new movement, as a corporate responsibility, before Friends united in a settled pattern of missionary service. Among non-Friends the famous haystack meeting of Williams College students had occurred in 1806 and had resulted in a high resolve to spread the Christian Gospel; by midcentury the missionary tide was at the flow.

By 1865 a Provisional Committee on Foreign Gospel Service had

---

[10] *Journal* of Daniel Wheeler.

been formed by British Friends; by 1870 it became the Friends Foreign Mission Association, independent of London Yearly Meeting. During that decade British Friends encouraged and fostered the new missionary efforts of both British and American Friends. As they had helped to open the way for the evangelical course of American Friends, so they accepted its corollary, mission work, before American Friends bodies had formed mission boards of their own. Indiana Yearly Meeting followed London Friends shortly by organizing a Foreign Missionary Society in the same year.

As there had been a Quaker form of renaissance in the last half of the seventeenth century there was now another kind in the last half of the nineteenth century, with new patterns of extension. By 1900 American Friends were serving in nine foreign mission fields. The first of the general conferences of Friends, held at Richmond in 1887, heard reports from Indiana Yearly Meeting on the work of Samuel Purdie in Mexico; Evi Sharpless, under Iowa Yearly Meeting, in Jamaica; Philadelphia Yearly Meeting in Japan; Kansas Yearly Meeting in Alaska; New England Yearly Meeting in Syria and at Ramallah; Ohio Yearly Meeting in China; and prospective work in India with Esther Baird.

All of these new efforts made missionary work a main and uniting topic as Friends of the 1887 conference started on a course that would result in the formation of the Five Years Meeting. At this conference the representatives approved the formation of a board on missions and submitted the idea to the several Yearly Meetings. In 1892 the second conference heard from the Yearly Meetings and again approved the formation of a mission board. In 1894 representatives of several Yearly Meetings met at Wilmington, Ohio, and formed the American Friends Board of Foreign Missions. The first work of the new board was not so much administrative as consultative and cooperative, with the Yearly Meetings carrying administrative responsibilities.

By 1907 further plans opened the way for the Yearly Meetings to place their fields of service under the new united work, and by 1912 Kansas, Indiana, Western, Oregon, New York, Wilmington, and North Carolina had turned their fields to the newly formed American Friends Board of Foreign Missions. In 1918 New England Yearly Meeting turned their field in Palestine to the united program.

In 1918 the Five Years Meeting recommended the formation of a Home Mission Board, uniting the work of the Evangelistic and Church Extension Board with that of social service and the committee on welfare and condition of the Negroes. By 1920 thirty projects of work in America were reported under this new board. The work of the Home Mission Board, after ten years, was merged with foreign work in the American Friends Board of Missions. This placed under one board an undue scope of responsibilities, which were later distributed to separate committees or boards.

## FIELDS UNDER THE FRIENDS UNITED MEETING

*Africa*

Almost a century after the Church Missionary Society of London (non-Friends) had sent missionaries to what is now called Liberia (1812) on the west coast of Africa, American Friends started mission work in Kenya (1902) on the east coast. The earlier work in Liberia was, in part, due to the awakening conscience on slavery, called by Livingstone "the open sore of the world," with its traffic in human life and incredible brutality. In 1851 Eli and Sybil Jones visited Liberia, which by that time had been set up as a republic to resettle the freedmen from America.

Here in Africa was the beginning of a human drama continent-wide in scope and soul-deep in its pathos and in its hard-won achievements. Africa is a land forced to leap over centuries into the modern period in a change that is breathtaking in speed and scope. What would normally require several centuries has been crowded into a few generations. Africa has been earth's most exploited area as commercial interests have moved in. Missions in Africa have not been able to escape wholly the spirit of colonialism, yet in large measure have kept alive the deeper stream of human understanding out of which national independence can survive. The outcome cannot be predicted, but Friends in Kenya have had an opportunity to share in the unfinished, unfolding drama. Never since the "holy experiment" of William Penn have Friends had so great an opportunity to affect the destiny of a nation.

The Friends mission began at the turn of the century. Willis R. Hotchkiss, trained in the Cleveland Bible Institute under Walter and Emma Malone, spent four years of service in Africa and returned

in 1899 urging Friends to open a mission among the Kavirondo of
Kenya. Friends Africa Industrial Mission was formed as Arthur
Chilson, Edgar T. Hole, and Willis Hotchkiss were sent to East
Africa in 1902 to find a location for missionary service. The purpose
stated by the board included "teaching them habits of industry and
ultimately establishing a self-supporting native Christian Church."
The work was developed under four departments — industrial, educational, medical, and evangelical (church extension). These four emphases have made for a balanced program out of which came East
Africa Yearly Meeting of Friends, established in 1946. It is the largest
Friends Yearly Meeting in the world, with a membership of over
thirty thousand.[11] The property and the administration of the work
have been transferred from the American Friends Board of Missions
to East Africa Yearly Meeting.

As Kenya came to independence in 1963, African Friends educated in the Friends mission came into positions of responsibility in
the new government. Perhaps the most striking example of Quaker
influence was the membership of a woman Friend on the Legislative
Council of Kenya.

Starting under the pastoral-evangelical branch of Friends this
body in Africa has drawn the interest of nearly all Friends. The
mission staff has included British and European Friends as well as
Americans. In 1961 the Friends World Committee held its triennial
meeting in Kenya with representatives from many countries, and
with the largest attendance the World Committee had ever experienced.

With the movement of African Friends from the rural areas of
western Kenya to the cities, adjustment to urban life has become a
great problem. Attention is now turning to Friends who have moved
to the cities. New Meetings and meetinghouses are being established
and activities are being developed to meet the needs in the new urban
centers. British Friends have also responded generously to the need
and through a center in Nairobi are working with these African
Friends. This is a cooperative movement, significant not only for
African Friends but also as an encounter of pastoral and nonpastoral

---

[11] Statistics on Friends Meetings have doubtful meaning when given in total
figures, for some Yearly Meetings list only adult and preparatory names. The African membership includes only adults.

forms of religious practices. Here also the mission and service streams meet. Under the Friends Service Council of London and Ireland Yearly Meetings a community center has been established and the African pastoral Friends Meeting uses the buildings for its own worship and work.

Schools for boys and girls in the western Kenya mission have brought African young people to the next level of educational need, and they are now asking for a Friends college in their area. This is by no means assured, but responsible Quaker educators are raising the question as a present-day issue.[12] Earlham College has included a program that has deeply involved faculty and students in the evolving educational pattern of Kenya.

The move from one stage to another of relationship between foreign workers and the nationals is never marked by distinct steps. When culture meets culture, as in Kenya, there are always complexity and many tensions to be understood and overcome; but among Friends these are generally tensions of growth. African Friends, being the largest body in mission-service work, have meant much in the intercultural experience of Friends. Creativeness within the Society of Friends has entered a new stage in which African Friends have a special role.

### Syria-Palestine

The "Holy Land" has always had a unique lure for the Christian churches and it early became a mission field.[18] The Presbyterians preceded Friends there by about forty years. In 1869 Eli and Sybil Jones, New England Friends, found there a school for boys but none for girls. A small school for girls was started by Friends, and English Friends under the Committee for Foreign Gospel Service supported it until 1888 when it was turned to New England Yearly Meeting. Theophilus Waldemeier, a German teacher in the British Syrian schools, joined Friends and with Eli Jones encouraged New England

---

[12] Considerable thought had been given to this question when two Friends college presidents, Landrum Bolling of Earlham and Milo C. Ross of George Fox, visited the African field in 1968 to survey the needs.

[18] Rufus M. Jones, *Later Periods of Quakerism II;* Macmillan and Co., Ltd., London, p. 893-905. Ch. XVII and XVIII give a full review of this period of awakening.
The later occupation within what was formerly called Palestine has led to the newer designation of "Jordan" and "Israel."

Friends to take responsibility. Two centers had developed, one at Brumanna in Lebanon, taken over by English Friends, and one at Ramallah under New England Yearly Meeting.

Under the leadership of American, English, and Arab Friends three schools have been maintained — one at Brumanna in Lebanon and two at Ramallah in Jordan — on elementary through high school levels. They have survived three wars and remain as centers of understanding and renewal despite very difficult circumstances. Friends Meetings have been established in these two areas and constitute Near East Yearly Meeting.

The work of Friends in the Holy Land represents a unique experience in which two faiths, Christianity and Islam, have met. This has added to the broad spectrum of relationships while it has called for a somewhat different approach in meeting Quaker responsibilities. The work in Ramallah and Brumanna is reflected across the entire Arab world in which Quaker-trained leaders are serving.

*Mexico*

When Samuel Purdie went to Mexico in 1871 with the approval and the support of the Friends Foreign Missionary Association of Indiana Yearly Meeting, it was not with the idea of establishing a mission station. He was a young schoolteacher from New York Yearly Meeting, serving in North Carolina. As a conscientious objector during the Civil War he became burdened with the need for peacemaking. The internecine conflicts of Mexico suggested to him an opportunity to proclaim and practice the gospel of peace. He was not a recorded minister; nor was preaching his main service. His paper *El Ramo de Olivo (The Olive Branch)* was his main channel of communication. He printed textbooks for the little school which he had established. He translated and printed some Quaker "Lives" of Stephen Grellet, William Penn, and Elizabeth Fry, and other literature. Calls for these productions came from several other Spanish-speaking countries.

Within a decade a chapel was built, two schools were started (including a girls' boarding school), and a printing press had been set up. What had started as a visit under personal concern had become a mission. By the time Samuel Purdie left the mission in 1895 several other Friends had come and helped to develop the work.

Six Monthly Meetings, with eight native pastors, and six hundred members of the Society of Friends witnessed the success of the visit that became a mission.

There are now two established Meetings. One is in Mexico City with membership in Pacific Yearly Meeting, having a broad international fellowship. The other is in Victoria, related to Friends United Meeting, having only Mexican membership, being pastoral in form. Another Meeting under the Evangelical Friends Alliance is planned for Mexico City. The work in Mexico has represented yet another experience unique in its nature, with the church-and-state encounter presenting peculiar problems. Certainly there have been no more heroic examples of Christian loyalty than those of Mexican Friends.

*Jamaica*

In 1655 Admiral Penn, father of William Penn, wrested Jamaica from Spanish control, adding it to the British Empire. This opened the island to colonization, and in the stream of migrants Friends came in considerable numbers. George Fox had visited there in 1671 and reported that there was "great convincement." By 1740 a Friends Meeting and a school had been established. The background of the native population presented moral conditions not conducive to the rearing of Quaker families or the building of strong Meetings. How this colony of Friends disappeared is not fully known. Some of them may have returned to England while others migrated to America.

The Spanish and the British imported large numbers of slaves from Africa. As a result, the population of Jamaica did not have the cultural cohesiveness that tribalism and family customs provided in Africa. Poverty, ignorance, and the lack of inherited mores have made the work of Friends in Jamaica different both in degree and in character from that in any other mission field.

It was not until 1881 that Evi Sharpless, from Iowa Yearly Meeting, opened the first mission work of Friends in the island. The Yearly Meeting in 1883 adopted Jamaica as its mission field and the first Meeting was established in 1885. In 1941 Jamaica was set off as a Yearly Meeting and now has three Quarterly Meetings with seventeen local Meetings.

Education was a major emphasis of Friends as they gathered

boys and girls into their centers and schools. Today varied services are rendered at Highgate in northeast Jamaica. The continuation school has developed a flexible program of education designed to meet the specific needs of students. Swift-Purcell Boys Home offers trade training on a modest scale. Friends Craft Industries not only trains students and older people but also furnishes a limited amount of employment and a sale for the products of the industry, such as furniture and baskets.

At Seaside, Happy Grove School offers a program on a coeducational basis through the high school level. Two Meetings in Kingston bring the work of Friends to the business and urban level of Jamaican life, somewhat different from that in the other Quaker centers. As Jamaica came to independence some Friends were prominent in key government positions.

*Cuba*

In 1898 the Spanish-American War wrested Cuba from Spanish control and opened it to further political and commercial penetration by America. Hardly had their independence been achieved when an opportunity was opened for a Friends mission to the island; by 1900 the new work was under way. Benjamin F. Trueblood had sparked the concern, urging Friends to start the mission, and Zenas L. Martin, superintendent of Iowa Yearly Meeting, was sent to Cuba to survey the need and decide upon a location. Sylvester Jones and May Mather, graduating from Penn College in 1900, were married and immediately left for Cuba accompanied by Emma Phillips, a worker in Mexico, as the first missionaries to Cuba.

By 1901 the first school was established and two years later the first Monthly Meeting was opened. Twenty-five years later the work had progressed and new Meetings had been started whereby Cuba Yearly Meeting of Friends was established by the Five Years Meeting of Friends. At the crest of the educational development there were three schools — Puerto Padre Elementary School, preparing students for high school; Banes Friends School, with a vocational program; and Holguin Friends School, with secondary standing.

After years of successful work the Yearly Meeting in Cuba now faces the question of survival. The authoritarian government has taken over all Friends schools, and the Meetings, so far as can be

A New Order Emerges

known, exist as a remnant whose future may be determined by the nature of the Cuban government. A Meeting at Miami, Florida, made up of refugee Cuban Friends, has been given special help by North Carolina Yearly Meeting and the Friends United Meeting (Five Years Meeting).

*Canada: Among the Doukhobors*

The work with the Doukhobors is more of a service than a missionary kind.[14] These unusual people came in the late 1800's to Canada as refugees from persecution in Russia. As "spirit wrestlers" they adopted the title, "The Christian Community of the Universal Brotherhood," based on love of all men. Dissenters from the Russian Orthodox Church, and persecuted for nearly two centuries, they came to think of persecution as a normal way of life. During their history they even considered themselves as descendants of the three men of the Bible who came through the fiery furnace of affliction.

In many respects their ideas were similar to those of Friends, but their way of life was marked by extremes. With the kind of background they had known in Russia it is readily understood why they might have felt that every man's hand was against them. They were especially averse to controls and became a problem even under the milder forms of regulation required by the Canadian government.

Some of them developed a great sensitivity toward the welfare of animals, refusing even to use the milk of cows and turning them loose on the range, believing they were to be enjoyed much as flowers and that "the living should not live on the living." They were diverse in their ideas, some of them holding to moderate views while others required protection by government when their extreme visionary ventures threatened the lives of their own men, women, and children.

As early as 1818 Stephen Grellet and William Allen had visited them in Russia. With the help of English Friends and Count Tolstoi they were aided in their migration to Canada. English and Philadelphia Friends were sensitive to their needs, helping to educate their children and serving as interpreters between them and the Canadian government when their views and practices were in conflict. The American Friends Service Committee turned attention to them and under its auspices Emmett Gulley of Oregon Yearly

[14] *Ibid.*, p. 836.

Meeting spent several years of very important and sacrificial service seeking to penetrate the inherited hostile attitude of some of them toward present-day realities. This loving attempt to promote understanding was not of a formal mission type but represented one of the most unusual services that Friends have ever attempted.

*Alaska*

In 1867 Alaska was purchased by the United States and the way was opened by government for the churches in the field of education. In 1886 when Kansas Yearly Meeting approved the opening of a mission in Alaska, workers were not lacking. Elwood W. Weesner of Kansas and Francis W. Bangham of Wilmington, Ohio, were sent the following year by Kansas Yearly Meeting. They located on Douglas Island and started a school, followed shortly by a Sunday School, a meeting for worship, and a small orphanage. There were about 1,500 Indians on this island, and the traditional concern of Friends for Indians may have been one incentive for responding to the opportunity. Five years later there were forty members of the Friends Meeting.

Kansas Friends continued in this mission for twenty-five years, releasing it to the Presbyterians in 1912; they then turned to the fields being sponsored under the American Friends Board of Foreign Missions of the Five Years Meeting.

In 1892 Oregon Friends sent a worker to serve under Kansas Yearly Meeting and in 1894 opened a mission station of their own at Kake, in the island chain. Here also school and Meeting were started in a dual ministry. Health habits were taught and the disastrous use of liquor, fostered by white traders, was opposed. When Kansas Yearly Meeting turned their field to the Presbyterians, Oregon Friends did the same and gave their support to the work of the mission board under the Five Years Meeting.

In 1895, when California Yearly Meeting was set off, a concern for service in Alaska was expressed and Anna Hunnicut offered herself as a missionary to that area.[15] The young people's Society of Christian Endeavor and the Women's Missionary Union offered support and, accompanied by Lizzie Morris, she started service in southeastern Alaska under Oregon Yearly Meeting.

---

[15] Christina Jones, *op. cit.*, p. 242-255.

Through an appeal by Friends to Dr. Sheldon Jackson, United States General Agent of Education in Alaska, doors were opened. Indians of the Kotzebue Sound had asked for teachers. In 1897 Charles Replogle, who was serving on Douglas Island under Kansas Yearly Meeting, visited California Yearly Meeting and presented the need for mission service to the Eskimos of Kotzebue Sound; the Yearly Meeting approved entering that field. Robert and Carrie Rowe Samms were sent to open the work. They were soon joined by Anna Hunnicut for this new field north of the Arctic Circle.

The mission helped to establish a government hospital and schools in the area. Training of Eskimo pastors for village churches was later developed and work formerly done by missionaries was largely taken over by the native people. By 1949, with 3,000 members in ten local Meetings, a Quarterly Meeting was organized. An airplane purchased by California Yearly Meeting has greatly facilitated transportation over long distances and rugged terrain.

All of the above fields, with the exception of Alaska and the Doukhobors, were involved in the transfer of work to the American Friends Board of Foreign Missions. They became thereby integral parts of the Five Years Meeting, giving it a worldwide responsibility in areas that presented very diverse issues.

With the maturing of Friends mission work in these areas there has been a growth in depth of understanding as to the real nature of problems that must be faced when differing cultures meet and when the distinction between Christianity-in-depth and the American form and expression of Christian faith and practice must be understood. The mission work of evangelical-pastoral Friends has brought to the Society of Friends a far-flung frontier that has helped to give all Friends a kind of world and cultural awareness within the Quaker fellowship itself.

These have developed under the compulsion of Christian faith and experience. A new spiritual frontier of understanding, within geographic areas, now confronts the Society of Friends on a world scale as these many and exciting new Friends Meetings have been brought into the Quaker fellowship. The Friends World Committee has recognized this wider relationship and is helping in the spiritual integration on what might be called a new level of the Society of Friends.

As indicated above, the first incentives to mission work came from British Friends quite as much as from Americans. Though there is not space to tell the whole story, the work of Philadelphia and Canada Yearly Meetings in Japan is an important part of the total development. Whatever the branches of Friends, they have often met in common service when they could not wholly agree on other aspects of their life.

*The Tennessee Hills*

The story of Friends movements and settlements in Tennessee is related in part in a previous chapter. These settlements were on the migration routes from South to North.[16] In 1799 Lost Creek Quarterly Meeting was formed and the settlements of Friends seemed promising, but the migrations which came into full force during the early 1800's depleted the area. The coming of the Civil War put a severe strain on the peace-minded Quakers caught within the Confederacy. When the war was over the small Friends groups were greatly reduced. Despite those conditions they retained their heritage of social concern, established a school for Negroes at Maryville, and assisted the Cherokee Indians who refused removal westward under the government program.

The chief evidence of their spiritual vitality is Friendsville Academy, established in 1857 and continuing today. In 1870 a young Quaker doctor, Jeptha D. Garner of North Carolina Yearly Meeting, came to the area to start his medical career. His work in the Tennessee hills revealed the condition of people, most of them non-Friends. The waves of migration had rolled past them and they were caught in the economic dead-ends of the post-Civil War period. Dr. Garner called on Friends of North Carolina and other Yearly Meetings of the East for support. Public schools were established and Quaker teachers were recruited.

A Quarterly Meeting was established and later transferred from North Carolina Yearly Meeting to Wilmington (Ohio) Yearly Meeting. In 1920 the Home Mission Board of the Five Years Meeting became interested in the work and undertook responsibility for it. Meetinghouses have been erected and teachers for schools have been found and placed. Some of the Meetings in what is now called

---

[16] William Williams, *Journal*, 1828.

Friendsville Quarterly Meeting are self-supporting. A farm project for improving the agriculture of the area has been a demonstration center.

## Fields Outside the Friends United Meeting

*California Yearly Meeting Fields*

As California Yearly Meeting came into the Five Years Meeting it retained its own fields. These included not only Alaska but also fields opened in Central America in the same year that the Five Years Meeting was organized. As was common among Friends missions, the first attack was on illiteracy. Friends had come with the open Bible to the "land of the tightly closed Bible." The Bible was not only "closed" because of the Catholic policies but also by the inability of the people to read.

The Amigos Schools in Guatemala now include grades one to nine and have an enrollment of about two hundred fifty boys and girls. These schools have spread to neighboring countries, and a school in Honduras has an enrollment of eighty. The Berea Bible Institute in Guatemala trains pastors and leaders, with twenty-four enrolled. Youth organizations and Sunday Schools are fostered. Training in better agricultural methods is conducted by a trained farm adviser. There are seventy-five Monthly Meetings organized into eleven Quarterly Meetings with a membership of over 1,700 and with the number of "professed believers" over ten thousand.

California Friends are also active among Mexican and Japanese neighbors in California. They have fostered local Meetings made up largely of these Friends. When the evacuation of the Japanese in the late war was ordered by the United States government, California Friends and representatives of the American Friends Service Committee befriended the Nisei in their time of frustrations and removal.

*Oregon Yearly Meeting Mission*

When Oregon Yearly Meeting withdrew from the Five Years Meeting in 1926 it approved continuing its missionary support under the American Friends Board of Missions until certain missionaries should terminate their work on the African field.[17] When this agree-

---

[17] Ralph K. Beebe, *A Garden of the Lord*, a history of Oregon Yearly Meeting; The Barclay Press, 1968. Ch. VII. Also from literature provided by Jack Wilcutts, superintendent of Oregon Yearly Meeting.

ment ended the Yearly Meeting then turned to the problem of locating a mission field of their own. Their minute of concern had stated: "Recognizing the importance of uniting our forces in foreign missionary work we pledge ourselves to such action as necessary to formulate a missionary program that will challenge our entire membership, and to use our best endeavor to secure their united support."

A new field seemed providentially opened to them when in 1930 a mission station at La Paz, Bolivia, was offered. Situated 12,000 feet in altitude in a country known for its tin, La Paz has been called the "tin roof of the world." This work had been opened as an extension by Guatemalan Friends. Juan Allyon, a young Spanish-Indian from La Paz, came to Guatemala in 1920 for training in the Bible School. In 1924 he and his wife, commissioned by Friends in the Central American station, opened work at La Paz.

The work soon outgrew the financial ability of Guatemalan Friends and an appeal was made by Esther Smith to Oregon Yearly Meeting to assume the responsibility. In 1930 the field was officially adopted by Oregon Yearly Meeting. Carroll and Doris Tamplin were the first appointees from the Yearly Meeting, arriving at La Paz in 1931. In spite of considerable opposition and threats and attacks on members of the Bolivian Friends group, they were soon able to report two hundred "believers" in twelve villages and cities. Dark days of persecution threatened the existence of the mission, but a revival of interest led to a new level of hope and growth. A chapel, a mission home, and other buildings were erected, a Bible Training School was established, portions of the Bible were translated and distributed, and schools were opened as more missionaries were added to the staff.

The Yearly Meeting realized that "a Bible Training School in Bolivia must include more than a building, trained teachers and student prospects. Because of the extreme poverty of the Aymara Indian it would be impossible for him ever to have enough money to attend school." A farm was purchased in 1947 to help meet the problem. It offered work for students and food for the school and the mission. The original group coming in with the farm included thirty-three families of Indians. A trained agricultural worker was sent to the field. Though in political changes of the Bolivian government this school was lost, it produced more than a hundred graduates in twelve years.

Friends were active in supplying medical aid. Lacking doctors, some missionaries took simple courses in medicine. Registered nurses were later sent to the field. In cooperation with the government, vaccine was supplied for combatting smallpox and typhoid, and some patients were sent to La Paz for treatment. Courses in hygiene were taught to local pastors who then made this information a part of their ministry.

By 1955 there were more than one thousand members, with seven day schools and one night school having two hundred students. The mission in Bolivia was well on its way toward becoming the Bolivian Friends Church, carrying administrative responsibilities. The mission had encouraged this move toward the indigenous, self-directing church.

In 1951 plans were made for the establishment of the "national church."

> The plan was, that at the end of the first year, the older churches were to assume the entire obligation of the salaries of their pastors. An Executive Committee of six nationals and one missionary was set up to work out the details of the actual functioning of the work under national leadership, to evangelize and to teach tithing. The mission was to continue mainly in the field of education, counselling, and in helping develop new groups and work.

In 1952 the plan was adopted and the Bolivian Friends Church became a reality. Bolivian leadership and administration were further developed and progress was slowly made toward transfer of church property titles from the mission to the Bolivian church. Pastors and teachers are now paid by the Bolivian Friends Meetings.

George Fox Friends School, established by 1965 with additional grades added to the elementary curriculum, is recognized by the Bolivian government.

The report in 1968 indicates "a membership of over 5,000 in one hundred and twenty-five congregations . . . twenty-one grade schools with an enrollment of nearly seven hundred . . . financial income of the National Church [Friends] has increased tenfold in ten years." The work in South America reaches across the Bolivian boundary and includes work in Peru, as a part of the total unified program.

At home the Oregon Friends have established an Indian mission outpost at Sprague River in Oregon and support a Korean Friends church in Portland. A Korean pastor visits in port at the Seaman's Center, calls in homes, and works with Korean, Chinese, Japanese, Philippine, and Yugoslav sailors.

## Kansas Yearly Meeting Mission

After Kansas Yearly Meeting severed membership with the Five Years Meeting they continued support of the American Friends Board of Missions until the term of service for Arthur B. and Edna Hill Chilson was concluded in Kenya. During the next four years Arthur Chilson served as superintendent of Kansas Yearly Meeting. They again looked toward Africa for a new mission station to be developed under Kansas Yearly Meeting. Arthur and Edna Chilson were available for a venture that was by no means new to them. With their daughter Rachel they sailed for Africa in 1933 believing that under divine leading a new place would be found. It was the same faith which had led Arthur Chilson, Edgar T. Hole, and Willis Hotchkiss, thirty years earlier, through British East Africa (Kenya) to a site that they were convinced was God's chosen location for their services.[18]

This second venture was, for Arthur Chilson, much like the first. There were the same obstacles of jungles, threatened diseases, hazardous camping in areas teeming with wild animals, and new tribes with languages unknown to him except for the bits of Swahili that opened the way of communication. Farther inland, beyond their former station in Kenya, they came to Ruanda-Urundi (now Burundi). This territory, formerly known as German East Africa, had been mandated to Belgium following the First World War. The war had ended the earlier German Lutheran mission under the state church. A Danish Baptist mission now occupied the territory.

Here the Chilsons found a friendly welcome and such aid as the Danish Baptists could give. By mid-1934 the new mission had been started, coffee trees were planted, bricks were burned for substantial buildings, and the mission was on its way as a station to be known as Kibimba.

---

[18] Edna H. Chilson, *Ambassador of the King;* private printing, 1943; a story of the life and work of Arthur B. Chilson.

As Friends on the raw American frontier were required to use every imaginative device for building cabins or sod houses and for opening farmsteads, so on the African frontier there was also need for ingenuity. Some lines from the account by Ralph Choate depict the experiences of the Chilsons:

> . . . on the bleak Kibimba hilltop . . . the cold dampness of the walls of the new temporary house . . . with mold on your shoes, clothes and books . . . lizards staring at you with their beady little reptilian eyes . . . flies, mosquitoes, worms, cockroaches . . . a temporary home whose wall hadn't even dried before you must move in, in order to get in and out of an even wetter tent . . . a return from a quick trip . . . to see that your grass-thatched home hasn't been burned . . . [but also] that sudden moment of happiness . . . a letter from your loved ones . . . a long awaited remittance . . . the sight of fold on fold of rugged hills . . . eucalyptus groves, acres of banana trees, cattle on open hillsides . . . the singing of birds . . . the spring carpet of wild flowers . . . an occasional snatch of song sung to a well-loved tune and know that some child or young person is singing the Gospel message . . . .[19]

Within two years a school had been established with an attendance of three hundred forty-five pupils, and four or five hundred persons were attending the church gatherings. Visions were rapidly being fulfilled. The site was selected for a future hydroelectric installation for light and power for the area and the mission station. By 1936 the African Friends Meeting was organized, outschools were established, and plans were made for a new brick church building.

Arthur Chilson was gifted as a builder. His ministry of the hands as well as of the Word fitted him for these exacting days. As he had been followed in the Friends Mission at Kaimosi in Kenya by Fred and Alta Hoyt, Fred Hoyt having a similar ability in building and mechanical skills, so in Kibimba he was joined by Ralph Choate, husband of their daughter Esther, in the broad service of spirit, mind, and hand. On the last day of the year 1935 the Choates had arrived. They were followed by others and with this increased staff and support the new mission became the Burundi Quarterly

---

[19] Ralph K. Choate, *Dust of His Feet,* a brief history of the mission.

Meeting of Friends in 1959. In 1961-1962 the property of the mission was turned to the national church body, a discipline in the national language was prepared, and the self-administrative church began rising into its own, as Burundi became an independent nation.

As on other Friends mission fields, there were four foundation corners for the work — the evangelistic, with the concern for the church; the educational, with schools and informal training for all ages; the medical, which of necessity came more slowly; and the industrial, which marked the work from the beginning, with its training in skills so essential to physical and spiritual well-being. It has all been encompassed and undergirded with spiritual concern and centered in the proclaiming of the Gospel of Christ.

It has been said that "missionaries are people, only more so"! This new work in Burundi represented a total concern for the whole person. Arthur Chilson, teamed with Edna Chilson, was an intrepid Christian missionary, with few rivals among Friends. When he died in 1939 he had been the pioneer in opening two mission fields and he had had the satisfaction of seeing the fulfillment of his vision.

The minutes of Kansas Yearly Meeting indicate not only an expanded, growing church in Burundi but also a dispensary with five registered nurses and a doctor, trips to outward areas for general clinics and baby clinics, over eight hundred mothers with babies coming for help each week; and a leprosarium with one hundred patients attended by a registered nurse. A hydroelectric system has been installed. A Teacher Training School has one hundred fifty-eight students, and about 1,200 are in Friends schools. A girls' school is operated for training in homemaking. A Bible Institute is conducted in cooperation with the World Gospel Mission and the Free Methodists. A broadcasting system, the only government-licensed station in the area, has been installed to carry the news of the mission program with its good news of the Gospel.

In association with the broadcasting system an electronics school is conducted. Programs in education, agricultural methods, medical information, and cultural ideas are broadcast to a wide area in East Africa. The programs, in five languages, are presented by Africans.

*Ohio Yearly Meeting Missions*

No other country has held a greater lure for Christian missions than has China. It was an ancient civilization at the time Europe was coming to birth, and its traditions, culture, and institutions were firmly established by the time Christian missionaries arrived. About 1294 A.D. the Roman Catholics started their missionary efforts. In 1807 the London Missionary Society sent Robert Morrison, who opened the first small beginning of Protestant efforts. Penetrating the language barrier in speech and writing was the initial problem of all missionary groups, especially in China, and their first major attempt was in translation of parts of the Bible.

IN MAINLAND CHINA. By the time Ohio Friends opened their work in 1890 there were forty mission boards with nearly 2,000 missionaries working in China. Esther H. Butler, a teacher, became concerned for missionary work, took training in nursing, and in 1887 entered service in a Methodist mission with the intention of starting a Friends mission after a period of apprenticeship. Encouraged and supported by Friends of Ohio Yearly Meeting she opened a "Quakerage" near Nanking in 1890. For thirty-four years she served with Ohio Friends in China. Here, as in other Friends fields, it was the physical needs which first presented an opportunity. An orphanage was conducted, a training school for "Bible women" was opened, and soon a Friends Girls Seminary was established.

In 1913 Walter and Myrtle Williams came to supervise this work and helped expand the mission into wider service. In 1922 a building for girls of high school grades was erected; eventually the boys' school, started in 1905, was merged with it in a coeducational institution including all grades.

Almost paralleling the educational work was the medical service. Esther Butler, having taken nurses' training and having served in the medical department of the Methodist mission, was prepared for dispensary work. This beginning led to an expansion of the service as Dr. Lucy A. Gaynor came to the field and a hospital was opened in 1895.

The coming of Dr. George F. DeVol in 1900 opened up an expanding service for Friends in China and brought into Friends missionary work a family whose members were destined to play an important part both in China and in India. His wife, Isabella French DeVol, was also a doctor. Their two sons, Charles E. and Dr. Ezra DeVol, followed in their parents' footsteps of spiritual concern in

China, as did their daughter, Catherine DeVol Cattell, in India. Membership of Friends in China rose to one thousand.

Friends from other Yearly Meetings spent several years under Ohio Yearly Meeting in China. From Kansas Yearly Meeting came Carson W. and Vercia Pitts Cox, serving for thirteen and fifteen years respectively. Carson Cox, literally giving his life, died there in 1932. In 1899 William A. and Julia B. Estes were sent by New England Friends. Many more Friends from Ohio and other Yearly Meetings served in China with the Ohio Friends Mission. They cannot be listed here, though their work was indispensable for the accomplishments of the mission.

ON FORMOSA. In the mid-1940's, civil conflict forced all missionaries to leave China. Ohio Friends transferred their work to Formosa, leaving their mainland Chinese friends to carry on the work.

Chester Stanley and Charles Matti surveyed the conditions on Formosa, looking for areas in which mission work could be started. Charles and Elsie Matti, coming from mainland China, were prepared by experience for another chapter of service with the Chinese.

The work on Formosa seems to have captured the interest of younger people especially. What had started in 1954 in a rented chapel spread in a work of extension. Daily Vacation Bible Schools were held. Young people were drawn together in conferences. A conference held in 1956 started a fresh extension by Chinese Christians, by which Sunday Schools and inspirational meetings were conducted. By 1957 there were thirty-four members, as Charles and Leora DeVol came to direct the work when Charles and Elsie Matti left. Charles DeVol taught in National Taiwan University.

Two general areas of work developed, one to the north, in the area of Taipei City, and the other to the south at Chiayi. Membership increased and by 1959 there were three centers in the north and seven in the south. To accommodate the expanding work four church buildings, four "parsonages," and three missionary residences were built. By 1966 twenty-three Meetings had been established. They have attracted not only the people of the villages, but also the educated Chinese and government people.

IN INDIA. Everett Cattell has indicated three stages in the Indian mission: the first period, when the orphanage was central to the program of service; the second, in which the outreach into the villages was the emphasis; and the third, in which the establishing of a self-governing church was effected.

Two young women opened the field in 1892. Esther E. Baird, a graduate nurse, and Delia Fistler, a teacher, felt called to mission work and in conference with other Friends they discovered that they were not alone in their concern. The Woman's Foreign Missionary Society and other Friends were ready to help them. At the time of their call a Methodist mission in India was looking for workers. The meeting of the need and the persons for it seemed providential. This gave them a time of apprenticeship, similar to that of Esther Butler in China. Esther Baird, being a nurse, was assigned to the medical department of the Methodist mission and Delia Fistler to a training school for Christian workers.

In 1895, ready for a venture on their own, they located in Nowgong in the state of Chhatarpur. Their first service came in ministry to starving people during famine. Not only were they pressed to find clothing, food, and medical aid, but also to care for orphans left at their door as desperate parents fled from the famine in search of food. Many parents planned to return for their children as soon as food and relief could be found. Most of them never returned, and over fifty children were left in the house that became an orphanage.

They had come to preach the Gospel in whatever way might open, and now, though they had not mastered the language, they were preaching it in the most effective way, by their lives of service. This was the language of love which crossed all barriers.

Breaking through the traditions around them they opened a girls' school. After some convincing of their neighbors, girls were enrolled. In the meantime, pastoral visitation was continued in which counsel and ministry to the ill were carried on. After Dr. Abigail Goddard of New England came, a hospital was started. A residence guesthouse was opened and the hospital for women and children was added. Dr. Ruth Hull and Alena Calkins, a registered nurse, came and with this added service the mission took on greater proportions.

Indian messengers were trained for Gospel ministry in about 1,500 villages of the area. The orphanage was a training center. The school they had started grew and by 1902 the first Friends meeting for worship was held. A core of believers had been established and would be a central dynamic force for the expanding work.

The school added technical and vocational training, helping to lift the standards of the area and prepare young people for vocations in their communities. A farm program was added for this purpose, but was partially ended as the government undertook similar training.

With the coming of Dr. W. E. DeVol and his wife the hospital was enlarged. Everett and Catherine DeVol Cattell came in 1936 with Everett Cattell as the superintendent of the mission work. This was a period of consolidation of gains.

There followed a period of twenty years when Milton Coleman, Clifton Robinson, and Robert Hess each worked with a team of Indian evangelists, spending a week in a village with a preaching-teaching-healing ministry throughout the Bundelkhand States and bringing the message of Christ. By the end of this period Bundelkhand Yearly Meeting was set off and the church was made responsible for all the mission work there except the hospital. Missionaries were deployed into other areas, mostly in types of work in which they cooperated with other missions: Clifton Robinson to International Christian Leadership, Anna Nixon to the Evangelical Fellowship of India, Milton Coleman to famine relief work with the Mennonites, and Robert Hess to the principalship of Union Biblical Seminary at Yeotmal.

Everett Cattell relinquished this position in 1957, coming to Ohio as superintendent of the Yearly Meeting. In 1960 he became president of Malone College. As in other fields, far more persons served than can be named here.

### Central Yearly Meeting (Indiana) Mission

Seven years before Central Yearly Meeting was formed in 1926, Friends were working in Bolivia under their personal concern, supported by individuals and some Meetings in Indiana. These workers, before and after the work was taken over by Central Yearly Meeting, went to the Bolivian field without definite provisions for support. Theirs was a service to be rendered in faith that the Lord would lead Friends at home to provide their financial needs.

The first efforts came from Union Bible Seminary at Westfield. Emma Morrow (Langston) and Mattie (Blount) Marca, students at the seminary, expressed their sense of call to Bolivia and with the prayers and the support of only a few persons they sailed to their future field of service in 1919. Without any previous training in the Spanish language they arrived and slowly acquired the ability to communicate with the Bolivians.

By the time Central Yearly Meeting was established there were other Friends who felt called to the field and in a few years mission stations were opened in several places, from the lowlands to the highlands, and Bible study groups were brought together. The members of these groups often became the native ministers and teachers who opened new opportunities for evangelistic work.

From the beginning the main emphasis has been on gospel ministry. Preaching points have been opened as the American and native workers found opportunity for extension work. Preaching, Bible Schools, and Day Schools have been the main methods employed. Along with these opportunities came medical services which consisted largely in helping those who were ill to get to doctors, clinics, or hospitals insofar as these services were available. The missionaries received some informal training whereby they could give "shots" and do simple forms of dental work.

There are now five areas of service with forty churches or outposts and an average attendance of twelve hundred. Besides these there are nine Day Schools with three hundred forty pupils and one Bible School for training leaders, with twenty persons enrolled. Meetings have been drawn together into five Quarterly Meetings as the church on the field has taken form. There are now eight missionary families on the field, and Bolivian Christians have assumed greater responsibility for leadership.

*Rocky Mountain Yearly Meeting*

The mission work at Rough Rocks, Arizona, is presented in Chapter 10, "Quakers and Indians."

### Work by Women Friends

In large measure the foreign mission work has been a women's program in most Christian churches. The first missionary organizations among Friends were generally women's associations.[20] It required time and education to bring men into the program in significant numbers. As other denominations developed laymen's missionary

---

[20] Christina Jones, *op. cit.*, Ch. V.

organizations, the concept of missions as a sound program within a total world responsibility gradually made its way and issued in a "men and missions" movement.

In 1888 a conference of women Friends was called to meet in Indianapolis. Twelve Yearly Meetings were represented. This conference gathered up the groups then existing in some of the Yearly Meetings into the Women's Foreign Missionary Union of Friends in America. This was followed by similar conferences, bringing Friends women in all Yearly Meetings under the world concern. Phebe S. Aydelott of New England Yearly Meeting was the first president of the new organization. Eliza Armstrong (Cox), the first secretary, became a chief moving spirit in the women's missionary enterprise among Friends. The organization, including women from Yearly Meetings that are not members of the Five Years Meeting, has been a factor in bringing Friends together.

The women's missionary group has now become the United Society of Friends Women. Their concerns have become more inclusive as projects have been developed in support of departments of work other than that of missions. As the mission has become the church or the Yearly Meeting, the total need has required the larger service in all departments of Five Years Meeting work.

### REFLECTIONS ON MISSIONS

Though the scope of this volume is limited mainly to Friends Yearly Meetings of western America, it is in order to include the work of British Friends at Szechwan, Chengtu, in west China, where the work was primarily educational. In cooperation with other Christian bodies West China Union University was established. Henry Hodgkin, Robert and Margaret Simkin, and Arnold and Lois Vaught were among the Friends serving there for several years. Likewise in mid-India, British Friends worked for several years and from their efforts Mid-India Yearly Meeting developed. British Friends have withdrawn from this field.

In China the missions had to live under the stigma of gunboat diplomacy as foreign countries came in to quell disturbances and enforce treaties for their own lucrative trade. It is little wonder that the future unfolded as it did — in an enforced leaving of missions from China. In recent years the churches of other nations have

Alma Swift Surrounded by Jamaican Boys and Girls

Eliza Armstrong Cox

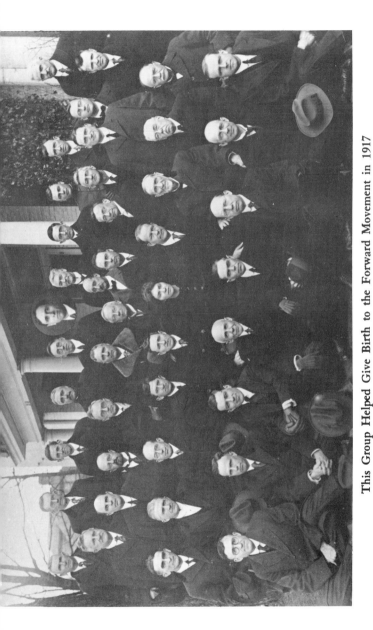

**This Group Helped Give Birth to the Forward Movement in 1917**

*Bottom Row* (left to right): B. Willis Beede, Clarence E. Pickett, Paul J. Furnas, W. Spencer Hadley, Stacy J. McCracken, Samuel H. Hodgin, Edgar H. Stranahan, David E. Henley.

*Second Row:* J. Edwin Jay, H. Edwin McGrew, Raymond Biniford, Harry N. Wright, David M. Edwards, Elizabeth Edwards, Levi T. Pennington, Timothy Nicholson, John R. Cary, Absalom Rosenberger.

*Third Row:* Robert E. Pretlow, Ellison R. Purdy, Alvin T. Coate, Willard O. Trueblood, Albert J. Brown, Isaac T. Johnson, Albert G. Shepard, Theodore Foxworthy, Charles O. Whitely, Richard R. Newby, J. Passmore Elkinton, Wilbur K. Thomas, Errol D. Peckham.

*Top Row:* Ancil E. Ratliff, Allen D. Hole, Walter C. Woodward, John H. Johnson, Harlow Lindley, William O. Mendenhall, Andrew F. Mitchell, Ross A. Hadley, Henry Bogue, Charles M. Woodman, Stephen M. Hadley. Alexander C. Purdy (picture not shown).

learned how much they needed to hear the voice of China, not simply to lift their own voices in this centuries-old country. When representatives of all nations have been brought together in church conferences and cooperative work, the representatives from China have been recognized as outstanding in their message and leadership. Ministry and visitation from China and other "receiving" nations to America, though of a different kind, have been well received. Missions have become "the younger churches" in many lands.

### Evangelism and Church Extension

The main thrust of the Quaker frontier was in the concern for outreach which came to be known as Evangelism and Church Extension. This was not new to Friends. No one reading the first years of Quaker history in England can miss their evangelical faith and spirit, though the word *evangelism* had not yet been coined. That early upthrust of spiritual awakening was far from the quietism and the self-protection that settled down on Friends in the following century.

The difference in the sense of mission of the first and third centuries lay not in the depth of concern but in the forms of expression. Something new had come but its roots were three centuries deep. Individual concern, expressed in visitation and preaching, changed to a group appeal patterned after that of the evangelical churches around Friends.

The evangelical wave was at its crest when the three general conferences were being held and the Five Years Meeting was being established. Though evangelism was a leading concern of most of the Yearly Meetings it was among the last of the departments of the Five Years Meeting to be financed and implemented with staff and program. A Board on Evangelism and Church Extension was formed early but had little to report except to review briefly what was occurring in the Yearly Meetings. For financial and other practical reasons publications, missions, peace, and other concerns needed a central organization, but evangelism was a responsibility within the Yearly Meetings themselves.

Revivalism as a mass form had become an accepted way in many Meetings. Jeremiah Hubbard, who later became noted for his work with the Indians of Oklahoma, is reported to have held the first revival meeting among Friends, at New London in Western Yearly Meeting He was "eldered" for this innovation, but this did not end the movement. Though revival meetings are still conducted in some areas the method has, with exceptions, largely run its course and evangelism as a year-around responsibility of the Meeting is replacing the once-a-year efforts of the past.

The Board on Evangelism and Church Extension was later merged with the Home Mission Board, where it practically disappeared as a distinct function of the Five Years Meeting. This lapse of recognition can be attributed in part to disagreement among Yearly Meeting representatives. There was a lack of unity on the evangelical-pastoral methods. In the session of the Five Years Meeting in 1907 Allen C. Thomas of Baltimore stated that he belonged "to a Meeting, and to a Yearly Meeting, where there are no pastors." And he added, "I must say that a good deal in these papers [on evangelism] does not seem to fit our case." He appealed for individual, voluntary responsibility rather than "professional leadership."

In the same session an Indiana Friend suggested that, instead of "thunder-calls of revival," Friends should pay attention to their non-resident members as nuclei for new Meetings, and that "true evangelism is not a two weeks' substitute for a congregation's all-year-round activity." Whatever effect these differing views or emphases had on this aspect of work, the chief reason for the lapse of attention lay mainly in the fact that the Yearly Meetings were nextdoor to these needs and did not need or want direction from the Five Years Meeting.

Even so there was always an aspect of the extension work which could be met chiefly in the overall program of the Five Years Meeting. This is seen in the report on Evangelism and Church Extension in 1912, which reviewed possible development of new Meetings in large cities. The movement of Friends from farms to cities was emphasized. That kind of extension would not likely be done adequately with less than a strong department on the Five Years Meeting level, but the central organization was not yet ready for it.

Following the sessions in 1917, the Inter-Church World Movement was organized, including the evangelical Christian Churches of America, bringing new life and vision as the First World War ended. It was a time of inflation both in finances and in church planning.

In April 1919, the Executive Committee, cooperating with other Christian churches, authorized the launching of the "Forward Movement," with goals that proved to be impossible of reaching but which led to some advanced moves. Levi T. Pennington was released temporarily from the presidency of Pacific College (now George Fox College) and gave important leadership to the movement.[21] It was not necessary for the Forward Movement to reach all of its stated objectives in order to serve many needs of Friends.

This program overbrimmed any one department and represented a total responsibility of the Five Years Meeting, but at heart it was a work of evangelism and extension. The report of 1922 indicated a penetration into Meetings with a broadened outlook on the world task of Friends and "the establishment of the principle of a united financial appeal for the agencies of the Five Years Meeting." Many Meetings greatly increased their interest in and support of the Five Years Meeting work.

The work of Evangelism and Church Extension at last came into its own when in 1962 the first full-time secretary was appointed and adequate funds were appropriated for getting under way. The Men's Movement had been formed in the meantime and teamed with the Board in starting new Meetings in new areas. In cooperation with California Yearly Meeting a new Meeting was established at Phoenix, Arizona. This was done with the goodwill of the unprogrammed Meeting in Phoenix. In Knoxville, Tennessee, a Meeting was opened in cooperation with Wilmington Yearly Meeting.

A Friends Extension Corporation was formed whereby loans were made to new Meetings. Besides Phoenix and Knoxville other Meetings were assisted in getting under way — Maryville, Tennessee; Southwood and Irvington in Indianapolis; and Jamestown in North Carolina. Iowa Yearly Meeting had established a new Meeting at Fairfield, and California and Oregon Yearly Meetings for years have opened several new Meetings on the Pacific coast.

There was now a fresh movement and the Five Years Meeting was ready for it. A "Partnership Program," which paired Meetings

[21] The Forward Movement had its rise in the home of David M. Edwards, then president of Earlham College, where a group of concerned Friends met in a meeting for prayer and conference that was, in their view, an experience of unusual vision and power (see picture and names). Levi T. Pennington, *Rambling Recollections of Ninety Happy Years;* Metropolitan Press, Portland, Oregon, 1967; p. 83-85.

of America with those of other countries, was started. A new world awareness was in evidence and the Five Years Meeting moved beyond the usual pattern of "missions" to a recognition and the inclusion of them as non-American Yearly Meetings.

With the new age of speed in transportation and communication, American Friends face a new frontier. Maine is now closer to California than Ohio was to Indiana a century ago. Consequently the future of Friends in their extension work lies in closer cooperation through the Friends United Meeting. No other aspect lies nearer to Friendly concern than the *message* and the *Meeting,* and with these the work of Evangelism and Church Extension is especially concerned. It might be said that Friends of the Yearly Meetings, portrayed in this movement, believe that their future is a matter of extension or extinction.

CHRISTIAN EDUCATION

From the beginning Friends believed in the Bible, loved it, read it, and memorized much of it. But not until the midnineteenth century did they begin to study, discuss, and interpret it. It was a sacred book, but it was, for all intellectual purposes, a closed book.

Rufus M. Jones states well the attitude of Friends just before the dawn of Bible study.

> The prevailing theory, in conservative circles, was that the revelation of truth was too sacred to be openly discussed and argued about. It was to be read with reverence and awe, somewhat as one feels on entering a holy place where God is to be met, but it [the Bible] was not to be "worked over" by the intellect . . . . [T]he Bible was never read publicly in Friends' meetings before 1860."[22]

Friends had heard and read the arguments by which interpretations had divided Christendom into contending bodies. Sundry "notions," as they saw it, had replaced the spiritual experience of the "life out of which the Scriptures came." To the more conservative Friends the new emphasis on Bible study represented an apostasy, if not heresy.

An innovation of Bible study started outside Friends circles about

---

[22] Rufus M. Jones, II, *op. cit.,* p. 885.

1780 when Robert Raikes Bible classes opened the gate to what would become the Sunday School movement in the Christian churches. In 1804 the British and Foreign Bible Society was organized with many Friends as enthusiastic members, and in 1808 many Friends in America became members of the Philadelphia Society. Friends started their own Bible Association in the 1820's.

Levi Coffin was instrumental in calling together a conference of young Friends at New Garden (Guilford), North Carolina, out of which a Sabbath School was started, before 1820. This may have been the first one among American Friends. The attempt met the usual conservative opposition. Once started it was bound to spread, and Bible study later included the full age range of Friends.[23]

Not until 1737 were children considered members of the Society of Friends.[24] When children became members they must be instructed in the faith of Friends. The Bible, a century later, would become a part of their education. Some English Friends encouraged this new movement among American Friends. In 1832 Hannah Chapman Backhouse, a member of the Gurney family, came to Indiana and started Sunday afternoon Bible classes.[25] This work by English Friends was very influential on the American frontier.

Bible study had hardly become *study* in this period. Attenders would read and memorize passages, then recite them to the class and comment on them. It was exciting and popular, revealing the latent hunger for intellectual experience and expression. Hannah Chapman Backhouse also started classes in New York and New England. Her work was firmly opposed by many Friends as "an entering wedge" and the beginning of "trouble in Israel." The Bible was used in Friends schools and when these closed there was further incentive toward the Sunday School movement.

In the visit of Joseph John Gurney to America in 1837-1840, the full impact of Bible study was felt. He had written in his memoirs, *"Never pass a day without reading a portion of Scripture in private;* meditate on these things; give yourselves wholly to them."[26] The interest in Bible study came toward full tide among Friends follow-

---

[23] Levi Coffin, *Reminiscences;* Robert Clark & Co., Cincinnati, Ohio, 1880, p. 71-73.

[24] Rufus M. Jones, I, *op. cit.,* p. 108.

[25] *Ibid.,* II, p. 886-888.

[26] *Ibid.,* p. 888.

ing the Gurney visit. The *Friends Review,* beginning in 1847 in Philadelphia, followed the Gurney line and was sympathetic with Bible Schools and foreign mission work. That influence was felt in the West.

By 1857 one hundred and thirty-eight Meetings in Indiana reported having Bible Schools. Various terms came to be used — *Bible Schools, Scripture Schools, First Day Schools,* and, later, *Sunday Schools.* Levi Coffin visited Indiana about 1823 when the western part of the state was largely undeveloped. At Honey Creek (in present-day Western Yearly Meeting), he started a Sabbath School, the first in that part of the country.

By 1829 White Lick Meeting received a report: "We of the committee appointed to open a First day school and select teachers have attended thereto, and find in our opinion the school beneficial; near eighty young persons attend . . . the committee thinks it best to continue the school. . . . " In 1859 Indiana Yearly Meeting appointed a "General Committee on First Day Scripture Schools."[27]

When in 1902 the Five Years Meeting convened in its first sessions three Yearly Meetings — Baltimore, North Carolina, and New England — requested Bible School literature and specifically a "Quarterly distinctly our own." In 1907 a committee was appointed to report at the sessions five years later. In 1912 a Bible School Board was appointed which opened a publications headquarters at Fairmount, Indiana, with Wilbur K. Thomas as the first editor, and adopted a graded lesson series for Bible Schools. The Five Years Meeting was now presenting to Friends the basic literature for teachers, adult classes, intermediate level, and children. A young people's paper, *Youth's Friend,* was issued. Other Quaker literature was printed as supplementary helps.

By 1919 the office had been moved to Richmond and occupied a part of the building that served as headquarters of the Five Years Meeting. In 1922 a Publication Board was appointed, with Alvin T. Coate as chairman, to care for the financial aspects of the work and to supervise the bookstore opened at that time. A board on Religious Education was appointed with Edgar H. Stranahan as the first chairman. The board was ecumenical in spirit, joining the International

---

[27] Rufus M. Jones *Papers;* Haverford College library.

Council on Religious Education which, in 1950, became a department within the National Council of Churches, in which the Five Years Meeting (Friends United Meeting) holds charter membership.

In 1938 the Young Friends Board became a department of the Board on Religious Education, the parent organization. There were three departments: Children, Youth (Young Friends activities), and Adult. What began one hundred and fifty years ago has now moved to a scope and level of service of significance far beyond any expectation which the little Sabbath School at New Garden in 1818 could have held.

The objectives of Christian Education, as stated in a pamphlet, *The Education Task for Friends,* in 1967, provide opportunities for persons

1. to enter into a vital and loving relationship with God, who is experienced supremely through the living Christ as both the revelation of God in history and the Word of God in man;
2. to gain a true spiritual life by responding to Christ within as light, grace, love of God, and Inward Teacher;
3. to know, understand, and live in the light of truth as found in the scriptures;
4. to increasingly understand and desire to do the will of God, accept the cost of Christian discipleship, love and serve God in all human relationships;
5. to grow in Christian fellowship together with those gathered into Christ; that they may be bearers of the light of God in Christ into the darkness of each personal and social situation.

The Board earlier had stated that "timeless Truth must be communicated to growing persons in timely language and with timely methods." In the field of publications for Christian Education the Yearly Meetings could do together what they could not do separately. The circulating of over 80,000 pieces of literature annually to the Meetings gives evidence of strength through united effort. Much of the printed material has been developed in ecumenical-type relations with other churches, but the Quaker accent in faith and in method has been maintained. In leadership training programs, in laboratory schools and conferences at Richmond, in Yearly Meetings, and in local Meetings teaching for learning has been advanced as a major, practical contribution to Friends Christian Education work.

## YOUNG FRIENDS

Young Friends have not allowed the Five Years Meeting to settle into comfortable, traditional grooves. They have been a growing edge in Quaker history. There is always a disturbance-by-growth as one generation helps to fulfill the life of those preceding it. Traditions can be both barriers and carriers — barriers to new and better ideas, but also carriers of hard-earned values from the past. Discerning between the two is never easy. The only real option is to provide not only for youth and adult work, but also for a creative encounter between the two, through discussion and through united action.

This was a conscious philosophy behind the incorporation of Young Friends activities in the Five Years Meeting. Young Friends saw in Quakerism the personal nature of religious experience and the need for application of Christian faith in their world. In a sense, they started over again within the existing framework of relationships.

In 1907 a commission was appointed by the Five Years Meeting to study and report on the possibilities of Young Friends work. In 1912 the commission reported that

> we have a large body of intelligent Young Friends, about twenty-five percent of our entire membership, who are more faithful in attendance upon meetings for worship than the adult membership, but who are not attending and are not being adequately used in Monthly Meeting activities.

Young Friends conferences during the preceding summer had drawn them together. It was estimated that there were 10,000 young Friends in Christian Endeavor Societies and other groups. A Board of Young People's Activities was appointed by the Five Years Meeting with Willard O. Trueblood as chairman. Thomas E. Jones, "that vigorous, capable and aggressive young man," was made field secretary, and the movement was on its way. Study material was prepared on *The History and Ideals of the Society of Friends.* This proved to be popular and furnished a basis for discussion in Yearly Meetings and summer conference groups.

Again, inspiration came from English and Philadelphia Friends. Ernest Taylor of London and Alfred C. Garrett of Philadelphia presented the work of Young Friends in their respective areas. In

England, under the name of Tramps, visits had been scheduled among several Meetings where Young Friends groups had been established.[28] John S. Hoyland had led in bringing four hundred Young Friends together in England in 1911. The organization of Young Friends was placed under the Home Mission and Extension Committee, which seemed to be the logical parent body.

For several years employed secretaries were generally temporary or part-time. The work depended largely on voluntary leadership, and excellent plans for Young Friends' activities often failed of accomplishment as the planners graduated from school or moved into their life careers. Later it became evident that the work of Christian Education and that of Young Friends overlapped, and the latter was made a subcommittee of the Christian Education department. Having a parent organization in the Board of Christian Education with its employed staff helped to keep the Young Friends work moving along. When finally the Young Friends department of the Board was able to employ secretarial help it seemed that the two (Christian Education and Young Friends) still belonged together. The dividing lines between the departments relating to children, youth, Young Friends, and adults were never really clear and they were now seen to require a closely related program which belonged, chiefly, in the field of Christian Education.

Under this arrangement the Young Friends movement within the Five Years Meeting has developed a greater scope of activities. The Young Friends department, under a full-time secretary, has had a vigorous program in recent years, including seminar, national conferences, and the African youth program. The work of mission fields has been opened to them, and Young Friends in areas outside the United States have felt the contagion and developed their own forms of Young Friends activities. This has helped to open a total relationship of Young Friends around the world as those of other branches of Friends have also met and discovered one another in new and exciting fellowships. Out of these experiences the association of Young Friends of North America has been formed. Whatever the future of Friends in the world may be, these groups of Young Friends will be a creative edge.

---

[28] *Minutes,* Five Years Meeting, 1912, p. 193ff.

STEWARDSHIP AND FINANCE

There is perhaps no other word that gives focus to the meaning of Christian responsibility better than *stewardship*. Yet it often evokes little more than dollar imagery. It represents an idea which also carries a sense of responsibility.

Yet because it involves all of life it includes money, without apology, for in a sense money is the coinage of all that one has. As "the love of money is the root of all evil," so the love of God and one's world neighbors is the root of all good. It is with that emphasis that the Board on Stewardship and Finance has tried to develop its work.

Only within the past few years has this aspect of Five Years Meeting work come to its present level of effective service. In 1960 a very representative Board was appointed to replace the smaller committee, and a full-time secretary was employed, with office help.[29]

Two major aspects of this department are its depth-and-breadth view of stewardship and its effort to help local Meetings in their own efforts for adequate interpretation and support. Raising support for Five Years Meeting activities has in a sense been secondary, but the results have justified these approaches and offered new opportunities of extension.

The Five Years Meeting during the later period ceased to be an American body with missions in other lands and became the Five Years Meeting of Friends *in the world*. The Board of Stewardship and Finance has extended its help to the younger Yearly Meetings in Africa and Jamaica.

The Board has helped to personalize the United Budget of the Five Years Meeting. In cooperation with other departments through the "Partner Projects" for service in Africa, Jamaica, Jordan, Cuba, Mexico, and the Tennessee mountains and among the Indians of Oklahoma, the Board has helped the Friends United Meeting to a new awareness of itself as a world body. This program has been closely linked with the Board on Missions and the Board on Evangelism and Church Extension.

The departments of the Five Years Meeting have been drawn together more closely in a spirit of unity and mutual concern, and

---

[29] *Minutes*, Five Years Meeting, 1960.

the Yearly Meetings integrated more fully into one body. During the first six years of this department the total income for Five Years Meeting work has increased by nearly forty-five percent, but the more important result has been the unifying of the member Yearly Meetings in their united services and the spiritual deepening of the stewardship concern. The Friends United Meeting has moved measurably beyond the limiting concept of an organization to that of an organism, and the work in stewardship and finance has had a major responsibility in it.

## Vocations and Ministry

The pastoral system came, representing a historic change in Quaker practices, but there was not a parallel change in the spirit and the method of Quaker Meetings. The pastoral garment was not sufficiently tailored for the Quaker body. To change the figure, there was no structured order of responsibility by which pastors felt released to do their best work. The methods that gave the Methodists their name and their pastoral tradition were a heritage of that body. But not so with the Friends! For Friends the result was not truly a pastoral system but was pastoralism without a system.

There were no requirements placed upon the pastor other than those of the Meeting he served. Having no long, inherited pastoral tradition, the system had to create its own; and the available pattern was that of the Protestant clergy. It was by no means easy for a located pastor to be sure, not only of the work expected from him, but also of his own future. He had foregone the making of a living for his family by business, profession, or farming. He was dependent upon an uncertain support for the service he was asked to render. In most cases, at the beginning of the pastoral course, the minister for the local Meeting had to supplement his income by other means.

This had a two-way result. He could not afford the necessary educational preparation; and the lack of preparation undercut his usefulness. The Meeting required a high level of service from him but was not ready to help him prepare for it. It was like asking him to work without tools.

This raised the right question: Was the Meeting or the Yearly Meeting willing to undergird the pastoral method it had accepted? This was the continuing issue. The result has been evident in the loss of pastoral leadership. Young people of ability have sometimes failed to see a future for themselves — or for the church in general — in pastoral service.

In recent years this question has awakened Friends of the pastoral areas to the necessity not only of employing leadership but also of helping in the preparation of persons for the responsibility. Friends colleges have generally furnished courses of study in the pastoral field. They have also offered some graduate-level training in specialized courses. In this work they have linked their efforts with those of the Yearly Meetings. There being no Friends seminary, many young people have attended the institutions of other churches, generally with the blessing and the encouragement of Friends.

Early in the history of the Five Years Meeting a Committee on Ministerial Training was appointed to coordinate, in some measure, the efforts of the Yearly Meetings. The concern for reorganization of the Five Years Meeting, when given plan and implementation in the sessions of 1955, resulted in the appointment of a Board on Christian Vocations, with representatives from all Yearly Meetings, and the employment of a full-time secretary. This lifted the whole concern to a new level.

By 1960 the new board (organized in 1958) had gotten under way. In the consideration of its responsibility it recognized "the blurred image of the contemporary parish minister" and the student doubt as to "whether the church is dead serious about its central mission." From its very beginning this department has seen its task to be that of encouraging commitment to Christian discipleship as a vocation and to the full scope of ministry in today's world.

Its studies and plans have ranged over the total life of Friends as seen in all occupations in which ministry has meant far more than that of the local pastorate. New ministries have been recognized and, especially in cooperation with the Earlham School of Religion, creative breakthroughs of diverse services have been undertaken in new fields. Now the settled pastor in a local Meeting is urged to help train all members of the Meeting to perform the ministry incumbent upon them in business, the professions, farming, and wherever life can be creatively expressed. His training must be based on the wider view of ministry, whereby his service as minister in a local Meeting becomes more important than ever before.

The Board on Vocations and Ministry represents a new venture in the solving of an old and basic problem. No other department of the Friends United Meeting offers more opportunity for creative thought and service, and no other concern is more crucial, not only for the future of pastoral Friends but also for their total ministry. In facing the issue this department of service overbrims the old barriers of pastoral-nonpastoral concepts whereby a new depth and a new scope may prove to be one of the most creative aspects of inter-Yearly Meeting relationships.[30]

### Toward a New Level of Life

Even while some separations were taking place the Five Years Meeting was experiencing a development that was destined to open a new level of support for a wider scope of service. The program was expanding and new staff members were employed to foster the added services. The old building in downtown Richmond had served well the needs of its time, but it was proving inadequate. A new day had arrived.

In 1940 Isaac and Adah Woodard purchased the large home of Isaac Woodard's grandparents, Isaac and Mary Evans, north of Richmond and presented it to the Five Years Meeting as a center for small conferences and other services. Its large hilltop expanse was an attraction for Five Years Meeting building expansion and the invitation to build there was accepted.

It was a historic occasion, a day of fulfillment, when in 1955 the Five Years Meeting in session adjourned to meet on the Quaker Hill grounds for the dedication of a beautiful new colonial-type building that would house the Central Offices for the next stage of service. Under the leadership of Ernest Lamb the entire Five Years Meeting area, from coast to coast, had been given the opportunity to contribute, and the new building was dedicated free of debt. This new building was, in itself, an added invitation to expanding the work.

At this period the Five Years Meeting surveyed the need for certain changes that would integrate its membership as a central body, give more representative strength to the departments of work, and undergird it with better financial support. As a result new strength

[30] Lorton Heusel, *Training for the Shared Ministry*, printed lecture for Cincinnati Monthly Meeting, 1967.

and an enlarged program brought the Five Years Meeting to a new level of unity and strength far beyond that of previous years.

By 1960 a definite turn upward in the organization and services of the Five Years Meeting had been effected. A wide survey was made among the Meetings and a plan for reorganization (approved in 1955) was enlarged into a more adequate program. In the new development three additional Boards were implemented with plans and finances for secretarial help. These were the boards on Evangelism and Church Extension, Christian Vocations, and Stewardship and Finance. The *American Friend* and *Quaker Action* (a promotional publication) were united, forming *Quaker Life* as a family-type journal.

All boards were strengthened by giving them not only a more representative membership but also a plan for annual meetings. Finances were provided for the additional expenses and the Yearly Meetings began to feel a greater responsibility as members of the Five Years Meeting. More fully than ever before, the Five Years Meeting belonged to the Yearly Meetings as a functioning body.

It was agreed that the sessions should be held every three years and a change in name was ordered to fit the new facts. In 1965 the Executive Council, under direction of the Five Years Meeting, chose the new name, Friends United Meeting, under which the sessions were held in 1966. A spirit of renewal, or rebirth, is evident in a new period of reintegration and outreach.

# Chapter 13

## INTO THE QUAKER FOURTH CENTURY

After the two major separations of 1828 and 1854, a period of integrative movements followed even while some later separations were taking place. Some of those integrative moves have been reviewed in preceding pages and require only a summary in order to indicate the trend which they signify.

Beginning with the Peace Association (1867) there followed the Associated Executive Committee of Friends for Indian Affairs (1869); the general conferences of Orthodox Friends (1887-1897); some conferences on peace and on work for Indians and Negroes; the formation of the Five Years Meeting and the Friends General Conference, representing separate moves within each of two branches (1902); the American Friends Service Committee (1917); the Friends World Committee for Consultation (1937); the Friends Committee on National Legislation (1943); and the Evangelical Friends Alliance (1966).

The All American Friends conferences held in 1929 and 1957 have moved Friends toward a better understanding of their diversities. These conferences have in turn resulted in smaller conferences on the regional and local levels.

Some of the above organizations included all Friends, whereas others were limited to certain branches. Some were intended for cooperative action only, whereas others represented organizational union. Distinction between branches still remains in most areas today.

## NEW AND UNITED MEETINGS

A major intra-Quaker movement during this separating-integrating period was the birth of new Meetings, chiefly in educational centers, across America.

The development of these new united Meetings was fostered by the Friends Fellowship Committee, formed in 1936. It grew out of the Message Committee, a subcommittee of the American Friends Service Committee, and in 1937 was affiliated with the Friends World Committee (American Section). In the 1950's it was united with the F.W.C.C. The new Meetings have generally reported to that body and, when ready for Monthly Meeting status, looked to it for official recognition.

The proliferation of new United Meetings near or within existing Yearly Meetings has seen an exciting development among American Friends, but at the same time it has introduced certain tensions. At times these have appeared as conflicts of interest, but more especially have raised the question of official recognition of new Monthly Meetings by the Friends World Committee (American Section) and the Friends Fellowship Council. This question is now being given further review.

Another activity of the Friends Fellowship Council was the fostering of the Wider Quaker Fellowship, in which members of other religious bodies may hold membership. These are persons who are inclined toward the Quaker way of thought and practice but are not prepared to accept more than an affiliated relation to the Society of Friends.

The open meeting for worship or silent waiting has appealed to many people. As few as two or three Friends may constitute a worship group. In many instances attendance grows and a worship group becomes a Monthly Meeting, with other worship groups or Preparative Meetings often associated. These sometimes meet in conference within a larger geographic area, and conferences become Associations. From these Associations four Yearly Meetings have developed: Pacific, Lake Erie, South Central, and Southeastern.[1]

*Pacific Yearly Meeting.*

This Yearly Meeting might be said to have had its beginning in 1880 with the establishment of College Park Meeting at San Jose, California. The Meeting was an object of controversy, centering in the request for a transfer of membership from Iowa Yearly Meeting by Joel and Hannah Bean. They had moved to San Jose in 1882, "to retire if possible from the conflict" which attended the wave of revivalism. Joel Bean had been clerk of Iowa Yearly Meeting for eleven years, 1867-1878, but like some other leading Friends could not go along with what he considered the "wild fire" attending the revival movement. The Meeting at San Jose was suspected of being too liberal and "in the mixture" with nonevangelical Friends.[2]

Years later other Meetings holding to the unprogrammed persuasion developed along the west coast. In 1932 Howard and Anna Brinton (a granddaughter of Joel Bean) called together representatives of these groups and the Pacific Coast Association of Friends was formed.[3] It became international in scope, including Friends Meetings in Canada, Hawaii, and Mexico, besides those in Washington, Oregon, Montana, Utah, California, Nevada, Arizona, and New Mexico. Being mainly a coastal Yearly Meeting, it has had special interest in the Asian countries on the Pacific rim in which Friends bodies exist, especially in Japan, China, and Korea.

There was a substantial growth of these groups, and in 1947 the Association became Pacific Yearly Meeting. It now has about 2,300 members in two Half-Yearly Meetings with four Quarterly Meetings and over forty Monthly and Preparative Meetings.

*Pacific Ackworth Friends School.* The Yearly Meeting has maintained an education program, one part of which is Pacific Ackworth Friends School. This school was started in 1942 for kindergarten through the eighth grade. The attendance includes about seventy-

---

[1] Full information on the development of new united Meetings may be secured from the Friends World Committee for Consultation (American Section), Philadelphia.

[2] Letter from Joel Bean to Rufus M. Jones, 1906; R. M. J. Papers, Haverford College library. Now available in several Friends college libraries.

[3] David C. LeShana, "Friends in California," a doctoral thesis, Ch. VI, reviews the development and inter-Yearly Meeting relationships with California Yearly Meeting.

five boys and girls. Responsibility for the operation rests largely upon the parents of the children. It is interracial and accents the peace principles of Friends. Its policy states that "our educational ideal is a school that is a community of families." Its plan is to remain small and flexible. Perhaps its spirit is, in part, shown by the lines which the school quotes from Wang-wei:

> You ask me
> What is the happiness here below?
> It is listening to the song of a little girl
> As she goes down the road
> After having asked me the way.

*Pacific Oaks College.* The college represents an imaginative educational development in which Friends of Pacific Yearly Meeting are directly involved. Starting in 1945, seven Quaker families who had been seeking ways to contribute to a more peaceful world founded Pacific Oaks Friends School and established a nursery school and informal adult education programs.

In 1947 it was incorporated under California laws; in the following years of growth it became the Pacific Oaks Association. This led to degree-granting status in 1958 and the accreditation of the college by the Western College Association. In 1961 it became Pacific Oaks. Though not including the name of Friends, it retained the Quaker philosophy which stems from its Quaker founders. Its work is closely planned with that of other educational institutions, including Whittier College. It is a participating institution with the University of California at Los Angeles in certain aspects of its work.

The original program for nursery and kindergarten children, as well as for parent education, continues; and the school affords also highly specialized training for teachers and workers who look toward professional service. In addition there is the John Woolman School at Nevada City, California, and the Argenta School in British Columbia, the latter sponsored jointly by Pacific and Canadian Friends.

It will not be necessary to trace in detail the development of the other new united Yearly Meetings. Their purposes are practically identical with those of Pacific Yearly Meeting, the oldest of the four. They follow the traditional methods of worship and outreach exemplified in London and Philadelphia Yearly Meetings.

## Lake Erie Yearly Meeting

This Yearly Meeting began in 1939 as the Lake Erie Association of Friends. It has developed a dual organization, continuing the Association and also forming Lake Erie Yearly Meeting in 1963. The annual meetings have alternated between points in eastern and southwestern Ohio. All local Meetings are unprogrammed and are located in large cities or college towns, chiefly in Ohio, Michigan, and Wisconsin. There is a membership of about eight hundred in twelve Monthly and Preparative Meetings in the Yearly Meeting and ten worship groups in the Association.

The Yearly Meeting participates in a "continuing committee," including representatives of Indiana (General Conference), Ohio (Conservative), and Wilmington (Friends United Meeting). The Committee occasionally calls representatives of these Yearly Meetings together in joint conferences.

## South Central Yearly Meeting

A fellowship of unprogrammed Meetings in Arkansas, Louisiana, Oklahoma, and Texas was begun in 1954. In 1961 the fellowship became a Yearly Meeting with about three hundred members in eleven Meetings and worship groups. It is now a member of Friends General Conference.

## Southeastern Yearly Meeting

Beginning as a conference of Friends groups in Florida, Georgia, and South Carolina, Southeastern Yearly Meeting was organized in 1962. Located in an area where Friends of all persuasions retire or visit, this Yearly Meeting includes those of the programmed and the unprogrammed backgrounds. Unlike the other three Yearly Meetings above, there is a flexibility and an accommodation to both forms whereby the Yearly Meeting hopes to play a unifying role within the Society of Friends. A pastoral Meeting, established in Miami for Cuban refugees, is conducted in the Spanish language.

## Costa Rica Friends

Though not representing a new union of Meetings, Costa Rica Friends must be included as a new migration and settlement of Friends during this period. At the end of the Second World War a small body of Friends with backgrounds mostly in Ohio or Iowa

Yearly Meeting (Conservative) migrated to Costa Rica, settling one hundred twenty-five miles from San Jose. Their purpose was to rear their families in an area free from militarism. Here they have built homes, a schoolhouse, and a meetinghouse. Their chief livelihood is dairying and cheese-making. There are eighty-five members, most of whom are living with the main body in a rural area. A few who live in San Jose hold regular meetings for worship.

### MERGING OF YEARLY MEETINGS

A parallel development has been the uniting of older Yearly Meetings.

#### Canadian Friends

The great separation of 1828 extended to the Canadian Quarterly Meeting, which had been set off by New York Yearly Meeting, in the area of present-day Ontario. In 1867 Canada Yearly Meeting (Orthodox) was established and, when the Five Years Meeting was organized, became affiliated with it. In 1834 Genesee Yearly Meeting (Hicksite) was established. In 1881 Canada Yearly Meeting (Conservative) was organized. In 1955 the three Yearly Meetings were united. By that time the pastoral system had virtually ended among Orthodox Canadian Friends and the new Yearly Meeting today has only unprogrammed Meetings.

#### Other Integrations

Though not within the geographical area of this book it is of interest to note integrations elsewhere. Philadelphia Yearly Meetings (Orthodox and Hicksite) were united in 1955. The development began with Young Friends holding united meetings and conferences. The American Friends Service Committee, formed in 1917, brought the two bodies closer together in service work. In 1933 disciplinary changes were made to allow the forming of united Monthly Meetings, and in 1945 the Philadelphia General Meeting was established, further preparing the way for complete union ten years later.

Along the east coast other unions have taken place. In 1945 — exactly one century after the separation — two Yearly Meetings of the Gurney and Wilbur persuasions were united as New England Yearly Meeting. The Yearly Meeting had not been divided by the earlier separation of the Orthodox-Hicksite bodies in 1827-1828. In

1955 Friends of the two New York Yearly Meetings, Gurneyite and Hicksite, were united, as were the two Baltimore Yearly Meetings of the two branches in 1968. All three of these Yearly Meetings now have both pastoral and nonpastoral Meetings, but the prevailing trend appears to be toward the nonpastoral form.

## THE EVANGELICAL FRIENDS

The latest integrative move among the Yearly Meetings was that of four evangelical bodies: Ohio, Kansas, Oregon, and Rocky Mountain Yearly Meetings. They did not think of themselves as independent Yearly Meetings. Independent of what? The word suggested independence from the Society of Friends, and they felt that their life and thought were firmly rooted in original Quakerism. They believed that though the outward expression of the pastoral-evangelical was greatly different from that of the first Quaker upthrust it was due, in the main, to the different circumstances of a different day, the root of evangelical faith and concern remaining the same.

### Association of Evangelical Friends

Of the three evangelical Yearly Meetings existing in 1902, only Ohio had remained outside the Five Years Meeting. After the other two had withdrawn and Rocky Mountain Yearly Meeting was organized the four were drawn together under a common view in faith and practice. Evangelical Friends from these and other Yearly Meetings held a series of conferences. In 1956 the Association of Evangelical Friends was organized. Membership in it is held by persons, not by Meetings or bodies of Friends.

Devoted to evangelical principles, it draws together for fellowship and discussion Friends who are ready to seek and share. This Association attracts many Friends, especially those of the four Yearly Meetings named above, but also many from those within the Friends United Meeting. Membership is based on a statement of faith, formulated by the Association. The conferences have continued, the eighth being held in 1968.

### Evangelical Friends Alliance

A major step was taken in the formation of the Evangelical Friends Alliance bringing together the four Yearly Meetings on the basis of a constitution with statements of purpose, policy, and faith.

As with the Association, the Alliance is not a separatist effort. Monthly and Quarterly Meetings cannot be received into membership from other Yearly Meetings. Membership is by Yearly Meetings only. The purpose is indicated, in part, in the following statement:

> The organization shall be an alliance of Friends yearly meetings which officially accept and propagate the evangelical doctrines of the Christian faith as herein defined. . . . The Evangelical Friends Alliance shall serve as the united voice and work for the mutual benefit of the member yearly meetings to pursue co-operatively the work of the Lord and to strengthen the work of the Friends church.

In general the statement of faith follows the views expressed in the Richmond Declaration of Faith, as written in 1887.

One of the questions facing the new organization, though not central to its concerns, was the practice of water baptism and outward communion by some Meetings in Ohio Yearly Meeting. This question was not taken lightly by the Alliance. The position clearly indicated in the constitution states, "We believe that both Christian baptism and communion are spiritual realities beyond the mere physical and outward ordinances." The present practice of those rites in some Meetings of Ohio Yearly Meeting is accepted by the Alliance, but the official statement points from the external to the inward and spiritual meaning. The practice of these ordinances, as in a few Meetings in Ohio, is not considered by those Meetings essential.

The major interests of the Alliance are reflected in its commissions on Church Extension, Missions, Youth, Christian Education, and Publications. The *Evangelical Friend* is their official journal. The Alliance is attempting a united mission work in Mexico.

The forming of the Alliance allows the member Yearly Meetings to speak with one voice on certain main issues. This also simplifies the approach for other Friends bodies in the conversations and encounters that will take place in the future. Though the evangelical alignment has a short history it is significant within the changing order of Friends bodies and is moving ahead into a unified program of service.

*Major Alignments of Friends*

There are now three associations of Yearly Meetings in America:

the Friends United Meeting, the Friends General Conference, and the Evangelical Friends Alliance. Conservative Friends Yearly Meetings have not developed an association but represent a fourth group of importance to the future of the Society of Friends in America. There has been a growing fellowship among them.

The Friends World Committee hopes to open the way for fellowship and encounter of all Friends groups. The conferences which it sponsors on the world, national, and regional levels are an important part in the inclusive movement of all Friends.

### OTHER INTEGRATIVE INFLUENCES

Four world conferences have been held: beginning in London in 1920, and continuing at Swarthmore, Pennsylvania, in 1937, at Oxford, England, in 1952, and at Guilford, North Carolina, in 1967. These conferences have not only brought Friends from all countries together, but have also encouraged numerous smaller conferences and discussion groups.

New centers of study or discussion have also emerged and have worked on the central issues of faith and theology, as well as those of practice. In 1966 the Association of Evangelical Friends sponsored a representative conference on doctrine at Colorado Springs. It was productive in promoting deeper understanding of Friends diversities.

In the summer of 1967 the Earlham School of Religion sponsored a small conference on the theological level. Though not all views of all Friends bodies could be reviewed, all branches of Friends were represented. Maurice Creasey, Director of Studies at Woodbrooke in England, Arthur Roberts of George Fox College and the Evangelical Friends Alliance, and Frances Hall of Friends General Conference served as a panel of speakers and discussion leaders. (See the picture and the names of attenders.) It proved to be a creative encounter which may be rightly appraised as a historic step. Though the Earlham School of Religion is presented in another chapter, it is well to see it within these integrative trends.

A small but significant center of thought is the Quaker Theological Discussion Group (also concerned for the above conferences), including in its membership Friends of every branch. It meets annually to discuss major topics in the field of Quaker life and publishes a quarterly, *Quaker Religious Thought*. It is a meeting place for those interested in theology as it relates to Quaker life and thought.

The quality and the number of fellowships formed and the mergers accomplished overshadow the separations and suggest the inescapable lure in a spiritual underflow of Quaker historical experience. New growth has risen out of it. Essentially Quakerism is an organism rather than an organization. Insofar as it is accepted as such it can be quality-tested by time and the live growth can be known and experienced. Reorganization and new structures inevitably follow, but the essence is spiritual and dynamic.

### ECUMENICAL RELATIONS

Though Quakers, especially in their first two centuries, were thought of as a people apart from other Christian bodies they have been cooperative when good causes drew them into community action. This has been true of all branches of Friends, in varying degrees.

With the coming in of the pastoral system another level of relationship has developed as pastoral associations were formed in local communities. These have sometimes fostered joint meetings and interchurch action on social issues. In the larger communities church federations have been formed, bringing Friends and the several church bodies into fellowship based on common work for community welfare.

In several states interchurch organizations have been formed. Friends of the pastoral Meetings have generally responded to these opportunities and carried their share of responsibility. In some cases the general association of churches has not seemed compatible with the Evangelical Yearly Meetings' views and ways, and churches nearer to their persuasion have offered other associations.

On the national level, cooperative organizations representing the Christian churches were formed for Missions, Christian Education, Stewardship, and other services.

The Federal Council of Churches, including membership of several Protestant church bodies, was established. The Five Years Meeting participated fully in its work. In 1950 there were eight interchurch agencies which, with the Federal Council of Churches, were merged into the National Council of Churches. The Five Years Meeting accepted charter membership in the constituting convention of 1950 and has cooperated fully with it. Friends of "Philadelphia

**"Christ in Quaker Faith and Mission" Conference, 1967**
Sponsored by the Earlham School of Religion

(left to right)

*Front Row:* Dean Freiday (Philadelphia), Logan Smith (Wilmington), James Higgins (Indiana), William Wagner (Indiana), Wayne Allman (Iowa), Francis Taylor (Philadelphia), Donald Good (Iowa), Herbert Huffman (Indiana), Earl Prignitz (Indiana).

*Second Row:* Charles Thomas (Indiana), Clarabel Marstaller (New England), Pearl Hall (New York), Errol Elliott (Indiana), Arthur Roberts (Oregon), Wilmer Cooper (Indiana), Lewis Benson (Philadelphia), Viola Purvis (New York), Dorothy Steere (Philadelphia), Leonard Hall (Indiana).

*Third Row:* Glenn Reece (Wilmington), Glenn Rinard (California), Maurice Creasey (London), Seth Hinshaw (North Carolina), Lorton Heusel (Indiana), Francis Hall (New York), Eugene Coffin (Indiana), Arnold Vaught (Baltimore), James Ellis (Wilmington), Clyde Johnson (Indiana), Wayne Conant (Kansas), Herbert Hadley (Philadelphia), Norval Webb (Western), John Pipkin (N.C.).

*Fourth Row:* Fred Littlefield (Kansas), Max Huffman (Indiana), Gerald Dillon (Oregon), John Grover (Indiana), Verlin Hinshaw (Kansas), David Stanfield (Indiana), Keith Sarver (California), Paul Goulding (Philadelphia), Canby Jones (Wilmington), Edwin Bronner (Philadelphia), Jack Willcuts (Oregon), Donald Moon (Western). Not in picture, George Badgley (New York).

and Vicinity" (now Philadelphia Yearly Meeting) were also charter members. Five Years Meeting departments have found valuable help in the departmental meetings under the National Council.

Most of the Yearly Meetings now constituting the Evangelical Friends Alliance have found their ecumenical fellowship within the National Association of Evangelicals and in the several conferences and organizations, local and national, which were compatible with their views.

It has been the genius of Friends to open new areas and types of service and, without credit or official responsibility, see them grow into wider usefulness. There are many instances of this in the work of the American Friends Service Committee. In other instances individual Friends, under their personal concern, have given leadership to new movements — such as the Yokefellow Movement, in which D. Elton Trueblood has been the leading figure. Beginning in concerned and scattered groups in 1950, the board of Yokefellow Associates was formed in 1954. Including both pastors and other members of several Christian churches, it represents an unusual and effective kind of ecumenical fellowship.

The formation of the World Council of Churches, interrupted by the Second World War, was effected in 1948. In 1940 the Five Years Meeting had approved membership in the World Council. The Executive Committee had recommended the qualification that, for Friends of the Five Years Meeting, "the basis of membership . . . is [accepted as] an affirmation of Christian faith rather than the formulation of a creed." But the Five Years Meeting in session accepted "wholeheartedly . . . the invitation" with no qualifying statement, though after long and serious discussion.

*Quakers and Christian Commitment*

Friends are ecumenical in depth, in that they share a central faith with their fellow Christians. They have often spoken of holding the "Christian faith as interpreted by Friends." They are Quakers, but they have recognized that the name, when overemphasized, can be a barrier to fresh thought and life.

# EPILOGUE

## The Historic Present

*The lines of movement, presented in the preceding pages, need to be drawn into focus, that a clearer view of the present may be seen as a fulfilling of the past.*

History has no stopping point. It is a moving blend of persons, ideas, and events within time. A moving picture film can be stopped or slowed down for a study of the action, but a period of history cannot be reduced to slow motion for a clear reading. The nearer the year under review, the more unclear is the reading, for it lacks the perspective of time, and it is blurred by its movement.

Though the achieving of a clear view of the present is difficult it must be attempted, for it is but the nearer part of the past. He who writes of the fast-changing present must know that his record is being outdated even as he writes. Furthermore, he is only one among others, with their varied viewpoints, who are as near to the scene as is he.

### Intra-Quaker Relations

What is the view for this decade of Friends history, especially within the scope of this writing? These Friends cannot be portrayed as wholly separate from the rest of the Society of Friends. They must be seen in wider perspective.

As the old geographic frontier was ending the new spiritual frontier was emerging. Friends are now brought face to face and mind to mind, almost despite any resistance to it. The world is shrinking and people are nearer to one another through increased travel and improved communication. Diverse as they are, each area of Friends must be reckoned with in any conceivable future.

### BELIEFS, WORDS, AND PRACTICE

One reason for the difficulty of understanding is the forming and re-forming of language. There is no settled vocabulary whose words mean the same to everyone, certainly not for every period. This has been well illustrated in the controversies that marked the antislavery movement.

It is not so easy for us to see the same problems of our own time. Present-day words that trouble us are: *liberal, orthodox, conservative, gradualist, activist, evangelical, pastoral, programmed, unprogrammed* (as related to Friends Meetings). Some of these words stand out in the minds of Friends as opposites, and in their extreme expression they may be. Words are necessary for communication, but they can quite as readily distort or prevent it.

God has had this problem among His contentious children, and His greatest answer was in the Word "made flesh [who] dwelt among us, full of grace and truth." The final test of truth is in the *incarnation* of Life.

The difficulty of words should not suggest brushing theological and doctrinal discussion to one side as unimportant; far from it. The problem suggests that we should try to say what we mean and mean what we say within the range of our own authentic experiences and the limitations of language. Not many of us are or need to be theologians in the scholarly sense of that word. That degree of theology has not marked deeply the history of Friends. They have emphasized the inner life, the personal, wordless experience of God. Though we can be thankful for Friends who help us in the realm of discerning thought, known as theology, we are not required to wait for a full understanding of their work; nor, happily, do they expect it of us.

Some Friends feel that a disciplined study of our faith is lacking and are concerned for the meeting of minds in theological discussion. Others are quite as certain that this emphasis is a deviation from the genius of Quakerism. They believe it represents that *from* which

Friends were originally led. There are Friends who do not align themselves definitely with either view. They also seek light, in their own way, and welcome those Friends who specialize in certain aspects of thought.

To yet others this does not represent the main distinction among Friends. They believe there is a basic difference between two main divisions in the realm of faith or belief, between orthodoxy and liberalism, whereas others see a basic difference in the nature of the meeting for worship — the open meeting and the ordered, or programmed, and the essential purposes of each.

Other alignments might be described as that of the vertical, God-man relationship and that of the horizontal, man-to-man relationship. This is by no means new, but it is being expressed among Friends in various ways today, sometimes in extreme forms. This fact is generally recognized by the main bodies of Friends who seek to bring worship and social action into one experience.

The nature of the Friends meeting for worship is being re-examined. Among pastoral Friends there are some planned efforts at achieving a wider participation by members and attenders. In some Meetings a flexibility has been developed, bringing a renewed sense of the meaning of worship as related to daily life experiences. Some of the unprogrammed Meetings have also been especially concerned for interrelatedness of the hour of worship and the other hours of the week. The danger in all meetings for worship, ordered or open, lies in their satisfaction with inherited ways, in forms that are considered ultimate and allow no rethinking. The experiences and the forms of worship are evolving and no Quaker Meeting has the final word.

In one of the pastoral Yearly Meetings a "team ministry" has been developed involving several Meetings, whereby the diverse needs of the Friends communities are met by members of a team, each member of which has special qualifications for certain specific needs. By this means one member of the team gives leadership in Christian Education, another in Young Friends work, etc. A team of five, for example, may care for seven or more Friends communities. All of them share in speaking. The members of the Meetings served are led into participation. Through a sense of common responsibility the Meetings are drawn together in a larger fellowship.

Educational emphases have been developed in western areas in recent years by which new ministries and new methods have evolved. These are receiving special attention in the Earlham School of Religion and in other centers of adult education. Some Friends pastors have accepted responsibility in the industrial ministry, in interracial work, and in inner-city service.

### GEOGRAPHY AND ATTITUDES

Viewed geographically, the Society of Friends in America has been divided, with important exceptions, by the Allegheny Mountains and the Potomac River. *East* and *West* have, in the past, become words that represent ideas about other Friends. These barrier ideas have sometimes been higher and broader, in faith and practice, than they were outwardly for the earlier Friends who pulled and pushed their wagons across the forbidding heights and ferried them over bridgeless rivers.

These barriers are being lowered and narrowed and Friends of diverse persuasions are meeting one another. This does not always result in erasing differences. Sometimes it accents them as mind-to-mind confrontation takes place, but the first confrontation does not generally end the meeting. A questing mind does not stop with a simple denial or a refusal to think further.

Whereto shall these new experiences lead? There seems to be no interest in *uniting* the branches of Friends, but there is an interest in *understanding* the differences. Friends know that *union* does not necessarily result in *unity*. Their history offers abundant proof. They are not concerned to carpenter some kind of organizational oneness, but to let the future grow as it will from the roots of experience and common concern. There is no better illustration than that given by Christ, of the vine and the branches — with its roots. The future of Friends must be formed, not by overbusy minds, but by the creative spirit of God working through them.

The geographic grouping of Friends Yearly Meetings has made Philadelphia a center which has deeply influenced all Yearly Meetings of that area, including those of the pastoral background, as well as the newer, united Associations and the Yearly Meetings (nonpastoral) in the West. The Friends General Conference has drawn together and includes most of these within the Philadelphia sphere of influence.

This area of Friends has carried the main load in support of Friends service agencies, whose headquarters have been located there, while Friends of the West have given their main support to missions. At the same time midwest offices of the service agencies have helped to awaken the western Yearly Meetings, and there is now a greater concern and a stronger support for them. Not so readily noticed is the large number of Friends from the West serving on the staff of these all-Friends bodies; and at one time most of the staff members of the American Friends Service Committee were from the pastoral Meetings of the West. There has been a two-way dependence between the main geographic areas of Friends, as many Friends from the East now serve in responsible positions in the West. Friends educational institutions of the East have helped in training leaders in the West.

Most recently the Evangelical Friends Alliance has drawn together the four evangelical-pastoral Yearly Meetings, formerly called independent, into a third major body. Their history is brief, but they are making progress in both unity and union, and they represent another sphere of influence.

Richmond (Indiana) has become a focal point of the larger number of pastoral Friends, though now including pastoral and nonpastoral Meetings in both East and West. The Five Years Meeting (Friends United Meeting) has furnished the organizational structure and the service outlet for these bodies, and has elements of both East and West within its membership. Its way, therefore, has not always been smooth. It may be that the tensions produced in its kinship with both spheres of influences have made it more creative than if it had been wholly of one or the other.

The former influence of London Yearly Meeting is still felt in the American West, though in less specific ways. The earlier reliance upon London's approval in the establishment of new Yearly Meetings has gone. But the London Epistle has had preferential consideration over those of all others in many of the pastoral Yearly Meetings. And visiting British Friends help them to remember their parentage.

The Friends World Committee, through an expanding program, including conferences and visitation, has given exposure of Friends to Friends on regional, national, and world levels. Under its concern certain relations between Friends and the rest of the world are maintained, as in the Quaker program at the United Nations.

SPIRITUAL LIFE AND SOCIAL CONCERNS

It has been said that the churches are answering questions which no one is asking. Overstatement though this is, there is a disturbing measure of truth in it. Friends have not wholly escaped this indictment. Their Queries read within their Meetings — along with their outward ministry — have often revealed their lack of relevance.

It would be far from the truth, however, to say that the Yearly Meetings within the evangelical-pastoral traditions have lacked a sense of social responsibility in their work. One cannot read the record of their missions without being aware of their broader concerns. A Friends missionary has not been simply a man with a Bible under his arm speaking to a circle of listeners. He has more often been a worker with tools of construction in his hand. He has also been a teacher and a doctor.

For instance, the work in Kenya at the beginning was *industrial* and was called the Africa Industrial Mission. But it also had departments of church extension, education, and medical service while being at the same time basically evangelical. In later years agriculture has been emphasized. From this, and from other missions, members have gone into important positions in their governments. The intention of missions has been to develop a core of Friends in the close fellowship of a Meeting, out of which a continuing range of service could be followed. Kenya is but a larger example of what has happened in countries from Africa to South America to Alaska. This type of outreach has also been pursued in home missions.

The Meetings and the Yearly Meetings which these Friends have helped to create offer a special opportunity for all Friends in their attempt to understand and serve in many areas of the world. "The most dramatic results," writes Everett Cattell, "came in Kenya — so dramatic indeed that today everybody wants to claim them." Many Friends who have been critical of the methods of missions are now eager to have a part in the results of that work.

While Friends of the pastoral-evangelical way have pursued their type of outreach, Friends of other branches have been concerned with what has been called social service, but which might more specifically be referred to as centers of reconciliation. Their projects have been broad, but also penetrating, seeking and speaking to the causes of unrest, hunger, and racial discrimination.

Those two kinds of work which, in an oversimplification of words, might be called missions and service, have now met each other and a new integration of thinking is slowly but surely taking place. Each has a contribution to make to the other. Indeed, they have never been entirely distinct. The two streams have, in some points of policy and program, become blended.

### The Disturbed Present

Though the full range of human problems has always existed in varying forms and degrees, some of these have struck with volcanic force at the present time. Chief of these are the demands for inter-racial and economic justice.

Friends, early involved in the first stage of emancipation of a race, dare not escape helping to complete what they helped to start. In some respects the second stage is more difficult than the first. The issues are too near and too complex for a complete analysis or for a simple remedy. There is much that Friends have to learn, but they know enough to begin. Their responsibility does not rest primarily in the measure of their knowledge, but in their willingness to pay the price of acting on the knowledge they have.

Answers to these problems must come in a growing spiritual awareness and relationship, in a true integration of the human family. The means by which this is accomplished varies with the different conditions and social context where Friends live. There is no common formula for immediate action.

At this point Friends are not of one view in the methods employed. In the minds of some Friends there is an urgency that requires immediate and "direct action," the quick breakthrough. As they view it, the problem will not wait! Other Friends fear what appears to them to be precipitate action, having the appearance but not the reality of a solution. Rationalizing and then doing nothing is perhaps the greater danger for most Friends. Racial and economic injustice unite to form one major issue and to invite many kinds of responses.

There is evidence of an awakening by all Friends to the total implications of their message. This is seen in responses from Oregon and California to North Carolina and Maine. A few examples can serve to illustrate. These are not necessarily the most important ones, and certainly are not all that could be cited within the Yearly Meetings with which this writing has been mainly concerned.

A Meeting in California resolved to meet the black community that had grown around it. A cooperative summer program was undertaken in which the Meeting, the Friends United Meeting, the Earlham School of Religion, and other Friends Meetings in the general area assisted. The children of the Meeting shared in the interracial experience and members gave time and talent to it. In preschool and Daily Vacation Bible School classes a new spirit was introduced, dispelling some of the white-black myths that prevent a true interracial community.

In North Carolina, a Friends Meeting has helped to open and support a downtown Church Center in cooperation with other churches. Interracial activities are encouraged as children are enrolled in existing programs at member churches. The work is interracial, educational, recreational, and also pastoral (in the work of visitation among families economically depressed). The statement of purpose indicates that "the old lines of 'churchification' are [to be] replaced by more meaningful ones."

A team of conscientious objectors from Oregon Yearly Meeting, working in Vietnam, give added evidence of the broader concern in both peacemaking and outreach. Friends of all branches are beginning to meet one another on many fields, as in Vietnam, where peace is being waged.

In a midland city the midwestern office of the American Friends Service Committee pioneered in an interracial development by which a community center was built, largely by cooperative weekend interracial work camps participated in by Young Friends of the area. The project expanded into a fair-employment effort, leading to a community agency in which large business firms are represented, by which many new kinds of job opportunities have been opened and filled on the basis of merit employment.

A Yearly Meeting on the east coast whose work includes more than race relations has supported the Poor Peoples Campaign in Washington, D. C.; cooperated fully with the Southern Christian Leadership Conference, collecting food and clothing for it; promoted discussion of civil disorders and the poverty problem; held dialogue sessions with the John Birch Society and the black nationalist groups;

conducted police education work with the police department of a major American city; purchased medical supplies in Canada to be sent in equal amounts to North and South Vietnam and the National Liberation Front; and given counsel to underprivileged youth facing the draft.

Friends have not agreed on activities in which violation of law was involved, just as they did not in the antislavery work of a century ago. Such demonstrations today have generally been unofficial, rising out of the concerns of the participants. When law violation has been involved, Friends have been open with it and have generally informed government authorities in advance of their activity. This is done with the sense of a higher loyalty to God and to truth as the Friends involved see it. It is not undertaken lightly or irresponsibly, and it has always been done peaceably. Friends who praise Levi Coffin's work in the Underground Railroad should remember that this was carried on in violation of laws of the states and much of it was done secretly. Whether that way of life and action was right, then or now, requires serious thought by Friends. The main question is loyalty to God as revealed in Christ and as experienced inwardly *now*.

The peace testimony has moved beyond refusal to bear arms although it is not forsaking that ancient stand. Two major concerns of Friends today are the abolition of conscription and the strengthening of world peacemaking forces.

The official attitude of Friends toward conscription may be well represented in the words of Lorton Heusel, General Secretary of the Friends United Meeting:

> As we reflect on the history of Friends and try to imagine the countless numbers in the generations of our tradition who have been caught in this problem — working for the sovereign rights of conscience, suffering for their beliefs, interceding with official-dom, offering assistance or asylum to those conscientiously opposed to the military system, writing, speaking and organizing on behalf of legislative campaigns, ministering to and counseling those in difficult straits, then we know that we can never lay this burden down until all men are free from the conscriptive power of the state.

In reviewing the social witness of Friends, *failure should not be overlooked*. Interracial membership has been rejected in some Meetings. Popular opinions in their neighborhoods have sometimes carried more weight with Friends than has the heritage of their Quaker ancestors. And the daily newspaper has sometimes had more influence than the New Testament when certain decisions were made involving interracial fellowship. In some Friends schools, both east and west, enrollment of students was for some years racially restricted. They now welcome an integrated faculty and student body.

For the most part the all-Friends agencies have served to integrate the interests of Friends in common concerns and joint service. However, there have been exceptions due to the nature of practical forms of activity and to varied interpretations of the nature of Friends responsibilities in social action. So long as Friends theorize about their responsibilities the areas of disagreement do not appear unduly serious. They can be discussed and, in some measure, resolved. When demonstration is made in a public way, and theory is implemented with certain forms of action, their diverse thinking is revealed. Friends are "conservative" or "liberal" not only in religious faith but also in political, economic, and racial attitudes. The old colonial-type barriers of more than a century ago are gone and Friends, now exposed to the same influences as are their non-Friends neighbors, tend to reflect community attitudes. The lines of cleavage which at one time ran between religious views now run through the entire range of their thinking.

Though these diversities are quite apparent, far greater unity has been evident in the vast range of forms and projects of service by the service agencies. These have had less attention than those on which Friends have disagreed. An amazing record that has focussed not only the attention of Friends, but also that of the nation and the world, on it has been made. The joint service of the American Friends Service Committee and the Friends Service Council (British), recognized in the Nobel Peace Prize of 1947, is evidence of this attention. Such work has had and will doubtless continue to have both the constructive criticism of most Friends and their support. "To see what love can do" is a continuing and underlying theme of the A.F.S.C. It will not prevent mistakes, but it offers an essential corrective and a central faith.

The Friends Committee on National Legislation being near the lawmaking bodies of the national government has been sensitive to its unique responsibilities as a Friends agency. The Committee has been, in many instances, invited by legislators to offer counsel and has helped Friends to express their views. In turn the Committee has presented information to Friends from inside the national legislative front.

One cannot read the early periods of Friends history, in England and later in North Carolina and other American Yearly Meetings, without recognizing the historic continuity of the work of the F.C.N.L. Like other practical service agencies, the Committee has evoked some criticism; but it has also enjoyed the support of most Friends. That this kind of work belongs in the service of Friends is clear to one who reads Quaker history.

## Of Waves and Tides

What finally can we say at this broad turn in the outlook and the service of Friends at the present time? They are living in a decade that seems to them stormy beyond that of any other period of their history. To a previous generation of Friends their days also appeared to be unusually disturbed.

It has been said that if the message of Jeremiah were distilled into one sentence it might well read, "God builds while He destroys." The collapsing of that which is not God-built and the disturbing pressure of growth of a new creation present a confusing view of the world, a world that is yet being made.

What is permanent and what is changing in the present cannot be readily discerned. The stormy present may find illustration in a view of the ocean. One who observes the restless sea must distinguish between the waves that curl into a foamy crest, fall of their own weight, then flow back into the depths, and the tide that rises with the moon-lift and brings the ocean inland. In human affairs it is not the noisy, heady waves of a period in history, but the divine powers of creation beneath the troubled years, that determine the future. The disturbances of our stormy days are evidence of God's presence and of men's resistance to His will. Within His creative purpose, found inwardly and expressed outwardly, Quakers find their way forward.

---

*There is that near you which will guide you; Oh, wait for it, and be sure you keep to it.* — Isaac Pennington

# APPENDICES

## 1. Purpose of the Appendices

In the preceding pages the work of Friends Yearly Meetings, departments of service, and all-Friends agencies is portrayed. These organizations were not simply groups; they were people — individual Friends — cooperating and serving, and they were far more in numbers than could be included by name in the text.

The following pages compensate in part for what the story could not do. Though only a few of the names can be given, they represent the service of others and will awaken memories of Friends who have worked with many of them.

All-Friends bodies have been included, because individuals in large numbers have crossed the dividing lines of Yearly Meetings and branches. North, South, East, and West are represented in forms of service in which Yearly Meeting backgrounds were less important, and the work of outreach, relief, and understanding were uppermost. They were simply Quakers, concerned and working.

Other information includes a parallel of historical events in Quaker history with national events; a bibliography of resources; letters that have not been published before, relating to Quaker concerns; and an outline of world membership of Friends.

## 2. Historical Parallels

### A Chronology

Events in American history which parallel those of the Quaker development present a backdrop against which Quaker history can be seen and, in some degree, interpreted.

The states listed, with their dates of admission to the Union, are restricted to those within which Friends Yearly Meetings covered within this book were organized.

The founding of other Christian churches suggests another and much larger religious stream paralleling that of the Quakers.

The dates represent the beginnings of events and institutions. Closing of institutions and ending of events are not indicated. Only secondary schools now existing and those evolving into colleges are given.

| U.S.A. | Dates | Quaker |
|---|---|---|
| First English colony at Jamestown .. | 1607 | |
| Separatist Congregationalists establish Plymouth Colony .......... | 1620 | |
| | 1624 | Birth of George Fox |
| First Dutch Reformed worship in New World .................... | 1626 | |
| First Baptist church, by Roger Williams ..................... | 1639 | |
| | 1649 | George Fox begins public ministry in England |
| | 1652 | George Fox climbed Pendle Hill, saw "a great people to be gathered" |
| | 1656 | First Quakers to America |
| | 1657 | *Woodhouse,* with Quaker passengers, sailed for New England |
| | 1659-1660 | Quakers martyred on Boston Common |
| | 1661 | Yearly Meeting for Friends in New England |
| The Carolinas established as a colony | 1663 | |
| | 1665 | Probable date first Friends family settled in North Carolina on Albemarle Sound |
| | 1672 | George Fox and William Edmundson visit American Friends Baltimore Yearly Meeting |
| | 1673 | Virginia General Meeting |
| | 1675 | West Jersey first Quaker colony |
| | 1680 | (approx. date) shipload of Friends from London to Charleston, South Carolina |
| | 1681 | Philadelphia Yearly Meeting |
| | 1682 | Beginning of William Penn's "Holy Experiment" in Pennsylvania |
| Dominion of New England established ......................... | 1686 | |
| Mennonites establish separate worship ......................... | 1690 | |

1691 Death of George Fox
1694 John Archdale (Quaker) appointed Governor General of Carolinas
1695 New York Yearly Meeting
1698 North Carolina Yearly Meeting

Presbytery of Philadelphia formed 1706
Yale College founded by Congregationalists ...................... 1707
Philadelphia Baptist Association formed ........................ 1707
1718 Death of William Penn

First Church of the Brethren (Dunker) congregation in America organized .................. 1723
First German Reformed church organized ...................... 1725
Wesleys organize "Holy Club" at Oxford, England .............. 1729
Jonathan Edwards' "Great Awakening" .......................... 1734
Moravians settle in Georgia ........ 1735
Princeton established to provide Presbyterian ministers .......... 1746 John Woolman (1720-1772) visit in the Carolinas
1751 (approx. date) first Quaker family settled at New Garden (Guilford)
Columbia University opened ...... 1754
1756 End of William Penn's "Holy Experiment"

Brown University founded by Baptists .......................... 1765
1768 Friends migrated to Tennessee from North Carolina
1769 (as early as) Friends settled in Monongahela valley
1770 Bush River Monthly Meeting (South Carolina)
1773 First Friends to visit in Ohio area

Pennsylvania Society for Abolition of Slavery ...................... 1775
Declaration of Independence ...... 1776 First Quaker separation; "Free Quakers" support War for Independence

Methodist Church established ...... 1784
The Northwest Territory opened .. 1787

Constitution ratified by states (Birth
of U.S.A.) ..................... 1789
George Washington inaugurated as
President ...................... 1789
North Carolina admitted to Union 1789
General Convention of Protestant
Episcopal Church organized .... 1789
Eli Whitney's cotton gin invented .. 1793

1799 (approx. date) Thomas Beals family
first Quaker settlers in Ohio Territory

First of camp meeting revivals in
the West ...................... 1800

1802 Migration from Bush River began

Ohio admitted to the Union ...... 1803
Louisiana Purchase of lands west of
the Mississippi River ........... 1803
British-American War ............ 1812

1813 Ohio Yearly Meeting

General Convention of the Baptists
organized ..................... 1814
Unitarian defection from Congrega-
tionalists ...................... 1815
Indiana admitted to the Union .... 1816 Tract Association of Friends
Illinois admitted to the Union .... 1818

1819 Underground Railroad started by
Vestal Coffin

General Synod of Evangelicals (Lutheran) Church ................ 1820
Santa Fe Trail being used ........ 1821 Indiana Yearly Meeting

1821 Benjamin Lundy published the *Genius of Universal Emancipation*

Rise of Mormons ................ 1823
American Sunday School Union ... 1824

1827 Hicksite-Orthodox separation in
Philadelphia
1828 Hicksite-Orthodox separation in
Ohio
1829 Bible Association of Friends in
America

Two "Christian" bodies unite to
form "Disciples" or "Christians" 1832
American Anti-Slavery Society .... 1833 Haverford College
1837 Joseph John Gurney visited America
1837 New Garden Boarding School (later

became Guilford College, 1889)

1837 Friends Boarding School, Mt. Pleasant, Ohio (transferred to Barnesville, Ohio, 1857)

Methodists and Baptists each divide over issue of slavery ............ 1845 Wilburite-Gurneyite separation in New England

1845 Salem Seminary (later Whittier College, Iowa — now closed)

Oregon Trail being used .......... 1846

Iowa admitted to the Union ...... 1846

Mormons settle in Utah .......... 1847 Friends Boarding School, Richmond, Indiana (later Earlham College, 1859)

Lutheran Church — Missouri Synod 1847 *Friends Review* (Gurneyite) founded

Mexican cession of Southwest Territory .......................... 1848

The Gold Rush .................. 1849

California admitted to the Union .. 1850

Y.M.C.A. organized .............. 1851 Site selected for White's Institute, in Iowa

1854 Wilburite-Gurneyite separation in Ohio

1857 Friends School in Tennessee (later Friendsville Academy)

1857 Friends Boarding School, Damascus, Ohio

1858 Western Yearly Meeting

Oregon admitted to the Union .... 1859 Buildings erected for White's Institute, Wabash, Indiana

Augustana (Swedish) Lutheran Church ...................... 1860 Iowa Yearly Meeting Boarding School (later Penn College, 1872)

Abraham Lincoln, President ...... 1861

Kansas admitted to the Union .... 1861

Nebraska admitted to the Union .. 1862

1863 Iowa Yearly Meeting

1865 Baltimore Association formed for reconstruction in North Carolina

1867 Canada Yearly Meeting

Ulysses S. Grant, President ...... 1869 Quakers commissioned by President Grant for Indian supervision

American Sunday School Convention (later International Council of Religious Education) ............ 1869

Dwight L. Moody revival campaigns 1870
                                   1871 Wilmington College, Ohio
                                       *Christian Worker* founded
                                   1872 Kansas Yearly Meeting
                                   1875 Illinois Yearly Meeting (Hicksite)
                                   1877 Conservative separation in Iowa
                                   1877 Conservative separation in Western
                                           Yearly Meeting
                                   1879 Conservative separation in Kansas
Young Peoples Society of Christian
  Endeavor ..................... 1885 Pacific Academy, Newberg, Oregon
                                       (became Pacific College, 1891; re-
                                       named George Fox College, 1949)
Student Volunteer Movement ..... 1886
                                   1887 First Conference on Unity, Rich-
                                       mond, Indiana
                                   1888 First Whittier Academy, California
                                       (became Whittier College, 1890)
                                   1890 Scattergood Friends Boarding School
                                       (Conservative), Iowa
                                   1892 Wilmington Yearly Meeting
                                   1892 Friends Bible Institute, Cleveland,
                                       Ohio (became Malone College,
                                       1957)
                                   1892 Friends Academy, Haviland, Kansas
                                       (joined to Friends Bible College,
                                       1917)
                                   1892 Second Conference on Unity
                                   1893 Oregon Yearly Meeting
                                   1894 The *American Friend* (uniting
                                       *Friends Review* and *Christian*
                                       *Worker*)
                                   1894 The American Friends Board of
                                       Foreign Missions
                                   1895 California Yearly Meeting
                                   1897 Third Conference on Unity
Spanish-American War ........... 1898 Friends University, Wichita, Kansas
                                   1899 Nebraska Central College (now
                                       closed)
                                   1902 The Five Years Meeting
                                   1902 The Friends General Conference
                                   1902 Friends Africa Mission (Kenya)
                                   1903 North Carolina Yearly Meeting
                                       (Conservative)
                                   1905 The *Evangelical Friend* published

Federal Council of Churches of
Christ ........................ 1908 Nebraska Yearly Meeting
1908 Greenleaf Academy, Idaho
First World War ................ 1914
America entered World War ...... 1917 Central Offices, Five Years Meeting,
at Richmond
1917 American Friends Service Committee
Interchurch World Movement .... 1919
1920 First World Conference of Friends
(London)
1926 Central Yearly Meeting (Indiana)
Herbert Hoover, President ........ 1929
1930 Pendle Hill School, near Philadel-
phia
1937 Second World Conference of
Friends (Swarthmore)
1937 Friends World Committee for Consultation
Three branches of Methodism unite 1939
America entered Second World War 1941 Quaker Hill (Richmond)
1943 Friends Committee on National
Legislation
United Nations .................. 1945
1947 Nobel Peace Prize to Friends
World Council of Churches ...... 1948
The National Council of Churches 1950
1952 Third World Conference of Friends
(Oxford)
1955 Five Years Meeting offices moved to
Quaker Hill
1956 The Association of Evangelical
Friends
The United Church of Christ
formed (uniting Congregational
Christian and Evangelical Re-
formed churches) .............. 1957 Rocky Mountain Yearly Meeting
1960 Earlham School of Religion, Rich-
mond, Indiana
1966 The Evangelical Friends Alliance
1966 First Conference on Doctrine at
Colorado Springs by Evangelical
Friends
1967 Fourth World Conference of Friends
(Guilford)
1967 Five Years Meeting name changed

to Friends United Meeting

1967 All-Friends Conference on Theology (Richmond) by Earlham School of Religion

United Methodist Church (uniting Methodist and Evangelical United Brethren churches) ............ 1968

Richard M. Nixon, President ...... 1969 Fifteenth meeting of Friends United Meeting (Five Years Meeting), sixty-seventh year

## 3. BIBLIOGRAPHY AND RESOURCES FOR THE TOPICS OF THIS BOOK

The books, articles, pamphlets, letters, and papers listed here are sources suggested for further research. Some of them have been used quite fully in this writing. Others have been sources for specific kinds of information. Yet others have been examined only to ascertain their usefulness as sources for further study.

They are listed with the topics and chapters to which they are mainly, though not exclusively, related.

### BOOKS, ARTICLES, AND PAMPHLETS

*Those Having General Background Material Relating to the Entire Book*

James Truslow Adams, *History of the United States,* Vol. I, 306 p.; Vol. II, 346 p.; Charles Scribner's Sons, New York, 1933.

Hugh Barbour, *The Quakers in Puritan England,* 272 p.; Yale University Press, New Haven and London, 1964.

E. G. Castle, *Approach to Quakerism,* 178 p.; Bannisdale Press, London, 1961.

Rufus M. Jones, *The Quakers in the American Colonies,* 603 p.; Macmillan and Co., Ltd., London, 1923.

———— *The Later Periods of Quakerism,* 1,020 p.; Vols. I and II; Macmillan and Co., Ltd., London, 1921.

Nelson Klose, *A Concise Study Guide to the American Frontier,* 269 p.; University of Nebraska Press, 1964.

John A. Krout, *United States to 1865* (Vol. I) and *United States Since 1865* (Vol. II); Barnes and Noble Inc., New York, 1961.

*Documentary Source Book of American History,* 656 p.; edited with notes by William Macdonald; Macmillan Company, New York, 1917.

T. Scott Miyakawa, *Protestants and Pioneers,* 306 p.; the University of Chicago Press, 1964.

Levi T. Pennington, *Rambling Recollections of Ninety Happy Years,* 188 p.; Metropolitan Press, Portland, Oregon, 1967.

Arthur O. Roberts, *Through Flaming Sword*, a spiritual biography of George Fox, 113 p.; Barclay Press, 1959.

—— *The People Called Quakers*, 18 p.; Barclay Press, 1965.

—— "Early Friends and the Work of Christ," *Quaker Religious Thought*, Vol. IX, No. 1 (spring 1967).

Elbert Russell, *The History of Quakerism*, 586 p.; Macmillan Company, New York, 1942.

—— *Elbert Russell, Quaker*, an autobiography, 376 p.; Friendly Press, Jackson, Tennessee, 1956.

William Warren Sweet, *The Story of Religion in America*, 492 p.; Harper & Row, New York, 1950.

Walter R. Williams, *The Rich Heritage of Quakerism*, 279 p.; William B. Eerdmans Publishing Co., Grand Rapids, Michigan, 1962.

Louis B. Wright, *Culture on the Moving Frontier*, 273 p.; Indiana University Press, 1955.

*Friends Face Their Fourth Century*, report of the Third World Conference of Friends; Oxford, 1952

*Travels of Robert and Sarah Lindsey*, 189 p.; edited by "one of their daughters"; Samuel Harris and Co., London, 1886.

## Chapter 1

Henry J. Cadbury, *The Church in the Wilderness*, 14 p. North Carolina Quakerism as seen by visitors, a historical lecture delivered to North Carolina Yearly Meeting, 1948.

Kenneth L. Carroll, "Elizabeth Harris, The Founder of American Quakerism," *Quaker History*, Bulletin of Friends Historical Association, Vol. 57, No. 2 (autumn 1968).

Fernando G. Cartland, *Southern Heroes* (Friends in War Time), 480 p.; Riverside Press, Cambridge, 1895.

Thomas E. Drake, *Quakers and Slavery in America*, 245 p.; Yale University Press, New Haven, 1950.

Amelia Mott Gummere, *The Journal and Essays of John Woolman*, 643 p.; Macmillan Company, 1922.

J. Floyd Moore, *Friends in the Carolinas*, 23 p.; private printing, 1964.

Patrick Sowle, "The Quaker Conscript in Confederate North Carolina," *Quaker History*, Bulletin of Friends Historical Association, Vol. 56, No. 2 (autumn 1967).

Stephen B. Weeks, *Southern Quakers and Slavery*, 400 p.; Johns Hopkins University Press, 1896.

*A Narrative of the Cruelties Inflicted upon Friends of North Carolina Yearly Meeting*, 1861-1865, 28 p.; printed in London, 1868.

*The Journal of John Woolman,* 233 p.; edited by Janet Whitney; Henry Regnery Company, 1850.

## Chapter 2

Addison Coffin, *Life and Travels,* an autobiography, 570 p.; William G. Hubbard, Cleveland, Ohio, 1897.

James M. De Garmo, *A History of the Hicksite Quakers and Their Doctrines,* 157 p.; Christian Literature Company, New York, 1897.

Charles P. Morlan, *A Brief History of Ohio Yearly Meeting* (Conservative), 191 p.; published by the Representative Meeting, Barnesville, Ohio, 1959.

James Harris Norton, *Quakers West of the Alleghenies and in Ohio,* to 1861; a Ph.D. thesis submitted to Western Reserve University, 1965.

Elbert Russell, *The Separation After a Century,* 72 p.; reprinted from the *Friends Intelligencer,* 1928.

H. E. Smith, *The Quakers, Their Migration to the Upper Ohio, Their Customs and Discipline,* 54 p.; private printing, 1928.

William P. Taber, Jr., "The Expanding World of Ohio Wilburites in the Latter Part of the Nineteenth Century," *Quaker History,* Vol. 56, No. 1 (spring 1967).

*A Journey in 1836, From New Jersey to Ohio,* 43 p.; from the diary of Elizabeth Lundy Willson, edited by William C. Armstrong; Shawnee Publishing Company, Morrison, Illinois, 1929.

Jeremiah Simeon Young, *A Political and Constitutional Study of the Cumberland Road,* 107 p.; University of Chicago Press, 1902.

*Journal of the Life and Travels of William Williams,* 272 p.; printed in Cincinnati, Ohio, 1828.

*Friends Miami Monthly Meeting Centennial,* a collection of printed papers in cover, prepared for the observance of 1903; 174 p.; Miami Monthly Meeting library, Waynesville, Ohio.

Bliss Forbush, *Elias Hicks, Quaker Liberal,* 355 p.; Columbia University Press, New York, 1956.

Robert W. Doherty, *The Hicksite Separation,* 157 p.; Rutgers University Press, 1967. A sociological analysis.

*Quaker Sesqui-Centennial,* 1812-1962; 111 p.; Ohio Yearly Meeting of Friends. Chiefly a statistical and pictorial review.

Walter Robson Journal; xeroxed copy, Haverford College library; regarding his visits to American Yearly Meetings, 1877.

## Chapter 3

Levi Coffin, *Reminiscences,* 732 p.; Robert Clark & Co., Cincinnati, Ohio, 1880.

*Narrative of the Life of Frederick Douglas,* 125 p.; an autobiography; published at the Anti-Slavery Office, Boston, 1847.

Walter Edgerton, *A History of the Separation in Indiana Yearly Meeting of Friends*, 352 p.; printed in Cincinnati, Ohio, 1856.

Willard Heiss, *Abstracts of the Records of the Society of Friends in Indiana*, 305 p.; from Encyclopedia, by William Wade Hinshaw, Vol. VII; Indiana Historical Society, 1962.

—— *A List of All the Friends Meetings That Exist or Ever Have Existed in Indiana*, 1807-1955; John Woolman Press, 1961.

—— *A Brief History of Western Yearly Meeting of Conservative Friends and the Separation of 1877*, 30 p.; John Woolman Press, 1963.

—— "Genealogy Honey Creek Monthly Meeting," reprinted from the *Indiana Magazine of History*, Vol. LIV, No. 8 (September 1958).

Harlow Lindley, "A Century of Indiana Yearly Meeting," *Bulletin of Friends Historical Society of Philadelphia*, Vol. 12, No. 1 (spring 1923).

Everett L. Cattell, *The Spirit of Holiness*, 103 p.; William B. Eerdmans Publishing Company, 1963.

*Benjamin Lundy*, Pioneer Quaker Abolitionist, 1789-1839, 30 p. A memorial compiled by the Lundy Memorial Committee of the John Swaney School Alumni and Society of Friends; including a sketch prepared by Fred Landon, librarian of the University of Western Ontario.

Richard P. Ratcliff, *Charles A. Beard, 1874-1948;* a native of Henry County, Indiana; Community Printing Company, New Castle, Indiana, 1966.

—— Histories of Spiceland Friends (Indiana).

(a) *Along the Banks of Brook Bezor*, 1838-1963, 90 p.

(b) *The Quakers of Spiceland*, 78 p.; Community Printing Company, New Castle, Indiana, 1968.

Wilma Reeve (Wildman), *One Hundred Years in Western Yearly Meeting*, 1858-1958. Chiefly a statistical record.

C. Clayton Terrell, *Quaker Migration to Southwestern Ohio*, 48 p.; private printing, 1967.

Opal Thornburg, *Whitewater, Indiana's First Monthly Meeting of Friends*, 1809-1959, 32 p.; private printing.

*Anniversary — Western Yearly Meeting*, 286 p. Semicentennial. Publishing Association of Friends, Plainfield, Indiana, 1908.

*Jericho Friends Meeting and Its Community*, 162 p.; compiled by Jericho Meeting for its fortieth anniversary; Edwards Brothers, Inc., Ann Arbor, Michigan, 1958.

*Reports on Wilmington College to Indiana Yearly Meeting*, 100 p.; typed and script, covering the period from the beginning of the college to the establishing of Wilmington Yearly Meeting.

## Chapter 4

References relating to this chapter have been listed mainly in Chapter 2 with the account of the separation of 1828.

*Chapter 5*

William Aarek, "Quakers in Norwegian History," the *Friends Quarterly*, Vol. 16, No. 2 (April 1968).

L. Frank Bedell, *Quaker Heritage*, 305 p. A story of Iowa Conservative Yearly Meeting; private printing, 1966.

Ephraim Bowles, *His Quaker Heritage*, 250 p.; edited by Joanna Bowles Mott; private printing, 1952.

John Frederick Hanson, *Light and Shade from the Land of the Midnight Sun*, 229 p.; Western Work Publishing Association, Oskaloosa, Iowa, 1903.

Louis Thomas Jones, *The Quakers of Iowa*, 360 p.; the State Historical Society, Iowa City, 1914.

Herbert C. Standing, *Iowa Yearly Meeting (Conservative)*, 63 p. A historical sketch, typed and duplicated; prepared for a church history seminar in the Divinity School, Drake University.

*West Branch Quarterly Meeting*, 1807-1957; 74 p.; private printing.

*Chapter 6*

Vera J. Casado, *Kansas Yearly Meeting in Panorama*, 43 p.; a pageant of seventy-five years' history.

Brief historical accounts of Friends settlements in Texas, by (a) Max Coleman, and (b) Nellie Witt Spikes and Ann Ellis, dated 1952. Typed copies.

Weston F. Cox, *The Community of Haviland, Kansas*, 61 p.; typed and duplicated by Friends Bible College Press. Written for a seminar in Wichita State University, 1966.

Henry C. and Melissa Fellow, *Semi-Centennial Historical Sketch of Kansas Yearly Meeting of Friends*, 1872-1921, 50 p.; published by Friends Book Supply, Wichita, Kansas.

Charles C. Howes, *This Place Called Kansas*, 236 p.; University of Oklahoma Press, 1952.

Sheldon Glenn Jackson, *A Short History of Kansas Yearly Meeting of Friends*, 95 p.; Days Print Shop, Wichita, 1946.

Emory Lindquist, "Kansas, A Centennial Portrait," 45 p.; reprinted from the *Kansas Historical Quarterly* (spring 1961).

*English Quakers Tour Kansas in 1858*, 16 p.; from the journal of Sarah Lindsey, edited by Sheldon Jackson. Taken from the *Kansas Historical Quarterly*, Vol. 13, No. 1 (February 1944).

*John Franklin Moore* (brother of Joseph Moore), two pages typed; written by their sister, Ellen Moore.

Herbert J. Mott, *Nebraska Central College, The Early Days*, 8 p., pamphlet; 1924.

*The Newman Collection*, 200 p. On the establishment of Friends Meetings in Kansas, typed and duplicated; assembled by Herman Newman in 1905.

Original manuscripts in the library of the Kansas State Historical Society, Topeka, Kansas.

Walter Prescott Webb, *The Great Plains,* 525 p.; Ginn and Company, 1931.

William Frank Zornow, *Kansas, A History of the Jayhawk State,* 417 p.; University of Oklahoma Press, 1961.

## Chapter 7

Ralph K. Beebe, *A Garden of the Lord,* a history of Oregon Yearly Meeting of Friends, 288 p.; Barclay Press, Newberg, Oregon, 1968.

Marie Haines, *Remembering 75 Years of History,* Oregon Yearly Meeting, 48 p.; Anniversary Booklet.

Dorothy O. Johansen and Charles M. Gates, *Empire of the Columbia,* a history of the Pacific Northwest, 685 p.; Harper & Row, New York, 1957.

Lela and Robert Morrill, *The History of Friends in Oregon,* 55 p.; typed, 1938.

## Chapter 8

Benjamin F. Arnold and Artilissa Dorland Clark, *History of Whittier,* 395 p.; Western Printing Corporation, Whittier, California, 1933.

T. Eugene Coffin, *Living Waters Flow West,* 89 p. A history of Friends churches established in California, (1955?), private printing.

Herbert E. Harris, *The Quakers and the West,* 175 p.; private printing by Whittier College, 1948.

David C. LeShana, *Friends in California,* a Ph.D. thesis, the University of Southern California; typed with cover, 1967.

Earl Pomeroy, *The Pacific Slope,* 404 p.; Alfred A. Knopf, New York, 1965.

## Chapter 9

Oscar F. Boyd, *The History of Wilmington College,* 98 p.; typed and duplicated, 1959.

Howard H. Brinton, *The Function of a Quaker College;* the Ward Lecture, 1951; given at Guilford College.

—— *Quaker Education in Theory and Practice,* 135 p.; printed as Pendle Hill Pamphlet No. 9; 1940.

Charles W. Cooper, *Whittier, Independent College in California,* 405 p.; Ward Ritchie Press, 1967.

Dorothy Lloyd Gilbert (Thorne), *Guilford, A Quaker College,* 359 p.; printed for Guilford College by Joseph J. Stone & Company, Greensboro, North Carolina, 1937.

Zora Klain, *Quaker Contributions to Education in North Carolina,* 333 p.; doctoral thesis, University of Pennsylvania, 1925.

Ethel Hittle McDaniel, *The Contribution of the Society of Friends to Education in Indiana,* 113 p.; the Indiana Historical Society, Indianapolis, 1939.

James M. Read, "State of the College Message," 1962; six typed pages.

Juliet Reeve, *Friends University, The Growth of an Idea,* 326 p.; Wichita Eagle Press, Wichita, Kansas, 1948.

Opal Thornburg, *Earlham, The Story of the College,* 484 p.; Earlham College Press, 1963.

*Annual Reports* of the presidents of Wilmington College.

"Scattergood School," a historical article in the *Cedar County Historical Review,* August 1960.

"Souvenir of Friends Schools," 108 p.; reprinted from *Western Work,* Oskaloosa, Iowa, undated: about 1900.

For a complete list of Friends schools and colleges in America write: Friends Council on Education, 1515 Cherry Street, Philadelphia, Pennsylvania 19102.

William J. Reagan, *A Venture in Quaker Education at Oakwood School,* 159 p.; published by Oakwood School, New York, 1968.

### Chapter 10

David Bailey, *A Short Account of My Concern on Indian Affairs,* 27 p.; pamphlet covering years after 1827, undated.

Harold E. Fey and D'Arcy McNickle, *Indians and Other Americans,* 220 p.; Harper and Brothers, New York, 1959.

Henry Harvey, *History of the Shawnee Indians,* 316 p.; Ephraim Morgan and Sons, Cincinnati, Ohio, 1855.

William T. Hogan, *American Indians,* 190 p.; University of Chicago Press, 1961.

Jeremiah Hubbard, *Forty Years Among the Indians,* 200 p.; Phelp Printers, Miami, Oklahoma, 1913.

Rayner W. Kelsey, *Friends and the Indians,* 291 p.; New Era Printing Company, Lancaster, Pennsylvania, 1917.

Rupert N. Richardson, *The Commanche Barrier to South Plains Settlement,* Glendale, California, 1933.

Lawrie Tatum, *Our Red Brothers and the Peace Policy of President Ulysses S. Grant,* Philadelphia, 1899.

### Chapter 11

Lorton Heusel, *Training for the Shared Ministry;* lecture given to Cincinnati Monthly Meeting, 1967.

D. Elton Trueblood, *The Paradox of the Quaker Ministry;* the Quaker Lecture, 1960; given at Indiana Yearly Meeting.

Margaret Hadley Weesner, *A Survey of the Status of Music in Western Yearly Meeting,* 15 p.; typed and duplicated, 1963.

Lela Gordon Chance, *Repentant Rebel,* 145 p.; Vantage Press, 1969. Memoirs of a Quaker woman minister.

## Chapter 12

Edna H. Chilson, *Ambassador of the King,* 265 p. A biography of Arthur B. Chilson; private printing, 1943.

Eliza Armstrong Cox, *Looking Back Over the Trail,* 69 p.; published by the Woman's Missionary Union of Friends in America, 1927.

Arthur Garratt Dorland, *A History of the Society of Friends in Canada,* 343 p.; MacMillan Company of Canada Ltd., at St. Martin's House, 1927.

Merle L. Davis, *Fifty Years of Service,* 75 p. Reviewing the work of the American Friends Board of Missions; private printing, 1944.

Elizabeth H. Emerson, *Walter C. Woodward, Friend on the Frontier,* 316 p.; private printing, 1952.

Willis H. Hall, *Quaker International Work in Europe Since 1914;* 310 p.; a thesis presented to the University of Geneva for the Doctor of Political Science degree, 1938. An excellent study having also a "treasury" of references as bibliography, and valuable for research work. Cover title in French, the text in English.

Christina H. Jones, *American Friends in World Missions,* 299 p.; Brethren Publishing House, Elgin, Illinois, 1946.

Herman H. Macy, *What About the Ordinances?* 40 p.; Barclay Press, 1955.

Levinus K. Painter, *The Hill of Vision,* 153 p.; the story of the Quaker movement in East Africa. Printed by the English Press, Ltd., Nairobi, Kenya, 1966.

Russell E. Rees, *Christian Education for Friends;* the Quaker Lecture, 1963; given at Western Yearly Meeting.

Edith F. Sharpless, *Quakerism in Japan,* 46 p. A brief account of the origins and the development of the Religious Society of Friends in Japan; private printing, 1944.

Walter R. Williams, *Those Fifty Years,* with Ohio Friends in China, 315 p.; private printing, 1940.

*The Peace Testimony of Friends,* 72 p.; edited by Lyle Tatum. Published by the Friends Coordinating Committee on Peace, Philadelphia, 1967.

*Minutes,* Conferences on Unity, 1887, 1892, 1897, with stenographic reports. Conferences leading to the formation of the Five Years Meeting.

*Minutes,* Five Years Meeting (now Friends United Meeting), 1902-1966.

Everett L. Cattell, *The Christian Mission,* 24 p.; John Woolman Press, Indianapolis, 1963.

## Chapter 13

Roland H. Bainton, *Friends in Relation to the Churches,* the Ward Lecture, 1954; given at Guilford College.

Edwin B. Bronner, *Quakerism and Christianity,* 21 p.; Pendle Hill Pamphlet No. 152; 1967.

Henry J. Cadbury, *The Place of Friends Among the Churches;* the Quaker Lecture, 1957; given at Western Yearly Meeting.

Charles F. Thomas, *The Nature and Mission of the Church,* 76 p.; published by Friends United Meeting, 1965.

*The Nature of the Church,* according to the witness of the Society of Friends, by the committee on Christian relationships of the Religious Society of Friends in Great Britain; prepared for presentation to the Commissions on the Church, set up by the Continuation Committee of the World Conference on Faith and Order.

"Quakers and Ecumenism," *Quaker Religious Thought,* Vol. X, No. 1 (summer 1968); a symposium by A. Burnes Chalmers, Gerald W. Dillon, Dean Freiday, T. Canby Jones, and John H. Yoder.

*American Quakers Today,* edited by Edwin B. Bronner, for the Fourth World Conference of Friends, 1967.

### Epilogue

Gerald Bailey, *The Politics of Peace,* 39 p.; the Lilly Lecture in Religion, 1962; Earlham College Press.

Lewis Benson, "The Future of the Quaker Vision"; reprinted from the *Friends Quarterly,* April 1967.

Edwin B. Bronner, "Changing Patterns in Race Relations in the U.S.A." The *Friends Quarterly,* Vol. 16, No. 4 (October 1968).

Henry J. Cadbury, *Negro Membership in the Society of Friends,* 213 p.; reprinted from the *Journal of Negro History,* Vol. XXI, No. 2 (April 1936).

Lorton Heusel, *A Search for Identity,* a lecture given at Friends United Meeting, 1966.

Harold Loukes, *The Quaker Contribution,* 128 p.; Macmillan Company, New York and the SCM Press, Ltd., Great Britain, 1965.

Robert Leach and William Hubben, "The Quaker Spectrum in America — Another Look"; the *Friends Quarterly,* Vol. 15, No. 11 (July 1967).

"Barnesville Conference Papers," *Quaker Religious Thought,* Vol. III, No. 2 (autumn 1961). An approach to the nature of Quakerism, by Chris Downing, Wilmer A. Cooper, and Lewis Benson.

"The Future of Quakerism," *Quaker Religious Thought,* Vol. VIII, No. 2 (autumn 1966). A symposium by Roland H. Bainton, Everett L. Cattell, and Maurice A. Creasey.

D. Elton Trueblood, *The People Called Quakers,* 298 p.; Harper & Row, New York, 1966.

James F. Walker, *The World-wide Society of Friends;* the Ward Lecture, 1964; Guilford College.

*Report of the Fourth World Conference of Friends* (1968).

*Seek Find Share,* study volume number two for the Fourth World Conference of Friends (1967).

Rufus M. Jones, *A Service of Love in War Time;* 284 p.; the Macmillan Company, 1920.

Elmore Jackson, *Meeting of Minds;* 220 p.; McGraw-Hill Book Company, Inc., 1952. A Quaker-initiated study on methods of reconciliation.

Howard E. Kershner, *God, Gold, and Government,* 146 p.; Prentice-Hall, Inc., 1957.

## PAPERS AND LETTERS

Letter, Joel Bean to Rufus M. Jones, 8 p.; typed and duplicated. Written from San Jose, 1906, reviewing the development of the revival movement. (R. M. J. Papers, Haverford College library)

Letter, from Levi Coffin to his cousin, Emory D. Coffin, November 3, 1849; in original script and typed copy.

Letter, from James M. Davis to Rufus M. Jones, November 10, 1898; an explanation of his reason for naming the Friends college at Wichita, Friends University; typed in photostat. (R. M. J. Papers, Haverford)

Letter, from David Hadley, Western Yearly Meeting, to Rufus M. Jones, August 2, 1901; regarding criticism of the *American Friend;* both script and typed in photostat. (R. M. J. Papers, Haverford)

Letter, from Rendel Harris (England), December 18, 1898, to Rufus M. Jones at a time of serious illness in his home; script in photostat. (R. M. J. Papers, Haverford)

Letter, by Albert Emmons, July 13, 1929; reflections written on his 94th birthday, covering the experiences of Friends on the Iowa frontier.

Letter, from Thomas Newlin, then president of Pacific College, to Rufus M. Jones, August 16, 1897; regarding controversy in Oregon Yearly Meeting; script in photostat. (R. M. J. Papers, Haverford)

Letter, from Henry Stanley Newman to Rufus M. Jones, November 25, 1895; regarding the Conference at Manchester; script and typed copy, in photostat. (R. M. J. Papers, Haverford)

Letter, with three-page inclosure, by Dilwyn J. Rogers, giving some brief data regarding Ansel Rogers and the Rogers family.

Letter, from Edmund Stanley to Rufus M. Jones, undated — 1892 to 1902; regarding the name of Friends University. (R. M. J. Papers, Haverford)

Copy of "Bill of Sale" of a Negro slave by which he was set free in Indiana; transfer from Thomas Newlin to James Guthrie. (Guilford College library)

Abel Bond's Foot Travels, from the Atlantic to the Pacific, 52 p.; an autobiography, typewritten.

Alpheus Briggs, *Education in North Carolina Yearly Meeting,* 23 p.; typed and duplicated, 1930. (Guilford College library)

Papers and Letters, regarding the John Brown Band, as related to the raid on Harpers Ferry and the two Quaker boys involved. They include typed copy of the original letter to the mother of the Coppoc boys from her sister; a letter from Harpers Ferry by Edwin Coppoc to his Uncle Joshua of Winona, Ohio, shortly before his death on the gallows; and some sketches from the *Salem Era* (Ohio), 1881, regarding Edwin Coppoc.

Papers, regarding John Frederick Hanson, 30 p.; dated 1937; a family history including some autobiographical material concerning Iowa Yearly Meeting, his visit among Norwegian and other Friends of Europe, and various experiences in America. (George Fox College library)

Treatise in Defense of Evangelical Quakerism, three typed pages, by Alpheus Briggs. (Guilford College library)

*List of Meetings, Indiana Yearly Meeting, 1800-1828*, 12 p.; made from original manuscript of Clarkson Butterworth, about 1900.

Papers, regarding Dougan Clark at the time of the controversy over water baptism and "The Supper," 1894-1896.

Papers and Letters, regarding the baptism of Dougan Clark: letters to Timothy Nicholson from E. C. Siler, Robert W. Douglas, J. Walter Malone, and Rufus M. Jones; "Propositions Submitted to Dr. Dougan Clark" from the Preparative Meeting of Ministers and Elders of Whitewater Monthly Meeting. All of these dated 1894.

*Frank Herbert Clark, A Principal of Friends Academies*, one typed page. By his daughter Evelyn Clark.

*Memoir of Anson Cox*, 48 p.; an autobiography of one who was prominent in the development of Friends Meetings in Idaho.

Journal, by John Jones (Indiana), 30 p.; typed and duplicated. This is a somewhat detailed story of his visit among Kansas and Iowa Friends.

White Lick Monthly Meeting of Friends, 19 p. (Rufus M. Jones Papers, Haverford)

Algie I. Newlin, "Quaker Trails to the West"; typed and duplicated. (Guilford College library)

Paper, by Ella Newlin, 11 p.; 1935; typed and duplicated. A personal review of the early frontier years viewed from the Conservative Friends experiences.

Harlow Lindley, "Thomas Beals, First Friends Minister in Ohio," 3 p.; typed; from the *Ohio State Archeological and Historical Quarterly*, Vol. LIII, No. 1 (January-March, 1944).

*Tribute to Frank D. Roberts*, 19 p.; prepared by Greenleaf Idaho Friends, to one who gave several years in developing the academy.

Henry Townsend, "A Principal of Friends Academies"; a brief sketch; two typed pages.

*An Account of the Sufferings of Friends of North Carolina Yearly Meeting*, in their testimony against war, 1861-1865, 28 p.; published by the Peace Association of Friends in America, 1868.

Paper by E. Hicks Trueblood, "Historical Sketch of Blue River Monthly Meeting (Indiana)," 7 p.; typed and duplicated; 1815 to 1895.

Extracts, from epistles and old records regarding the separation of 1854 — giving both the Gurneyite and the Wilburite views.

*The Testimony of the Society of Friends, On the Continent of North America,* 21 p.; a reflection by Orthodox Friends, following the separation of 1828. Prepared by a "General committee . . . assembled in Philadelphia the 27th of the 7th month, 1829."

*Slavery Within Its Limits,* a narrative on the subject by the Meeting for Sufferings of North Carolina Yearly Meeting, 40 p.; printed in Greensboro, North Carolina, 1848.

## 4. Some Hitherto Unpublished Letters

With one exception these letters are from the files of the late Rufus M. Jones, and were written to him during his service as editor of the *American Friend.* The controversies of the period were focussed mainly in that journal, which, in 1894, merged the *Christian Worker* (1871) and the *Friends Review* (1847).

The letters are presented here with a minimum of editing by which parts that had no bearing on the main concern have been deleted, as indicated. Certain grammatical changes have been made out of respect for the writers who would have made them had they anticipated publication.

Their peculiar value lies largely in the fact that they are *letters.* They represent candid views such as person-to-person correspondence would invite. Out of a large number of letters found in research these are chosen as representing certain diverse views and controversies of a half-century or more ago.

The letters from the files of Rufus M. Jones are reprinted by consent of Mary Hoxie Jones, his daughter. Their inclusion in this book has been decided after consultation with several concerned Friends. These and several other letters are being offered to all Friends college libraries in their original unedited form.

---

Mary Moon Meredith was probably the most prominent woman Friends minister in the later years of the nineteenth century. With her husband, Franklin Meredith, she held evangelistic meetings from North Carolina to Oregon and California.

Barclay, Kansas 11.6,1894

Rufus M. Jones
Dear Friend

Our hearts have been touched with such sympathy, interest and appreciation of thy work as editor of the American Friend. We feel constrained to write a message of assurance to thee of our high esteem of thy editorials and general management of the Friend.

We believe for a time like this thou hast been raised up. Thy editorial on the question of the ordinances of Nov. 1st was most excellent, and we are truly grateful for such a hand at the helm now.

Very truly thy friends,
Franklin Meredith
Mary Moon Meredith

P. S. We are now at Barclay, Kansas in a very gracious revival.

---

No other names in the history of Ohio Yearly Meeting are more respected than those of Walter and Emma Malone. For years the Bible School at Cleveland was under their care, and their name has been given to Malone College, which evolved from their work.

The history of the adoption of water baptism by some Meetings in Ohio Yearly Meeting may not be widely known among Friends. Here Walter Malone expresses his disapproval and gives a page from his memory of the first public practice in Ohio Yearly Meeting.

THE MALONE STONE CO.
General offices
5 Euclid Ave., Cleveland, O

Cleveland, Ohio
Sept. 13, 1894

Rufus M. Jones,
Haverford, Pa.

Dear Friend:

I was glad to receive thy letter and to know of the good time thee had in the west. I wish I could have been with thee. I did think something of it but it was impossible to get away.

Yes, we were very sorry indeed for the occurrence at our Yearly Meeting. . . . I will give thee a little account of it, and thee can put in what thee pleases of it or none of it. (I do not know that it is necessary as I wrote about the same to Timothy Nicholson, and thought perhaps thee would like to know the inside of it.) (I was called home Fifth Day evening by the illness of my wife, and the death of an aged member of our meeting kept me over till the Seventh Day afternoon.)

Reaching Damascus, the man that drove me out said there was a Memorial Meeting for David B. Updegraff going on in the Meeting house so I went in. There was no one on the platform except Dr. [Dougan] Clark, John Pennington and A. H. Hussey, and just as I got in at the close of the meeting Dr. Clark announced that he had felt for a long time that he wanted to be baptized and was going to ask John Pennington to do it then. I was quite taken off my feet and had nothing to say as that was the first I had heard. . . .

John Pennington asked if there were any others who wanted to be baptized and if there were to come forward and be baptized with Dr. Clark, and some six or eight came forward and John Pennington took a pitcher of water and poured a little on each one's head as they bowed there around the table. Then they tried to make a great hurrah about it and wanted everyone to come forward and shake hands with them etc., but some of us did not feel like doing it and did not, so the meeting closed (. . . I found out that it was a meeting that Dr. Clark had been holding each afternoon, called his Pentecostal Meeting).

Nothing was said about the occurrence until the next day when I was invited to Ezra French's to dine. That was where Dr. Clark was making his home and he invited me into his room to have a little talk so I went and he voluntarily gave me a little history of the occurrence which was about as follows: That he had been feeling for sometime like he wanted to be baptized. I know that A. H. Hussey had pressed it upon him very hard as well as John Pennington. A. H. Hussey insisted on his being baptized in the meeting house, but all his other friends together with Sarah Jenkins and John Pennington advised him not to be, saying it would be better in private so he decided, as it was much his preference, to be baptized privately. But all the afternoon while he was preaching he said that John Pennington and A. H. Hussey were talking and groaning and keeping up a great noise and when he sat down John Pennington had turned clear over and said he must be baptized in public and it must be done now. [He said] that the Holy Ghost was leading them and that was the thing to do, and A. H. Hussey insisted that the Holy Ghost was leading so he yielded, not that he felt that way himself, but they so insisted that they were being led by the Holy Ghost, that he just yielded to them.

After he told me this I gave him my view of it and said I would like to see John Pennington, A. H. Hussey and him together and talk the matter over a little and he said he would be very glad to do so, and I left it to him to make the arrangements for me to see them.

Then after the meeting in the evening was over he came up, took me by the hand and said he wanted to assume the responsibility of the whole affair, and I said, "Yes, but thee told me the truth this afternoon, and I want to see you three together." A. H. Hussey came up and said the Holy Ghost was leading them. Dr. Clark said that he had not intended to be baptized at that time, but they insisted so much that he finally gave up to them, but in the meantime they made Dr. Clark sign a written statement, I suppose clearing them. I do not know what it was, did not ask to see it and they would none of them meet me, so thee can see that I lay a large part of the blame on John Pennington and A. H. Hussey. A. H. Hussey had been around over the Yearly Meeting making a boast of water baptism and said he was going to have it in Ohio Yearly Meeting, and a number took that as the reason he insisted on having it done in public, but I think it was as good a thing as could have happened for us under the circumstances for we had a good opportunity to explain our views of matters which we did.

· · · · ·

. . . They had John Pennington bring his right of membership into our Yearly Meeting and he had only had it there about a week, and A. H. Hussey appointed him chairman of the Committee on Gospel services and did it so quickly that the clerk thought he had appointed him on the committee that had just finished, so we could all see that something was up. When this committee brought in their report at the close of Yearly Meeting we expressed our views and said that we did not assume the responsibility of some of the conduct of the meeting [as given in the] minute. . . . I wish I could give thee the whole inside of it but thee can get the history of it anyway.

After discussing this for an hour or so they [the Yearly Meeting] put it to a rising vote and twice as many rose in favor of putting the minute on record as those that were against it, so there were only a few that thought [the baptism] was right at all. The rest of us had an opportunity to express ourselves and I think it did more good than anything that could possibly have come up any other way. Water baptism lost a great many friends by the matter in our Yearly Meeting.

I presume now that they have caused Dr. Clark to lose his position in Earlham they will be satisfied. He has nothing now to live on and they have nothing to give him. . . .

Thy Friend and Brother,<br>Walter Malone

---

John Henry Douglas was probably the most influential Friend in the beginning and development of revivalism among Friends. His influence was felt from New England to California as he led in the evangelistic efforts of his day. His first letter (1901), represents the fear of many that the *American Friend* was moving toward a heretical course. His second letter (1913) reviews the rise of the revival movement and his part in it.

Pasadena, Cal.<br>7/24/1901

Rufus Jones
My Dear Friend,

I have refrained from writing to thee for a long time having felt that I had done all that I could to advise and criticise etc., I knew that sooner or later a break would come, and it seems to be upon us now, as shown in thy late editorials. All I need to say now is, be careful and wise and loving.

Thee knows that we were not satisfied with the old *Friend* and the [*Friends*] *Review* was published which I took from the first. Then there came a time when our work demanded a different paper. This led to launching the *Christian Worker*. I worked hard to help start it. It served a grand purpose and greatly helped with the aggressive work. The two papers went on, with but little friction until these were united [in the *American Friend*] when everybody seemed determined to support the new paper.

From various causes many became uneasy with the teachings and influence of the *American Friend* not any more because of what it said, than of what it did not say. Some way many of our workers did not find in it what they needed in sympathy and help. The strong clear-cut doctrinal food and instruction we used to find in the *Worker* were wanting. Then there seemed to many of us a very strong sympathy, if not endorsement of the Higher Criticism. This seemed very evident when the paper became the champion of the Haverford Summer School work. When books and lecturers were advertised, [with] most of which very many who were conversant, [found] . . . very unsatisfactory.

The [*American*] *Friend* seemed to insinuate that [none] except ripe scholars had [any] business to have anything to do with the teachings of Higher Criticism, when the fact is that very many first-class scholars and divines have written, spoken and warned us of the danger of said criticism. Then again every time any one has attempted to enter a warning voice in the *American Friend* they have *always* been met with severe rejoinders . . . [opposing] such writers as Woodward, Malone, Pinkham, C. T. Prichard, Wood and others; and the paper seemed always to go hand in hand with those who opposed these writers.

These are a few things which have been seen and felt by many good Friends, and there has been a growing demand for a change in the A. F. or [else] a new paper. It looks now as though the latter might be forthcoming. I am very sorry we could not have in the A. F. all we need in a church paper. I believe Friends generally have hoped and prayed to that end, and it will be very hard for many to give up that hope.

What will be the outcome? Can two papers be supported, like the two papers in England representing two schools of thought? If so I do hope that great care will be taken not to make an unnecessary war upon each other. . . .

The saddest thought to me is that many have been poisoned and their faith weakened, and others have become bewildered by the many voices claiming to be wise above that which is written. It is a trying time for the young and intelligent who are wading through the labyrinths of modern thought. Many are enchanted with the study of Biology, Evolution, High Criticism etc.

The demand seems to be for science and philosophy in every thing; so that revelation has to wait for the diagnosis of a host of doctors, and thus many lives of talented men are wasted. . . . To edit a paper now is no light task and I know of no other way than to do it with a very few essential things in view, [such as] the salvation of the lost, the sanctification of the believer, the edification and unity of the church and the glory of God.

I write the above as a personal letter of sympathy and regret. No one was more pleased with thy being editor of the A. F. than myself, although I know of [thy] lack of experience in the work of the church especially as evangelist, or pastor and [that thee] could not know the needs of the work as those of greater experience, but I expected thee would be in the field and join with us as occasion offered in our soul-saving work and church extension. . . .

Thy Friend and Brother<br>
John Henry Douglas.

---

Whittier, Cal.<br>
Apr 23 1913.

Levinus Painter,
My Dear Friend

Your letter of the 18th is now before me. It interests me greatly. The subject of your letter has been the absorbing theme of my long life. To be definite as to the time and the places where the revivals first appeard cannot be stated very definitely. . . .

During all these years a very strong effort was made to uphold the testimonies and practices of early Friends. There were a few intelligent spiritually minded Friends who looked upon all this struggle to perpetuate and uphold Quakerism on traditional lines as entirely a mistake and failure. J. J. Gurney stood at the head of this class. These few prayed much that the eyes of the blind might be opened and that God would once more arise for the redemption of His people. They prayed for a revival.

I remember well those prayers, offered by certain of our ministers. Occasionally there were noticed some signs of awakening but such was the presure of tradition and formalism that everything was suppressed. But about 1852 a few breaks were made. Some of our young people were converted and began to give testimony to their experience. This was the time when after deep conviction and great suffering, I yielded to be saved . . . from that time until now, my whole life has been devoted to pleading with men to be reconciled to God. I opened my mouth in confession. After this, here and there, others were led in the same way.

It required the greatest watchfulness and care that we might not offend the Elders. We passed through many painful experiences for several years. The church was afraid that creaturely activity and excitement might come into the church. Many of these dear Friends were deeply concerned for our well-being, but were so fearful that they and we suffered. In spite of all a revival spirit was taking hold of our people. It manifested itself in families. The power of the Lord would come upon the family meetings or "sittings" as they were called then, so that frequently mouths would be opened in prayer or testimony. Tears were abundant, the people . . . asked to be prayed for.

These meetings became more frequent and spread into different parts until quite a revival wave was reaching our people in the different yearly meetings. Then several families would meet together and most blessed results followed. Then occasionally meetings would be held in school houses. The church became deeply concerned and made strong efforts in many places to stop these family meetings. It was held that they were out of the order of the Society of Friends, but the work went on, and spread far and near. In a few places the intolerant spirit [was] manifested towards those who were engaged in this service so that a ranter spirit was provoked and some harm done to the new move. . . . [I]n every place where the ranter spirit was manifested it was brought about by undue efforts to suppress the revival spirit and efforts.

We had now come to a time of very great importance. There was quite a strong tension manifesting itself and some friction appearing in some places. In the providence of God a very strong encouragement was given to the revival spirit and work by that never to be forgotten Sabbath night meeting during [Indiana] Yearly Meeting in 1860. . . . It is well written up in Rhoda M. Coffin's journal. This meeting was attended and approved by many leading Friends among them Lindley M. Hoag, Sybil Jones, Rebecca Updegraff and others. It had been on my heart for years and I could not rest until it was granted. Then the revival wave rose higher and higher in many parts of America. It was fully endorsed when the General Meeting plan was adopted and a committee appointed in about 1869. Great results followed. Soon the missionary spirit appeared, and Foreign Missions established, many were called into the ministry and became successful soul winners. Soon pastors were needed for the flock of young converts, and the system came upon us without convention or any human effort. The Lord led and the church followed. . . .

We have enjoyed a very successful 50 years of revival. I have some fears that the wave is abating. There is danger of professionalism, and human planning. Intellectuality can never take the place of spirituality. The Gospel is the only power of God unto salvation. In all ages this has been successful, and will be in the future and nothing can take its place. *Sin* is the great destroyer, Jesus Christ and Him Crucified is the remedy for soul sickness and death. The Lord bless thee.

Thy Friend and Brother
John Henry Douglas.

---

The Quaker educators of the midwest and Pacific areas held similar views, revealing again the cleavage that, in general, ran between church and college. Robert L. Kelly was at this time acting president of Penn College.

Oskaloosa, Iowa
1/18/1901

Rufus M. Jones
My Dear Friend,

You receive many letters and I always hesitate to add to your burdens along this line. I cannot resist the temptation however to say a word or two in reference to your "An Editorial Letter" of yesterday. . . .

Two weeks ago I attended Quarterly Meeting at New Providence, Iowa, preaching on Saturday. . . . In the course of that talk I was very deeply impressed with the necessity of your adhering to the course you are pursuing in *The American Friend*.

There must be a conciliatory spirit shown on both sides of this discussion. There are *dangers* as well as elements of truth on *both* sides, but in the meantime I feel that the business of the Friend's Church is to preach the pure and simple Gospel of Christ and let it come straight from the shoulder.

In my lecture, "The Relation Between Philosophy and Religion," which was given at New Providence [Iowa] Sunday night I said the same things you say in your "Letter.". . . After much study I feel that is the proper attitude to take, and I feel so secure in the position that I am sure I could not easily be made a partisan on either side. I shudder for what extreme partisanship *may* do for our church. Policy, and what is much more important than that, *truth* lies in the path you have marked out. . . . Let's hold our forces together.

Very fraternally,
Robert L. Kelly

---

Among evangelical Friends there was disagreement on the second coming of Christ. Some Friends believed there was to be a visible return of Christ to earth, while others considered the question speculative and not in keeping with a spiritual interpretation of the New Testament. Joseph Moore, president of Earlham College, represents in this letter to the *American Friend* those who held to the latter view. His second letter, commending the stand taken by the *American Friend,* stands in contrast to the views of some other correspondents.

Earlham College
Richmond, Indiana
4/24/97

Rufus M. Jones
Dear Friend,

I want to be right and to commend the right and in this spirit I heartily agree with thy two [recent] editorials. . . .

As the matter often looks to me it would almost seem that it is harder for the church to see the coming of Christ as he was revealed at Pentecost and as he is even more fully and graciously revealed today, than it was for the Jews to see Him as He was revealed in the flesh as Jesus of Nazareth.

I can but often grieve that there are so many teachers whose strength is largely bestowed in a way to turn people away from the present and the possible to what may be far distant, for aught we know. Life is *now* to be received and *lived* in the gladness of heroic service rather than a holding out of expectation of what will happen in a year or a century.

If the church could see a coming of Jesus in the mighty stirring of the

multitudes in our day, if it could see that He has come to secure the brotherhood of man and that he is seeking in the church for a mighty and all-conquering army, if instead of compromising with sin in divers ways [the church] would rise up at the Captain's call "against the rulers of this world's darkness," if we could see that God wants to do mightier things through us in our day than He has done for any age as we are "workers together with him," if we could see these things we should find that it is enough for us *now* to know that he is *here*.

I am not writing for the American Friend but simply to second thy motion to practical Christianity by the acceptance of a present-risen Christ who is calling to his church to let him do more for it than he has ever yet done.

Very truly thy friend,
Joseph Moore

---

Earlham College
Richmond, Ind.
Jan. 21, 1901

Dear Rufus Jones:

*Keep on!* I do not say this for fear there will be any swerving but to express approval — heartily.

Thy editorial letter in last number of *The American Friend* renews the idea of what the paper and its editor are rightly set to do.

There are probably enough people who can give "cold theological definitions." A journal like *The American Friend* cannot fit itself to people's various theological and other systems.

Our little systems have their day
They have their day and cease to be.
They are but broken lights of Thee
And thou O lord art more than they.

Yes, hold us to the central Sun.

Very truly thy friend,
Joseph Moore

---

The controversies that brought tensions and some separations among Friends in America were resolved amicably by British Friends. The issues were brought candidly before a conference held at Manchester in 1895. Henry Stanley Newman, editor of the *Friend,* writes to Rufus M. Jones his evaluation of the conference and the issues.

Bishopsgate, London, E.C.
Broad Street, Leominister,
25,x1,1895

Dear Friend,

The Manchester Conference will mark an era in the history of our Society in England. We have found for some years past that whilst our Home Mission work was laying hold of thousands of the strong Anglo Saxon working men of our country and many of them were being converted and not a few being received into membership that our Church was *losing grasp* of the highly educated and intelligent young men and women belonging to our best old Quaker families who were receiving first class curriculum at College and then *drifting* theologically.

If our Society was thus to lose its best, after years [this] might settle our fate. Every Christian Church *must* face modern criticism and modern scientific thought. It is not the slightest use ignoring it by burying our head in the sand. This Conference is the effort *for the first time* in our Society to *face* this emergency and I want thee to quietly make the best and fullest use thou can of the double number of the "Friend" (Conference Number) that we sent thee. . . . President Mills and others in your land have spoken to me about the future problems that confront us which many good Friends your side of the stream do not yet dream of, but our church will have to face them to *grow* and grow *strong*. The addresses by Rendel Harris and Thomas Hodgkin are golden. Thou wilt see my own remarks . . . (on page 77). A recent leader in the *Friend* on "Modern Criticism" also gives my views on another department of the subject, but it may be rather strong food for some in America. Use thy own discretion and may God guide thee.

> Thy Brother Editor,
> Henry Stanley Newman

P.S. The speech of Alexander Maclaren at the Conference was very fine. See also a letter from Rendel Harris in the *Friend* for the 29th instant, and the notes on the Conference by "a Stranger."

5. "FAMILY TREE" OF AMERICAN YEARLY MEETINGS (opposite 382)

6. OVER-ALL ASSOCIATIONS

ASSOCIATION OF EVANGELICAL FRIENDS
*Chairmen*

Harold B. Winn . . . . . . . . . 1956-1968    Stanley Brown . . . . . . . . . . 1968-

EVANGELICAL FRIENDS ALLIANCE
*President*

Harold B. Winn . . . . . . . . 1966-

FRIENDS GENERAL CONFERENCE
*Chairmen*

| | | | |
|---|---|---|---|
| Dr. O. Edward Janney | . . . . 1900-1920 | Clarence E. Pickett | . . . . . . 1955-1959 |
| Arthur C. Jackson | . . . . . . . 1920-1941 | Barrett Hollister | . . . . . . . . . 1959-1968 |
| Bliss Forbush | . . . . . . . . . . . 1941-1949 | William Hubben | . . . . . . . . . 1968- |
| George A. Walton | . . . . . . . 1949-1955 | | |

## Secretaries

| | | | |
|---|---|---|---|
| Henry W. Wilbur | 1905-1915 | Lawrence McK. Miller, Jr. | 1954-1965 |
| J. Barnard Walton | 1915-1951 | George B. Corwin | 1965-1967 |
| Earle Edwards | 1951-1954 | Lawrence McK. Miller, Jr. | 1967- |

## FRIENDS UNITED MEETING
### Secretaries

PART-TIME
Joseph John Mills ........ 1914-1917

FULL-TIME
Walter C. Woodward .... 1917-1942

Percy M. Thomas (acting) 1942-1944
Errol T. Elliott .......... 1944-1957
Glenn A. Reece .......... 1957-1967
Lorton G. Heusel ........ 1967-
David O. Stanfield (assoc.) 1968-

### Business Managers (Book Store)

Richard E. Kendall ...... 1955-1959
Merle Brauer ............ 1960-1964

Clyde Johnson ............ 1965-1968
Thomas Cooper .......... 1968-

### Editors the American Friend

(For two years, 1867-1868, a journal called the *American Friend* was published and edited at Richmond, Indiana, by an editorial committee. The *American Friend* (new series) was first published in 1894, uniting the *Christian Worker* and the *Friends Review*.)

Rufus M. Jones .......... 1894-1906
Herman Newman ........ 1907-1912
S. Edgar Nicholson ...... 1913-1917
Walter C. Woodward .... 1917-1942
Murray S. Kenworthy
(acting) .............. 1942-1943

James R. Furbay (acting) 1943
Errol T. Elliott .......... 1943-1957
Merritt Murphy .......... 1957-1960
Earl Conn *(Quaker Life)* 1960-1964
Xen Harvey *(Quaker Life)* 1964 —

### Department Secretaries

CHRISTIAN EDUCATION
Jeanette Hadley .......... 1937-1941
Lillian White Shepard .... 1941-1945
Charles Thomas .......... 1945-1950
Leonard Hall ............ 1950-1955
Russell Rees ............ 1955-1963
Earl Prignitz ............ 1964-

CHRISTIAN SOCIAL CONCERNS
William Merton Scott .... 1950-1957
Milton H. Hadley ........ 1957-1962
Herbert S. Huffman ...... 1962-

EVANGELISM AND CHURCH EXTENSION
T. Eugene Coffin ........ 1962-

MISSIONS
Mahalah Jay ............. 1894-1907
Morton C. Pearson ....... 1907-1908
Charles E. Tebbetts ....... 1908-1917

Ross A. Hadley .......... 1917-1921
Milo S. Hinckle .......... 1922-1923
B. Willis Beede .......... 1923-1932
Errol T. Elliott .......... 1932-1934
Merle L. Davis (acting) .. 1934-1935
Merle L. Davis .......... 1935-1953
Charles A. Lampman ..... 1953-1955
Ernest Lamb (acting) .... 1955-1956
George A. Scherer ........ 1956-1960
Norman E. Young ....... 1960-1966
Harold V. Smuck ........ 1966-

STEWARDSHIP AND FINANCE
Leonard Hall ............ 1955-1959
David O. Stanfield ........ 1960-1968

VOCATION AND MINISTRY
David E. Henley ........ 1960-1964
James Higgins ........... 1964-

## 7. Over-all Agencies

### AMERICAN FRIENDS SERVICE COMMITTEE

#### Chairmen

| | | | |
|---|---|---|---|
| Rufus M. Jones | 1917-1928 | Henry J. Cadbury | 1944-1960 |
| Henry J. Cadbury | 1928-1934 | Harold Evans | 1960-1963 |
| Henry Tatnall Brown | 1934-1935 | Gilbert F. White | 1963- |
| Rufus M. Jones | 1935-1944 | | |

#### Secretaries

| | | | |
|---|---|---|---|
| Vincent D. Nicholson | 1917-1918 | Colin W. Bell | 1959-1968 |
| Wilbur K. Thomas | 1918-1929 | Stephen G. Cary (acting) | 1968 |
| Clarence E. Pickett | 1929-1950 | Bronson P. Clark | 1968- |
| Lewis M. Hoskins | 1950-1959 | | |

### FRIENDS COMMITTEE ON NATIONAL LEGISLATION

#### Chairmen

| | | | |
|---|---|---|---|
| Murray Kenworthy | 1943-1946 | Delbert Replogle | 1955-1958 |
| Sumner A. Mills | 1947-1948 | Charles J. Darlington | 1959-1965 |
| David E. Henley | 1949-1953 | Stephen L. Angell, Jr. | 1966-1968 |
| Samuel R. Levering | 1954 | | |

#### Secretaries

| | | | |
|---|---|---|---|
| E. Raymond Wilson | 1943-1962 | Edward F. Snyder | 1962- |

### FRIENDS WORLD COMMITTEE FOR CONSULTATION

#### Chairmen

| | | | |
|---|---|---|---|
| Carl Heath | 1938-1947 | Elsa Cedergren | 1959-1961 |
| D. Elton Trueblood | 1948-1952 | James F. Walker | 1962-1964 |
| Errol T. Elliott | 1952-1958 | Douglas V. Steere | 1965- |

#### Secretaries

| | | | |
|---|---|---|---|
| Frederick J. Tritton | 1938-1946 | Ranjit M. Chetsingh | 1954-1956 |
| Leslie D. Shaffer | 1947-1948 | Herbert M. Hadley | 1956-1962 |
| Frederick J. Tritton | 1948-1950 | Blanche W. Shaffer | 1962- |
| Harry T. Silcock | 1950-1954 | | |

#### F.W.C.C. — AMERICAN SECTION

(United with the former Friends Fellowship Council)

#### Chairmen

| | | | |
|---|---|---|---|
| J. Passmore Elkinton | 1938 | Dorothy G. Thorne | 1956-1960 |
| Alvin T. Coate | 1939 | A. Ward Applegate | 1961-1967 |
| J. Hoge Ricks | 1939-1943 | Edwin B. Bronner | 1968- |
| Thomas E. Jones | 1944-1946 | | |
| D. Elton Trueblood | 1947-1948 | | |
| Alexander C. Purdy | 1948-1955 | | |

#### Secretaries

| | | | |
|---|---|---|---|
| Leslie D. Shaffer | 1937-1946 |
| Allen J. White | 1947-1948 |
| Leslie D. Shaffer | 1948-1950 |
| James F. Walker | 1950-1962 |
| Herbert M. Hadley | 1962- |

# 8. PRESIDENTS OF FRIENDS COLLEGES

## EARLHAM COLLEGE

| | | | |
|---|---|---|---|
| Barnabas C. Hobbs | 1867-1868 | Robert L. Kelly | 1903-1917 |
| Joseph Moore | 1868-1883 | David M. Edwards | 1917-1929 |
| William P. Pinkham | | William C. Dennis | 1929-1946 |
| (acting) | 1883-1884 | Thomas E. Jones | 1946-1958 |
| Joseph John Mills | 1884-1903 | Landrum Bolling | 1958- |

## FRIENDS UNIVERSITY

| | | | |
|---|---|---|---|
| Edmund Stanley | 1898-1918 | S. Arthur Watson | 1947-1952 |
| William O. Mendenhall | 1918-1934 | Lloyd Cressman | 1952-1956 |
| David M. Edwards | 1934-1939 | Lowell E. Roberts | 1956-1964 |
| W. A. Young | 1939-1946 | Roy F. Ray | 1964- |
| Charles A. Reagan (acting) | 1946-1947 | | |

## GEORGE FOX (PACIFIC) COLLEGE

| | | | |
|---|---|---|---|
| Thomas Newlin | 1891-1900 | Gervas A. Carey | 1947-1950 |
| Henry Edwin McGrew | 1900-1907 | Paul E. Parker | 1950-1952 |
| W. Irving Kelsey | 1907-1911 | (Adm. committee) | 1952-1954 |
| Levi T. Pennington | 1911-1941 | Milo C. Ross | 1954- |
| Emmett W. Gulley | 1941-1947 | | |

## GUILFORD COLLEGE

| | | | |
|---|---|---|---|
| Louis Lyndon Hobbs | 1888-1915 | Raymond Binford | 1918-1934 |
| Thomas Newlin | 1915-1917 | Clyde A. Milner | 1934-1965 |
| (Executive committee) | 1917-1918 | Grimsley Taylor Hobbs | 1965- |

## HAVERFORD COLLEGE

| | | | |
|---|---|---|---|
| Joseph Gibbons Harlan | 1857 | Archibald MacIntosh | |
| (Vacancy) | 1857-1863 | (acting) | 1945-1946 |
| Samuel James Gummere | 1863-1874 | Gilbert F. White | 1946-1956 |
| Thomas Chase | 1874-1886 | Archibald MacIntosh | |
| (Vacancy) | 1886-1887 | (acting) | 1957 |
| Isaac Sharpless | 1887-1917 | Hugh Borton | 1957-1967 |
| William Wistar Comfort | 1917-1940 | John Royston Coleman | 1967- |
| Felix Morley | 1940-1945 | | |

## MALONE COLLEGE

| | | | |
|---|---|---|---|
| Byron L. Osborn | 1957-1960 | Everett L. Cattell | 1960- |

## NEBRASKA CENTRAL COLLEGE

| | | | |
|---|---|---|---|
| D. R. Haworth | 1899-1901 | Stephen S. Myrick | 1910-1911 |
| D. B. Gilbert | 1901-1902 | Floyd W. Perisho | 1911-1912 |
| Samuel L. Haworth | 1902-1903 | Eli H. Perisho | 1912-1917 |
| Emmet E. Hadley | 1903-1904 | Homer J. Coppock | 1917-1921 |
| Eli H. Perisho | 1904-1907 | Ora W. Carrell | 1921-1953 |
| Stacy J. McCracken | 1907-1910 | (College closed) | |

## SWARTHMORE COLLEGE

| | | | |
|---|---|---|---|
| Edward Parrish | 1864-1871 | William Wilfred Birdsall .. | 1898-1902 |
| Edward Hicks Magill | 1872-1889 | Joseph Swain | 1902-1921 |
| William Hyde Appleton | | Frank Aydelotte | 1921-1940 |
| (acting) | 1889-1890 | John W. Nason | 1940-1953 |
| William Hyde Appleton .. | 1890-1891 | Courtney Craig Smith .... | 1953- |
| Charles De Garmo | 1891-1898 | | |

## WHITTIER COLLEGE

| | | | |
|---|---|---|---|
| Charles E. Tebbetts | 1901-1907 | Walter F. Dexter | 1923-1934 |
| Thomas Newlin | 1907-1915 | W. O. Mendenhall | 1934-1943 |
| Absalom Rosenberger | 1915-1918 | William C. Jones | 1944-1951 |
| Harry N. Wright | 1918-1923 | Paul S. Smith | 1951- |

## WILLIAM PENN COLLEGE

| | | | |
|---|---|---|---|
| John W. Woody | 1873-1876 | Henry Clark Bedford | 1931-1934 |
| William B. Morgan | 1876-1879 | B. F. Andrews (acting) | 1934-1935 |
| Benjamin Trueblood | 1879-1890 | Henry Randolph Pyle | 1935-1936 |
| Absalom Rosenberger | 1890-1900 | Henry Edwin McGrew | 1936-1942 |
| Robert L. Kelly (acting) .. | 1900-1901 | Errol T. Elliott | 1942-1944 |
| Absalom Rosenberger | 1901-1909 | Cecil Hinshaw | 1944-1949 |
| David M. Edwards (acting) | 1909-1910 | Forrester C. Stanley | |
| David M. Edwards | 1910-1917 | (interim) | |
| Stephen M. Hadley (acting) | 1917-1918 | Charles S. Ball | 1949-1958 |
| Henry Edwin McGrew .... | 1918-1927 | S. Arthur Watson | 1958-1964 |
| H. Linneus McCracken .... | 1927-1931 | Duane Moon | 1964- |

## WILMINGTON COLLEGE

| | | | |
|---|---|---|---|
| Lewis A. Estes | 1871-1874 | Beverly Oden Skinner .... | 1928-1931 |
| Benjamin F. Trueblood ... | 1874-1879 | Oscar F. Boyd (acting) ... | 1931-1932 |
| David Dennis | 1879-1881 | Walter L. Collins | 1932-1940 |
| James B. Unthank | 1881-1903 | S. Arthur Watson | 1940-1947 |
| Albert J. Brown | 1903-1912 | Samuel D. Marble | 1947-1959 |
| Samuel H. Hodgin | 1912-1915 | W. Brooke Morgan (adm. | |
| J. Edwin Jay | 1915-1927 | head) | 1959-1960 |
| Henry G. Williams | 1927-1928 | James M. Read | 1960- |

(For Friends Bible College, a later development, see Index)

## 9. YEARLY MEETING OFFICIALS

All omissions of names and dates are due to unavailable records
E.F.A.: Evangelical Friends Alliance
F.G.C.: Friends General Conference
F.U.M.: Friends United Meeting

### BALTIMORE YEARLY MEETING — F.G.C.*

---

* The two Baltimore Yearly Meetings united in 1968 with Ellis T. Williams as clerk.

## Clerks

MEN'S MEETING

| | |
|---|---|
| Phillip E. Thomas | 1827-1832 |
| William Stabler | 1833-1840 |
| Thomas P. Stabler | 1841 |
| Phillip E. Thomas | 1842 |
| Thomas P. Stabler | 1843-1849 |
| William Stabler | 1850-1851 |
| Benjamin Hallowell | 1852-1867 |
| William Wood | 1868-1875 |
| Darlington Hoopes | 1876-1877 |
| Levi K. Brown | 1878-1886 |
| Edward Stabler, Jr. | 1887-1898 |

WOMEN'S MEETING

| | |
|---|---|
| Rachel Mason | 1827 |
| Hannah P. Wilson | 1828-1829 |
| Rachel Mason | 1830-1835 |
| Eliza Marsh | 1836-1842 |
| Martha E. Tyson | 1843-1847 |
| Margaret E. Hallowell | 1848-1862 |
| Mary G. Moore | 1863-1872 |
| Mary L. Roberts | 1873-1874 |
| Mary C. Cutler | 1875-1882 |

| | |
|---|---|
| Priscilla Matthews | 1883 |
| Anna F. Matthews | 1884-1890 |
| Elizabeth M. Koser | 1891-1898 |

JOINT

| | |
|---|---|
| Edward Stabler, Jr. | 1899-1903 |
| Elizabeth M. Koser | 1904-1911 |
| Elizabeth Koser Wilson | 1912-1914 |
| Edward C. Wilson | 1915-1917 |
| Edward C. Wilson | 1919-1921 |
| William S. Pike | 1922-1930 |
| Bertha L. Broomell | 1931 |
| William S. Pike | 1932 |
| William S. Pike | 1933-1935 |
| Esther Foulke Sharpless | 1936-1946 |
| J. Harold Passmore | 1947-1951 |
| Edna P. Legg | 1952-1956 |
| Margaret L. Matthews | 1957-1959 |
| Bliss Forbush | 1960-1962 |
| Harry S. Scott, Jr. | 1963-1967 |

UNITED

| | |
|---|---|
| Ellis T. Williams | 1968- |

## Secretaries

| | |
|---|---|
| O. Edward Janney | 1928 |
| Bliss Forbush | 1929-1943 |
| LaVerne H. Forbush | 1944 |
| William Machensen | 1945-1950 |

| | |
|---|---|
| ——— ——— | 1951-1952 |
| Marshall O. Sutton | 1953-1958 |
| Theodore H. Mattheiss | 1959-1967 |

## BALTIMORE YEARLY MEETING — F.U.M.*

### Clerks

| | |
|---|---|
| Hugh Balderston | 1828-1840 |
| John P. Balderston | 1841-1845 |
| Hugh Balderston | 1846-1849 |
| Richard H. Thomas | 1850-1851 |
| Hugh Balderston | 1852 |
| Richard H. Thomas | 1853-1855 |
| Francis T. King | 1856-1884 |
| James C. Thomas | 1885-1896 |

| | |
|---|---|
| Allen C. Thomas | 1897-1920 |
| John R. Cary | 1921-1928 |
| J. Hoge Ricks | 1929-1947 |
| Edward F. Raiford | 1948-1952 |
| Emmet M. Frazer | 1953-1958 |
| Elizabeth E. Haviland | 1959-1967 |
| Ellis T. Williams | 1968- |

### Secretaries

| | |
|---|---|
| Lewis C. Moon | 1923-1929 |
| D. Elton Trueblood | 1930-1934 |
| W. Bruce Hadley | 1935-1937 |
| Jesse A. Stanfield | 1938-1943 |

| | |
|---|---|
| Harold N. Tollefson | 1944-1950 |
| Marlin D. Dawson | 1951-1959 |
| Arnold B. Vaught | 1959-1967 |

* See the preceding footnote.

## CALIFORNIA YEARLY MEETING — F.U.M.
### Clerks

| | | | |
|---|---|---|---|
| Levi Gregory | 1896-1897 | Oscar O. Marshburn | 1952-1962 |
| John Chawner | 1897-1917 | Warren O. Mendenhall | 1962-1967 |
| Allen U. Tomlinson | 1917-1947 | Glen Rinard | 1967- |
| Blaine G. Bronner | 1947-1952 | | |

### Superintendents

| | | | |
|---|---|---|---|
| John Shober Kimber | 1916-1919 | R. Ernest Lamb | 1943-1949 |
| Harry R. Keates | 1919-1927 | Donald E. Spitler | 1949-1958 |
| Frank W. Dell | 1927-1936 | Keith Sarver | 1958- |
| Harley M. Moore | 1936-1943 | | |

## CANADA YEARLY MEETING — CONSERVATIVE
### Clerks

| | | | |
|---|---|---|---|
| William Richardson | 1904-1923 | Howard Clayton | 1943-1945 |
| Albert Pollard | 1924-1927 | Elma M. Starr | 1946-1947 |
| ———— ———— | 1928-1942 | | |

## CANADA YEARLY MEETING — F.U.M.
### Clerks

| | | | |
|---|---|---|---|
| Adam Spencer | 1867-1876 | William I. Moore | 1899-1905 |
| William Spencer | 1877 | William Harris | 1906-1915 |
| Hannah Hane Cody | 1878 | Joseph P. Rogers | 1916 |
| William Wetherald | 1879 | William Harris | 1917-1923 |
| Howard Nicholson | 1880-1881 | Arthur G. Dorland | 1924-1935 |
| Ira Clark | 1882 | Raymond G. Booth | 1935-1939 |
| Howard Nicholson | 1883 | Arthur G. Dorland | 1940-1945 |
| Thomas Walker | 1884-1885 | Howard Clayton | 1946-1954 |
| Howard Nicholson | 1886-1888 | UNITED | |
| John T. Dorland | 1889-1890 | Howard Clayton | 1955-1957 |
| Thomas Harris | 1891-1892 | Mable B. Willson | 1958-1961 |
| John R. Harris | 1893-1898 | C. LeRoy Jones | 1962- |

### Secretaries (United)

| | | | |
|---|---|---|---|
| Mary Needler Hinde | 1958-1959 | Fred Haslam | 1960- |

## CENTRAL YEARLY MEETING (INDIANA)
### Clerks

| | | | |
|---|---|---|---|
| J. Carl Root | 1926-1933 | J. Edwin Newby | 1934-1968 |

### Superintendents

| | | | |
|---|---|---|---|
| Frank Reichenbach | 1926-1929 | William Barnard | 1944 |
| Corman Cox | 1930 | R. Lloyd Wilson | 1945 |
| Grant Hinshaw | 1931 | William I. Cook | 1946-1948 |
| Frank Reichenbach | 1932 | Donald E. Cassady | 1949-1960 |
| J. Carl Root | 1933-1936 | Fred O. Lee | 1961-1962 |
| Joshua Stauffer | 1937-1938 | J. Russell Butler | 1963-1968 |
| A. O. Cassady | 1939-1943 | | |

## GENESEE YEARLY MEETING (CANADA) — F.G.C.
### Clerks
C. Harold Zavitz ......... 1928-1929    Charles A. Zavitz ......... 1930-1939

## ILLINOIS YEARLY MEETING — F.G.C.
### Clerks

MEN'S MEETING

| | |
|---|---|
| Jonathan W. Plummer .... | 1875-1883 |
| Oliver Wilson ............ | 1884-1897 |
| Clarence Mills ............ | 1898-1900 |
| Oliver Wilson ............ | 1901 |
| Clarence Mills ............ | 1902-1913 |
| Albert T. Mills ........... | 1914-1918 |
| Clarence C. Mills ........ | 1919-1920 |
| Clement B. Flitcraft ...... | 1921-1924 |
| Theodore J. Smith ........ | 1925-1927 |
| Luella W. Flitcraft ....... | 1928-1933 |
| Charles A. Whitney ....... | 1934-1939 |
| William Mackensen ....... | 1940 |
| Charles A. Whitney ...... | 1941-1943 |
| George H. Watson ....... | 1944-1949 |

| | |
|---|---|
| Charles H. Harker, Jr. .... | 1950-1952 |
| Beulah G. Nelson ........ | 1953-1954 |
| France D. Hole .......... | 1955-1957 |
| Robert O. Byrd .......... | 1958-1959 |
| Clifford Haworth ......... | 1960-1961 |
| Chester A. Graham ....... | 1962-1964 |
| Helen Jean Nelson ........ | 1965-1966 |
| Orval Lucier ............. | 1967-1968 |

WOMEN'S MEETING

| | |
|---|---|
| Caroline Lukens .......... | 1875-1880 |
| Elizabeth H. Coale ....... | 1881 |
| Caroline Lukens .......... | 1882-1884 |
| Elizabeth H. Coale ....... | 1885-1886 |
| (United with Men's Meeting) | |

## INDIANA YEARLY MEETING — F.G.C.
### Clerks

| | |
|---|---|
| David Evans ............. | 1828-1829 |
| Benjamin Hopkins ........ | 1830 |
| David Evans ............. | 1831-1837 |
| John T. Plummer ........ | 1838-1839 |
| William Kinney .......... | 1840 |
| John T. Plummer ........ | 1841-1842 |
| William Kinney .......... | 1843-1844 |
| Samuel Silver ............ | 1845 |
| Samuel Morris ........... | 1846-1847 |
| John T. Plummer ........ | 1848-1851 |
| David Evans ............. | 1852-1853 |
| John T. Plummer ........ | 1854-1856 |
| David Evans ............. | 1857-1860 |
| William Parry ............ | 1861 |
| Robert Hatton ........... | 1862-1866 |
| William Parry ............ | 1867-1868 |
| Robert Hatton ........... | 1869 |
| William Parry ............ | 1870-1872 |
| Aaron Wright ............ | 1873 |
| Robert Hatton ........... | 1874 |
| William Parry ........... | 1875-1879 |

| | |
|---|---|
| Davis Furnas ............. | 1880-1894 |
| George R. Thorpe ........ | 1895-1901 |
| Aaron B. Chandler ....... | 1902-1907 |
| Emil P. Yeo ............. | 1908-1909 |
| Aaron B. Chandler ....... | 1910-1911 |
| George R. Thorpe ........ | 1912 |
| J. Lindley Mendenhall .... | 1913-1914 |
| George R. Thorpe ........ | 1915-1916 |
| Elizabeth S. Darlington ... | 1917 |
| J. Lindley Mendenhall ..... | 1918-1919 |
| Finley Tomlinson ........ | 1920 |
| J. Lindley Mendenhall .... | 1921-1923 |
| Ruth A. Chandler ........ | 1924-1929 |
| George H. Swain ......... | 1930-1931 |
| Finley Tomlinson ........ | 1932 |
| J. Lindley Mendenhall .... | 1933 |
| M. Sherman Pressler ...... | 1934-1942 |
| Lawrence W. Furnas ..... | 1943-1957 |
| Rita E. Rogers .......... | 1958-1960 |
| Louis P. Newmann ....... | 1961- |

## INDIANA YEARLY MEETING — F.U.M.
### Clerks
Benjamin Hopkins ........ 1821    George Carter ............ 1822

Benjamin Hopkins ....... 1823-1824
James Pegg .............. 1825-1826
Elijah Coffin ............. 1827-1857
Charles Coffin ............ 1858-1884
Allen Terrell ............. 1885-1890
Elwood O. Ellis .......... 1891-1903
Timothy Nicholson ....... 1904-1911
Robert L. Kelly .......... 1912-1916
Ancil E. Ratliff ........... 1917
David M. Edwards ....... 1918
S. Edgar Nicholson ....... 1919-1925

Arthur M. Charles ........ 1926
Percy M. Thomas ........ 1927
Arthur M. Charles ........ 1928-1930
William J. Sayers ......... 1931-1943
Norval E. Webb .......... 1944-1948
Leslie Frazer ............. 1949-1950
Murray C. Johnson ....... 1951-1955
D. Elton Trueblood ....... 1956-1960
Raymond V. Breaker ..... 1961-1965
Harold C. Cope .......... 1966-

## Superintendents

Robert W. Douglas ....... 1888-1891
Allen Jay ................ 1892-1895
Samuel C. Mills .......... 1896-1897
Joseph O. Binford ........ 1898-1904
Ira C. Johnson ........... 1904-1914
Truman C. Kenworthy ... 1914-1917
Ira C. Johnson ........... 1918-1919
Aaron Napier ............ 1919-1920
Charles E. Hiatt .......... 1921-1932

Frederick E. Carter ....... 1933-1934
————— ————— .... 1935-1936
Milo S. Hinckle .......... 1937-1941
Murray S. Kenworthy .... 1942-1946
Logan W. Smith ......... 1946-1947
John Compton ........... 1947-1960
Kenneth R. Pickering ..... 1960-1963
William A. Wagner ...... 1964-

## IOWA YEARLY MEETING — CONSERVATIVE
### Clerks

MEN'S MEETING
Zimri Horner.. .......... 1877-1881
Peter Hobson ............ 1882-1886
Clarkson Penrose ........ 1887-1906
James E. Gooden ......... 1907-1917
William P. Young ........ 1917-1933
Wilson T. Emmons ...... 1934-1939

WOMEN'S MEETING
Julia Ann Stout .......... 1877
Ruth Newlin ............. 1878
Margaret Ann Tomlinson . 1879-1881
Eunice S. Beezley ........ 1882-1886
Deborah Standing ........ 1887

Leah J. Paxson ........... 1888
Deborah Standing ........ 1889
Almeida R. Wroe ........ 1890-1892
Leah J. Paxson ........... 1893-1902
Susanna E. Ramsey ....... 1903-1907
Mary B. Henderson ....... 1908-1920
Alza J. Binns ............ 1921
Alice L. Standing ........ 1922-1935
Jessie B. Jones ............ 1936-1939
    (United the Meetings)
Wilson T. Emmons ....... 1940-1945
John P. Williams ......... 1946-1958
Irving J. Smith ........... 1959-1966
Lewis G. Mott ........... 1967-

## IOWA YEARLY MEETING — F.U.M.
### Clerks

David Hunt .............. 1863
Willett Dorland .......... 1864-1866
Joel Bean ................ 1867-1875
Barclay Hinchman ........ 1876
Joel Bean ................ 1877-1878
Barclay Hinchman ........ 1879-1889
W. Jasper Hadley ......... 1890

Stephen M. Hadley ....... 1891-1928
Edgar Stranahan ......... 1929-1933
Carl Byrd ................ 1934
Percy M. Thomas ......... 1935-1938
Carl Byrd ................ 1939-1940
Edgar Stranahan ......... 1941-1943
Roy S. Williams .......... 1944-1954

Richard R. Newby ....... 1955-1957    John L. David ........... 1961-1968
Bernard L. White ........ 1958-1960    Lloyd Davis .............. 1969-

### Superintendents

John Henry Douglas ...... 1886-1890    Richard R. Newby ........ 1934-1942
Isom P. Wooten .......... 1891-1895    Paul Barnett ............. 1943-1945
Zenas L. Martin .......... 1896-1899    Charles A. Beals .......... 1946-1948
W. Jasper Hadley ......... 1900-1910    Kenneth L. Eichenberger .. 1949-1951
Harry R. Keats ........... 1911-1915    Orval H. Cox ............ 1952-1960
Charles O. Whitely ....... 1916-1928    Wayne C. Allman ........ 1961-
Moses T. Mendenhall ..... 1929-1933

## KANSAS YEARLY MEETING — E.F.A.

### Clerks

William Nicholson ....... 1872-1888    Gurney T. Hadley ........ 1947-1958
Edmund Stanley .......... 1889-1927    Warren Stanfield ......... 1959-1968
Frank Brown ............ 1928-1946

### Superintendents

Z. H. Powell ............. 1889-1892    M. F. Swafford ........... 1924-1929
W. P. Haworth .......... 1893-1895    Arthur Chilson .......... 1930-1933
Isaac A. Woodard ........ 1896-1898    Frank Davies ............ 1934-1936
Eliza H. Carey .......... 1899-1902    Richard L. Wiles ......... 1937-1946
Josiah Butler ............ 1903-1906    Frank Davies ............ 1946-1949
L. Clarkson Hinshaw ..... 1907-1915    Merle A. Roe ............ 1949-1966
M. F. Swafford .......... 1916-1918    Fred Littlefield .......... 1966-
Richard R. Newby ........ 1919-1923

## LAKE ERIE ASSOCIATION-YEARLY MEETING — UNITED

### Clerks

Robert Blood ............. 1963-1964    Esther W. Ewald ........ 1966-1968
Howard W. McKinney .... 1964-1966    Flora S. McKinney ....... 1968-

## MISSOURI VALLEY ASSOCIATION

### Clerks

Garnet Guild ............ 1951    Edgar Palmer ........... 1961-1962
Ruth Decker ............. 1952    Bryan Michener .......... 1963-1964
Wynona Leonard ......... 1953-1954    Lida Helson ............. 1965
William A. Mott ......... 1955    Lloyd Hulbert ............ 1966
Cornell Hewson .......... 1956-1958    Anne Moore ............. 1967
Cecil E. Hinshaw ........ 1959    Paul Brink .............. 1968
Domingo Ricart ......... 1960    Martin Cobin ........... 1969

## NEBRASKA YEARLY MEETING — F.U.M.

### Clerks

Cyrus R. Dixon .......... 1908-1909    John Fry ................. 1914
L. E. Kenworthy ......... 1910    Eli H. Perisho ........... 1915-1916
G. D. Weeks ............. 1911-1913    John D. Mills ........... 1917-1919

| | | | |
|---|---|---|---|
| Homer J. Coppock | 1920-1921 | Dale V. Benton | 1950-1956 |
| Ora W. Carrell | 1922-1927 | M. Herbert Watson | 1957-1960 |
| M. Herbert Watson | 1928-1946 | Lyman C. Platt | 1961-1965 |
| Russell Stands | 1947 | Don Finley | 1966-1967 |
| Ava C. Maris | 1948-1949 | | |

### Superintendents

| | | | |
|---|---|---|---|
| W. Jasper Hadley | 1908 | ——— ——— | 1934-1937 |
| John Fry | 1909-1910 | Aaron McKinney | 1938-1940 |
| Frank W. Dell | 1911-1914 | Glenn A. Reece | 1941-1944 |
| Theodore Foxworthy | 1915-1921 | Millard V. Powell | 1945-1949 |
| Charles Replogle | 1922-1924 | T. Clio Brown | 1950-1956 |
| Theodore Foxworthy | 1925-1928 | Lindley J. Cook | 1957- |
| Walter Wilson | 1929-1933 | | |

## NEW ENGLAND YEARLY MEETING — CONSERVATIVE
### Clerks

| | | | |
|---|---|---|---|
| Thomas B. Gould | 1845-1850 | Isaac P. Wilbur | 1882-1884 |
| Peleg Mitchell | 1851-1862 | John W. Foster | 1885-1901 |
| Valentine Meader | 1863-1873 | Job S. Gibley | 1902-1921 |
| Ethan Foster | 1874-1878 | Arthur Perry | 1922-1926 |
| Jonathan Chace | 1879-1881 | Henry H. Perry | 1926-1944 |

## NEW ENGLAND YEARLY MEETING — F.U.M
### Clerks

| | | | |
|---|---|---|---|
| John Rodmon | 1684-1689 | Abraham Shearman, Jr. | 1819-1845 |
| Walter Clarke | 1690-1706 | Samuel Boyd Toby | 1846-1866 |
| Thomas Rodmon | 1707-1717 | Samuel Boyce | 1867-1870 |
| Thomas Richardson | 1718-1743 | Charles Tucker | 1871-1876 |
| Christopher Townsend | 1744-1751 | William O. Newhall | 1877-1891 |
| Thomas Richardson | 1752-1759 | Timothy B. Huzzey | 1892-1895 |
| David Earle | 1760-1766 | John Ellwood Page | 1896-1907 |
| Isaac Lawton | 1767-1776 | Charles H. Jones | 1908 |
| Thomas Lapham, Jr. | 1777-1781 | Walter S. Meader | 1909-1923 |
| Thomas Arnold | 1782 | Lindley M. Binford | 1924 |
| Samuel Rodmon | 1783 | George L. Jones | 1925 |
| Caleb Greene | 1784-1785 | Lindley M. Binford | 1926-1940 |
| Samuel Rodmon | 1786 | Arthur L. Jones | 1941-1945 |
| William Almy | 1787 | (United, 1945) | |
| William Rotch, Jr. | 1788-1797 | Arthur L. Jones | 1945-1951 |
| William Almy | 1798-1800 | Winslow Osborne | 1952-1955 |
| William Rotch, Jr. | 1801 | George I. Bliss | 1956-1961 |
| Obadiah Davis | 1802-1807 | Thomas R. Bodine | 1962-1967 |
| Samuel Rodmon | 1808-1812 | Ruth F. Osborne | 1968- |
| William Rotch, Jr. | 1813-1818 | | |

### Superintendents

| | | | |
|---|---|---|---|
| Charles H. Jones | 1899-1900 | Charles H. Jones (acted) | 1903 |
| Frank E. Jones | 1901-1902 | Alfred T. Ware | 1904-1905 |

Thomas Wood ........... 1906-1915
Percy D. Macy ........... 1916-1917
Percy D. Macy ........... 1918
   Northern District
Tom A. Sykes ............ 1918-1919
   Central District
W. Carleton Wood ....... 1918
   Southern District
Alfred W. Hawkes ....... 1919
   Northern District
William J. Cleaver ........ 1919
   Southern District
Tom A. Sykes ............ 1920-1921
   Northern District

Charles W. Mesner ....... 1920-1921
   Southern District
Tom A. Sykes ............ 1922-1923
O. Hershel Folger ........ 1924
Thomas Wood ........... 1925-1927
Arthur Jones ............. 1928
   Northern District
James A. Coney .......... 1928
   Central District
Bertha V. Smith .......... 1928
   Southern District
James A. Coney .......... 1929-1945
   (Yearly Meetings united)

### Secretaries

James A. Coney .......... 1946-1950
Russell D. Brooks ........ 1951-1955

Milton H. Hadley ........ 1956
Louis J. Marstaller ........ 1957-1958

## NEW YORK YEARLY MEETING — F.G.C.
### Clerks

MEN'S MEETING
Nathaniel S. Merritt ...... 1871
Charles A. Macy ......... 1872-1874
Nathaniel S. Merritt ...... 1875-1878
Robert S. Haviland ....... 1879-1895
William H. Willits ....... 1896-1903

WOMEN'S MEETING
Mary Jane Field .......... 1867-1882
Amanda K. Miller ........ 1883-1888
Jane W. Carpenter ....... 1889-1893
Emily P. Yeo ............. 1894-1903
   (Meetings merged)

William H. Willits ....... 1903-1908
James S. Haviland ...... 1909-1914
Ellwood Burdsall ......... 1915-1930
Edward Cornell .......... 1931-1937
J. Franklin Brown ........ 1938-1939
Stephen Holden .......... 1940
J. Hibbard Taylor ........ 1941-1943
George B. Corwin ........ 1944-1945
Howard E. Kershner ..... 1946-1949
Horace R. Stubbs ......... 1950
Howard E. Kershner ...... 1951
Frank Orloff ............. 1952
Horace R. Stubbs ......... 1953-1955

### Secretaries

J. Elliott Janney .......... 1928-1931
Elizabeth M. Lantz ....... 1931-1943
Gladys Seaman ........... 1943-1961

Rachel Wood ............ 1961-1967
Viola Purvis ............. 1968-

## NEW YORK YEARLY MEETING — F.U.M.
### Clerks

MEN'S MEETING
Robert L. Murray ........ 1871-1874
Augustus Taber .......... 1875-1881
James Wood ............. 1882
Augustus Taber .......... 1883-1884

WOMEN'S MEETING
Maria Willets ............ 1871-1872

Ruth C. Hagler .......... 1873-1880
Caroline E. Ladd ......... 1881-1884
   (Meetings merged)
Augustus Taber .......... 1884-1890
Charles H. Jones ......... 1891-1893
James Wood ............. 1894-1925
L. Hollingsworth Wood ... 1926-1931
David F. Lane ........... 1932-1936

George H. Wood ......... 1937-1942
Ruth E. Craig ........... 1943-1947
George Badgley .......... 1948-1950
Alfred Henderson ........ 1951
Henry A. Wheeler ........ 1952
Alfred J. Henderson ...... 1953-1955

(Both New York Meetings united)
Arthur J. Stratton ........ 1956
Paul Schwantes .......... 1957-1961
George B. Corwin ........ 1962-1965
Frances B. Compter ...... 1966-1969

*Secretaries*

J. Lindley Spicer ......... 1909-1910
Richard R. Newby ........ 1910-1912
Albert G. Shepherd ...... 1916-1922
Mary E. Pennington ...... 1924-1925

Emmet Gulley .......... 1925-1928
Elizabeth L. Hazard ...... 1928-1950
George A. Badgley ....... 1950-
(Yearly Meetings united, 1955)

## NORTH CAROLINA YEARLY MEETING — CONSERVATIVE
### Clerks

MEN'S MEETING
Albert W. Brown ........ 1904-1914
Walter J. Brown ......... 1915-1921
Anderson M. Barker ...... 1922-1932

WOMEN'S MEETING
Julianna Peel Harvey ..... 1904-1910

Margaret F. Parker ....... 1911-1920
Mary J. Peele ........... 1921-1928
(Meetings merged)
Mahlon Newlin .......... 1933-1949
David H. Brown ......... 1950-1960
George C. Parker ........ 1961-

## NORTH CAROLINA YEARLY MEETING — F.U.M.
### Clerks

William Everigin ......... 1708-1711
John Symons ............. 1720
John Symons ............. 1722-1723
———— ———— .... 1724-1729
R. Wilson ............... 1730-1740
Joseph Roberson .......... 1741-1760
Francis Nixon ........... 1761-1771
Jacob Wilson ............ 1772-1775
Josiah White ............ 1776
Thomas White ........... 1777-1778
George Walton ........... 1779-1780
Benjamin Albertson, Jr. ... 1781-1786
Levi Munden ............ 1787-1794
Exum Newby ............ 1795
Levi Munden ............ 1796
Enoch Macy ............. 1797
Levi Munden ............ 1798
Thomas Jordan .......... 1799-1802
Barnabas Coffin .......... 1803
Thomas Jordan .......... 1804
———— ———— .... 1805-1811
Thomas White ........... 1812
Barnabas Coffin .......... 1813
Thomas White ........... 1814
Jeremiah Hubbard ........ 1815-1821

Elijah Coffin ............. 1822-1823
Jeremiah Hubbard ........ 1824-1826
Nathan Mendenhall ...... 1827-1829
Jeremiah Hubbard ........ 1830-1835
Nathan Mendenhall ...... 1836-1840
Aaron Stalker ........... 1841-1856
John R. Hubbard ......... 1857-1858
William Clark ........... 1859
Nereus Mendenhall ....... 1860-1871
Josiah Nicholson ......... 1872-1873
Isham Cox .............. 1874-1878
Josiah Nicholson ........ 1879-1880
Isham Cox .............. 1881-1884
Josiah Nicholson ........ 1885
L. Lyndon Hobbs ........ 1886-1916
Zino H. Dixon .......... 1917-1920
L. Lyndon Hobbs ........ 1921-1928
Samuel L. Haworth ...... 1929-1941
Algie I. Newlin ......... 1942-1945
Samuel L. Haworth ...... 1946
Seth B. Hinshaw ........ 1947-1952
Algie I. Newlin ......... 1953-1960
Byron Haworth .......... 1961-1965
J. Binford Farlow ........ 1966-1968

## Superintendents

Lewis W. McFarland .... 1915-1932
Murray C. Johnson ....... 1935-1941
(No superintendent) ..... 1942
Fredric E. Carter ........ 1943-1947

Isaac Harris .............. 1947-1952
Seth B. Hinshaw ......... 1952-1968
Victor Murchison ......... 1968-

## OHIO YEARLY MEETING
### Clerks

Horton Howard .......... 1813-1815
Isaac Wilson ............. 1816-1818
Elisha Bates ............. 1819
Benjamin W. Ladd ....... 1820-1824
Elisha Bates ............. 1825-1826
Jonathan Taylor .......... 1827

(Separation, 1828)
Elisha Bates ............. 1828-1831
Benjamin W. Ladd ....... 1832-1837
Benjamin Hoyle .......... 1838-1854
(Separation, 1854)

## OHIO YEARLY MEETING — CONSERVATIVE
### Clerks

(After the separation of 1854)
Benjamin Hoyle .......... 1854-1857
George Gilbert ........... 1858-1864
Asa Branson ............. 1865-1870
Edward Stratton ......... 1871-1872
Wilson Hall ............. 1873-1886
Barclay Stratton .......... 1887-1891
Barclay Smith ............ 1892-1898
Nathan R. Smith ........ 1899-1904

Jonathan Binns ........... 1905-1914
Carl Patterson ............ 1915-1925
W. Mifflin Hall .......... 1926-1936
Charles P. Morlan ........ 1937-1948
Louis J. Kirk ............ 1949-1958
James R. Cooper .......... 1959-1964
Jesse R. Starbuck ......... 1965-1968
Edward N. Kirk ......... 1969-

## OHIO YEARLY MEETING — E.F.A.
### Clerks

Jonathan Binns .......... 1854-1860
William Ratcliff .......... 1861
Jonathan Binns .......... 1862-1869
George K. Jenkins ........ 1870-1877
William J. Harrison ...... 1878-1885
Asa Pim ................. 1886
Edward G. Wood ........ 1887-1888

Asa Pim ................. 1889-1893
William J. Harrison ...... 1894-1898
Mahlon Perry ............ 1899-1902
Edward Mott ............ 1903-1919
Ralph S. Coppock ........ 1920-1953
Ora Lovell ............... 1954-1961
Harold Winn ............ 1962-

### Superintendents

J. Walter Malone ......... 1891-1904
Edward Mott ............ 1904-1914
John Pennington ......... 1915-1920
Samuel J. Mosher ........ 1920-1929
Homer L. Cox .......... 1929-1930
Claude A. Roane ......... 1930-1951

Walter R. Williams ....... 1951-1957
Everett L. Cattell ........ 1957-1960
Walter R. Williams ....... 1960
Chester G. Stanley ........ 1960-1968
Russell Myers ............ 1968-

## OHIO YEARLY MEETING — F.G.C.
### Clerks

MEN'S MEETING
David Hillis ............. 1829

Israel French ............. 1830-1831
George Cope ............. 1832-1839

James Hambleton ......... 1840
George Cope ............. 1841-1842
John H. Price ............ 1843-1844
Amos Wilson ............ 1845-1846
George Cope ............. 1847
Amos Wilson ............ 1848
Benjamin Marshall ........ 1849
Samuel Griffith ........... 1850-1851
Benjamin Marshall ....... 1852
John H. Price ............ 1853-1855
Jonathan Binns ........... 1856
John H. Price ............ 1857-1858
George Cope ............. 1859
Joseph S. Hartley ........ 1860-1877
William Stanton .......... 1878-1879
Joseph S. Hartley ........ 1880-1883

William Stanton .......... 1884
Joseph S. Hartley ........ 1885-1891

WOMEN'S MEETING
Mary Hall ............... 1829-1831
Lydia Hoag .............. 1832-1835
Mary Hall ............... 1836-1838
Mary Ann Updegraff ..... 1839-1871
Jane Edgerton ............ 1872-1888
Mary Anna Packer ........ 1889
Jane Edgerton ........... 1890-1891
(Meetings united, 1891)
Joseph S. Hartley ........ 1892-1900
Sarah C. Fox ............. 1901-1919
(Yearly Meeting laid down, 1920)

### PACIFIC YEARLY MEETING — UNITED
*Clerks*

Verne James ............. 1946-1947
Benjamin Darling ........ 1947-1949
Eubanks Carsner ........ 1949-1951
Phillip Wells ............ 1951-1954
Ruth Schmoe ............ 1954-1956

Catherine Bruner ......... 1956-1960
Harold Carson .......... 1960-1962
Edwin Morgenroth ....... 1962-1965
Madge Seaver ........... 1965-1968
Francis Dart ............. 1968-

### PHILADELPHIA YEARLY MEETING
From 1681 to the Separation in 1827

From the beginning (1681) to 1696 no presiding clerk, as such, was appointed. Proceedings were informal; various people were appointed to certain clerical tasks. Phineas Pemberton and Anthony Morris, in different years, signed epistles.

Phineas Pemberton ....... 1696-1701
Griffith Owen(?) ........ 1702
Caleb Pusey and Anthony
   Morris ................ 1704
Anthony Morris .......... 1710
Isaac Norris ............. 1711-1729
John Kinsey ............. 1730-1749
Israel Pemberton, Jr. ...... 1750-1759
John Smith .............. 1760
James Pemberton ......... 1761-1766
George Churchman ....... 1767

James Pemberton ......... 1768-1776
Isaac Jackson ............. 1777
James Pemberton ......... 1778-1781
John Drinker ............ 1782-1786
Caleb Carmalt ............ 1787-1788
Nicholas Waln ........... 1789-1794
Jonathan Evans .......... 1795-1807
John Cox ................ 1808
Jonathan Evans .......... 1809-1810
John Cox ................ 1811-1816
Samuel Bettle ............ 1817-1827

### PHILADELPHIA (ARCH STREET: ORTHODOX)
*Clerks*

MEN'S MEETING
Samuel Bettle ............ 1827-1830
William Evans ........... 1831-1861

Joel Evans ............... 1862-1864
Joseph Scattergood ........ 1865-1876
Clarkson Shepperd ....... 1877-1880

Joseph Walton ........... 1881-1896
Ephraim Smith ........... 1897
Ephraim Smith ........... 1901
William Evans ........... 1902-1905
William Bishop ........... 1906
Charles Carter ........... 1908-1911
Davis H. Forsythe ........ 1912-1923
John D. Carter ........... 1924-1928
D. Robert Yarnall ........ 1929

WOMEN'S MEETING
Anna P. Haines .......... 1901-1906
Rebecca S. Conard ........ 1908-1913
Jane W. Bartlett .......... 1914-1919

Anna Rhoads Ladd ....... 1920-1921
Mary R. Williams ........ 1922
Anna Rhoads Ladd ....... 1923-1927
Elizabeth B. Jones ........ 1928
Anna Rhoads Ladd ....... 1929

JOINT
D. Robert Yarnall ........ 1930-1939
Harold Evans ............ 1940
William Wistar Comfort .. 1941-1943
Harold Evans ............ 1944-1949
James F. Walker ......... 1950-1955
(Merged with Race Street Meeting)

## PHILADELPHIA (RACE STREET: HICKSITE)
### Clerks

Benjamin Ferris .......... 1827-1829
John Comly .............. 1830-1833
Joseph Parrish ........... 1834-1836
Benjamin Price, Jr. ....... 1837-1842
James Martin ............ 1843-1853
William Griscom ......... 1854-1864
Dillwyn Parrish .......... 1865-1872
Benjamin G. Foulke ...... 1873-1885
Emmor Roberts .......... 1886-1900
Isaac H. Hillborn ........ 1901-1903
Wesley Haldeman ........ 1904-1912
Joseph T. Foulke ......... 1913-1917
Morgan Bunting ......... 1918-1922
Walter H. Jenkins ........ 1923

Jane P. Rushmore ........ 1924-1925
George A. Walton ........ 1926-1928
Jane P. Rushmore ........ 1929
George A. Walton ........ 1930-1932
Thomas A. Foulke ........ 1933-1941
Gordon P. Jones .......... 1942-1949
William Eves III ......... 1949-1953
Charles Darlington ....... 1954
Philadelphia (Arch Street) united
  with Philadelphia (Race Street)
Charles Darlington ....... 1955-1961
David G. Paul ........... 1962-1965
Albert B. Maris .......... 1966-1967
Charles K. Brown III ..... 1968-

### Secretaries

RACE STREET
Jane P. Rushmore ........ 1911-1945
Richmond P. Miller ...... 1945-1964
Marguerite Hallowell (office) 1945-1956
ARCH STREET
William B. Harvey ....... 1918-1938

Edward W. Evans ........ 1938-1946
Howard G. Taylor ....... 1946-1955
  (United in 1955)
William Eves III ......... 1955-1964
Francis G. Brown ........ 1964-——

## ROCKY MOUNTAIN YEARLY MEETING — E.F.A.
### Clerks

Dale V. Benton .......... 1957-1962
Clyde Jacobson ........... 1962-1966

Olen R. Ellis ............. 1966-

### Superintendents

T. Clio Brown ........... 1957-1960
Walter P. Lee ............ 1960-1966

Merle A. Roe ............ 1966-

SOUTH CENTRAL YEARLY MEETING
Southwest Conference
Organized 1953 As a Conference
*Chairmen*

William D. S. Witte ..... 1954      Kenneth Carroll .......... 1958
John Barrow ............. 1955      Otto Huffman ............ 1959-1960
Marvin Fair .............. 1956      Wade Mackie ............ 1961-——
Lida Helson ............. 1957

Organized 1961 As a Yearly Meeting
*Clerks*

Kenneth L. Carroll ....... 1961-1963      Jane Lemann (acting) .... 1966
John Barrow ............. 1964      Jane Lemann ............. 1967
Paul Reagan (acting) ..... 1964      Paul Reagan ............. 1968
Kenneth L. Carroll ....... 1965      Warner Kloepfer (acting) . 1968
Cyril Harvey ............. 1966      Warner Kloepfer ......... 1969

SOUTHEASTERN YEARLY MEETING
Organized 1951 As a Conference
*Chairmen*

Caroline N. Jacob ........ 1951-1954      Rembert Patrick .......... 1959-1960
J. William Greenleaf ...... 1955-1958      J. William Greenleaf ...... 1960-1962

Organized 1963 As a Yearly Meeting
*Clerks*

Edwin C. Bertsche ........ 1963-1964      Carolyn N. Jacob ......... 1967
Leon Allen .............. 1965-1966      James O. Bond ........... 1968

SOUTHERN APPALACHIAN ASSOCIATION OF FRIENDS
*Clerks*

Donald W. Newton ...... 1959-1960      James H. Wagner ........ 1964-1965
Hibbard Thatcher ........ 1960-1962      Nelson Fuson ............ 1965-1968
Carl Denison ............ 1962-1963      Jack Kaiser .............. 1968-
Walter Hoose ........... 1963-1964

WESTERN YEARLY MEETING — CONSERVATIVE
*Clerks*

Albert Maxwell .......... 1877-1895      Arthur Stanley .......... 1920-1925
Abel Blackburn .......... 1895-1900      Harvey Pickett .......... 1926-1929
Albert Maxwell .......... 1900-1904      Arthur Maxwell ......... 1930
Luna O. Stanley ......... 1904-1917      Albert Maxwell ......... 1931-1962
Joseph Allen ............ 1918-1919      (Yearly Meeting discontinued, 1962)

WESTERN YEARLY MEETING — F.U.M.
*Clerks*

Barnabas Hobbs .......... 1858-1867      Amos Doan .............. 1867-1874

| | | | |
|---|---|---|---|
| Barnabas Hobbs | 1874-1878 | Albert J. Brown | 1918-1924 |
| Amos Doan | 1878-1884 | Albert L. Copeland | 1924-1943 |
| Hiram Hadley | 1884-1888 | Sumner A. Mills | 1943-1947 |
| Simon Hadley | 1888-1891 | Milo L. Hinckle | 1947-1952 |
| Thomas C. Brown | 1891-1901 | Marcus Kendall | 1952-1957 |
| Lewis E. Stout | 1901-1906 | Claude O. Wood | 1957-1962 |
| Thomas C. Brown | 1906-1910 | Frank Johnson | 1962-1967 |
| George H. Moore | 1910-1914 | Lowell Mills | 1967- |
| Willard O. Trueblood | 1914-1917 | | |

### Superintendents

| | | | |
|---|---|---|---|
| David Hadley | 1889-1894 | Richard R. Newby | 1923-1933 |
| Lewis L. Hadley | 1894-1896 | (No superintendent) | 1933-1937 |
| David Hadley | 1896-1900 | Frederic Carter | 1937-1943 |
| Thomas C. Brown | 1900-1905 | Glenn A. Reece | 1943-1957 |
| Lewis E. Stout | 1905-1909 | Norval E. Webb | 1957-1968 |
| Edward M. Woodard | 1909-1914 | Robert E. Garris | 1968- |
| Enos Harvey | 1914-1923 | | |

## WILMINGTON YEARLY MEETING — F.U.M.

### Clerks

| | | | |
|---|---|---|---|
| James B. Unthank | 1892-1903 | Howard F. McKay | 1940-1946 |
| Jonathan B. Wright | 1904-1907 | Burton S. Hill | 1947-1948 |
| Albert J. Brown | 1908-1915 | Jesse A. Stanfield | 1949-1952 |
| Mary Mills | 1916-1918 | Burritt M. Hiatt | 1953-1956 |
| W. Rufus Kersey | 1919-1922 | C. Vincent Fairley | 1957-1961 |
| C. Clayton Terrell | 1923-1929 | Clifton J. Warren | 1962-1964 |
| W. Rufus Kersey | 1930-1933 | James A. Terrell | 1965- |
| Wendell G. Farr | 1934-1939 | | |

### Superintendents

| | | | |
|---|---|---|---|
| Josephus Hoskins | 1893-1894 | Clyde Watson | 1926-1929 |
| Eliza Thorn | 1895-1896 | Jane M. Carey | 1930-1939 |
| Jesse Hawkins | 1896-1897 | Wendell G. Farr | 1940-1941 |
| Amos Cook | 1898-1901 | Ethel Wall | 1942-1944 |
| Josephus Hoskins | 1902-1907 | Adam H. Flatter | 1945-1948 |
| Levi Mills | 1908-1911 | David O. Stanfield | 1949-1952 |
| Josephus Hoskins | 1912-1913 | Robert J. Rumsey | 1953-1961 |
| Amos Cook | 1914-1918 | James W. Ellis, Jr. | 1962-1968 |
| Murray Kenworthy | 1919-1921 | Lawrence Peery | 1969-—— |
| Harold McKay | 1922-1925 | | |

## 10. MISSIONARIES

These persons have served in Africa, Alaska, Bolivia, Central America, China, Cuba, Formosa, India, Jamaica, Japan, Mexico, Ramallah (Palestine), Rough Rock (Arizona), Southland Institute (Arkansas), and Tennessee.

The asterisk (*) denotes service under married and maiden names listed separately.

## CALIFORNIA YEARLY MEETING

| Name | Field | Years of Service |
|---|---|---|
| Abbott, Fern* | C. A. | 1942-1945 |
| Adell, W. Robert and Mabel F. | C. A. | 1919-1924 |
|  |  | 1927-1932 |
| Acosta, Hortensia | C. A. | 1956- |
| Allen, Izabel E. | C. A. | 1919-1920 |
| Almquist, Lily I. | C. A. | 1922-1927 |
|  |  | 1934-1937 |
|  |  | 1956-1963 |
| Anderson, Myrtle S. | C. A. | 1920-1926 |
| Astleford, John | C. A. | 1941- |
| Astleford, Esther Hansen | C. A. | 1942- |
| Beard, Frances* | C. A. | 1941-1946 |
| Beck, Harold and Hulda | Alaska | 1951-1961 |
|  |  | 1965- |
| Benton, Bernice Guyor | Alaska | 1920-1921 |
| Bodwell, Charles L. | C. A. | 1904-1905 |
| Bodwell, Gertrude L. | C. A. | 1904 |
| Brown, Winfred and Myrtle | C. A. | 1948-1953 |
| Buckley, Clark J. | C. A. | 1902-1903 |
| Burbank, Raymond and Gertrude | C. A. | 1949-1954 |
| Burns, Maude | C. A. | 1912-1916 |
| Cammack, Irvin H. and Dorothy N. | C. A. | 1909-1914 |
| Cammack, Lenora | C. A. | 1947-1949 |
| Canfield, Raymond G. and Virginia W. | C. A. | 1967- |
| Castro, Dr. Anhel | C. A. | 1944-1945 |
| Castro, Mildred | C. A. | 1942-1944 |
| Chance, Sylvester and Rachel M. | Alaska | 1917-1927 |
| Cox, Bertha S. | Alaska | 1905-1909 |
|  |  | 1922-1928 |
| Cox, Nina O. | Alaska | 1928-1937 |
| Cox, Wilson and Lucy | Alaska | 1909-1912 |
|  |  | 1914-1916 |
| Downs, Ira and Parolee | Alaska | 1932-1944 |
| Eckels, Wilson and Ruth | Alaska | 1948-1955 |
|  |  | 1960-1961 |
| Enyart, Paul C., Jr., and Winifred A. | C. A. | 1965- |
| Elliott, Richard and Jean | Alaska | 1964-1965 |
| Ford, Helen Kersey | C. A. | 1917-1933 |
| Foster, Anna Hunnicutt | Alaska | 1897-1906 |
| Geary, James V. | Alaska | 1905-1909 |
| Geary, Eva Watson | Alaska | 1906-1909 |
| Gilmore, Robert and Maurine | C. A. | 1960-1964 |
| Glover, Richard | Alaska | 1901-1904 |
| Gooden, William T. and Lizzie M. | Alaska | 1905-1912 |
| Hadley, J. Perry and Gertrude M. | Alaska | 1917-1922 |
| Hadley, Martha E. | Alaska | 1899-1904 |
| Hainden, Mr. and Mrs. Elmer M. | Alaska | 1908-1914 |
| Hare, Rhoda | Alaska | 1911-1913 |

| | | |
|---|---|---|
| Haworth, Matilda L. | C. A. | 1915-1949 |
| | Alaska | 1956-1957 |
| Henley, William F. and Maria W. | Alaska | 1922-1927 |
| Howland, Clara | C. A. | 1914-1949 |
| Hunnicutt, Martha | Alaska | 1911-1937 |
| Kelly, Thomas J. | C. A. | 1902-1903 |
| King, Delbert H. and Bertha | Alaska | 1922-1930 |
| Lund, Herbert C. and Agnes | C. A. | 1947-1950 |
| McNichols, John and Joyce | C. A. | 1954- |
| Miller, Julia | Alaska | 1956-1957 |
| Miller, Marilyn | Alaska | 1965-1967 |
| Miller, Paul and Patsy | Alaska | 1955-1964 |
| Miller, Virginia | C. A. | 1955- |
| Moline, Donald and Ruth | Alaska | 1960-1963 |
| Munsell, Ward | C. A. | 1911-1915 |
| Myers, Eli, Minnie, and Pauline | Alaska | 1907-1912 |
| Nickel, Glenna | Alaska | 1961-1963 |
| Oakley, Helen L. | C. A. | 1927-1937 |
| | | 1947-1963 |
| Parrish, Stella | C. A. | 1909-1914 |
| Pearson, John Howard | C. A. | 1930-1935 |
| Perisho, Earl and Janice | Alaska | 1961- |
| Peterson, David R. and Christine | C. A. | 1955-1965 |
| Ratcliff, Sara Wade | C. A. | 1949- |
| Replogle, Charles and Mary | Alaska | 1914-1922 |
| Richards, Bernard | C. A. | 1967- |
| Richards, Wilma Rhinesmith | C. A. | 1944-1948 |
| | | 1967- |
| Ridgeway, Helen Ruth | C. A. | 1959- |
| Roque, Lillian | C. A. | 1965 |
| Sams, Robert and Carrie | Alaska | 1897-1902 |
| | | 1912-1918 |
| | | 1929-1947 |
| Sandusky, Abe and Susan | C. A. | 1920-1921 |
| Saveker, Merny B. | C. A. | 1921-1959 |
| Schanz, Anna | C. A. | 1944-1948 |
| Schneider, David R. and Chloe* | C. A. | 1941-1944 |
| Sentmier, Arthur and Alice | Alaska | 1922-1923 |
| Sharpless, Homer and Evelyn | C. A. | 1961- |
| Sharpless, Shirley | Alaska | 1963-1964 |
| Sickles, Leslie G. and wife | Alaska | 1908-1912 |
| Smith, Isaac A. and Effie A. | C. A. | 1926-1930 |
| Smith, R. Esther | C. A. | 1906-1947 |
| Stanton, Helen Scott | C. A. | 1937-1942 |
| Stanton, Mae Burk | C. A. | 1909-1913 |
| | | 1916-1952 |
| Stanton, W. Lester | C. A. | 1913-1916 |
| | | 1919-1952 |
| Stevens, Frederic | C. A. | 1927-1931 |
| Still, Josephine | C. A. | 1940- |
| Stolberg, Eugene and Delores | Alaska | 1963-1966 |

| | | |
|---|---|---|
| Stratton, Elizabeth | Alaska | 1914-1920 |
| | | 1925-1935 |
| Sylvester, Elizabeth P.* | C. A. | 1925-1929 |
| Tamplin, Carrol G. and Doris M. | C. A. | 1926-1928 |
| Thomas, Dana Harold and Otha C. | Alaska | 1902-1906 |
| Thomas, Gary and Carol | Alaska | 1967- |
| Thomas, William and Esther | C. A. | 1944 |
| Vore, Charles and Sammye S. | C. A. | 1945- |
| Wagner, William and Dorothy | C. A. | 1959-1964 |
| Wallace, Vard B. | C. A. | 1923-1925 |
| Wallace, Mabel Hollister | C. A. | 1922-1925 |
| Walton, Alfred and Priscilla | Alaska | 1904-1908 |
| Watson, William and Victoria | Alaska | 1918-1922 |
| Westbrook, Delos and Doris | Alaska | 1938-1951 |
| White, Esther Bond | C. A. | 1904-1908 |
| White, Milton and Margaret | Alaska | 1912-1917 |
| White, Truman J. | C. A. | 1907 |
| Wildman, Cora | C. A. | 1906-1921 |
| Williams, Bion B. | C. A. | 1915-1917 |
| Wing, John B. | C. A. | 1957- |
| Wing, Waynel R. | C. A. | 1963- |
| Witt, Marlin | Alaska | 1967- |
| Wistar, Casper | C. A. | 1909-1910 |
| Woodward, Ronald | Alaska | 1959-1960 |
| York, Herbert and Vera | Alaska | 1908-1911 |
| Zimmer, Alice C. | C. A. | 1904-1907 |

## CANADA YEARLY MEETING

### All Japan Field

| Name | Years of Service |
|---|---|
| Binford, Gurney | 1891-1899 |
| Binford, Gurney and Elizabeth S. | 1899-1936 |
| Wright, William V. and wife | 1889-1891 |

## CENTRAL YEARLY MEETING

| Name | Field | Years of Service |
|---|---|---|
| Bardales, Rene and Lois | Bolivia | 1954-1959 |
| | | 1961-1964 |
| Barnard, John and Ethel | Bolivia | 1950-1956 |
| Barnard, Mary* | Bolivia | 1929-1930 |
| Barnard, William | Bolivia | 1930-1941 |
| Blount, Mattie* | Bolivia | 1919-1928 |
| Briles, Ruth and Eula | Bolivia | 1922-1931 |
| Canaday, Emma | Bolivia | 1924-1928 |
| Culp, Donald and Gladys | Bolivia | 1929-1931 |
| Enyart, Arthur | Bolivia | 1930-1936 |

| | | |
|---|---|---|
| Enyart, Paul and Mary Barnard* | Bolivia | 1930-1939 |
| | | 1941-1949 |
| Fulton, James and Grace | Bolivia | 1966- |
| Greene, Max and Lessie | Bolivia | 1955-1964 |
| | | 1966- |
| Hendrickson, Imogene | Bolivia | 1944-1951 |
| | | 1953-1960 |
| | | 1962-1964 |
| | | 1965- |
| Hinshaw, Byrdie | Bolivia | 1928-1930 |
| Hinshaw, Alva | Bolivia | 1919-1927 |
| | | 1928-1937 |
| | | 1938-1953 |
| Hinshaw, Mabel | Bolivia | 1919-1927 |
| | | 1928-1935 |
| | | 1941-1948 |
| | | 1949-1953 |
| Hinshaw, Sarah* | Bolivia | 1942-1948 |
| | | 1949-1953 |
| Holmes, Andrew R. | Bolivia | 1941-1954 |
| Hunnicutt, Martha | Alaska | 1936-1938 |
| Hunt, Esther | Bolivia | 1927-1938 |
| | | 1953-1960 |
| | | 1962-1968 |
| Langston, Emma Morrow | Bolivia | 1921-1928 |
| Indiana Friends | | 1928-1951 |
| Central Friends | | 1951-1962 |
| Langston, Walter | Bolivia | 1921-1928 |
| Indiana Friends | | 1928-1951 |
| Central Friends | | 1951-1959 |
| Lee, Fred and Edith | Bolivia | 1935-1942 |
| | | 1944-1951 |
| | | 1952-1958 |
| | | 1963-1966 |
| Marca, Mattie Blount* | Bolivia | 1929-1939 |
| | | 1940-1943 |
| Merrill, Joseph and Grace Barnard | Bolivia | 1967- |
| Mishkoff, Mr. and Mrs. Paul | Bolivia | 1936 (dec.) |
| Morrow, Emma* | Bolivia | 1919-1921 |
| Morrow, Mary | Bolivia | 1927-1928 |
| Indiana Friends | | 1928-1945 |
| Nahrwold, William and Lillian | Bolivia | 1936-1941 |
| | | 1958-1964 |
| Rich, Perry | Bolivia | 1926-1937 |
| Rich, Perry and Bernice | Bolivia | 1939-1947 |
| | | 1951-1957 |
| | | 1961-1965 |
| Richard, Bernard and Ruby | Bolivia | 1948-1954 |
| | | 1958-1962 |
| Rhoades, Walter | Bolivia | 1928-1936 |
| Smith, Samuel and Gladys | Bolivia | 1941-1948 |

Schwartz, Fred and Pauline .................... Bolivia    1935-1944
                                                           1946-1952
                                                           1954-1961
                                                           1963-1968
Suarez, Sarah Hinshaw* ....................... Bolivia    1953-1957
Terry, Jack and Winona ....................... Bolivia    1955-1958
Thornburg, Lola ............................. Bolivia    1927-1928
        Indiana Friends ................                  1928-1936
Warrick, Rhoda ............................. Bolivia    1927-1931

## FRIENDS UNITED MEETING

| Name | Yearly Meeting | Field | Dates of Service |
|------|----------------|-------|------------------|
| Adams, Ellis and Sue ...... | Indiana | Africa | 1957-1959 |
| Alber, Charles and Ruth .... | Indiana | Africa | 1957-1961 |
| Allen, Eva H. .............. | New England | Jamaica | 1912-1913 |
| Allen, M. Elizabeth ......... | London | Jamaica | 1900-1922 |
| Allen, Roberta .............. | Nebraska | Africa | 1956-1958 |
| Andrews, Alsina M. ......... | Iowa | Jamaica | 1897-1945 |
| Andrews, Dr. B. F. and Bertha | Iowa | Mexico | 1900-1906 |
|  | Western | Jamaica | 1937- |
| Andrews, Sarah B. .......... | Iowa | Jamaica | 1896-1898 |
| Arms, Lora P. .............. | Iowa | Jamaica | 1915-1934 |
| Bailey, Moses M. and Mabel G. | New England | Ramallah | 1920-1921 |
| Baker, Eloise .............. | London | Africa | 1965-1967 |
| Baker, Florence ............ | Iowa | Jamaica | 1899-1902 |
| Baldwin, John A. and Mildred J. |  | Southland Inst. | 1917-1918 |
| Ballard, Mary A. J. ......... | Indiana | Mexico | 1920- ? |
| Ballinger, Edith Caroline .... | North Carolina | Mexico | 1889-1891 |
| Ballinger, Julia L. ........... | North Carolina | Mexico | 1883- ? |
| Barlow, Earle and Laurita ... | Baltimore | Jamaica | 1955-1960 |
| Barnett, Paul and Alice ...... | Iowa | Africa | 1945-1949 |
| Barrett, Leslie and Winnifred . | New England | Africa | 1963-1965 |
| Bassett, T. Robert and Irene .. | Non-Friend | Ramallah | 1951-1952 |
|  |  |  | 1961-1965 |
| Bassett, T. Robert .......... |  |  | 1966-1967 |
| Beeson, Dr. Wilbur B. and Miriam .............. | Indiana | Africa | 1954-1957 |
| Biddlecum, Florence ........ | Indiana | Tennessee | 1960-1964 |
| Biddlecum, Homer .......... | Indiana | Tennessee | 1956-1964 |
| Binford, Micajah M. and Susie R. ................. | Indiana | Mexico | 1873-1875 |
| Binford, Myra C. ........... | North Carolina | Jamaica | 1940-1945 |
| Blackburn, Dr. Elisha and Virginia .............. | Ohio | Africa | 1903-1916 |
| Blackburn, Grace .......... | Baltimore | Africa | 1948-1953 |
| Bond, Dr. A. A. and Myra ... | Western | Africa | 1916-1951 |
| Bradley, Allan and Mary .... | London | Africa | 1955-1960 |
| Branen, Orah .............. |  | Mexico | 1913- ? |
| Brightman, Lloyd and Imogene | New England | Africa | 1962-1965 |
|  |  | Ramallah | 1965-1966 |

| | | | |
|---|---|---|---|
| Buckingham, Thomas and Norma .............. | New York and Wilmington | Ramallah | 1955-1957 |
| Burgess, Donald ............ | London | Jamaica | 1963-1968 |
| Burgess, Ray ............... | London | Jamaica | 1963-1968 |
| Carter, Annice ............. | Western | Ramallah | 1929-1932 |
| | | | 1935-1941 |
| | | | 1957-1959 |
| | | Africa | 1959-1962 |
| | | | 1963-1966 |
| Cassell, Marie .............. | Indiana | Tennessee | 1950-1951 |
| Caughey, John and Mary .... | Ohio (Con.) | Africa | 1956-1960 |
| Chant, Franklin and Lillian R. | Indiana | Tennessee | 1939-1941 |
| Charles, Leslie and Kathleen . | London | Africa | 1959-1963 |
| Charles, Sarah R. ........... | Indiana | Mexico | 1913-1923 |
| Chilson, Arthur B. and Edna H. | Iowa and Kansas | Africa | 1902-1927 |
| Clark, Earl ................ | Kansas | Tennessee | ? |
| Cole, Catherine ............ | Non-Friend | Africa | 1963-1965 |
| Conover, C. Frank and Blanche A. .............. | Iowa | Africa | 1913-1928 |
| Cope, Robert E. and Ardelle F. | Iowa | Jamaica | 1932-1934 |
| Cope, Lois M. .............. | Ohio | Africa | 1920-1926 |
| Courtney, Albert and Ola .... | Iowa | Jamaica | 1901-1906 |
| Cox, Henry D. and Alma W. . | Kansas | Cuba | 1910-1942 |
| Crossman, Hurford and Winifred ................ | Ann Arbor | Africa | 1962-1964 |
| Crossman, Helen ........... | New England | Ramallah | 1913 |
| Darnell, Carl and Eunice .... | Indiana | Tennessee | 1950-1953 |
| | | | 1962-1966 |
| Davies, Alan and Anne H. ... | London | Africa | 1958-1960 |
| Davis, Merle L. and Carrie ... | Kansas | Cuba | 1919-1929 |
| Davis, Laura ............... | North Carolina | Ramallah | 1939-1940 |
| Davis, Myrtle .............. | Indiana | Mexico | 1899-1902 |
| DeWitt, Paul and Hortense L. | Non-Friend | Africa | 1968- |
| Dillon, Josiah and Mary ..... | Iowa | Jamaica | 1887-1889 |
| | | | 1888-1890 |
| Dorrell, Homer and Gladys .. | Western | Africa | 1956-1960 |
| | | | 1962-1966 |
| Dorrell, Mabel ............. | Non-Friend | Africa | 1959-1961 |
| Dugdale, Ned and Dottie .... | Indiana | Africa | 1965 |
| Ellis, Mary Louise ......... | Iowa | Cuba | 1904-1908 |
| | Nebraska | Mexico | 1911-1912 |
| Estock, Dr. A. B. and Lilah M. | Ohio | Africa | 1912-1917 |
| Farlow, Margaret (Davis) ... | North Carolina | Jamaica | 1945-1952 |
| Farquhar, Esther L. ......... | Wilmington | Cuba | 1920-1923 |
| Farr, Gilbert L. and Anna M. | Iowa | Jamaica | 1891-1903 |
| | | | 1892-1903 |
| Farr, Faye ................. | Iowa | Jamaica | 1914-1918 |
| | Wilmington | | 1943-1949 |
| Farr, Wendell G. ........... | Iowa | Jamaica | 1912-1918 |
| | Wilmington | | 1943-1949 |

| | | | |
|---|---|---|---|
| Flatter, Adam and Naomi ... | Wilmington | Jamaica | 1949-1951 |
| Fletcher, Helen ............. | Wilmington | Africa | 1951-1961 |
| Foley, Rolla ................ | Western | Ramallah | 1939-1946 |
| Ford, Helen Farr ........... | Iowa | Jamaica | 1892-1900 |
| | | | 1901-1902 |
| | | | 1906-1913 |
| | | Africa | 1914-1931 |
| Ford, Helen Kersey ......... | California | Africa | 1933-1948 |
| Forde, Jefferson W. ......... | Western | Jamaica | 1901-1902 |
| | | | 1906-1913 |
| | | Africa | 1914-1948 |
| Garrett, Rufus .............. | Iowa | Jamaica | 1895 |
| Garwood, Juanita G. ........ | Indiana | Mexico | 1885-1893 |
| George, Jessie C. ............ | | Jamaica | 1889-1891 |
| Gilchrist, Laura ............. | | Ramallah | 1910-1911 |
| Goddard, Alvano C. ......... | New England | Ramallah | 1930-1931 |
| Goom, Kenneth and Helen .. | London | Africa | 1955-1959 |
| Grant, Elihu and Almy C. ... | New England | Ramallah | 1901-1903 |
| Green, Peter and Hope ...... | London | Africa | 1957-1960 |
| Green, William E. ........... | New York | Jamaica | 1886-1888 |
| Griffith, Georgie ............ | Iowa | Jamaica | 1895-1900 |
| Grimshaw, Arthur and Lily .. | Non-Friend | Africa | 1955-1956 |
| Gulley, Emmett W. and Zoe H. | Oregon | Mexico | 1919-1922 |
| Hadley, David and Ruth .... | Indiana | Africa | 1959- |
| Hadley, Jeanette ............ | Baltimore | Africa | 1968- |
| Hadley, Lena ................ | Kansas | Cuba | 1912-1922 |
| Hadley, Mary Glenn ........ | Iowa | Africa | 1962- |
| Hagerty, Mahlon and Edith .. | Phoenix (Ariz.) | Africa | 1962-1964 |
| Hahn, Margaret ............. | Germany | Africa | 1955-1957 |
| Haisley, Phillip ............. | Indiana | Africa | 1964-1966 |
| Hall, Marilyn ............... | Non-Friend | Africa | 1968- |
| Haramy, John J. ............. | Syria | Ramallah | 1921-1922 |
| Haramy, Ruth S. ............ | Indiana | Ramallah | 1921-1922 |
| Hare, Lizzie M. ............. | Indiana | Mexico | 1895-1900 |
| Haviland, Carrie E. ......... | Baltimore | Cuba | 1913-1920 |
| Haviland, Edna C. .......... | New England | Ramallah | 1920-1927 |
| Haviland, Elizabeth E. ...... | Baltimore | Africa | 1926-1932 |
| | | Ramallah | 1936-1937 |
| | | Africa | 1938-1940 |
| Haviland, Katherine ......... | New England | Ramallah | 1926-1935 |
| Haworth, Charles C. and | | | |
| Orpha R. ................. | Nebraska | Cuba | 1902-1913 |
| | | Mexico | 1908 |
| | | Cuba | 1919-1922 |
| Hawthorne, Mabel .......... | Nebraska | Africa | 1948-1964 |
| Hayes, Lillian E. ............ | Indiana | Jamaica | 1921-1922 |
| Henderson, Philip and Carolyn | Non-Friend | Africa | 1962-1964 |
| Henderson, Elam and Elda .. | New England | Jamaica | 1909-1910 |
| Hendrick, Cora A. .......... | Kansas | Mexico | 1921-1931 |
| Henry, Mildred ............. | Wilmington | Africa | 1958-1961 |
| Hiatt, John C. and Esther A. . | Iowa | Jamaica | 1886-1887 |

| | | | |
|---|---|---|---|
| Hiatt, Merrill L. ............ | | Ramallah | 1928-1929 |
| Hill, Hershel and Janetta .... | North Carolina | Tennessee | 1951-1954 |
| Hilty, Hiram and Janet B. ... | New York | Cuba | 1943-1948 |
| Hinckle, Milo S. and Addie M. | Indiana | Maine | 1917-1922 |
| | | | 1924-1925 |
| Hinshaw, Edwin and Dorothy | Indiana | Africa | 1958-1962 |
| Hockett, Francis and Rachel . | Indiana | Mexico | 1900-1905 |
| Hoeksema, Marvin and Doris | Iowa | Africa | 1968- |
| Holding, Minnie Cook ...... | Kansas | Cuba | 1903-1907 |
| | | Mexico | 1907-1913 |
| | | Cuba | 1914-1919 |
| Holding, Raymond S. ....... | Western | Cuba | 1902-1907 |
| | | Mexico | 1907-1913 |
| | | Cuba | 1914-1919 |
| Hole, Edgar T. and Adelaide W. .............. | Ohio | Africa | 1902-1923 |
| | | | 1903-1923 |
| Hollingsworth, William ..... | Western | Africa | 1959-1961 |
| Hollinshead, Estelle ......... | London | Africa | 1959- |
| Hoover, Alta .............. | Iowa | Jamaica | 1925-1934 |
| Hoover, Jennie M. .......... | Iowa | Jamaica | 1914-1929 |
| Hoover, Luella J. ........... | Iowa | Jamaica | 1925-1927 |
| Hotchkiss, Willis R. ......... | | Africa | 1902-1903 |
| Houghton, Richard .......... | Baltimore | Africa | 1958-1960 |
| Hoyt, Fred N. and Alta H. .. | Kansas | Africa | 1912-1946 |
| Huffman, John and Karolyn . | Wilmington | Africa | 1967- |
| Hussey, Timothy and Anna .. | New England | Jamaica | 1885 |
| | | Ramallah | 1889, 1894 |
| | | | 1896-1899 |
| | | | 1900-1905 |
| | | | 1909-1910 |
| Hutchison, Donn .......... | Non-Friend | Ramallah | 1967- |
| Jenkins, F. Raymond and Cecilia C. ............... | Indiana | Southland Inst. | 1922-1925 |
| Johnson, Barclay and Anna .. | Indiana | Southland Inst. | 1899-1903 |
| Johnson, Henrietta .......... | New England | Ramallah | 1889-1893 |
| Johnson, Jessie ............. | North Carolina | Mexico | 1892-1894 |
| Jones, Alice W. ............. | New England | Ramallah | 1906-1915 |
| | | | 1919-1929 |
| | | | 1939-1949 |
| Jones, Mack and Amy ...... | Indiana | Jamaica | 1946-1950 |
| Jones, Charles M. ........... | New England | Ramallah | 1889, 1895 |
| Jones, Christina H. ......... | Western | Ramallah | 1922-1930 |
| | | | 1944-1953 |
| Jones, A. Willard .......... | Western | Ramallah | 1922-1930 |
| | | Africa | 1943-1944 |
| | | Ramallah | 1944-1953 |
| Jones, Eli and Sybil ........ | New England | Ramallah | 1869- ? |
| Jones, Sylvester and May M. . | Iowa | Cuba | 1900-1927 |
| | | | 1942-1943 |
| Joyce, Jennie E. ............ | Nebraska | Cuba | 1905-1910 |

| | | | |
|---|---|---|---|
| Lock, Louis and Shirley ..... | New York | Africa | 1951-1961 |
| Longstreth, Leona ........... | Kansas | Mexico | 1903-1904 |
| Lung'aho, Thomas and Leah . | East Africa | Africa | 1963- |
| McClean, Bertrell S. ......... | Iowa | Cuba | 1912-1922 |
| McClean, Clarence .......... | Iowa | Cuba | 1912-1922 |
| McCracken, Mary B. ........ | Kansas | Cuba | 1917-1923 |
| McMillin, Fred ............. | Iowa | Tennessee | 1928-1938 |
| MacKenzie, Mary ........... | | Ramallah | 1913- ? |
| Macy, Evalena .............. | Kansas | Cuba | 1920-1923 |
| Macy, Florence O. (Parker) .. | Indiana | Africa | 1905-1909 |
| Mardock, Keith and Joyce ... | Indiana | Africa | 1964-1966 |
| Marriage, Gertrude .......... | Iowa | Jamaica | 1897-1900 |
| | | | 1903-1907 |
| Marriage, Margaretta (Sein) . | Iowa | Mexico | 1888-1905 |
| Marshburn, Oscar and Olive . | California | Africa | 1963-1965 |
| Martin, Susie J. ............. | Iowa | Cuba | 1902-1930 |
| Martin, Zenas L. ............ | Iowa | Cuba | 1901-1930 |
| Martinez, Emma Phillips .... | Indiana | Mexico | 1893-1900 |
| | | Cuba | 1900-1946 |
| Matthews, Norman and Rubie | F.G.C. | Africa | 1963-1966 |
| Meader, Eunice ............. | New England | Ramallah | 1913-1915 |
| Mendenhall, Lloyd H. and | | | |
| Bertha L. ................ | Iowa | Cuba | 1915-1919 |
| Mendenhall, Herschel and | | | |
| Mildred ................. | Iowa | Africa | 1958-1960 |
| Meredith, Clifford and Ruby . | | Jamaica | 1949-1951 |
| Metcalfe, Edna ............. | New England | Ramallah | 1911-1912 |
| Michener, Dr. R. Bryan | | | |
| and Edith ............... | Kansas | Africa | 1930-1938 |
| | | | 1967- |
| Michener, Paul H. and | | | |
| Margaret M. ............. | Iowa | Jamaica | 1928-1933 |
| Miles, Carrie ............... | | Tennessee | 1921- ? |
| Mills, Robert and Carol ..... | Western | Africa | 1955-1964 |
| Mills, Newlin .............. | Western | Africa | 1965- |
| Montgomery, Elizabeth ...... | Non-Friend | Africa | 1958-1961 |
| Moon, Lewis C. ............ | Wilmington | Africa | 1919 |
| Moon, Ruthanna C. ......... | Ohio | Africa | 1919 |
| Moore, Raymond and Edna .. | California | Tennessee | 1954-1956 |
| Moore, Floyd and Lucretia ... | North Carolina | Ramallah | 1946-1947 |
| Morgan, Clara R. ........... | Kansas | Mexico | 1898-1909 |
| Morgan, Everett E. ......... | Kansas | Mexico | 1898-1911 |
| Morris, Gladys ............. | Iowa | Tennessee | 1924-1925 |
| Morris, Joan ............... | Non-Friend | Africa | 1955-1968 |
| Morris, Rodney ............. | New York | Africa | 1955-1968 |
| Nagler, Marion ............. | Western | Africa | 1963-1964 |
| Neatby, Helen .............. | London | Africa | 1956-1958 |
| Neiger, Lillie A. ............ | Western | Mexico | 1884-1890 |
| Newsom, Belva ............. | Western | Ramallah | 1926 |
| Newsom, Clara Mary ........ | Western | Ramallah | 1929- ? |
| Nixon, Frederick F. and | | | |

| | | | |
|---|---|---|---|
| Reynolds, Julia .............. | Baltimore | Ramallah | 1951-1956 |
| Riley, Paul ................. | Western | Africa | 1966-1967 |
| Ridgeway, Helen ............ | Kansas | Africa | 1948-1959 |
| Roberts, Clyde E. ........... | Nebraska | Mexico | 1911-1925 |
| | | | 1928-1932 |
| Roberts, Lou Flora S. ........ | Nebraska | Mexico | 1911-1925 |
| Roberts, Ida M. ............ | Western | Mexico | 1904-1907 |
| Roberts, Mary .............. | | Ramallah | 1929- ? |
| Rosenberger, Absolom ....... | Iowa | Ramallah | 1909-1913 |
| Rosenberger, Florabel P. ..... | Iowa | Ramallah | 1910-1913 |
| Rothe, Horst and Ingeborg .. | Germany | Africa | 1949-1958 |
| Rountree, Wilfred and Della . | New England | Ramallah | 1897-1902 |
| Russell, William and Sabina .. | | Southland Inst. | |
| Sanders, Edwin and Marian .. | Pacific | Africa | 1965-1967 |
| Sarfas, Eirene .............. | London | Africa | 1954-1966 |
| Scantland, Dwight E. ....... | | Ramallah | 1949- ? |
| Scherer, George and Lucille .. | Indiana | Ramallah | 1956-1957 |
| Schmudlach, Maude A. ...... | Non-Friend | Africa | 1966-1968 |
| Schoonover, Kermit and Grace | Kansas | Ramallah | 1935-1938 |
| Schroeder, Paul and Nina .... | California | Africa | 1965 |
| Scoltock, Leah T. ........... | Iowa | Jamaica | 1903-1910 |
| Scott, Charles and Charlotte .. | Western | Tennessee | 1946-1950 |
| Sharpless, Evi .............. | Iowa | Jamaica | 1881-1887 |
| Sherman, Anna C. .......... | Iowa | Jamaica | 1911-1913 |
| Shirk, Kenneth and Martha .. | Indiana | Ramallah | 1965-1968 |
| Short, Elsie ................ | Indiana | Africa | 1960-1968 |
| Short, Warren ............. | Indiana | Africa | 1960-1968 |
| Simkin, Margaret .......... | New York | China | 1907- ? |
| Simkin, Margaret T. ........ | New England | China | 1923-1944 |
| Simkin, Robert L. .......... | New York | China | 1907-1944 |
| Smith, Caleb and Jeannette .. | New England | Africa | 1963-1965 |
| Smith, Florence Mae ........ | New England | Jamaica | 1928-1946 |
| Smith, Gladys (Jones) ....... | Iowa | Jamaica | 1918-1923 |
| Smith, Logan and Opal ...... | Indiana | Jamaica | 1951-1955 |
| | | Africa | 1959-1961 |
| Smuck, Harold V. and Evelyn | Western | Jamaica | 1950-1951 |
| | | Ramallah | 1957-1962 |
| | | Africa | 1962-1966 |
| Snyder, Lois ................ | Western | Ramallah | 1957-1966 |
| Spann, Charles E. and Mary .. | Iowa | Africa | 1910-1913 |
| Spoon, Pearl ............... | Kansas | Tennessee | 1946-1948 |
| | | Africa | 1948-1965 |
| Stalker, Roxie ............. | Western | Africa | 1917-1923 |
| Stanley, Sada F. ............ | Iowa | Jamaica | 1900-1946 |
| Stinetorf, Roscoe and Louise A. | | Ramallah | 1929 |
| Stratton, Janice ............ | Non-Friend | Africa | 1963-1966 |
| Stratton, John ............. | New York | Africa | 1963-1966 |
| Sutton, James E. ........... | Philadelphia | Ramallah | 1923-1935 |
| Sutton, Phyllis M. .......... | Non-Friend | Ramallah | 1927-1935 |
| Swift, Arthur H. ........... | New England | Jamaica | 1889-1909 |
| Swift, H. Alma ............. | Iowa | Jamaica | 1893-1934 |

| | | | |
|---|---|---|---|
| Swift, Naomi George ........ | | Jamaica | 1888-1893 |
| Taber, Ervin G. and | | | |
| Margaret C. .............. | Western | Mexico | 1886-1898 |
| Taylor, Lewis and Margaret .. | Western | Africa | 1964-1966 |
| Terrell, Clayton ............. | Wilmington | Cuba | 1908 |
| Terrell, Eva (Woody) ....... | Wilmington | Cuba | 1904-1910 |
| Thomas, Auretta M. ........ | Indiana | Mexico | 1910-1913 |
| Tice, Solomon R. and | | | |
| Amanda R. .............. | Indiana | Mexico | 1905-1920 |
| Totah, Ermina Jones ....... | New England | Ramallah | 1927-1928 |
| Totah, Evan Rae Marshall .... | Iowa | Ramallah | 1927-1944 |
| Towle, Philip and Virginia ... | New England | Africa | 1962- |
| Townsend, Jesse R. and | | | |
| Elizabeth R. .............. | | Jamaica | 1883-1887 |
| Turner, John S. and Luella M. | Indiana | Mexico | 1897-1900 |
| Vail, Homer and Rebecca .... | Indiana | Africa | 1965- |
| Votaw, Roy C. and Ruth T. .. | California | Cuba | 1929-1932 |
| Wagoner, William and Joyce . | Iowa | Jamaica | 1958- |
| Walls, William A. .......... | Canada | Mexico | 1880-1892 |
| Wardell, Michael J. and Mina | London | Africa | 1958-1960 |
| Weaver, Clara .............. | Indiana | Africa | 1955-1964 |
| Weeks, George D. and Sarah . | Iowa | Mexico | 1897 |
| Wellons, Esther L. .......... | North Carolina | Jamaica | 1938-1947 |
| Wellons, Harry A. .......... | Baltimore | Jamaica | 1938-1947 |
| Whinnery, Mary B. (Egbert) . | Indiana | Mexico | 1909-1910 |
| White, Barbara ............. | | Ramallah | 1946- ? |
| White, Charles S. and | | | |
| Nellie M. ................. | Iowa | Jamaica | 1897-1898 |
| White, Edwin and Jocelyn ... | Indiana | Africa | 1965- |
| White, Martha E. (Miller) ... | California | Jamaica | 1933-1938 |
| | | | 1954-1956 |
| White, Mary E. ............. | Iowa | Jamaica | 1895-1946 |
| White, Mildred ............. | Indiana | Ramallah | 1922-1947 |
| | | | 1949-1954 |
| Wilhite, Harold and Marjorie | Oregon | Africa | 1951-1955 |
| Williams, Roy and Ada ...... | Iowa | Jamaica | 1958-1959 |
| Wines, Leonard and Edith ... | Kansas | Africa | 1948-1955 |
| Winslow, Ellen A. .......... | New England | Ramallah | 1925 |
| Winston, Laura A. .......... | North Carolina | Mexico | 1885- ? |
| Wise, Genevieve ............ | California | Africa | 1965- |
| Wolfley, Eugene and Frances . | Iowa | Jamaica | 1963-1966 |
| Wolford, Harry C. and Anna B. | Indiana | Southland Inst. | 1903-1922 |
| Woody, Martha J. .......... | North Carolina | Cuba | 1900-1919 |
| Wright, Ora E. ............. | Indiana | Cuba | 1918-1923 |
| Wyatt, Eric and Gladys ...... | London | Africa | 1964-1968 |
| Yates, Howard and Margaret . | Wilmington | Tennessee | 1948-1961 |
| | | | **1965-1967** |
| Yow, Howard and Lalah .... | North Carolina | Africa | 1946-1950 |

## KANSAS YEARLY MEETING
### All Africa Field

| Name | Years of Service |
|------|------------------|
| Bales, Marvin and Ethel | 1956-1965 |
| Brown, Clayton and Luella | 1940-1961 |
| Brown, Randall and Sara | 1952-1966 |
| Cain, Donald and Patricia | 1963- |
| Chilson, Arthur | 1933-1938 |
| Chilson, Edna | 1933-1945 |
| Chilson, Rachel | 1946- |
| Choate, Ralph and Esther | 1935- |
| Custer, Geraldine | 1947- |
| Ehlinger, Lawrence and Delores | 1952-1966 |
| Ferguson, Willard and Doris | 1962- |
| Ford, Arthur and Faith | 1938- ? |
| Fuqua, Gary and Ann | 1966- |
| Jones, Twila | 1954- |
| Kellum, David and Mae | 1959- |
| Kellum, Robert and Esther | 1960- |
| Miller, Alfred and Ruth | 1945-1965 |
| Morris, James and Doris | 1950- |
| Muck, Dr. Floyd and Leora | 1945-1953 |
| Rawson, Edward and Joan | 1966- |
| Rawson, Dr. Perry and Marjorie | 1945- |
| Ridgeway, Helen | 1938-1946 |
| Riley, David and Annie | 1955- |
| Stuart, Reta | 1955- |
| Thomas, Clyde and Mary | 1945-1951 |
| Thomas, George and Dorothy | 1945- |
| Thornburg, Paul and Leona | 1954- |
| Wheeler, Eli and Alice | 1945-1947 |
| Wheeler, Lyle and Janet | 1956- |

## OHIO YEARLY MEETING

| Name | Field | Years of Service |
|------|-------|------------------|
| Allen, Eva | India | 1906 |
| Baird, Esther | India | 1892-1938 |
| Banker, Max and Ruth Ellen | India | 1949-1955 |
| Bolitho, Walter and Geneva | India | 1928-1932 |
| Butler, Esther | China | 1887-1921 |
| Calkins, Alena | India | 1927-1950 |
| Carmichael, Eva | China | 1904 |
| Cattell, Everett and Catherine | India | 1936-1957 |
| Coffin, Merrill M. and Anna | India | 1923-1929 |
| Coleman, Milton and Rebecca | India | 1945 |
| Cox, Carson W. | China | 1919-1932 |
| Cox, Vercie P. | China | 1919-1934 |
| Crowl, Annie L. | China | 1916-1918 |

| | | |
|---|---|---|
| DeVol, Charles E. | China | 1926-1943 |
| | | 1946-1950 |
| | Formosa | 1957- |
| DeVol, Frances H. | China | 1940 |
| | India | 1949 |
| DeVol, Dr. George | China | 1900-1917 |
| DeVol, Dr. Isabella | China | 1897-1920 |
| DeVol, Leora | China | 1926-1940 |
| | | 1946-1948 |
| | Formosa | 1957- |
| DeVol, Dr. William E. | China | 1940-1942 |
| | India | 1949 |
| Earl, John | India | 1932-1935 |
| Earle, Robert and Elizabeth | India | 1938-1946 |
| Earle, Ruth Thurston | India | 1927-1935 |
| Edgerton, Annie V. | India | 1898 |
| Estes, Julia | China | 1899-1902 |
| Estes, Wilbur A. | China | 1899-1905 |
| Farmer, Freda | Formosa | 1959- |
| Fleming, Dr. Mary R. | India | 1925-1928 |
| Fistler, Delia | India | 1892-1916 |
| Freer, Norma | India | 1945 |
| Gaynor, Dr. Lucy A. | China | 1892-1912 |
| Girsberger, Freda | China | 1923-1942 |
| Goddard, Dr. Abigail | India | 1906-1910 |
| Hess, Robert and Esther | India | 1952 |
| Hill, Mary A. | China | 1909-1910 |
| Hixon, Martha B. | China | 1913-1915 |
| Holme, Margaret A. | China | 1894-1930 |
| Hull, Dr. E. Ruth | India | 1928-1940 |
| Hutson, Ella Ruth | China | 1947-1950 |
| | Formosa | 1953- |
| Kinder, James | India | 1930-1935 |
| Kinder, Judith | India | 1931-1935 |
| Kirkpatrick, Amanda | China | 1888-1891 |
| Lewis, Nellie | India | 1929-1935 |
| Matti, Charles A. | China | 1925-1942 |
| | | 1946-1950 |
| | Formosa | 1953-1957 |
| Matti, Elsie | China | 1925-1940 |
| | | 1946-1950 |
| | Formosa | 1953-1957 |
| McGowen, Dr. Edith | China | 1904 |
| Moore, Emily R. | China | 1919-1923 |
| Moore, Howard W. and Mary Evelyn | Formosa | 1954 |
| Morris, Clinton | India | 1912-1915 |
| Mostrom, Rachel | China | 1923-1940 |
| Murray, Effie | China | 1894-1906 |
| Naylor, R. Ethel | China | 1919-1940 |
| Naylor, Roberta | China | 1930-1936 |
| Nixon, Anna | India | 1941 |

| | | |
|---|---|---|
| Oliver, Emma D. | China | 1907-1913 |
| Pennington, Eva | China | 1903-1904 |
| Robbins, Dr. Oona Mae | China | 1923 |
| Robinson, Clifton and Betty | India | 1947 |
| Rogers, Alison and Inez Cope | India | 1921-1927 |
| Shimer, Harriet | China | 1913-1919 |
| Smith, Margaret | India | 1913-1928 |
| Stanley, Lenna M. | China | 1891-1920 |
| Stewart, Matilda | China | 1925-1927 |
| Tsao, Dr. Li Yuin | China | 1912-1918 |
| Williams, John and Geraldine | China | 1947-1948 |
| Williams, Myrtle M. | China | 1909-1923 |
| Williams, Walter R. | China | 1909-1927 |
| Wood, Carrie B. | India | 1907-1948 |
| Wood, Mary | China | 1906-1913 |
| Thompson, Kathy | India | 1963- |
| Zinn, Russell and Esther | Formosa | 1958- |

## OREGON YEARLY MEETING

| Name | Field | Years of Service |
|---|---|---|
| Brown, Oscar and Ruth | Bolivia | 1960-1964 |
| Cammack, Edwin and Marie | Bolivia | 1968- |
| Cammack, Forrest and Orpha | Bolivia | 1956-1968 |
| Cammack, Helen | Bolivia | 1932-1937 |
| | | 1938-1944 |
| Cammack, Paul and Phyllis | Bolivia | 1948-1961 |
| Chapman, Ralph and Marie | Bolivia | 1944- |
| Clarkson, Everett and Alda | Bolivia | 1958-1967 |
| Comfort, Eugene and Betty | Bolivia | 1960- |
| Gulley, Estel | Bolivia | 1931(?)-1939 |
| Hibbs, Leland and Iverna | Bolivia | 1951-1957 |
| Knight, Roscoe and Tina | Bolivia | 1945-1966 |
| | Mexico | 1966- |
| Maurer, Nicholas and Alice | Bolivia | 1966- |
| Moon, Silas and Anna | Alaska | 1887-1893 |
| | | 1894-1906 |
| Nordyke, Quentin and Florene | Bolivia | 1961- |
| Pearson, Howard and Julia | Bolivia | 1931(?)-1950 |
| Puckett, Paul and Martha | Bolivia | 1963-1966 |
| Roberts, Mark and Wilma | Bolivia | 1953-1964 |
| Scott, Charles and Charlotte | Bolivia | 1960-1963 |
| Stansell, Ronald and Carolyn | Bolivia | 1967- |
| Tamplin, Carroll and Doris | Bolivia | 1930-1945 |
| Thomas, David and Florence | Bolivia | 1957- |
| Willcuts, Jack and Geraldine | Bolivia | 1947-1958 |

## PHILADELPHIA YEARLY MEETING
### All Japan Field

| Name | Years of Service |
|---|---|
| Bailey, Nichola | 1952-1954 |

Binford, Elizabeth ....................................... 1899-1936
Binford, Gurney ......................................... 1893-1936
Borton, Hugh and Elizabeth .............................. 1928-1931
                                                          1934-1936
Bowles, Gilbert ......................................... 1901-1941
Bowles, Luanna J. ....................................... 1927-1928
Bowles, Minnie P. ....................................... 1893-1941
Braithwaite, G. Burnham and Edith L. .................... 1922-1935
Clark, Rosamond H. ...................................... 1921-1923
Clevenger, Janice A. .................................... 1957-1959
                                                          1962-
Cobin, June P. .......................................... 1967-1968
Coleman, Horace E. and Elizabeth ........................ 1907-1927
Cosand, Joseph and Sarah Ann ............................ 1885-1900
Dillon, Edith ........................................... 1896-1903
Dixon, Alice L. ......................................... 1926-1929
Domingo, Delia .......................................... 1963-1965
Ellis, Sara ............................................. 1902-1915
Foulke, Eliza A. ........................................ 1963-1964
Gifford, Alice C. ....................................... 1911-1920
Gundry, Mary Ann ........................................ 1889-1905
Haines, Mary M. ......................................... 1892-1895
Hawkins, Violet ......................................... 1925-1932
James, Margaret S. ...................................... 1922-1924
Jones, Catherine ........................................ 1915-1916
Jones, Esther B. ........................................ 1914-1924
Jones, Thomas E. ........................................ 1918-1924
Knapp, Donald ........................................... 1950-1951
Lester, Mary Ann ........................................ 1965-1967
Lewis, Alice G. ......................................... 1905-1924
Lewis, Mary H. .......................................... 1908-1909
Longstreth, Sarah M. .................................... 1903-1905
Miho, Fumiye ............................................ 1960-1967
Miller, Edna ............................................ 1929-1933
Newlin, Edith ........................................... 1918-1927
Nicholson, Herbert V. ................................... 1915-1939
Nicholson, Madeline W. .................................. 1920-1939
Nicholson, Samuel and Anna Margaret ..................... 1960-1967
Pearson, Bruce and Barbara .............................. 1954-1958
Rhoads, Esther B. ....................................... 1917-1918
                                                          1921-1940
                                                          1946-1960
Rhoads, Margaret W. ..................................... 1921-1922
Rittenhouse, Jane A. .................................... 1954-1957
Roudebush, Lillie ....................................... 1947-1950
Sharpless, Edith F. ..................................... 1910-1943
                                                          1951-1956
Smith, Sarah A. G. ...................................... 1933-1935
Taber, Inez E. .......................................... 1905-1910
Taylor, Howard G. and Mary R. ........................... 1958-1960
Taylor, Kathryn ......................................... 1967

| | |
|---|---|
| Thomas, Helen | 1936-1937 |
| Wright, William V. and Isabel | 1888-1891 |
| Zollinger, Margaret | 1959-1962 |

### ROCKY MOUNTAIN YEARLY MEETING
### All Rough Rocks Mission (Indians)

| | |
|---|---|
| Brown, Bessie Franc | 1962-1964 |
| Brown, Richard and Ruth | 1964-1965 |
| Byerly, John and Helen | 1958 |
| Cammack, Albert and Ruth | 1967-1968 |
| Ellis, Vern and Lois | 1956-1962 |
| | 1965- |
| Gafford, Mary | 1957-1962 |
| | 1963- |
| Glass, Nick and Helen | 1962-1964 |
| Huff, Jane | 1964-1965 |
| Johnston, Roy and Frances | 1956-1958 |
| | 1962-1963 |
| Schram, Don and Mary | 1959-1960 |
| | 1964-1965 |
| Thomas, George and Dorothy | 1961-1963 |

## 11. OUTLINE OF WORLD MEMBERSHIP

Compiled by the Friends World Committee
As of 1967

### Africa (42,014)

| | | | |
|---|---|---|---|
| Burundi | 1,362 | Pemba and Zanzibar | 147 |
| Kenya | 32,155 | South Africa | 142 |
| Madagascar | 8,208 | | |

### Asia (1,864)

| | | | |
|---|---|---|---|
| China (no figures) | | Japan | 266 |
| India (Bundelkhand) | 240 | Jordan and Lebanon | 130 |
| India (Mid-India) | 268 | Taiwan | 960 |

### Australasia (1,597)

| | | | |
|---|---|---|---|
| Australia | 929 | New Zealand | 668 |

### Europe (23,991)

| | | | |
|---|---|---|---|
| Denmark | 53 | Netherlands | 117 |
| France | 83 | Norway | 91 |
| Germany and Austria | 530 | Sweden and Finland | 154 |
| Great Britain | 21,040 | Switzerland | 123 |
| Ireland | 1,800 | | |

### North America (120,701)

| | | | |
|---|---|---|---|
| Canada | 814 | United States | 119,887 |

### South and Central America (6,391)

| | | | |
|---|---|---|---|
| Bolivia | 3,000 | Jamaica | 635 |
| Costa Rica | 71 | Mexico | 197 |
| Cuba | 319 | Peru | 400 |
| El Salvador and Honduras | 299 | | |
| Guatemala | 1,470 | | 196,558 |

## (U.S.A., CANADA, AND MEXICO)

### Friends United Meeting

| | | | |
|---|---|---|---|
| Alaska | 1,140 | New England | 1,678* |
| Baltimore | 1,623* | New York | 3,329* |
| California | 7,605 | North Carolina | 14,856 |
| Canada | 407* | Western | 12,235 |
| Indiana | 12,765 | Wilmington | 4,249 |
| Iowa | 5,499 | | |
| Mexico | 197 | | 65,943 |
| Nebraska | 360 | | |

### Evangelical Friends Alliance

| | | | |
|---|---|---|---|
| Kansas | 9,264 | Rocky Mountain | 1,606 |
| Ohio | 7,324 | | |
| Oregon | 6,202 | | 23,396 |

### Unaffiliated

| | | | |
|---|---|---|---|
| Pacific | 1,689 | Other Meetings | 372 |
| Southeastern | 364 | | |
| | | | 2,425 |

### Friends General Conference

| | | | |
|---|---|---|---|
| Baltimore | 1,623* | New York | 3,329* |
| Canada | 407* | Philadelphia | 15,965 |
| Illinois | 1,200 | South Central | 326 |
| Indiana | 689 | | |
| Lake Erie | 494 | | 26,711 |
| New England | 1,678* | | |

### Conservative

| | | | |
|---|---|---|---|
| Iowa | 800 | Ohio | 856 |
| North Carolina | 270 | | |
| | | | 1,926 |

### Central Yearly Meeting 497

---

* Since these Yearly Meetings have an affiliation with both Friends United Meeting and Friends General Conference, membership has been divided so that there is no duplication of statistics.

# INDEX

Besides the usual form of indexing, a few topical arrangements are presented here. For the sake of non-Quaker readers certain aspects of Quaker faith and practice are listed under "The Quakers." These references do not presume to give a complete historical interpretation of these aspects of Quaker life, but indicate references to them within the scope of this history. For further information and interpretation of Quakerism, many books may be found in most Quaker libraries.

The complex pattern of Quaker Meetings across America makes difficult their identification within the large structure of the Society of Friends. By far the larger number are of the Orthodox or Gurneyite tradition and therefore these have not been given a specific identifying name or initial.

Some of the Meetings are initialed for the Yearly Meeting to which they belong. For others, it has seemed preferable to indicate the state in which they exist. The text, in many cases, will offer more complete identification.

The Conservative and Hicksite Meetings, being fewer in number, are initialed with "C" or "H"; United Yearly Meetings have the "U" identification.

Friends whose writings have helped in the preparation of this history, as indicated in footnotes, have been included, giving but one page reference in which the name appears.

It should be noted that names of persons, places, Meetings, and institutions have not been selected for their importance above others necessarily, but because they were pertinent to the story being told. The object of the writing and indexing of this volume has been to present the total sweep of the westward Quaker movement, not the history of any one Yearly Meeting.